# Testing in the Professions

*Testing in the Professions* focuses on current practices in credentialing testing as a guide for practitioners. With a broad focus on the key components, issues, and concerns surrounding the test development and validation process, this book brings together a wide range of research and theory—from design and analysis of tests to security, scoring, and reporting. Written by leading experts in the field of measurement and assessment, each chapter includes authentic examples as to how various practices are implemented or current issues observed in credentialing programs.

The volume begins with an exploration of the various types of credentialing programs as well as key differences in the interpretation and evaluation of test scores. The next set of chapters discusses key test development steps, including test design, content development, analysis, and evaluation. The final set of chapters addresses specific topics that span the testing process, including communication with stakeholders, security, program evaluation, and legal principles. As a response to the growing number of professions and professional designations that are tied to testing requirements, *Testing in the Professions* is a comprehensive source for up-to-date measurement and credentialing practices.

**Susan Davis-Becker** is a Partner with ACS Ventures, LLC, USA.

**Chad W. Buckendahl** is a Partner with ACS Ventures, LLC, USA.

The NCME Applications of Educational Measurement
and Assessment Book Series

**Editorial Board:**

Brian E. Clauser, National Board of Medical Examiners, Editor
Robert L. Brennan, The University of Iowa
Wayne Camara, ACT
Michael J. Kolen, The University of Iowa
Suzanne Lane, University of Pittsburgh
Rebecca Zwick, Educational Testing Service

**Technology and Testing: Improving Educational and Psychological Measurement**
*Edited by Fritz Drasgow*

**Meeting the Challenges to Measurement in an Era of Accountability**
*Edited by Henry Braun*

**Fairness in Educational Assessment and Measurement**
*Edited by Neil J. Dorans and Linda L. Cook*

**Validation of Score Meaning in the Next Generation of Assessments**
*Edited by Kadriye Ercikan and James W. Pellegrino*

**Testing in the Professions: Credentialing Policies and Practice**
*Edited by Susan Davis-Becker and Chad W. Buckendahl*

# Testing in the Professions

Credentialing Policies and Practice

Edited by
Susan Davis-Becker and
Chad W. Buckendahl

NEW YORK AND LONDON

First published 2017
by Routledge
711 Third Avenue, New York, NY 10017

and by Routledge
2 Park Square, Milton Park, Abingdon, Oxon, OX14 4RN

*Routledge is an imprint of the Taylor & Francis Group, an informa business*

© 2017 Taylor & Francis

The right of Susan Davis-Becker and Chad W. Buckendahl to be identified as the authors of the editorial material, and of the authors for their individual chapters, has been asserted in accordance with sections 77 and 78 of the Copyright, Designs and Patents Act 1988.

All rights reserved. No part of this book may be reprinted or reproduced or utilized in any form or by any electronic, mechanical, or other means, now known or hereafter invented, including photocopying and recording, or in any information storage or retrieval system, without permission in writing from the publishers.

*Trademark notice*: Product or corporate names may be trademarks or registered trademarks, and are used only for identification and explanation without intent to infringe.

*Library of Congress Cataloging in Publication Data*
A catalog record for this book has been requested

ISBN: 978-1-138-79427-6 (hbk)
ISBN: 978-1-138-80644-3 (pbk)
ISBN: 978-1-315-75167-2 (ebk)

Typeset in Minion Pro
by Cenveo Publisher Services

# Contents

*List of Contributors*   vii
*Preface*   xi
*Acknowledgments*   xiii

1 **Credentialing: A Continuum of Measurement Theories, Policies, and Practices**   1
  CHAD W. BUCKENDAHL

2 **A Validation Framework for Credentialing Tests**   21
  MICHAEL T. KANE, BRIAN E. CLAUSER, AND JOANNE KANE

3 **Test Design: Laying out the Roadmap**   41
  SUSAN DAVIS-BECKER AND TIMOTHY J. MUCKLE

4 **Specifying the Content of Credentialing Examinations**   64
  AMANDA L. CLAUSER AND MARK RAYMOND

5 **Content Development and Review**   85
  CYNTHIA G. PARSHALL AND BELINDA BRUNNER

6 **Estimating, Interpreting, and Maintaining the Meaning of Test Scores**   105
  WALTER D. WAY AND KATHLEEN A. GIALLUCA

7 **Data and Scale Analysis for Credentialing Examinations**   123
  RICHARD M. LUECHT

8 **Communication with Candidates and Other Stakeholders**   153
  ELLEN R. JULIAN AND BRIAN BONTEMPO

9 **Security Issues in Professional Certification/Licensure Testing**   178
  JAMES A. WOLLACK AND GREGORY J. CIZEK

10 **Using Standards to Evaluate Credentialing Programs**   210
   LAWRENCE J. FABREY

11 **Legal Issues for Credentialing Examination Programs**   228
   S. E. PHILLIPS

*Index*   277

# Contributors

**Brian Bontempo**, Ph.D., is the founder and CEO of Mountain Measurement, Inc. a Portland, OR based company which provides psychometrics, analytics, and data visualization services to the assessment industry. Brian served as a commissioner for the National Commission on Certifying Agencies (NCCA) and on the Main Committee responsible for the development of the 2016 NCCA Standards for the Accreditation of Certification Programs. His areas of expertise include psychometrics, Item Response Theory (IRT), Rasch modeling, Computerized Adaptive Testing (CAT), licensure and certification, data visualization, scoring, and reporting.

**Belinda Brunner** has previously held positions overseeing certification activities for the American Health Information Management Association (AHIMA) and the Joint Commission on Allied Health Personnel in Ophthalmology (JCAHPO). She joined Pearson VUE in 2007, and in her current role as Director of Testing Services Strategy, she formulates test development solutions and assists in test design activities for Pearson VUE's global clients.

**Chad W. Buckendahl**, Ph.D., is a Partner with ACS Ventures, LLC in Las Vegas, NV. His research interests include legal issues, standard setting, test evaluation, and validity. Dr. Buckendahl has designed and led validation studies for licensure and certification tests in architecture, dentistry, dental hygiene, education, and law. He received a Ph.D in educational measurement and an M.L.S. in legal studies from the University of Nebraska, Lincoln. Dr. Buckendahl also serves on technical advisory committees for education and credentialing programs; and as a psychometric reviewer and previously served as a psychometric reviewer and chair of the National Commission for Certifying Agencies.

**Gregory J. Cizek** is Guy B. Phillips Distinguished Professor of Educational Measurement and Evaluation at the University of North Carolina at Chapel Hill. His research focuses on standard setting, test security, validity, and testing policy. Previously, he managed national licensure and certification programs, worked on a state assessment program, and he began his career as an elementary school teacher. He has served as President of the National Council on Measurement in Education (NCME), member of the National Assessment Governing Board, and Secretary of Division D and the Professional Licensure and Certification Special Interest Group of the American Educational Research Association (AERA).

**Amanda L. Clauser** is a psychometrician at the National Board of Medical Examiners. She earned her doctorate in Educational Measurement and Psychometrics from the

University of Massachusetts and her Master's from the University of Pennsylvania. Her research interests include applications of evidence-centered design, score reporting, and performance assessment. Her professional experience is primarily in licensure and certification testing, qualitative research, and student growth models.

**Brian E. Clauser** graduated from the University of Massachusetts at Amherst with a focus on research and evaluation methods. For the past twenty-four years he has done psychometric research at the National Board of Medical Examiners. He has published on issues related to automated scoring of complex assessments, validity, standard setting, applications of generalizability theory, and differential item functioning. He is past editor of the *Journal of Educational* Measurement and the current editor of the NCME book series.

**Susan Davis-Becker** is a Partner with ACS Ventures, LLC. She has provided psychometric consultation to a variety of educational and credentialing testing programs including psychometric oversight, designing and evaluating test development activities, psychometric analysis, and overall quality assurance. Dr. Davis-Becker received her Ph.D. in assessment and measurement from James Madison University. She has served on committees for the Institute for Credentialing Excellence (ICE) and the National Council on Measurement in Education (NCME). Her research interests include test design, standard setting, and score reporting.

**Lawrence J. Fabrey**, Ph.D., is Senior Vice President of Psychometrics for AMP, a PSI Business (PSI/AMP). He is responsible for psychometrics, test development, and test scoring for numerous certification organizations, and had served in that role for 27 years with Applied Measurement Professionals. Larry previously worked with the American Nurses' Association and the National Board of Medical Examiners. He served as psychometrician and chair for the National Commission for Certifying Agencies. He received the NOCA Service Award and co-chaired the committee to revise the NCCA accreditation standards. Larry holds a Ph.D. in Educational Psychology from the Pennsylvania State University.

**Kathleen A. Gialluca** is a psychometrician with extensive experience in test development and computer-based testing. She has worked with corporate clients, test authors, and colleagues to revise tests, write items, and design and conduct assessment-related research studies. She has managed test development projects from the initial design phase through final production and documentation, and has overseen the operational psychometric activities as well. Her experience ranges from standardized instruments assessing psychological characteristics to adaptive computer-based exams assessing professional competence. She is currently a Senior Research Scientist at Pearson, where she serves as senior advisor for test design issues.

**Ellen R. Julian**, Ph.D., is a psychometrician who helped computerize several large examination programs and developed a variety of innovative item types. After years in testing-program management, she is returning to her roots by building a psychometric consulting service within the larger Inteleos certification organization to help other certification programs improve their examinations with sound advice, data analyses, and meeting facilitation. She received her measurement training at Florida State University, which emphasized theoretically sound practical solutions to real-world problems. Dr. Julian is an ANSI/ISO 17024 Psychometric Assessor.

Contributors ix

**Joanne Kane** is the Associate Director of Testing at the National Conference of Bar Examiners in Madison, WI. Her research centers on issues in legal licensure and educational assessment. She was previously a post-doctoral fellow at Princeton University; her work at the Woodrow Wilson School of Public and International Affairs focused on fairness and social justice in the context of public policy evaluation.

**Michael T. Kane** has been the Messick Chair in Validity at the Educational Testing Service since 2009. He served as Director of Research at the National Conference of Bar Examiners from 2001 to 2009, and as a professor in the School of Education at the University of Wisconsin from 1991 to 2001. Prior to 1991, Dr. Kane served as VP for research and development and as a senior research scientist at ACT, as Director of Test Development at the National League for Nursing in New York, as a professor of education at SUNY, Stony Brook, and as Director of Placement and Proficiency Testing at the University of Illinois, Urbana-Champaign. His main research interests are validity theory and practice, generalizability theory, licensure and certification testing, and standard setting. Dr. Kane holds a Ph.D. in education and an M.S. in statistics from Stanford University and a B.S. and M.A. in physics from Manhattan College and SUNY, Stony Brook, respectively.

**Richard M. Luecht** is a Professor of Educational Research Methodology at the UNC-Greensboro where he teaches graduate courses in applied statistics and measurement. His research includes technology integration in assessment, psychometric modeling and estimation, and formative assessment engineering design. He has developed algorithms and software programs for automated test assembly and helped introduce the computerized adaptive multistage testing framework used by a number of large-scale testing programs. Prior to joining the UNCG faculty, Dr. Luecht worked for ACT and for the National Board of Medical Examiners. He is currently a technical advisor for many state departments of education and large-scale testing organizations.

**Timothy J. Muckle**, Ph.D., is the Senior Director of Testing Programs at the National Board of Certification and Recertification for Nurse Anesthetists. He is responsible for overseeing test development and psychometric quality of the National Certification Examination, the development of innovative item types, and the development of assessment components of the NBCRNA's Continued Professional Certification (CPC) program. He took a B.S. degree in Mathematics from the University of Notre Dame, and a Ph.D. in Educational Psychology from the University of Illinois at Chicago. His research interests include computerized adaptive testing, alternative item types, and performance-based assessments using simulation.

**Cynthia G. Parshall**, Ph.D., is the Principal Consultant with Touchstone Consulting. She holds a Ph.D. in Educational Measurement and Research and an M.Ed. in Instructional Computing. Dr. Parshall's work focuses on the intersection of technology and assessment, especially in the design of innovative item types to improve assessment fidelity and in the application of action design tools to help our examinees be their best selves. She is the lead author on the book *Practical Considerations in Computer-Based Testing*.

**S. E. Phillips** is an independent consultant in assessment law, attorney, and former professor of educational measurement at Michigan State University. Dr. Phillips has taught courses in psychometrics and assessment law, served as an expert witness in a number of testing cases, served on Technical Advisory Committees for numerous testing programs and twice taught a graduate seminar on Assessment Law at the University of Iowa.

Dr. Phillips' publications include the seminal reference book *Assessment Law in Education* (2010), and legal issues chapters in *Educational Measurement* (2006), *Setting Performance Standards* (2012), *Accessible Tests of Student Achievement* (2011) and *Fairness in Educational Assessment* (2016).

**Mark Raymond** is Research Director and Principal Assessment Scientist at the National Board of Medical Examiners. He has 30 years of experience working and consulting with licensing agencies, professional associations, and universities on matters related to test development and psychometrics. His scholarly interests include job analysis and test blueprinting, generalizability theory, and performance-based assessment. He serves on editorial boards for journals in healthcare and testing, and recently coedited the *Handbook of Test Development* (2nd ed.). Mark received his doctorate in Educational Psychology from Penn State in 1985.

**Walter D. Way** is Chief Research Scientist – Digital Transformation at the College Board. Dr. Way has over 25 years of assessment experience in a variety of settings. He is a nationally known expert on computer-based testing and has worked on testing programs in higher education, licensure and certification, and statewide K–12 assessment. Dr. Way received his Ph.D. in Educational Measurement and Statistics from the University of Iowa.

**James A. Wollack** is a Professor of Quantitative Methods in the Educational Psychology Department and the Director of Testing & Evaluation Services and the Center for Placement Testing at the University of Wisconsin–Madison. His research focuses on test security, item response theory, test construction, and placement testing. He is currently on the Governing Council for the National College Testing Association and the Executive Committee for the Conference on Test Security, and has served on the NCME Board of Directors and as past-chair of the Measurement Services Special Interest Group of AERA.

# Preface

*Susan Davis-Becker and Chad W. Buckendahl*

This volume is focused on current practices in credentialing testing (e.g., certification, licensure) as a guide for practitioners working with these types of programs whether large or small, general or highly specialized. However, practitioners who work in educational settings, particularly areas of secondary education and adult learning, will likely find value in the chapters within this volume due to growing overlap in the types of measurement policies and practices observed in these areas. The chapters included herein are focused on the key components of the test development and validation process (e.g., design, development, scoring, analysis, reporting) as well as overarching issues and concerns (e.g., context/policy of credentialing, validity, security, communication, evaluation). Each chapter addresses current practices, theory, and research within a given topic area, but also includes authentic examples as to how various practices are implemented or current issues observed in credentialing programs.

The volume begins with an exploration in Chapter 1 of the various types of credentialing programs and how these represent key differences in the intended interpretations and uses of test scores; and the evidence needed to support these uses. The topic of collecting and evaluating evidence for supporting scores is more fully explained in Chapter 2 dedicated to validity. The next series of chapters discuss the key test development steps. This process begins in Chapter 3 with test design and questions that should be addressed to properly plan the subsequent test development steps.

In Chapter 4, the next major step is determining the content of the exams through practice analysis or similar processes. The development process continues with creating content and Chapter 5 describes the various types of measurement modes along with key considerations for the development within each. In Chapter 6, the process then shifts to creating a scoring plan by which performance can be estimated and evaluated for all examinees across items, forms, and years. Analysis procedures are described in Chapter 7 that can be used to evaluate item and form level performance.

The final four chapters address specific topics that span the testing process. This section of the volume begins in Chapter 8 with a discussion of communicating with stakeholders as they transition from applicants to candidates to members of the credentialed community. Similarly, the topic of security is critical through test development, administration, and reporting, and Chapter 9 on security discusses how practitioners can be proactive to protect their programs. Following the development of a credentialing program, many practitioners seek an external evaluation or recognition through accreditation or audit and Chapter 10 discusses the various options for doing so. Finally, given the stakes involved in the decisions being made from credentialing test results, programs should be prepared in the event of legal challenges and the final chapter discusses legal principles and seminal cases and how they impact practices today.

Our goal for this volume was to create a comprehensive source that delved into the current measurement practices in credentialing testing based on several motivating factors. First, credentialing testing continues to expand. In addition to the growing number of professions and professional designations that are tied to testing requirements, different types of credentials are emerging, including micro-credentials and badges. More than ever, practitioners need a guide that helps identify the link between various key policy issues, practice options, and professional standards. It is important to acknowledge the level of measurement specificity and validity evidence that is expected when using scores to make various types of decisions.

Second, we wanted to highlight some of the many connections and areas of overlap between practices in educational testing and credentialing testing. So often, the context of credentialing is discussed in testing volumes as a stand-alone section or chapter suggesting that practices in this area are unique from those found in other areas. Although some differences do exist in the policy and contextual factors between credentialing and education, many of the practices follow the same fundamental steps and guidelines. One theme that practitioners will glean from this volume is that research and recommendations from other areas of testing (e.g., education, industrial and organizational psychology) can be interpreted within the policy and context factors that are faced by credentialing practitioners.

Third, and relatedly, the lines are becoming blurred regarding what types of testing falls within each domain. Traditionally, tests delivered in schools are thought of as educational and tests delivered to individuals seeking a job or advanced designation are thought of as credentialing. However, we now have students in schools taking tests at the end of their high school career to determine if they are ready for college and career, which largely mimics the nature of credentialing (i.e., determining if someone is prepared for performing in a given environment or role). Conversely, one can find instances of credentialing exam results being used to evaluate educational or training programs. Given that the purposes of testing in these two domains are showing more similarities, it is important to better understand how professional expectations align with said purposes so that practitioners can ensure they will have validity evidence to support these anticipated uses.

Our hope is that this volume helps advance the science and practice of testing in credentialing as other such volumes in this area as *Certification: The ICE Handbook* (2nd ed.) (Knapp, Anderson, & Wild, 2009), *Licensure testing: Purposes, procedures, and practices* (Impara, 1995) and *Understanding testing in occupational licensing* (Fortune, 1985). These volumes have served as foundational references in this field and a guide for many practitioners.

# Acknowledgments

This volume was assembled with assistance from a great number of individuals. In addition to the authors who contributed their insights and research efforts, a number of volunteer reviews also supported this process by providing feedback during the writing process. We would like to thank Grady Barnhill, Kirk Becker, Matthew Burke, Adrienne Cadle, Sarah Carroll, Andrew Dwyer, Chuck Freidman, Kurt Geisinger, Jefferson Glassie, Deborah Harris, James Impara, Deirdre Knapp, Tim Konold, John Mattar, William Mehrens, Gerald Melican, Kimberly Swygert, Richard Tannenbaum, John Twing, Ada Woo, and Cynthia Woodley. Their assistance with this project was invaluable in ensuring the quality of the content and representation of best practices in our industry.

# 1 Credentialing

## A Continuum of Measurement Theories, Policies, and Practices

*Chad W. Buckendahl*

**Overview of Credentialing**

In concept, testing in the professions may elicit images of candidates preparing for their medical boards or the bar exam. Although this is an accurate picture for these respective professions, the area of credentialing has greatly expanded. Shimberg (1982) noted that at the time, more than 800 professions were licensed and that it was a dramatic increase since the early 1900s when regulatory agencies began to engage in the credentialing process. Schmitt (1995) indicated that the number of professions offering a credential had again increased. More recently, the number of occupations that require a license is greater than 1,100 (Morath, 2015) with this figure representing approximately 30% of workers in the United States (Kearney, Hershbein, & Boddy, 2015). This expansion is not surprising as new or existing professions often try to emulate established professions such as, medicine, dentistry and law, that have long been concerned with developing and maintaining systematic processes for entry into the profession. Emerging professions have the responsibility of persuading their state legislators of the necessity to protect the citizenry from unlicensed or unregulated practitioners who do not have the requisite education, training or competence for safe and effective practice.

This public protection component of state licensure is required to establish the process, but the profession also benefits from a defined scope of practice and protection from competition from less skilled, educated or qualified practitioners. The success that the established professions have had in establishing the credibility of their credential and the brand associated with it has led to numerous other professions striving to build their own credentialing process and programs as a strategy for communicating to the public the importance and distinction of a particular set of knowledge, skills, and abilities. Similarly, earlier volumes have explored a range of test development and validation activities within occupations, particularly focusing on licensure and certification (Fortune, 1985; Impara, 1995; Knapp, Anderson, & Wild, 2009). Extending this work to broader treatments of credentialing is important. Throughout this chapter, the term "profession" is used to be broadly inclusive of all occupations that rely on credentials to help define it.

This expansion of the credentialing concept spans the continuum of measurement practices that may have previously been associated separately with education, licensure, certification, and employment eligibility. However, as is discussed in this chapter, the lines that distinguish these traditional disciplines in the credentialing field are blurring. The result is that practitioners and policymakers need to have a greater breadth of understanding about how measurement theories, policies, and practices apply within and across these areas. The risks of failing to gain this breadth of understanding are also discussed in this chapter as external forces—political and legal—can influence how measurement principles are applied and interpreted in practice. Within the chapter, the term "credentialing" is used to be inclusive of the range of credentials that different sponsors may offer. The distinctions among the types of credentials are discussed below. An important first step in understanding credentialing programs is how they are used and why individuals may seek to obtain a given credential.

## *Purposes*

Similar to the range of credentials available in professions, there is a range of purposes as to why certain credentials exist and how scores from examinations should be interpreted and used. For many credentialing programs, the emphasis is on public protection, specifically to distinguish candidates who are at least minimally qualified from those who are not. The idea of public protection stems from a profession's belief or regulatory authority's responsibility that the members of the public would not be able to distinguish qualified versus unqualified performance. For professions involving risk to the public, such as those in architecture, aviation, education, healthcare, or law, an incompetent practitioner can produce lasting, negative consequences.

The concept of public protection is often associated with certain types of credentialing (e.g., licensure, certification), but some programs exist to certify or recognize individuals who have demonstrated specialized knowledge, skills, and abilities in a particular domain or subdomain within a profession (e.g., specialty certification). Other credentials are closely tied to education or training and designed to serve as evidence of learning a particular domain of knowledge or skills associated with something that would be valued in the market (e.g., assessment-based certificates). As an expansion of these historical purposes, an emerging, yet poorly defined class of credentials is also being observed (e.g., micro-credentials, badging). These newer credentials may provide recognition for a range of reasons and be only loosely connected to sound measurement principles. The range of options for candidates and the differentiation for consumers can make understanding credentialing challenging. Beyond programmatic and public purposes, there are some important incentives for participants to engage in a credentialing program.

From a candidate's perspective, the purpose of seeking a credential may be to demonstrate sufficient competence to be eligible to practice in a given profession. Beyond the entry-level expectations of a profession, there are often market-based incentives for candidates to demonstrate a particular depth of abilities that distinguish themselves from others in their field. More broadly, a credential may be considered by employers as part of eligibility requirements for employment purposes.

## *Sponsors of Programs*

Similar to the range of intended uses and interpretations of scores from credentialing examinations, there is a range of sponsors for these programs. Agencies or organizations that award and enforce credentials may assume responsibility for development and validation of tests associated with their credentials (e.g., National Commission on Certification of Physician Assistants [NCCPA]). At the same time, some professions have formed federations where one or more intermediary agencies have been formed to be responsible for development and validation of the program's examination(s) (e.g., National Council of Architectural Registration Boards [NCARB], American Board of Dental Examiners [ADEX], Federation of State Boards of Physical Therapy [FSBPT]). Members of the federation (e.g., state licensing boards) contribute to the process and then agree to accept the results of the examination(s) to facilitate efficiency in the process.

For some credentials, membership associations or trade groups may serve as the sponsor for the credentialing program (e.g., American Physical Therapy Association [APTA] for physical therapy specialties, National Strength and Conditioning Association [NSCA] for personal training). For some professions, this may be a single association (e.g., APTA) whereas for others, there may be multiple membership associations or programs that compete for credibility and market share among members of the eligible population (e.g., NSCA). In addition, some credentialing programs are sponsored by organizations that are then seeking to assign or place individuals somewhere within divisions of the parent organization (e.g., agencies like the Army, Navy, Federal Bureau of Investigation, National Security Agency within the U.S. Department of Defense). However, sometimes these credentials begin to have value in the workforce or labor market beyond just the requirements of the sponsoring organization.

The sponsorship and development of credentialing programs by organizations that may be viewed as employers necessitates a discussion of how the intended uses of credentialing examinations can be positioned as intersecting with purposes of education programs and employment decisions.

## *Overlap with Education and Employment Testing*

As is discussed in more detail in the next section, some credentials are closely associated with specific educational training programs or experiences. In these situations, the development and validation processes will often mimic the processes observed in educational achievement testing programs. In a more historical meaning of the term, however, the meaning of the credential is interpreted relative to what occurs in practice and not directly associated with a given curriculum, instructional or training program.

Because many credentials are used as an important source of evidence for demonstrating qualifications, it is not surprising that they are frequently included as part of eligibility requirements in an employment process. This raises the question of whether credentialing examinations should be interpreted as employment tests. Although the purpose of a credentialing examination may be to simply distinguish between those candidates who are minimally competent or not, in some cases, those individuals who do not possess the credential are deemed not to meet the requirements for employment. The *Standards for Educational and Psychological Testing* (AERA, APA, & NCME, 2014; *Standards*) make a distinction among tests that are used for selection, placement, and promotion in the employment process from those examinations that are used to make a determination of minimum qualifications that may be used to screen out candidates who do not meet these minimum expectations. Employment tests are sometimes used to rank candidates – for example, interviews may be granted only to those candidates in the higher score groups, especially if the number of available positions is very limited. This ranking function requires that the exam produce scores of adequate information and reliability across the entire score range, rather than just near the passing point. Although seemingly subtle, it is an important distinction that has implications for development, gathering validation evidence, and legal defensibility of the examinations (see Chapter 11).

Suffice it to say, the proliferation of credentials for a range of purposes has led to an increase in the gray area that may have historically distinguished educational assessments, credentialing examinations, and employment tests. Some of this overlap can be attributed to semantics and a lack of clarification of the intended purpose of each program. More concerning is that some of the overlap is attributable to programs expanding purposes beyond the limits that may have been originally intended. Within the educational assessment sector, we have observed policies that incorporate student achievement results for purposes of school and educator accountability. In higher education, the results from licensure and certification exams are used to evaluate or serve as a proxy for outcomes evidence as part of program accreditation. These additional uses can be particularly problematic when organizations or training programs make evaluations based on subscores that lack appropriate psychometric characteristics to support the use. Although perhaps reasonable as policy in concept, the measurement community has been appropriately critical of these expanded uses of assessment when the policies are implemented without the necessary evidence and validity evaluation to support the interpretations and uses of the scores and decisions.

The characterization of credentialing programs can often be confusing and interpreted to mean different things depending on the particular profession and context. Although attempting to explain how or why the confusion emerged would likely be futile, it is important for readers to understand the distinctions among the common types of credentials they may encounter in practice. The next section illustrates these types, highlighting similarities and differences. It should also be noted that because there are different considerations under each country's respective legal and regulatory systems, the credentialing discussions in this chapter are drawn from interpretation and use in jurisdictions in the United States of America. Although some will be analogous to other countries, jurisdiction-specific requirements will be controlling.

## Focus of Credentialing Programs

A variety of credentials are often consolidated into a single group of programs that have a testing component. Although convenient for communicating that the outcome of participating in such a process is a credential that communicates something to the public, all credentials are not equivalent in terms of what they mean and how they are interpreted. Further, semantics can interfere with understanding how credentials are administered and enforced. It also helps to understand how credentialing emerged as an important component in the development of professions.

Credentialing, particularly as it relates to licensure and certification has a long history. Schmitt (1995) provides a summary of how licensure specifically developed since approximately 2000 BC when tariffs were imposed on medical practitioners as part of an effort to regulate practice. Many of the early examples of attempts to regulate professions were related specifically to healthcare. Given that licensure and certification programs are often designed around efforts to protect the health, safety, and welfare of the public, it stands to reason that professionals in the healthcare sector would be associated with these criteria. However, the effort to define and regulate professions extended beyond government agencies.

The Guild system that emerged in the 13th to 15th centuries began to establish rules for membership, expectations for training through apprenticeships, and also member-determined expectations for entry (Schmitt, 1995). The purposes of these efforts were likely less about ensuring competency of members, but rather control of the profession and ultimately the market by limiting the number of individuals who were included to prop up prices and wages. Although the Guilds may have functioned more like trade unions, this initial shift from government regulation to regulation by a profession could be interpreted as the precursor to more self-regulation or certification programs that are sponsored by associations or similar membership organizations within professions. However, as particular trends ebb and flow, the push for regulation of professions has observed similar periods of stronger or weaker support.

One of the reasons for the push for deregulation of certain professional credentialing requirements in the mid-1800s was that for professions like physicians and attorneys, there was a perception that the education programs training these individuals were of much better quality than had been at the time of the initial implementation of the licensing laws. As a result, perhaps the need for regulation had become outdated. However, by the late 1800s, this belief seems to have diminished with the growth in the number of schools and training programs coupled with concerns about the quality and consistency of practitioners who were representing themselves as having a particular skill set (Schmitt, 1995). Since that time, the number of professions regulated by states or professional associations has continued to grow.

It seems to be a case of history repeating itself because in this discussion of reasons for developing and enforcing a credential, the conversation about the need has gone on for decades and yet many of the arguments for why some credentials exist today are still ongoing. Within many professions, there is a belief that graduation from an accredited training program should be sufficient evidence that candidates have achieved at least the knowledge, skills, and abilities to have earned an entry level credential. At the same time, there are stakeholders in these professions who argue that having matriculated through one of many potential educational programs alone is insufficient without an independent demonstration of minimum competence.

Considering the hundreds of professions, specializations, and skill sets that are now credentialed, at what point have we gone too far where the intent and the value of a credential is diluted? Take, for example, a case in which a woman challenged a state's Barber, Cosmetology/Barber, Esthetics, Electrology and Nail Technology Licensing Board for the right to provide African hair-braiding services without a license after being ordered to cease and desist offering the service (Romboy, 2012). The court in this case noted that the specific hair-braiding service was beyond the scope of the public protection interests of the licensing board. The lingering measurement question is whether the collection of evidence supports the intended interpretation and use of the credential examination and its role in the credentialing program.

There is a difference between this extreme example and representing oneself in a profession without the proper abilities and credentials. However, because credentialing has expanded so much, so too, have the reasons for development of the credential. Where public protection was a historical, primary intent, today, professions without recognized, credible credentials are at risk of being seen as less than professional and are at further risk of allowing external forces to regulate their profession for them. Fortunately, psychometricians have not succumbed to the siren song of credentialing within its profession. This distinction between government-regulated versus profession-regulated is part of the next section that describes the types of credentials and related characteristics observed in practice

## *Licensure*

Perhaps the most widely known credentials are those that can be classified into the licensure category. Most laypersons can name a number of professions that require a license to practice including architects, attorneys, educators, and physicians. Shimberg (1982)

provides a useful definition of licensure that is drawn from the U.S. Department of Health, Education, and Welfare (1977) that states that licensing is:

> The process by which an agency of government grants permission to an individual to engage in a given occupation upon finding that the applicant has attained the minimal degree of competency necessary to ensure that the public health, safety, and welfare will be reasonably well protected.
>
> (p. 15)

With some exceptions (e.g., private pilot licenses issued by the Federal Aviation Administration), licensure is a function of the state or territorial jurisdiction where an individual seeks to practice. Therefore, each jurisdiction may have different requirements for eligibility, examination, and maintenance of the credential. Although there are varying degrees of reciprocity and shared efforts for efficiency in many professions, the landscape to obtain and retain a license can be daunting. As noted above, the focus of licensure is for public protection. The logic of this focus is that the regulation of a government agency can serve as an intermediary between the prospective practitioner and the public as prospective consumers to help evaluate minimum competency. Competency can be defined as the ability to do something successfully or efficiently.

It is important to note the focal point of licensure—minimum competency. Unlike an academic achievement test that may seek to evaluate mastery of a domain or an employment test that might be used to help evaluate who is the best candidate for a particular position, the measurement focus of licensure is on those knowledge, skills, and abilities that are directly related to the health, safety, and welfare of the public. This can create challenges for users who seek to co-opt the results of these tests for other uses including outcomes assessment for higher education programs, selection or placement into academic programs, or selection or placement for employment purposes.

Licensure programs generally include multiple sources of evidence prior to determination of whether the credential has been earned. This is common for many credentialing programs. Specifically, licensure programs will generally include an educational requirement, a background check of the individual, and a requirement to pass one or more examinations. Some licensing programs may also require some amount of experience as part of the eligibility requirements. Therefore, a license can be interpreted as a regulated barrier to enter a profession.

Although having a license is necessary to represent oneself with a protected title or legally practice for professions that require it, the nature of the licensing process and its examinations are different from employment tests. Having a license to practice does not guarantee an individual employment. The *Standards* speak to this distinction in that a credentialing examination may serve as an eligibility screener as part of the employment process, but the scores of the tests are not designed to predict effective performance on the job or distinguish among qualified candidates. Rather, the validity evidence should be sufficient to support a claim that the individual possesses the necessary minimum amount of competence to enter the profession. The credential that an individual earns in this mandatory process is a license, but licensure is best characterized as a process that, after obtaining the initial license, there is a requirement for continued maintenance of the license.

Individuals holding a license are usually required to pay administrative fees to the regulatory agency for monitoring and enforcement. In addition, the licensing program will have additional requirements for the credential beyond the fees to ensure that the practitioner remains current and that the individual holding the license continues to practice in good standing. Some of the ways that regulatory agencies ensure maintenance of the credential is through continuing education, participation in profession-specific activities, or, in rarer instances, retesting after a certain period of time. The purported goal of the maintenance process is to ensure that license holders continue to be reasonably current with respect to changing practice. Debate among professionals about whether learning activities such as continuing education are really a substitute for periodic demonstration of competence is ongoing. However, treatment of that topic is beyond the scope of this chapter and is closely tied with particular professions and their related credentialing programs.

As noted as the outset of this section, there is semantic confusion over how credentials are characterized. For example, licensure is considered mandatory for practice and requires a demonstration of competency. Similarly, certification requires a demonstration of competency, but is generally considered voluntary. Registration is considered mandatory, but usually without the requirement for a demonstration of competency. The challenge, then, is that the distinct meaning of each of these types of credentials is confounded when certifications or registrations function as de facto licenses in many jurisdictions (e.g., certified educators, certified public accountants, registered nurses). Therefore, the generic designation of each of these different types as a credential is often viewed as more inclusive with the particular label or program branding being secondary to the requirements of the program and how the credential is interpreted and used in practice. The next section highlights the similarities and differences that certification shares with licensure.

## *Certification*

Although sometimes interpreted by the public as interchangeable with the expectations for a license, it is not, although certification represents a large and growing segment of the credentialing sector. There are hundreds of these credentials, many of which are widely recognized. For example, physicians may seek to achieve nationally recognized specialty certifications such as emergency medicine or family medicine. Attorneys may seek jurisdiction-specific specialty certification in family law or estate planning. Or an accountant or financial analyst may seek certification as a Chartered Financial Analyst. Similar to licensure, certification examinations require candidates to demonstrate a minimally acceptable level of competency in the domain of interest. These demonstrations generally occur through written and/or performance-based examinations that are developed using methods and processes described by authors in the subsequent chapters of this volume.

In contrast to the predominantly state level oversight of licensure programs, certification programs are often developed by an association, vendor, or the profession itself. Many certification programs, like the medical board specialty exams noted above, are national or even international in scope. However, some certification exams may only be recognized within a given jurisdiction (e.g., county code enforcement official, restaurant food safety manager). Some of the specialty certification areas for attorneys noted above may only be offered or supported within a particular jurisdiction with oversight provided by the bar association within the jurisdiction. Because many certifications are national or recognized across jurisdictions, reciprocity is not as much of an issue. However, for some certifications (e.g., crane operators, selected nursing specialties, personal training) there is a competitive landscape for recognition of programs that may require additional efforts to educate the public on the similarities and differences among competing programs. The role of intermediary to the public is within the program itself. This can create an uneasy relationship between broader goals of public protection and business interests unless conflicts of interest and activities that could be interpreted as self-serving can be minimized.

Also similar to licensure examinations, the focus of a validity argument for certification examinations is to ensure that evidence supports an interpretation of at least minimally qualified performance. Demonstrations of competency are based on the knowledge, skills, and abilities related to the definition of performance in the respective domain. The concept of minimally qualified, though, can create intuitive misconceptions that may appear to be counterintuitive to actual practice. For example, the expectations for an individual to achieve a particular medical specialty certification require a medical license and then additional demonstrated competency and maintenance beyond the entry level of performance required for licensure. Although minimally qualified for the interpretation of the credential, the demonstrated skill set goes beyond the expectations for obtaining a license to practice. Illustrating the concept with the medical specialty example, not all physicians will achieve a specialty certification; however, the lack of this credential does not preclude these individuals from practice entirely.

Certification programs, too, generally include multiple sources of evidence prior to determination of whether the credential has been earned. Similarly, programs will often have a combination of eligibility requirements that may include education, experience, or prerequisite credentials that are a precursor to then taking one or more examinations to earn the credential. However, a key departure from the characteristics of a licensure program is the voluntary nature of certification.

For certifications that are truly voluntary, it is not necessary to have the credential to practice. However, for some professions, earning a particular certification may be viewed as distinguishing themselves in the market or as a tacit expectation. Similar to licensure, possession of a certification does not constitute an expectation of employment, but may be used in the employment process as a preferred characteristic of applicants. If a certification is used as an eligibility requirement—whether to practice or for employment—the use of the credential shifts from being voluntary to mandatory. This can lead to the need for certification programs to collect additional evidence to support the interpretation and use of scores for this purpose. This potential overlap of credentialing and employment purposes was also noted above and is discussed in greater depth by Phillips (see Chapter 11). Similar to licensure, evidence for certification programs should be sufficient to support a claim that the individual possesses at least the necessary minimum level of competence to perform the job.

For many certification programs, there are maintenance requirements that are similar to those for licensure. These requirements will be unique to the program, but may include such activities as continuing education, professional involvement, or retesting after a period of time. As is the case with licensure, there is debate within a number of professions about whether the maintenance requirements for the credential should require demonstration of continued competence or enhanced competence. Psychometrically, we would frame the question as one of defining the meaning of the credential at a point of initially earning the credential versus a period of time when it may need to be renewed. For certifying programs, the discussion also extends beyond measurement questions to ones of policy and governance. Compelling arguments have been made for both interpretations without consensus in the credentialing industry.

### *Registration*

Having some regulatory similarities with licensure in that jurisdictions may mandate registration, the protection that the regulation affords is often one of title, rather than of the practice itself. The concept is analogous to a trademark or similar protection of intellectual property. In practice, this means that individuals who engage in the activities of the profession may do so, but may not use the regulated title associated with it (Schmitt, 1995; Shimberg, 1982). Registration is considered a lower standard than licensure and certification because individuals are generally only required to provide their name and contact information. Although some registration programs will have additional requirements, demonstration of minimally qualified abilities with respect to competency standards are required rarely. However, this also communicates that there is generally a much lower risk to the public with respect to the health, safety, and welfare associated with licensure and many certification programs. Because registration programs are not competency based, there are generally no requirements for maintenance of the credential beyond keeping contact information up to date and often paying an administrative fee.

As has also been noted with licensure and certification, the vocabulary used to characterize credentials can quickly blur. For example, a Registered Dental Hygienist is a licensed profession while the National Registry of Emergency Medical Technicians characterizes its programs as a certification. The legacy characterizations and branding associated with programs reinforces the use in this volume of the synthesizing language of credentialing as it relates to these widely used terms. Licensure, certification, and registration have comprised historical treatments of credentialing. As the workforce evolves, the emergence of newer credentials has led to additional types of credentials that may be observed in practice. Some of these are discussed in the next sections.

## *Assessment-based Certificates*

With traditional credentialing programs there is often consideration, but not intentional alignment with a particular education or training program. This is because there are often different educational philosophies that guide training programs that ultimately lead to diversity among practitioners. In contrast to these approaches, an assessment-based certificate functions more like an educational assessment program that uses formal measurement to ensure that student-candidates have learned the objectives associated with the role on which the certificate is based. Similar to educational assessment programs, there is an intent for the curriculum or learning objectives, instruction, and assessment to function in close alignment in the context of the intended meaning of the credential. The nature of the relationship between training and assessment will often provide distinguishing evidence of whether the program is better characterized as a certification or an assessment-based certificate.

These certificates are often considered voluntary and can be used to enhance a particular skill set within a particular profession. However, when applied in workforce settings, the use can shift to purposes that may be more similar to mandatory or employment (e.g., selection, promotion, retention) uses. One example of an assessment-based certificate program where there is alignment between education/training and assessment is the food safety manager program, ServSafe®, sponsored by the National Restaurant Association. Another example of an assessment-based certificate is the Rigging and Signalers Certificate sponsored by the Carpenters International Training Fund, illustrating that a program may be designed to measure a focused set of skills within an employment setting for specific sectors within an industry. Similar to registration, there are typically no maintenance requirements for an assessment-based certificate.

For credentials that involve the application of formal measurement principles, the psychometric considerations that are discussed in subsequent chapters of this volume are similar. Test development and validation activities for the credentialing examination programs already discussed are generalizable. This means that if an author discusses an illustration of how a method applies to a licensure examination, it is likely that the practice can also be observed across the range of credentialing programs. Assessment-based certificates, though, have curricular and instructional design elements that overlap with practices that will be more familiar within educational assessment programs. Concerns regarding psychometric integrity begin to rise as discussed in the next section about another emerging area of practice in credentialing.

## *Micro-credentials and Badging*

As the other chapters of this volume demonstrate, developing and supporting credentialing decisions is a nontrivial validation effort. When a score from a credentialing examination is used to make an assertion about whether a candidate is competent to enter into a profession or as an eligibility criterion for employment in an occupation that requires a certain level of certification, the evidence that supports that assertion is likely to be challenged. In many instances, the inferences underlying these scores are based on compensatory decision rules that permit candidates to overcome weaknesses in some parts of the domain with strengths in other parts of the domain. Although many fields such as architecture, dentistry, medicine, and airplane pilots require conjunctive demonstrations of competency, there are assumptions underlying those determinations and an expectation that each of these decisions can be psychometrically supported. As an extension of this conjunctive concept, there has been an emergence of micro-credentialing and badging in an effort to further specify elements within domains and make inferences about an individual's competency.

One of the goals of these additional efforts is to provide stakeholders with a more refined picture of the abilities of an individual with respect to focused learning or a desired competency. As a result, this class of credentials has a range of interpretations and therefore an often undesirable range of psychometric quality associated with them. At the heart of these credentials is the question of the intended meaning and the interpretation by users. For example, some digital badges are awarded simply for participation at a conference or an event. These awards have little value beyond public recognition and generally have no psychometric properties. They are similarly analogous to the recognition credentials observed in some professions (e.g., Fellow, Diplomate) that may be based on factors other than an independent determination of competence. Another use might be to enhance an existing credential by requiring candidates to demonstrate greater depth of their abilities within a particular subdomain. A combination of these smaller elements of the domain may provide a perception of greater confidence in an individual's abilities on these topics, but depending on the evidence to support the assertion, it comes with a potentially high psychometric price tag.

The intended interpretation and use of the micro-credential or badge can lure users into a trap of placing greater faith in these credentials without an understanding of whether there is sufficient validity evidence to support it. So, the risk to the user is that the representation of competency may not be supported by sound measurement evidence. Similar risks are evident for the sponsoring program and the psychometric community. From the programmatic perspective, without a concerted effort to educate stakeholders, each additional micro-credential or badge that is associated with a core credential has the potential to dilute the meaning and value of the brand if stakeholders begin to rely too much on the adjunct information. The risks for psychometric practice are numerous and include specification of the domain, dimensionality, measurement error, and decision rules about threshold competency. Because micro-credentialing and badging are not yet well defined, future volumes about credentialing may be able to provide greater clarity. At this point in time, the purpose of including this brief treatment of the topic is designed to raise awareness among practitioners who may have opportunities to develop solutions. As this is a more recent trend in credentialing, subsequent chapters in this volume do not focus on it.

Because the branding of a credential may not appropriately convey the intended interpretation and use of scores, the development of a validation framework that aligns with the specific purpose is important. Such a framework would provide a roadmap for credentialing programs to organize, prioritize, collect, and evaluate evidence in support of the intended purpose of the program. In the next section, a suggested validation framework for credentialing programs is discussed along with an illustration from a licensure examination program.

## Validation Framework for Credentialing

The *Standards* recommend collecting and evaluating categories of evidence that reflect decades of research regarding validity theory (see Chapter 2). The *Standards* provide broad guidance for test developers, sponsors, and users, but do not prescribe methods for demonstrating compliance. At the same time, the *Standards* are necessarily less descriptive on a number of factors that impact validation activities, but are contextual for the respective program. In their evaluation of the *National Assessment of Educational Progress*, Buckendahl et al. (2009) suggested three categories that could be used as an organizing framework for validation: operational, policy, and innovation. However, beyond these high-level descriptions, the authors did not provide additional input regarding how such a framework would be constructed or what would be included in an output of such an effort. Buckendahl (2013) expanded on these categories in an effort to provide more explicit guidance about how to develop a framework and use it as an organizational tool for programs and practitioners. For purposes of reference, practitioners are defined here to mean individuals responsible for design, development, implementation, evaluation, and redevelopment of operational testing programs. The intent of this framework is to help practitioners, many of whom are not psychometricians, organize and prioritize their validation efforts. Each organizing source of evidence is described here.

### *Operational*

The operational aspects of the framework proportionally represent the largest and most common component that practitioners consider when creating a test development and validation plan. This element can be further subdivided into five sources of evidence suggested by the *Standards*: test content, response processes, internal structure, relations to other variables, and consequences of testing. To emphasize the contextualized nature of validation, it is important to note that each credentialing program's framework will be similar, but how it is designed and implemented will be unique to its respective interpretations and uses. As a result, one should not interpret these organizing sources as a specific profile or as being equally weighted in importance. Rather, each source and its corresponding evidence will contribute differentially relative to the intended uses and interpretations. This is particularly important when evaluating evidence collected in each of these categories of the framework. Because validation (see Chapter 2) and sources of operational evidence are discussed at length by the authors in this volume, the discussion here is limited to a high-level description and an illustration for how a credentialing program might construct such a framework.

*Policy*

Knowing that policies—internal and external—influences credentialing programs, it is reasonable that policy considerations are a component of the operational development and validation of examinations within a credentialing program. However, policies that were unknown or not considered at the outset can redirect validation priorities and efforts midcourse. The policy aspect of the organizing framework is included as a placeholder to remind programs of the dynamic elements of policies or legislative actions that can modify intended interpretations and uses that also influence practices. Within the framework, this element refers to the uncertainty of policies that can emerge during a program's lifecycle. This aspect could be characterized as the most dynamic of the sources of evidence that may be necessary for a program because it is difficult to appropriately plan. Although programs may be able to anticipate some policy changes, it is unlikely that programs can accurately anticipate all of them. Henderson-Montero and Buckendahl (2010) noted that programs' and, specifically, measurement professionals' ability to adapt to continually changing environments can greatly influence the success of a program.

*Innovation*

Changes to policy can challenge programs to respond to changing validation needs. However, these policy initiatives or questions may be relatively short term. The innovation component of the validation framework is intended to focus on the system level design characteristics that may shape the program in the future. As a result, these validation efforts may be conducted concurrently with, but distinct from, the operational and policy related validation activities. The challenge of maintaining current evidence while preparing for the future is nontrivial. As such, credentialing programs often neglect to discuss the strategic, program design features necessary to transition to the next evolutionary phase of operation. For example, a credentialing examination program transitioning from paper-pencil to computer-based administration, or from linear to item-level adaptive delivery requires organized validation efforts to ensure a smooth transition. Studies to identify, collect, and evaluate the necessary supporting evidence may occur over multiple operational development cycles before fully migrating to the new phase of the program. Consideration of future validation needs can help credentialing programs be better prepared and reduce the risk of failing to address challenges that may not have previously existed in the program.

Under the validation framework described above, credentialing programs can begin to identify, prioritize, collect, and evaluate evidence that contributes to their intended interpretation and use of test scores. The next section discusses how a credentialing program could apply the framework in practice.

## Application of the Validation Framework

The example credentialing program described in this section is informed by the components of a clinical licensure examination program in dentistry that is used to determine eligibility for candidates seeking to enter the profession. Although inspired by an actual program, it is important to note that the framework is intended to illustrate how a program might construct its own and should not be construed as representing any existing credentialing program. As a brief overview of what could be included in a clinical examination program, there may be a combination of written and performance-testing components. Written examinations would be intended to measure candidates' clinical judgments in the respective domains of the profession, while the performance examinations would be designed to measure the integration of cognitive and psychomotor skills for each of the disciplines through job-related tasks. This example is used throughout this section as context for illustrating the validation framework.

The framework can serve multiple purposes. First, it is intended to help credentialing programs organize and prioritize the evidence they need to support the interpretation and use of scores from their program. However, a secondary use is one of communication to stakeholder groups. Specifically, an organizing framework like the one illustrated in Table 1.1 can be used to communicate the multiple validation efforts credentialing programs may use during development or revision. This approach may be particularly valuable when there is a range of stakeholders (e.g., candidates, training programs, regulatory authority, profession, public). For interested readers, note that the range of stakeholders suggested for a credentialing program is similar to the diverse constituencies experienced in educational assessment and accountability programs that to confront a variety of stakeholders who want to use assessment scores for a variety of purposes that range from student achievement to school and educator accountability. As a related part of its value to communication, a message can be shared with stakeholders of the extent to which the framework is comprehensive. In a practical sense, this type of information can be useful for resource requests and planning.

Rather than separating the interpretation and use argument as suggested by Kane (2013), practitioners in the credentialing community may want to consider these characteristics as prerequisite context to the organizing framework. The argument then serves as a point of reference for evaluating evidence. For the illustrative licensure examination program discussed in this section, the first step in applying the framework begins with an articulation of the intended interpretation and use of test scores, a rationale for each use, and a description of anticipated, but unintended interpretations and uses.

## *Intended Interpretation and Use*

Although most readers may have visited a dentist at some point, they may not be familiar with the examination processes for prospective candidates. The licensure process for dentistry in most jurisdictions in the U.S. involves a series of examinations that are intended to measure cognitive and psychomotor abilities. In focusing on clinical examinations in dentistry, the primary intended interpretation and use of test scores are to provide reasonable assurance to the public that entry-level dentists have demonstrated the job-related, clinical judgments and skills that are necessary for safe, independent, entry-level practice. An unintended goal would be to distinguish among degrees of competency. A secondary intended interpretation and use of test scores from the program may be to provide descriptive feedback to dental schools regarding the extent to which students have demonstrated the entry-level clinical judgments and skills related to licensure within the major disciplines that define the profession. However, even this use is limited by the intersection of the measurement focus of a licensure examination as opposed to an educational assessment.

With respect to the dental licensure program, there is a combination of cognitive and psychomotor measurement approaches used to evaluate entry-level competency.

Table 1.1 Illustrative Validation Activities for a Credentialing Examination for Evaluating Clinical Judgments and Skills in Dentistry

| Content | Operational | | | | Policy | Innovation |
|---|---|---|---|---|---|---|
| | Response Processes | Internal Structure | Relations to other Variables | Consequences | | |
| Practice analysis including survey of practitioners | Alignment of test design with cognitive and psychomotor skills | Analysis of item and form performance | Candidates' performance with training courses | Disciplinary record of credentialing agency | Exam results compared with class rank or GPA | Simulation technologies for skills exam |
| Item, task, and scoring criteria development and editing | Cognitive labs to evaluate intended processes for simulated tasks | Equating and scaling analyses to retain meaning of passing score | Candidates' performance on practice exams | Impact of program on curriculum, instruction, and practice | Overlap of training program content with exam | Alternative item types for written exam |
| Independent review of job-related content and cognitive processes | Analysis of rater performance and decision consistency | Dimensionality and drift studies to evaluate stability and exam security | Analysis of potential disparate impact | Impact on workforce capacity | Responding to comparability with other exam programs | Additional quality control methods for written and skills exams |
| Standard setting to establish passing score | | | | | Responding to unintended uses of the exam or legal challenge | |

Each major discipline (e.g., diagnosis and treatment planning, operative, prosthodontic, endodontic) is measured with a separate examination to reflect the different abilities associated with each. Passing each clinical examination indicates that the candidate has demonstrated minimally competent clinical judgments and skills consistent with entry level practice to safely and independently be eligible to enter the profession.

### *Rationale for Each Intended Use*

The justification for the primary intended use reinforces what Shimberg (1982) characterized as the purpose of licensure, specifically, to protect the public. The program's primary purpose is further supported through state-level legislation that requires state boards of dentistry to regulate entry into the profession. Expectations for the profession are then described in varying levels of detail in state-level Practice Acts that serve as a basis for formal studies that specify the domain. In Chapter 4, Clauser and Raymond discuss the content specification process for credentialing process in greater detail.

A justification for the additional uses of scores from the program is that training programs in the field seek feedback on the effectiveness of the curriculum they have adopted and outcomes of instructional practices. This is similar to expectations that any educational or professional training programs would have regarding feedback from formal measurement activities. Therefore, providing aggregate, descriptive feedback on candidates' performance can serve as feedback to these institutions. However, these secondary interpretations and uses of scores are more difficult to justify in practice.

### *Anticipated, Unintended Interpretations and Uses*

Like many credentialing programs where educational training programs are designed to broadly align with expectations of the profession of interest, there is often a desire to use results from the credentialing examinations for evidence of successful outcomes for programmatic accreditation purposes by third parties. Although it may seem intuitive that results from the credentialing examination serve as evidence for the program, this is where the desire by training programs to receive the descriptive information noted above can transform into an unintended consequence. Specifically, the results from credentialing examinations are rarely designed to serve as a comprehensive assessment for program evaluation. Credentialing examinations focus on knowledge, skills, and abilities needed for the purpose of the credential, and generally are designed to maximize measurement information around the passing score. As a result, with the exception of assessment-based certificates, the alignment with a specific educational program is unintended.

Therefore, all components of an educational training program that might prepare a *student* will not necessarily contribute to that purpose when evaluating a prospective *candidate*. This discussion only provides one example of an anticipated, unintended interpretation and use. Additional unintended uses may include the use of these domain scores to evaluate the effectiveness of faculty or to inform selection decisions for specialty residency programs. Clearly, many more unintended uses can be anticipated. However, it reinforces the need to note these limitations at the design or revision phase of development and to communicate them through program documentation, candidate information, and score reports to mitigate unintended uses and to educate stakeholders.

*Illustrative Validation Activities*

Using the context of the program as described above, Table 1.1 shows a sample of the validation activities that a clinical licensure examination program could use in an initial design. These validation activities should be considered representative of the types of studies a credentialing program like this might consider. However, it should not be interpreted as what a comprehensive validation plan might entail. Nor should the studies be interpreted as equivalent in terms of their value to the credentialing program. The validation activities and studies are organized by the respective framework category or subcategory.

The information provided in Table 1.1 suggests a number of potential validation opportunities for a credentialing examination program, but does not specify how these would occur or on what schedule. The implementation of the plan is a critical next step in moving from concept to actualization. This is where the context of the program and the input from stakeholders will be particularly valuable to be able to prioritize which activities are more important in the short, intermediate, and longer term to respond to evolving program needs. The validation activities presented above are designed to serve different stakeholder group interests. For example, most of the operational activities are intended to support the core purpose of the program—that is, to provide sound evidence to support credentialing eligibility decisions. This has an outcome of assisting candidates, regulatory bodies, and indirectly, training programs, in contributing to the public protection goal. Similarly, in the innovation part of the framework, the examination program might be characterized as the primary stakeholder, but may serve to respond to efficiencies or technological advances in the profession as they become more feasible.

With respect to the policy considerations, these stakeholders are related entities to the program (e.g., regulatory bodies, jurisdictional uniqueness), and can be influential in terms of how the program functions or evolves. Collectively, these three organizing characteristics of evidence—operational, policy, and innovation—combine to inform a credentialing program's validation efforts and resource prioritization. Although the need to develop a validation framework may seem clear to measurement practitioners, the diversity of stakeholders involved in the program will contribute to deliberations about how to implement it. There is not a simple resolution to this challenge. However, the next section attempts to discuss how the integration of policy and practice in credentialing programs is critical to the development and related psychometric considerations.

## Integrating Policy and Practice

Similar to assessment challenges in other segments of the industry, psychometric theory and practice operate within other systems including business, legal, policy, and practical. There are multiple factors that practitioners consider when developing and implementing credentialing programs. Integrating psychometric practice in the context of credentialing policies is one of these important considerations. Promoting integration, however, requires drawing on education and training practices to effectively bridge the gap between science and practice.

*Assessment Literacy*

The appropriate design of credentialing programs requires an understanding of the development and validation methods commonly employed by measurement practitioners.

Closing this gap necessitates what is sometimes characterized as assessment literacy. Communicating technical measurement concepts in accessible language that can be understood by subject matter experts and policymakers occurs in other testing disciplines such as education and employment. However, unlike the education context, in credentialing programs there may be fewer experiences with assessment and appropriate uses. Studies have consistently suggested there is limited assessment literacy among educators and administrators (Brookhart, 2011; Plake, Impara, & Fager, 1993). These challenges extend to policymakers and practitioners in the credentialing community (e.g., Buckendahl, Davis-Becker, & Russell, 2011). And more recent work suggests that methods for evaluating assessment literacy are weak at best (Gotch & French, 2014). Undoubtedly, measurement practitioners continue to face a consistent challenge on this topic.

Therefore, a level of assessment literacy that aligns with the needs of the credentialing program should be sought with concerted efforts to assist with development of some core concepts (e.g., validity, reliability, fairness) and how these will be strengthened, observed, and documented in the program. As with other policy environments, assessment literacy becomes an ongoing component of the program because staff, boards, and committees will continuously turnover within the system. Although each credentialing program will have unique assessment literacy needs, striving for contemporary, appropriate practices will encourage a culture of continuous improvement. The level of sophistication of a program's assessment literacy and its outreach efforts to involve a wider range of stakeholders will also be a function of the stakes associated with the interpretations and uses of scores from its program. At a minimum level, programs are encouraged to understand the risk of legal challenge for their program and to ensure that validation activities are responsive to these concerns.

## *Accreditation*

As an external indicator of quality, some credentialing programs participate in accreditation programs. While the *Standards* are considered voluntary and perhaps aspirational, accreditation standards require a minimum level of compliance to achieve and maintain accredited status. As a result, these accreditation standards may support levels of accountability to stakeholder groups. Within the credentialing sector, three of the more common sets of accreditation standards for which credentialing programs make seek external recognition include International Standards for Organization (ISO) 17024, National Commission for Certifying Agencies (NCCA), and Institute for Credentialing Excellence (ICE) 1100. Although each of these sets of accreditation standards includes expectations from the *Standards* related to development and validation activities, they are more inclusive of broader programmatic elements. For example, the ISO 17024 and NCCA standards require evidence of programmatic governance and have an expectation of a clear separation between education and certification functions. There is also an expectation for representation by the public so that the programs are not designed solely for the benefit of its members or the profession. Similarly, the ICE 1100 accreditation standards were developed for assessment-based certificate programs where there is an expectation of instructional design that is aligned with content specification and an assessment. These programs function similarly to end of course (EOC) assessments observed in many state's academic assessment and accountability programs. Fabrey (Chapter 10) and Buckendahl and Plake (2006) describe in more detail some of the processes, expectations, and models for these types of external reviews.

Although participation in accreditation programs like the ones described in this section is generally voluntary, there are motivations for accreditation beyond the desire to seek a third party mark of quality. For some professions (e.g., crane operators, alcohol and drug counselors in California), credentialing program accreditation may be required as part of federal or state regulation. Under these circumstances, the mandatory nature of the accreditation becomes a "need to have" as opposed to a "nice to have" characteristic of the program. As discussed further in a later section of this chapter, there may be business considerations for why a program seeks accreditation. In addition, programs may also seek external accreditation as an additional layer of protection for legal or ethical challenges that they may face.

### *Legal Considerations*

Although programs may seek third-party accreditation as described above, this does not suggest that a program is immune to external challenge. Because legislation and court decisions can change, an evaluation of the legal defensibility of a program should not be interpreted as absolute. Further, the *Standards* caution users that legal requirements may override professional expectations. However, this caution is somewhat disconcerting because practitioners look to the *Standards* and related publications for guidance as to how the profession has defined best practices. In Chapter 11, Phillips discusses a number of legal considerations for credentialing programs along with important court decisions related to these programs. Of particular note for credentialing programs is the grey area between what constitutes testing for a credential and testing for employment. The *Standards* include a chapter specifically to help practitioners make this distinction as well as the different types of validation activities and evidence that may be necessary to support these different uses. Phillips and Camara (2006) discuss legal considerations that range across educational and credentialing programs. Recent court decisions (see Chapter 11) have further blurred these lines and raised questions for practitioners about the types of validity evidence that may be needed. The use of credentialing examinations as part of the employment process has raised legitimate questions about validation practices. Generally, challenges to credentialing programs will be raised on questions of fairness for protected classes. As a result, evidence that the content of the examination is sufficiently job-related, that content is not biased, scores and decisions are reliable, and that passing scores have been appropriately established are prioritized in the evidence collection and evaluation.

### *Business of Credentialing*

The role of credentialing in verification of candidate qualifications is often undertaken by professions, associations, or similar agencies. In many instances, these credentials are monopolistic in that there is only one option for an individual seeking a particular credential. Credentials for airline pilots, architects, and physician assistants are illustrations of these types of programs. From a business perspective, this is a desirable situation when there is sufficient market demand along with a sufficient population of interested candidates to support sustainability of the program. Conversely, some credentials operate in a competitive environment where the same or very similar credentials may be sought by candidates from different associations or agencies. This leads to efforts to differentiate a particular program in the market relative to its competitors. For these programs, business considerations are an important aspect of an evaluation of feasibility that occurs prior to the test development and validation activities described throughout this volume. Examples of credentials that operate in competitive arenas include nursing specialties, personal training, and food safety. This competitive environment is similar to the education sector where there are a number of vendors that offer commercially available and customized products and services to local and state education agencies.

**Summary**

As an introduction to credentialing, this chapter provided context for readers who may be unfamiliar with the purposes and range of strategies that are used by professions, associations, and organizations. Credentialing programs often emerge from a real or perceived need to identify individuals with certain knowledge, skills and abilities, and may be mandatory, voluntary, or some combination of requirements for individuals. The chapter discussed and contrasted types of credentials that are commonly used in the workforce—specifically, licensure, certification, registration, assessment-based certificates, microcredentials, and badges. Each of these credentials communicates something to the public about the individual who possesses the credential and perhaps the profession, association, or organization that awarded the credential. Because the context of the program directly influences the support for using test scores for a defined purpose, I also presented and discussed a suggested validation framework that programs could adapt to organize the prioritization, collection, and evaluation of evidence.

Similar to many educational programs, the purpose of credentialing programs is often to determine whether a candidate has met an acceptable level of competency to hold the credential. This purpose differs from a selection activity within employment testing in that the goal is not to predict future performance or rank order candidates. Rather, the purpose is to evaluate threshold competence at the time the credential is awarded. Another difference is in the area of credential maintenance and whether the purpose is to support continued competency, enhanced competency, or both. Finally, I discussed some of the challenges of integrating policy and psychometric practice within credentialing along with some of the unique characteristics of these programs when compared with the larger educational assessment arena. As credentialing programs have continued to increase in number and expand in scope, so, too, have the challenges for practitioners to ensure that appropriate methods and practices continue to evolve.

**References**

American Educational Research Association, American Psychological Association, & National Council on Measurement in Education (AERA, APA, & NCME) (2014). *Standards for educational and psychological testing*. Washington, DC: American Educational Research Association.

Brookhart, S. M. (2011). Educational assessment knowledge and skills for teachers. *Educational Measurement: Issues and Practice, 30*(1), 3–12.

Buckendahl, C. W. (2013, April). *A practitioner's guide to validation framework development*. Paper presented at the annual meeting of the National Council on Measurement in Education, San Francisco, CA.

Buckendahl, C. W., Davis-Becker, S., & Russell, S. (2011, February). *Defining and developing assessment literacy among stakeholders*. Presentation at the annual Innovations in Testing Conference of the Association of Test Publishers. Phoenix, AZ.

Buckendahl, C., Davis, S., Plake, B., Sireci, S., Hambleton, R., Zenisky, A., & Wells, C. (2009). *Evaluation of the National Assessment of Educational Progress: Final Report*. Washington, DC: U.S. Department of Education.

Buckendahl, C. W., & Plake B. S. (2006). Evaluating tests. In S. Downing & T. Haladyna (Eds.), *Handbook of test development* (pp. 725–738). Mahwah, NJ: Lawrence Erlbaum Associates.

Fortune, J. C. (1985). *Understanding testing in occupational licensing*. San Francisco, CA: Jossey-Bass.

Gotch, C., & French, B. (2014). A systematic review of assessment literacy measures. *Educational Measurement: Issues and Practice, 33*(2) 14–18.

Henderson-Montero, D., & Buckendahl, C. W. (2010, May). *Psychometric challenges in a rapidly changing environment*. Paper presented at the annual meeting of the National Council on Measurement in Education. Denver, CO.

Impara, J. C. (Ed.). (1995). *Licensure testing: Purposes, procedures, and practices*. Lincoln, NE: Buros Institute for Mental Measurements.

Kane, M. T. (2013). Validating the interpretations and uses of test scores. *Journal of Educational Measurement, 50*(1), 1–73.

Kearney, M. S., Hershbein, B., & Boddy, D. (2015, January 27). Nearly 30 percent of workers in the U.S. need a license to perform their job: It's time to examine occupational licensing practices. Washington, DC: The Brookings Institution. Retrieved from: www.brookings.edu/blogs/up-front/posts/2015/01/26-time-to-examine-occupational-licensing-practices-kearney-hershbein-boddy

Knapp, J., Anderson, L., & Wild, C. (2009). *Certification: The ICE handbook* (2nd ed.). Madison, WI: Omnipress.

Morath, E. (2015, November 14–15). License law is nixed in D.C. *The Wall Street Journal*. Retrieved from: http://wsj.com

Phillips, S. E., & Camara, W. J. (2006). Legal and ethical issues. In R. L. Brennan (Ed.), *Educational measurement* (4th ed., pp. 701–732). Westport, CT: American Council on Education and Praeger.

Plake, B. S., Impara, J. C., & Fager, J. J. (1993). Assessment competencies of teachers: A national survey. *Educational Measurement: Issues and Practice, 12*(4), 10–12.

Romboy, D. (2012, Aug. 10). Court sides with woman in hair braiding case. Salt Lake City, UT: KSL.com. Retrieved from: www.ksl.com/?nid=960&sid=21638994

Schmitt, K. (1995). What is licensure? In J. C. Impara (Ed.), *Licensure testing: Purposes, procedures and practices* (pp. 3–32). Lincoln, NE: Buros Institute for Mental Measurements.

Shimberg, B. (1982). *Licensing in the occupations: A public perspective*. Princeton, NJ: Educational Testing Service.

# 2 A Validation Framework for Credentialing Tests

*Michael T. Kane, Brian E. Clauser, and Joanne Kane*

The basic function of credentialing programs is to decide whether candidates have achieved a level of mastery in some domain of knowledge, skills, and judgment (KSJs). The focus is on the level of achievement in the domain and on the adequacy of that level of achievement for some purpose (e.g., licensure, credentialing). So a core concern in validating credentialing tests is the extent to which the test content reflects the KSJ domain (as addressed by "content-related validity evidence"), but there are six additional concerns that can loom as large or larger in validating credentialing programs. First, the KSJs in the domain need to provide a reasonable and appropriate basis for the decisions that are to be based on the test scores (e.g., for licensure, KSJs that are required in practice). Second, the testing program should be of high psychometric quality (in terms of decision consistency, equating, scaling, and standard errors around the passing score). Third, the scores should be free of extraneous sources of variance that would be large enough to interfere with the proposed score use. Fourth, if the testing program has an adverse impact on any protected group, this impact should reflect real differences in the populations rather than defects in the testing program. Fifth, the cut scores used to make decisions should satisfy the "Goldilocks Criterion," being not too high and not too low. Sixth, the program should be as transparent as possible. These issues are discussed in detail in various chapters in the book. This chapter will develop a general validation framework for evaluating the impact of these and other issues on the validity of credentialing tests.

This chapter provides an overview of the major validity issues in credentialing and a framework for efforts to plan for, collect, and organize the validity evidence needed to evaluate credentialing programs. The basic function of credentialing programs is to certify that a test taker possesses at least a minimally acceptable level of competence in some domain of knowledge, skills, and judgment (KSJ domain) that is needed for effective performance in some area of activity or practice. Candidates who pass the test and meet any additional requirements (e.g., for education, experience) are awarded a credential (e.g., a license) attesting to their competence in the KSJ domain and candidates who fail the test do not get the credential. Many test-based credentials serve as requirements for engaging in certain kinds of practice (e.g., professions, skilled occupations, and potentially hazardous activities like flying an airplane). Credentialing decisions tend to be high stakes because the goal of encouraging effective performance in practice (e.g., piloting an airplane, practicing medicine) is important, and because the credentials are valuable to the candidates.

Testing programs tend to be evaluated mainly in terms of their psychometric properties. However, we argue here that credentialing programs should in fact be evaluated (or validated) in terms of a number of properties, including not only their psychometric properties but also their objectivity, their freedom from bias and extraneous sources of variance, their transparency, and more generally their effectiveness in maintaining and improving practice.

It would be desirable to observe candidate performance in the kind of activity that is of interest as the basis for credentialing, but this is often not feasible for reasons of safety and practicality; we don't evaluate candidates for medical licensure by having them provide critical care for real patients. Rather, we generally evaluate the candidates on some domain of knowledge, skills, and judgments that are considered critical for effective performance in practice. Adequate competence in the KSJ domain is assumed to be a necessary (but not sufficient) requirement for effective performance in practice.

For credentialing programs to achieve their goals, it is necessary that mastery of the KSJ domain that is assessed be required for effective performance in practice. For a professional licensure examination, we would expect the KSJ domain to include a substantial subset of the kinds of knowledge, skills, and judgments needed for safe and effective entry-level performance in professional practice, and we expect that adequate mastery of the KSJ domain would be critical in the sense that its absence would pose an unacceptable risk to the public (see Chapter 4).

A credentialing program tends to differ in many ways from the top-down selection procedures that are sometimes used for employment (Clauser, Margolis, & Case, 2006). Top-down selection tests are designed to rank order candidates in terms of general skills and aptitudes that are relevant to learning the job, and the employer or institution tends to select the applicants with the best scores because they are expected to have the best performance on the job. Credentialing tests are designed to assess KSJs that are developed in designated educational programs (e.g., professional schools), and the scores are used to make pass–fail decisions based on specified passing scores rather than rank ordering the candidates. Score scales are typically developed for credentialing tests, but these score scales are used mainly for technical analyses (e.g., calculating standard errors, reliability, decision consistency, item analysis, differential item functioning across groups, convergent and discriminant validity—see Chapter 7), to support statistical adjustments of scores across different test forms (equating, scaling—see Chapter 6), and to enhance interpretability.

Credentialing programs tend to be particularly important in democratic, meritocratic societies where certain privileges or opportunities (e.g., in licensed professions and occupations) are to be awarded based on demonstrated mastery of a KSJ domain needed for effective performance in practice. In these contexts, credentials of various kinds serve an important function in providing evidence that the holder of the credential has demonstrated a level of competence in the KSJ domain and is at least minimally prepared for practice (see Chapters 3 and 11). To the extent that the programs are successful, they provide assurance that credentialed practitioners have achieved an acceptable level of competence in the KSJ domain.

In the next two sections we outline a general, argument-based approach to validation and specify how credentialing test scores are typically interpreted and used (Argument-Based Validation and The Interpretation and Use of Credentialing Test Scores). We then outline a validity argument for credentialing programs (Validation: Evaluation of the Interpretation/use Argument). In the last main section (Perspectives on Credentialing), we consider the expectations of credentialing from three different perspectives: a psychometric perspective, an institutional perspective, and a candidate perspective.

## Argument-Based Validation

House (1980) and Cronbach (1988) proposed that test-score validation could be thought of as an evaluation of the claims based on the test scores, and Cronbach (1988) suggested that the analysis "should make clear, and to the extent possible, persuasive, the construction of reality and the value weightings implicit in a test and its application" (p. 5). The resulting *validity argument* would employ empirical data and conceptual analysis to evaluate the reasoning inherent in the intended interpretations and uses of the test scores (American Educational Research Association [AERA], American Psychological Association [APA], & National Council on Measurement in Education [NCME], 2014; Cronbach, 1971; Messick, 1989).

An evaluation of the claims based on the test scores requires a clear and complete statement of these claims (Crooks, Kane & Cohen, 1996; Kane, 1992, 2006, 2013; Shepard, 1993). One way to do this is to develop an *interpretation/use argument* (*IUA*) that lays out the chain of inferences leading from the observed performances on the test tasks to the proposed interpretations and uses of the test scores (Kane, 2013). The IUA would include a network of inferences and assumptions leading from the test performances to the score-based conclusions and to any decisions based on these conclusions.

So, we have two kinds of arguments. The IUA lays out the inferences and assumptions inherent in the proposed interpretations and uses of test scores, and the *validity argument* evaluates the plausibility of the IUA. If any part of the IUA is contradicted by the evidence, the interpretation/use as a whole would not be valid; therefore, it is important that the IUA not claim too much or too little.

### Interpretation/Use Arguments (IUAs)

The IUA plays the role that a formal theory plays in Cronbach and Meehl's (1955) proposal for construct validation. It specifies the inferences and assumptions inherent in the proposed interpretation and use of the test scores. The IUA should be developed as the intended uses of test scores are specified and the kinds of score interpretations needed to support these uses are identified, and it tends to get refined during the process of test development as testing materials and procedures are developed and evaluated. The goal is to develop a testing program and an IUA that are consistent with each other.

The IUA provides an explicit statement of what is being claimed and thereby provides a framework for validation. It also provides criteria for evaluating how well the proposed interpretation and use have been validated. If the IUA is coherent and fully represents the proposed interpretation and use, and if all of its inferences and assumptions are highly plausible (either a priori, or because of the evidence provided), the interpretation/use would be considered plausible, or valid. If any part of the IUA is refuted, the proposed interpretation/use would not be considered valid. Once the IUA is accepted, it provides a general basis for making validated claims about individual test takers. It is applied every time test scores are interpreted and used to make decisions, and it does not need to be developed anew for each test taker.

The IUA is a presumptive argument that is intended to fully represent the claims being made rather than a formal (mathematical or statistical) model that might represent a part of the reasoning justifying the claims being made. In Toulmin's (1958) model for presumptive inferences, each inference goes from a *datum* to a *claim*. The inference employs a *warrant*, which is a general rule for making claims of a certain kind based on data of a

Datum ⇒ [*warrant*] ⇒ {Qualifier} Claim

⇑                    ⇑

**Backing**        **Exceptions**

The *Warrant* is a rule for making claims based on data.

The *Backing* provides support for the warrant.

The *Qualifier* indicates the confidence with which the claim can be made.

*Exceptions* are conditions under which the warrant would not apply.

*Figure 2.1* Toulmin's Model for the Structure of Presumptive Inferences

certain kind (see Figure 2.1). Warrants generally require *backing*, or support. Some warrants may be plausible enough a priori, but most warrants require at least some backing.

Warrants can have *qualifiers*, which indicate the uncertainty of the inference. For some inferences, the qualifier may be qualitative (e.g., employing words like "usually" or "almost always"). Many of the inferences in IUAs for test scores can have quantitative qualifiers (e.g., standard errors or confidence intervals).

For example, a critical inference in the IUAs for all testing programs is the scoring inference, which takes us from observed performances (the data) on test tasks to the scores assigned to these performances (the claims). The warrant for these inferences is a scoring key or rubric. The backing for the warrant generally involves expert opinion based on research and other sources of information, and it can involve empirical data (e.g., from item analyses). In cases where scoring involves judgment, the qualifier for the scoring inference would typically include standard errors associated with less than perfect inter-rater agreement.

A presumptive inference yields a presumption in favor of its claim, but the inference may be modified or overturned in particular cases by special circumstances, and *conditions of rebuttal* specify conditions under which the warrant would not apply. For example, test takers with disabilities may need accommodations in testing materials or procedures. As a result, the IUA may have to be adapted to reflect the accommodations (see Chapter 3 of the *Standards*, AERA, APA, & NCME, 2014). The IUAs for the accommodated testing would rely on evidence that the accommodated form of the test is functionally equivalent to the standard form, so that the intended conclusions and decisions are comparable for all test takers (see Chapters 3 and 11).

For credentialing, the IUA would generally involve at least four inferences. A *scoring inference* takes us from a candidate's observed performances on the test tasks to evaluations or scores for the candidate's task performances, and perhaps to an observed score for the test. A *generalization/scaling inference* extends the interpretation from observed performances on a particular set of test tasks to a scaled score defined across all forms of the test and representing the candidate's standing on the KSJs assessed by the test tasks. An *extrapolation inference* extends the interpretation to the candidate's standing on the target KSJs needed for effective performance in practice. *Decision inferences* would award a credential to candidates who have demonstrated an acceptable level of competence in the KSJs (by passing the test and meeting any other applicable requirements), and would not award a credential to candidates who have not demonstrated an acceptable level of competence in the KSJs.

The IUA provides a general framework for interpreting and using the test scores for individual candidates. Although they may not be explicitly mentioned in discussing scores, the warrants for various inferences are an integral part of the IUA.

## Validity Arguments

The *validity argument* provides an evaluation of the proposed IUA and thereby provides a validation of the proposed interpretation and use of the test scores. Some of the evidence required for the validity argument will be developed during test development (e.g., the content relevance of the testing materials, and the scalability and reliability of the scores) as the testing materials and the IUA are refined. Additional empirical evidence for validity will typically be collected after the IUA and the testing program have been fully specified. The IUA provides a framework for the validity argument by specifying the inferences and assumptions that need to be evaluated.

The validity argument would start with a critical review of the IUA with particular attention to identifying any hidden assumptions or alternative plausible interpretations of the test scores. It would also provide a critical review of the inferences and assumptions built into the IUA. The point is to identify the most questionable inferences and assumptions, and to evaluate them critically. As Cronbach (1980) suggested, "The job of validation is not to support an interpretation, but to find out what might be wrong with it. A proposition deserves some degree of trust only when it has survived serious attempts to falsify it" (p. 103). An IUA that has undergone a critical appraisal of its coherence and the plausibility of its inferences and assumptions can be accepted as providing adequate justification for the proposed interpretation and use of the scores.

Different kinds of inferences will require different kinds of evidence for their evaluation. Scoring rules generally rely on expert judgment for their support. Generalization/scaling inferences make extensive use of statistical models and depend on evidence supporting the appropriateness and applicability of these models to the testing program and population under consideration. Extrapolation inferences rely on evidence indicating the extent to which the KSJs assessed by the test are critical for effective performance in practice. Score-based decisions require evidence that the procedures and criteria used in making the decisions are reasonable and fair.

Cronbach (1989) proposed four criteria for prioritizing the questions to be addressed in validation: prior uncertainty, information yield, cost, and leverage for achieving consensus in relevant audiences. Some assumptions may be accepted a priori or be based on analyses of procedures (e.g., sampling assumptions). Some assumptions (e.g., that time limits are adequate for most test takers) may be accepted on the basis of experience. Any questionable assumptions will require new empirical evidence in order to be considered plausible. Strong claims (e.g., causal inferences, or predictions of future performance in different contexts) typically require extensive empirical support.

In order to make a positive case for the proposed interpretations and uses of scores, the validity argument needs to provide adequate backing for all of the inferences in the IUA and to rule out challenges posed by plausible alternative interpretations. A refutation of any part of the IUA invalidates the IUA as a whole. It is therefore important to specify the IUA in enough detail so that the weakest parts of the IUA can be identified and evaluated. All parts of the IUA merit attention, but the most doubtful parts of the argument should get the most scrutiny. This focus is particularly important because, from a practical perspective, a program of validity research will never be exhaustive. The high-priority empirical studies will be those that are most likely to shift overall confidence in the interpretations, one way or the other.

## Necessary and Sufficient Conditions for Validity

The argument-based approach to validation is contingent in the sense that the evidence needed for validation depends on the proposed interpretation and use of the scores.

Given a proposed interpretation and use and its corresponding IUA, an argument-based approach specifies necessary and sufficient conditions for validity. The evidence needed to validate the proposed interpretation and use requires a conceptual analysis to establish that the IUA adequately represents the proposed interpretation and use of the scores, and it requires evidence (mostly empirical) to evaluate the inferences and assumptions in the IUA. Once an IUA that accurately represents the inferences and assumptions inherent in the proposed interpretation and use has been laid out, developing evidence that supports the plausibility of each of the inferences and assumptions in the IUA is a necessary condition for the validity of the proposed interpretation and use.

The argument-based approach also specifies a sufficient condition for validity. If the IUA accurately represents the proposed interpretation and use, and the IUA's inferences and assumptions are adequately supported by evidence, it is reasonable to accept the proposed interpretation and use as valid.

It is always possible that new evidence (e.g., indicating that a key assumption is not justified) will, in the future, overturn this conclusion about validity in some special cases or in general. The criteria for accepting the validity of a proposed interpretation and use are essentially the same as the criteria for accepting a scientific theory. Assuming that the theory has survived all plausible challenges to its claims, it can be accepted, presumptively (Cronbach, 1980).

That an acceptance of all of the inferences and assumptions in the IUA provides sufficient conditions for the validity of the proposed interpretation and use implies that it is not necessary to evaluate extraneous inferences or assumptions (those not in the IUA) that could yield a more ambitious interpretation of the scores or could provide indirect support for some of the inferences in the IUA. For example, the interpretation of scores on credentialing tests typically involves an inference from a failing score on the test to a claim that the candidate is not prepared to be fully effective in practice. However, IUAs do not generally require predictions of each candidate's future performance in practice, and therefore, it is not necessary to evaluate such predictions. (That said, the usefulness of predictive evidence should not be discounted. In a licensing context, where failing candidates are excluded from practice, it will be impossible to collect evidence that failing candidates pose a greater risk to the public than passing candidates. Nevertheless, evidence that candidates with high passing scores perform better in practice than those with low passing scores would provide support for the relevance of the KSJs to performance in practice.)

## The Interpretation and Use of Credentialing Test Scores

Credentialing tests are designed to assess readiness for some area of activity or practice. If assessing performance in practice directly were a viable option, it would probably be the preferred option. However, this approach is generally not feasible because it would require a representative sample of performance in actual practice for each candidate and most credentialing programs address broadly defined areas of activity (like the practice of a profession or skilled occupation) that would be very difficult, if not impossible, to sample adequately. Furthermore, for many areas of practice (e.g., a licensed profession, driving a car) it is illegal to engage in practice without supervision before getting the relevant credential (Clauser et al., 2006; Kane, 2004; Shimberg, 1981).

Rather than try to assess performance in practice, most credentialing program assess KSJs that are needed for effective performance in the area of activity for which the credential is intended. The KSJs would involve knowledge and the ability to apply this knowledge in practice (e.g., for a pediatrician, the KSJs would include knowledge of immunization schedules and methods), skill in performing various activities (e.g., diagnosing problems) and judgment about what to do in particular practice situations (e.g., in choice of available methods to address a problem). For professional licensure, the skills that are tested are mainly cognitive, but in some other cases (e.g., commercial airline pilots) some specific psychomotor skills (e.g., landing a plane in a simulator) may also be addressed. The KSJs are assumed to be needed for effective performance in practice, because many practice situations would require a practitioner to apply one or more of the KSJs in order to deal with the situations. For the credentialing program to be effective, it does not have to include all the KSJs used in practice, but it does need to include a substantial subset of KSJs that are critical for effective performance in practice.

The logic of credentialing programs is quite simple. The KSJs are needed for effective practice, and the credentialing test evaluates the candidate's level of mastery of the KSJs. Failing the test indicates that the candidate has an inadequate level of mastery of the KSJs, and is therefore not ready for practice, and should not be awarded a credential. Those who pass the test are deemed to have adequate mastery of the KSJs and are credentialed if they also meet all other requirements for the credential.

The testing program is designed to assess each candidate's level of competence in the KSJ domain. The tasks included in the credentialing test are designed to require KSJs from the relevant KSJ domain for their successful performance, and to have as few sources of irrelevant variance as possible (e.g., unusual item formats, unnecessarily complex wording). The task formats may include multiple-choice items, essays, simulations, performance tasks, or some combination of these formats. Test development would also involve the specification of the standardized conditions of administration and the specification of scoring rules.

The test tasks are generally designed to focus on the KSJs as they are used in practice, and therefore they generally require the candidate to apply KSJs to some hypothetical practice problem. Performance on the test tasks presumably depends mainly on the candidate's level of competence in the KSJs, but would also depend on other characteristics (e.g., verbal ability, familiarity with task formats, test-taking efficiency) that may not be related to performance in practice. The test tasks are designed to present realistic practice problems, but the test tasks/problems are not real practice tasks/problems. So there is always some question about the extent to which the results obtained in the testing context are applicable to the practice context.

The IUA flows from the test-task performance to conclusions about the candidate's mastery of the KSJs as they are used in practice. It involves a number of non-trivial assumptions: (1) that the test tasks reflect the target KSJs and that these KSJs are needed for effective practice in the sense that a low level of competence on the KSJs would lead to ineffective practice, (2) that the scoring is accurate and consistent, (3) that the KSJs included in the test are critical in the sense that their absence would make a substantial difference in practice effectiveness, and (4) that the passing score is appropriate. The use of the test scores for credentialing also assumes that the tests are psychometrically sound (e.g., in terms of reliability, equating), that they are fair to groups and individuals (with particular attention to minorities and other protected groups) and that the credentialing decisions are made appropriately and consistently.

Note that passing the test is not assumed to guarantee effective performance in practice, because a candidate might lack competencies (e.g., physical or interpersonal skills, conscientiousness) that are required for effectiveness in practice, but are not included in the KSJ domain. The credentialing test is viewed as a measure of KSJs that are necessary but not necessarily sufficient for effective performance in practice; as a result, passing the test does not ensure effective performance, and test scores are not necessarily expected to provide very accurate estimates of relative quality of performance in practice for individual candidates. Credentialing agencies try to fill the gaps and expand the range of critical KSJs that are assessed when that is feasible. The intention is to cover as many of the skills needed in practice as possible. This has led to the increased use of performance assessments and simulations in licensing examinations. Examples include high-fidelity simulations of practice situations, such as flight simulators, as well as a range of lower fidelity simulations. These efforts expand the KSJ domain and strengthen the IUA. In cases that involve the most serious and immediate risks (e.g., airline pilots, surgeons) resources are brought to bear to ensure that credentialing is associated with a very high likelihood of effective performance.

In many credentialing programs, passing the test is one of several requirements for the credential, including perhaps educational and experiential requirements. These additional requirements provide further support for the claim that credentialed individuals are prepared for practice in various ways. However, even with a range of such requirements in place, the credential does not guarantee effective performance in practice. The argument that candidates with low scores on the test are not adequately prepared for practice is generally stronger than the argument that candidates with high scores are fully prepared for practice.

### *Developing the Credentialing Test and the IUA*

Credentialing tests are designed to measure KSJs that are needed for effective performance in practice in the sense that serious deficiencies in these KSJs would interfere with effective performance in practice (or worse, make the candidate an unsafe practitioner). In designing the credentialing test, the goal is to employ test tasks and procedures that will support the proposed interpretation in terms of mastery of the KSJs and the proposed use of the test scores for credentialing (see Chapters 3, 4, and 5). A common first step in designing the test is the development of a fairly detailed definition of the practice domain using expert opinion, legal or other a priori definitions of the scope of practice, and empirical practice analyses (Clauser et al., 2006; Raymond, 2001). As part of this process, the relative importance or criticality of different activities in the practice domain can be estimated.

In designing the assessment itself, there are a number of decisions to be made, including the mode of presentation of the tasks (e.g., printed questions, computer/video presentation, simulations, or performance tasks) and the response mode (e.g., selecting options, providing an extended written response, performing certain tasks). These choices tend to involve various tradeoffs, and in a sense, all the tasks included in credentialing tests may be viewed as simulations of key aspects of performance in practice; the tasks differ in the fidelity with which the practice environment is simulated. Multiple-choice items can generally be considered very low-fidelity simulations, but they provide an effective way to collect data on a candidate's cognitive performances on a wide range of tasks. Flight simulators for pilots, standardized-patient based assessments for physicians, and driving tests come closer to approximating the practice setting, but observation of actual performance in practice is unusual in credentialing examinations.

The test tasks may be framed in terms of problems commonly encountered in practice, but even in high-fidelity simulations, the problems tend to be standardized and simplified in various ways, and the response options are also standardized. Most credentialing tests tend to focus on cognitive rather than physical or interpersonal activities. To the extent that actual performance tasks (e.g., in a driving test) or simulations are employed, they tend to focus on a few specific skills.

As noted earlier, the IUA for credentialing decisions is one-sided. If a candidate cannot handle test tasks involving the application of the KSJs to relatively simplified situations, we infer that they would have trouble applying the KSJs in more complicated, real practice contexts. However, successful performance in applying the KSJs to test tasks does not ensure that the candidate will be able to apply the KSJs equally well in more complex practice situations in the field. Again, the extent of this gap is likely to vary across settings. The challenges presented in an assessment for an initial license to practice medicine may be less complicated than some of those which will be encountered in practice. The challenges presented on an assessment for certification in a medical subspecialty may come closer to capturing the range of complexity that will be found in practice.

### *The Interpretation/Use Argument for Credentialing Tests*

As noted above, the IUA for a credentialing test typically involves four main inferences. First, each candidate's test performances are scored, yielding a score for each task included in the test that the candidate took. The warrant for this *scoring inference* is the scoring rule (e.g., scoring rubrics or a scoring key) for the test tasks.

Second, the task scores are then combined to derive a scaled score representing the candidate's overall level of competence in the KSJ domain assessed by the testing program (Kolen, 2006). A candidate's task scores may simply be summed to get an observed score, with the observed scores on different forms or versions of the credentialing test being equated to each other. Alternately, an item response theory (IRT) model may be used to generate an estimated latent score based on the task scores (Yen & Fitzpatrick, 2006). This *generalization/scaling inference* takes us from a claim about performances on a particular set of test tasks under particular conditions to a claim about level of competence in the KSJ domain, as assessed by the testing program; it takes us from an evaluation of actual, observed performances on a particular set of test tasks on a particular occasion to a more general claim about the candidates' level of competence in the KSJ domain as a whole, as represented by the scaled score. The equating and scaling models that are used to scale the scores are designed to generate a scaled score that reflects the expected result over replications of the testing procedure and is independent of the particular test form. The warrant for the generalization/scaling inference consists of the model-based procedures used to derive the candidate's scaled score from the candidate's task scores.

Third, the interpretation of the scaled score is then extended from a claim about expected performance over the test domain to a claim about the candidate's level of competence on the KSJs as they are applied in practice. The *extrapolation inference* extends the score interpretation from a claim about the KSJs as reflected in the test performances to a claim about the ability to apply the KSJs in practice. The warrant for the extrapolation inferences asserts that candidates who can effectively apply the KSJs to test tasks will generally also be able to effectively apply the KSJs to practice problems, and even more important, that candidates who cannot apply the KSJs to test tasks will generally not be able to apply the KSJs in practice. The extrapolation inference does not change the value of the scaled score, but it does extend its interpretation from the testing context to the practice context.

Fourth, a decision is made about the awarding of the credential by comparing the candidate's scaled score to the passing score. The warrant for this *decision inference* is usually a simple, binary decision rule. If the candidate's scaled score is at or above the passing score, the candidate passes the credentialing test. If the candidate's scaled score is below the passing score, the candidate fails the test.

The warrants for the four inferences in the IUA are employed as each candidate's test performances are interpreted and used to make a decision about whether to award the credential. First, the scoring inference applies a scoring rule (the warrant for the scoring inference) to assign a score to the candidate's observed performances on the test tasks. This inference assumes that the test was administered appropriately (i.e., using the standardized administration rules), that the candidate did not suffer from any unreasonable impediment (e.g., due to a disability) or have any unacceptable advantage (e.g., cheating), that the test and the testing procedures are appropriate given the credential, and that the scoring rule is appropriate. If the scoring involves judgment, it assumes that this judgment is consistent (interrater reliability).

Second, the generalization/scaling inference extends the interpretation from a claim about the candidate's performances on the test tasks to a more general claim about the candidate's level of competence in the KSJ domain, as estimated by the test (Brennan, 2001; Haertel, 2006). The scaled score is expected to be generalizable over replications of the testing procedure. It relies on statistical models of various kinds to take us from evaluations of the limited sample of candidate performances obtained on the test to a more general and abstract characterization of the candidate's performance. Depending on the statistical model being applied, the generalization/scaling inference could extend the interpretation to a "true score" (in classical test theory), to a "universe score" (in generalizability theory), or to a "latent score" (in IRT). These three models differ in their statistical and interpretive framework, but they all involve a generalization of the score interpretation from an evaluation of the candidates' actual test performances to a more abstract characterization of the candidate's expected score over replications of the testing procedure (either as a latent trait or as an equated scaled score). This inference assumes that the scaled score is dependable in the sense that it is not unduly distorted by variations in candidate scores over replications of the testing procedure (or random errors). Generalization/scaling inferences can be quite sophisticated and complex for high-stakes credentialing programs, involving statistical models for scaling, equating, and commonly, latent-trait models of various kinds (Brennan, 2013).

As mentioned previously, these models depend on important assumptions which are rarely fully satisfied. For example, commonly used IRT models require the test to be unidimensional. Credentialing tests are typically intended to sample items from distinct content categories. A licensing test for physicians might include items covering issues in surgery, internal medicine, pediatrics, obstetrics, and so on. The test specifications are constructed based on the assumption that content sampling is important. This assumption suggests that a test composed of content from multiple categories may not be unidimensional. This does not suggest that IRT models will not be useful with the resulting data; it does imply that the applicability of any models that are employed should be considered.

Sophisticated scaling models aside, the generalizability argument for these tests is likely to be complex. Generalization over randomly equivalent sets of items (the type of reliability analysis provided by coefficient alpha) is essential, but it is only a modest part of the case that must be made to generalize from the specific test instance to the assessed domain. One step in this process, which is often ignored, is generalization across occasions. No one is likely to be interested in how well a professional might perform on a single occasion unless they believe that the performance on that occasion is representative of performance in general. To the extent that variability over occasions is not investigated empirically, this limitation should be recognized in documentation for generalizability of the scores.

For multiple-choice tests, sampling across items (tasks) and occasions may provide compelling evidence of generalization, but with more complex assessments this is just the beginning of the story. Some credentialing examinations use human judges to score tasks; this raises issues about generalization across judges. Other examinations include computer-delivered simulations. Scoring algorithms for these assessments are typically developed by a panel of content experts. The usefulness of these algorithms is in part based on the assumption that the scores would be similar if the algorithm had been developed by an independent (but similarly qualified) panel. Relatively little evidence is available to support generalized expectations in this area, but the available evidence does not suggest that generalization over panels is a foregone conclusion (Harik et al., 2013).

Third, the extrapolation inference extends the interpretation from a claim about the level of competence in the KSJ domain, as measured by the test under standardized conditions, to a general claim about the candidate's standing on the KSJs as they are applied in practice. This inference assumes that the test tasks require application of the KSJs (and preferably application of the KSJs to descriptions or simulations of practice problems), and therefore assumes that the test scores provide an indication of the candidate's ability to apply the KSJs to practice situations. This part of the argument also assumes that the scores from the domain are not unduly influenced by sources of construct irrelevant variance (see Chapter 9). Dependence on multiple-choice items may result in construct underrepresentation because they fail to capture the full range of knowledge, skills and judgments required for practice, but the nearly universal familiarity with the format (at least among candidates from professions that require graduate level education) reduces the impact of format effects. The same is not true for credentialing examinations that include more complex simulations of the practice environment. With these types of assessments, familiarity with the format is almost certain to have an impact on the resulting scores. There is little empirical evidence about this effect. When a series of equivalent performance tasks are presented in sequence, it is straightforward to observe warm-up effects—if they exist—and such effects are likely to reflect increasing familiarity with the format rather than improvement in the proficiency of interest. Most tests that include this type of task present a relatively small number of tasks to each candidate: often just one of each type of task. One exception is found in the United States Medical Licensing Examination. Two studies of different formats used in that examination show clear improvement across the first several tasks presented during the test session (Clauser, Margolis, & Clauser, 2014; Ramineni et al., 2007).

Fourth, the credentialing decision awards the credential to candidates whose scores are at or above the passing score, and does not award the credential to candidates whose scores are below the passing score. The decision is one-sided in the sense that passing the test does not imply that the candidate is admitted to practice. In most cases, there are other requirements for practice (education, character, fitness). However, failing the test will generally prevent the candidate from practicing (to the extent that the credential is required for practice). In contrast with employment and selection decisions, which are top-down and seek to select in the best candidates, credentialing programs are mainly designed to select out candidates who lack adequate command of the KSJs, and therefore, are not deemed ready for practice in the area to which the credential applies.

This argument works in the sense that, if the inferences can be justified, it gets us from observed performances on the test tasks to a reasonable decision about the candidate's mastery of the KSJs that are critical for practice. Therefore, it provides a reasonable basis for most credentialing programs.

## Validation: Evaluation of the Interpretation/Use Argument (IUA)

Once the IUA and the credentialing test have been developed, the validation of the proposed interpretation and use of the credentialing test scores will involve an evaluation of the inferences in the IUA and their supporting assumptions. The validity argument provides an evaluation of the plausibility of the IUA and of its four inferences and their supporting assumptions.

### *Scoring Inference*

The warrant for the scoring inference is a scoring rule that assigns an observed score to each candidate's test performances. Expert judgment based on research findings regarding how the KSJs should be applied in practice typically provides backing for the scoring warrant. In cases where empirical evidence is lacking, the backing for the scoring rule may be based on expert consensus (see Chapters 3 and 6).

For test performances (e.g., performance tasks) that require judgment for scoring, the consistency of scoring can be evaluated by collecting data on interrater reliability, or generalizability over raters. The accuracy and consistency of scoring can be supported by documented quality control procedures.

In assigning a score to a candidate's test performance, we assume that there are no irrelevant factors that might interfere with performance or distort the score interpretation. To the extent that this assumption is not plausible in a specific case, we may need to adjust the assessment or the IUA for that case. For example, if procedures are adjusted to accommodate a candidate with a disability, it would be desirable to evaluate the comparability of such scores to scores obtained under standard conditions. In many cases, the main source of evidence for comparability is a lack of any clear indications that the two sets of procedures are not comparable.

Major exceptions to the scoring inference can occur if the test administration or scoring procedures were violated in some serious way (e.g., the test was defective, a rater made a mistake in recording a score, a candidate cheated). More subtle violations may occur if the scoring rule is based on expert opinion that is not supported by empirical evidence, legal requirements, or consensus practice guidelines.

### *Generalization/Scaling Inference from the Task Scores to a Scaled Score*

The generalization/scaling inference takes us from a candidate's task scores on a particular test administration to a scaled score representing the candidate's estimated level of competence over replications of the testing procedure (see Chapters 6 and 7). If an IRT model is used for scoring, the estimated latent score provides an estimate of the candidate's expected latent score over replications of the testing process. Alternately, various equating models can be used to transform the observed scores on particular test forms to scaled scores defined on some reference form. The justification of such equating procedures requires support for the appropriateness of the equating/scaling model, the fit of the model to the data, the sample sizes being large enough, and the equating errors not being too large (Kolen, 2006).

The generalization/scaling warrant also assumes that the random errors associated with observed scores and the impact of these errors on the scaled scores are not too large. Random error reflects the extent to which candidates' scores are likely to vary across replications of the test involving different tasks, occasions, or scorers, and this concern is addressed in analyses of reliability or generalizability and standard errors (or in IRT, the information function). Random errors can be controlled to a large extent through standardization and by employing large samples of observations. Credentialing tests often include many objective items, but it can be impractical to include many tasks in cases where the tasks require a lot of time to administer (e.g., performance tasks or high-fidelity simulations).

The backing for the assumption that random errors are not too large consists of empirical evidence that the observed score would not vary much over replications of the test. Credentialing tests typically involve generalization over several facets, including test tasks and variable testing conditions. In most cases, generalization over tasks is explicitly examined (via coefficient alpha, a G coefficient, or an IRT information function, for example). As noted earlier, generalizability over raters is usually examined in conjunction with scoring, in cases where this is appropriate. Other potentially important facets, including the occasion, format, and context of testing, are typically ignored, because it is often not practical to collect the required data. The fact that many test developers ignore these facets should not be taken as evidence that they will make a trivial contribution to overall error variance.

Standard errors plus equating error and confidence intervals based on the total error provide quantitative indications of our confidence in the generalizability of a candidate's observed score on a particular test administration thereby providing quantitative qualifiers for the generalization inference. Standard errors around the passing score or estimates of decision consistency are particularly relevant for credentialing tests.

Exceptions to the generalization/scaling inference can be triggered by indications that the observations are not representative of the test domain, or by indications that the testing conditions deviated in some significant way from the prescribed conditions.

### *Extrapolation from the Scaled Score to the Use of the KSJs in Practice*

The extrapolation warrant *extends* the interpretation from performance on test tasks to conclusions about the candidate's standing on the KSJs needed in practice (see Chapters 3, 6, and 7). Even if the test tasks are framed in terms of practice problems, the testing context is substantially different from the practice context. Therefore, the extent to which candidates' scaled scores reflect their abilities to apply the KSJs in practice is questionable. Answering questions about practice situations is different from addressing complex practice situations, and the test tasks tend to focus on simplified, decontextualized applications of the KSJs.

The test tasks included in credentialing tests are typically designed to assess command of the KSJs, particularly those that are frequently required in practice (Raymond, 2001) and that are critical for effective performance in practice. As a result, the steps taken in designing and developing the credentialing test make a case for the relevance of the test scores to the KSJs. To support this positive case further, the test tasks (including multiple-choice items) are often presented as practice-based problems, in which the candidate is asked to apply the KSJs to hypothetical practice situations. It is expected that test performance will reflect competence in the KSJ domain, because the test tasks are designed to reflect the KSJ activities.

The test tasks on credentialing tests (particularly high stakes programs) are reviewed and edited extensively to ensure, to the extent possible, that they are functioning as intended. The tests are designed and edited to minimize the impact of any source of irrelevant variance (e.g., unnecessarily complicated wording, ambiguity). Similarly, the test administration procedures are designed to provide an environment in which candidates with a good command of the KSJs can do well on the test. Testing methodology is intended to make it unlikely that a candidate with a good command of the KSJs would do poorly on the test (Clauser et al., 2006).

In the other direction, security procedures are designed to make it unlikely that a candidate without a good command of the KSJs would get a good score on the test through some inappropriate means (e.g., cheating, prior knowledge of the test tasks). The testing process is designed to provide a level playing field, although there have been several well-documented cases in which this process has been insufficient. This is a particularly problematic part of the process of ensuring the validity of score interpretations, both because the evidence is rarely made public and because candidates that attempt to cheat go to considerable effort to hide their fraudulent behavior (see Chapter 9).

Statistical analyses of testing data (e.g., factor analyses, correlations with alternate measures of some of the KSJs, empirical checks on factors like time limits, task sequencing) can provide checks on the proposed interpretation of the test scores in terms of the KSJs, but generally, there is no single criterion measure that can be used to validate the interpretation of the test scores in terms of the KSJs. If a serious effort is made to identify factors that would cause test performance to underestimate or overestimate competence in the KSJ domain, and no such differences are found, the extrapolation is likely to be accepted.

Exceptions to the extrapolation inference could involve cases in which the ability to apply the KSJs in the testing context could be substantially different from the ability to apply the KSJs in practice for some reason. For example, any disability that interferes with test performance more than it does with performance in practice would generate exceptions to the extrapolation inference. However, a disability that interfered with both performance on the test and in practice typically would not generate an exception (see Chapter 3 of the Standards, AERA, APA, & NCME, 2014, and Chapter 11 in this volume).

### *Credentialing Decision*

Credentialing tests are designed to support decisions about each candidate's readiness for effective performance in practice (see Chapters 3, 6, and 7). The warrant for these decisions is the decision rule which typically specifies that, if a candidate's scaled score is at or above the passing score, the candidate passes the test, and if the candidate's scaled score is below the passing score, the candidate fails the test.

The backing for the decision rule would include all the research and experience indicating that various KSJs are, in fact, critical for effective performance in practice—for example, evidence on the effectiveness of immunization supports a claim that KSJs related to immunization would be critical for the practice of family medicine, and rational analysis indicates that a familiarity with traffic laws is critical for safe driving. The applicable research base would include practice analyses indicating the situations and problems that are frequently encountered in practice (Clauser et al., 2006; Raymond, 2001) and research bases (scientific, clinical, legal, and analytic) indicating the KSJs that are critical for effective performance in dealing with these situations and problems. The basic assumption is that the KSJs are essential for effective performance in practice and therefore failure to achieve a reasonable level of competence in these KSJs would limit a practitioner's effectiveness in practice.

The backing for the decision rule would also involve evidence that the passing score is appropriate and will serve the purpose of the credentialing program (e.g., protection of the public). The choice of passing score is a critical issue for credentialing programs. The passing score is necessarily based on judgment (i.e., judgment of how good is good enough) and tends to involve a kind of Goldilocks principle. The passing score should be high enough to achieve the goal of the program (to protect the public from candidates who lack sufficient mastery of the KSJs to be effective in practice), but it should not be so high that it deprives qualified candidates of the opportunity to practice.

Note that the IUA outlined above does not include a predictive inference from a client's test score to a criterion measure of the client's future performance in practice. This kind of criterion-related inference is not needed for credentialing tests, and collecting the data needed to back such predictive inferences is not generally possible for credentialing tests. In most cases, it is difficult if not impossible to develop an adequate criterion measure of success in practice. Furthermore, in cases where it is illegal for individuals to engage in practice without a credential, it is not possible to collect practice data on failing candidates, and therefore criterion-related studies could not address the bottom line for credentialing, the pass/fail distinction. It should be noted, however, that this fact puts considerable weight upon the evidence for the appropriateness of the passing score, and in the absence of empirical evidence (distinguishing between performance of passing and failing test takers), this evidence is often based on expert judgment. This sort of judgmental evidence is likely to be convincing to the extent that: the experts making the judgments are competent to make the necessary judgments, the judgments are internally consistent and consistent across replication of the standard-setting process, and judges are not subject to any identifiable source of bias.

**Perspectives on Credentialing**

Credentialing programs can be evaluated from many perspectives (Cronbach, 1988; Dorans, 2012; Holland, 1994). These perspectives reflect different interests and points of view, and credentialing programs (as distinct from the tests per se) need to satisfy criteria associated with each. Here, we will focus on three pertinent perspectives: a psychometric perspective, an institutional perspective, and a candidate perspective. These different perspectives tend to be complementary, but in cases where the perspectives are in opposition, tradeoffs need to be made.

The psychometric perspective focuses on technical criteria in evaluating claims based on the test scores, particularly the reliability of the scores and their validity as measures of the target variable. Psychometric analyses tend to be abstract and hypothetical, relying on notions like latent variables, random sampling, and expected values (and variances) of a candidate's scores over hypothetical replications. The psychometric perspective provides a useful framework for developing tests that will yield reliable and valid estimates of the target variable, and it can also be helpful in designing decision rules. It does not, however, provide an evaluation of the certification program as a whole.

The institutional perspective reflects the concerns of the policy makers (e.g., state licensing agencies) who have responsibility for making the credentialing decisions based on the test scores. It focuses mainly on the effectiveness, efficiency, and fairness of the credentialing program. It is concerned about accuracy and precision, because these properties support claims about effectiveness, efficiency, and fairness. In contrast to the psychometric perspective, the institutional perspective tends to take a candidate's test score (observed or scaled score) as a fact on which a decision can be based, and gives less attention to unobservable true scores, standard errors, or latent variables.

The candidate perspective reflects the interests of test takers who are likely to view the test as a hurdle to be overcome or as a contest to be won (Dorans, 2012; Holland, 1994). Candidates may sometimes engage in illegitimate means to try to pass a credentialing test (e.g., by cheating), but as used here, the candidate perspective reflects the candidates' legitimate efforts and expectations. Candidates have a right to expect a "level playing field", and they tend to object to any aspect of the process that they see as interfering with their chance of success. They also have a right to know, at least in general terms, the criteria that will be used to evaluate their performance. Their main concerns are procedural fairness, relevance, and transparency.

The perspectives align in that they all value accuracy and precision in estimating each candidate's overall performance in the KSJ domain. They all value procedural fairness (i.e., treating all candidates in essentially the same way unless a specific accommodation is needed) and fairness as a lack of bias or irrelevant variance. They all favor transparency in the sense of providing accurate and fairly complete information about the testing program. They differ mainly in how they interpret these criteria and in the emphasis they place on the different criteria.

In the following subsections, we expand on the three perspectives and highlight some areas of alignment and potential conflict among them.

### The Psychometric Perspective

In psychometric models, a test taker's score is interpreted as an estimate of the test taker's standing on a target variable and the emphasis is on the validity (or accuracy) and reliability (or precision) of this estimate. Psychometric models tend to posit unobservable construct or trait values as the variables of interest, and they treat the observed score as an estimate of the variable of interest. The primary interpretation of certification test scores is in terms of the test taker's mastery of the KSJ domain, and therefore the variable of interest is the expected level of performance on the KSJ domain.

This perspective values standardization of testing procedures, test format, and test content, in order to enhance reliability of the scores and to promote the validity of the proposed interpretation by controlling as many potential sources of extraneous variance as possible. It values a broad sampling of the KSJ domain in order to support the plausibility of the generalization and extrapolation inferences. The psychometric perspective tends to be particularly concerned about errors of various kinds, random and systematic, in estimating target scores, and in controlling these errors. In general, the psychometric perspective emphasizes the technical adequacy of the testing program, as such, with particular emphasis on the consistency across replications and the plausibility of inferences from observed scores to expected performance over the target domain.

The psychometric perspective promotes fairness in several ways. The psychometric preference for standardization is motivated in large part as a way of controlling random errors, but it also plays a major role in promoting procedural fairness by limiting variation in testing conditions across test takers. The psychometric tradition has also provided an array of statistical methods for detecting differential item functioning and test bias (Camilli, 2006).

The psychometric perspective employs statistical models to get accurate and precise estimates of the target variable. Psychometric analyses tend to involve complex and sophisticated statistical models, and they tend to get more complex and sophisticated over time as better methods of estimation become available. These models are often difficult to explain (i.e., not transparent) to non-technical audiences, and it is not expected that candidates or the general public will understand them without a lot of effort. As a result, there can be conflict between the desire for accurate and precise estimates of the target variable and the desire for transparency. For example, a new estimation procedure that offers a modest gain in accuracy but involves a substantial increase in complexity would tend to be attractive to the psychometric perspective but could be less attractive to the institutional and candidate perspectives, both of which may put a higher value on transparency.

Each of the perspectives can be considered a precondition for the utility of a credentialing assessment. If a test score lacks adequate precision, and as a result, cannot support the institutional intention to protect the public nor the legitimate concerns of the candidates (e.g., fairness), it would not be considered acceptable. However, the judgment of what level of precision is acceptable involves tradeoffs among the different perspectives. For example, within the psychometric perspective higher reliability (or precision around the passing score) is considered preferable to lower reliability (or precision around the passing score), but it could be argued from the other perspectives that a broadly defined performance test might be preferred to a multiple-choice test with a higher reliability. Or, a longer, more reliable test might come at too high a cost or take too much time.

### *The Institutional Perspective*

The institutional sponsors (state agencies, professional and other certification agencies) of certification programs are accountable to the public in various ways, and therefore need to employ decision procedures that are clearly relevant to the purpose of the certification program, that are fair to all candidates, and that are highly transparent. Not only do the procedures need to *be* relevant, fair, and transparent, but they need to be *perceived* as relevant, fair, and transparent by the public.

The institutional perspective takes a more pragmatic view of testing than the psychometric perspective. Public officials and other institutional decision makers who are charged with making decisions that impact people's lives generally operate under mandates that put a particularly high value on relevance, fairness, and transparency. The psychometric concerns about validity and reliability are important in this perspective, mainly because they support the goal of making relevant, fair, and publicly defensible credentialing decisions.

Certification programs employ well-defined systematic procedures, largely to promote fairness by eliminating various potential sources of bias and random error that can arise in less standardized assessments. Porter (2003) has argued that objectivity (defined in terms of not being subjective, personal, or capricious) is highly valued in decision making in the public arena because it "provides an answer to a moral demand for impartiality and fairness" and suggested that:

> This modern sense of objectivity tends to idealize automatic or mechanical standards of knowledge, such as the reduction of judgment to a calculation. It comes close to achieving standardization, in the sense that knowledge should be independent of the person who produces it, and hence tends to disarm those who would suspect that prejudice or self-interest may have corrupted it. Such knowledge often travels well, because in principle it requires no familiarity with the individuals who appear in the guise of author.
>
> (Porter, 2003, p. 242)

Test scores and other standardized, quantitative measures tend to be highly objective. Passing scores are generally based on judgments, but once established, they provide an objective basis for decisions (see Chapter 6).

From the institutional point of view, the candidate is evaluated in terms of performance on a specific test administration. The emphasis is not on how well candidates might do on an infinite sequence of possible replications of the testing procedure, or on a latent variable, but on how well the candidates did on the actual test they took. Minimizing random errors of measurement is not as much of a concern as it is for the psychometric perspective. The focus is on the candidate's observed score, and on whether that score is above or below the passing score. The procedures are standardized and as objective as possible in order to promote fairness and transparency.

From the institutional perspective, tests are tools that can help make the decision-making process fairer and more effective than it would otherwise be. Tests must be reliable and valid enough to achieve that purpose, but these criteria for good measurement are not of primary concern. The examination is expected to be clearly relevant to the purpose at hand and reasonably reliable, but the bottom line is that the process must be relevant, transparent, and fair.

### *The Candidate Perspective*

The candidate perspective views tests as contests or as hurdles that the candidate wants to get over successfully and without too much trouble (Dorans, 2012; Holland, 1994). Some candidates may be disappointed by the outcome, but some negative decisions are an inherent part of the intent of credentialing programs. Most candidates are not particularly concerned about psychometric issues, as such, but they do expect the content of the test to be broadly representative of the KSJs, the tests to be administered and scored accurately and consistently, and the passing criteria to be reasonable, relevant, and consistent. The candidates are mainly concerned about passing the test, but they are also concerned about the fairness and appropriateness of the process (especially if they fail). It is important that test takers see the testing procedures and the decision rules as giving them a fair chance to succeed.

For the candidates to see the process as fair and relevant, the procedures used for test development, administration, scoring, and credentialing decisions need to be made available to the candidates in ways that are accessible and understandable to them—that is, the credentialing program should be as transparent as possible given the other constraints on the program.

Credentialing programs have to satisfy psychometric criteria in order to function effectively as assessments, but they also have to meet additional requirements in order to be satisfactory to candidates and institutional sponsors. Credentialing programs are not simply measurement procedures; they are programs that employ test scores to award credentials.

### Concluding Remarks

To validate score interpretations and uses is to provide a convincing argument for the claims inherent in the interpretation and use. Assuming that a clear and coherent IUA has been developed, the validation effort can focus on its inferences and assumptions. Some of the inferences may not need much support, but any inferences or assumptions that are questionable need to be evaluated before they are accepted.

We want some assurance that the candidates who get credentialed are adequately prepared for practice. We identify some KSJs needed for effective performance in practice, and develop test tasks that evaluate the candidate's mastery of the KSJs. Candidates who do well enough on the test to pass are credentialed, and those with scores below the passing score are not credentialed. General assumptions about practice play critical roles at various points (particularly in providing support for inferences from test tasks to conclusions about the KSJs and from claims about the KSJs to claims about performance in practice).

Although the argument is highly structured, and some parts of it depend on statistical models, much of the argument employs qualitative evidence (e.g., expert judgment) and reasoning rather than quantitative reasoning. The evaluation of observed performance, the extrapolation from scaled test scores to the KSJs, and the determination of the passing score may all be substantially supported by judges' understanding of patterns of practice and the relationship between the KSJs and effectiveness in practice activities.

The negative side of this argument is usually stronger than the positive side. If candidates perform poorly on the test, their level of competence in the KSJs is weak, and if they lack competence in the KSJ domain to a substantial degree, they are not likely to perform effectively in practice. The inferences in this sequence are all fallible and exceptions are possible, but the IUA provides a reasonable basis for awarding and withholding credentials.

Successful performance on test tasks indicates competence in the KSJs. However, the KSJs evaluated by the test do not exhaust the KSJs and other attributes needed for effective performance in practice, and candidates with good mastery of the KSJ domain may lack other skills or other characteristics (e.g., physical skills, interpersonal skills, diligence) that are necessary for success in practice. For the positive side of the argument to be as strong as the negative side, it would be necessary for the KSJs included in the test to include all or almost all of the characteristics relevant to effectiveness in practice.

This lack of symmetry is not a problem for credentialing tests; the expectation is that low scores on the test (i.e., those below the passing score) indicate an inadequate mastery of KSJs essential for effective performance in practice, and therefore that candidates with low scores will tend to be ineffective in practice. It is not necessary that high test scores be associated with superior performance or that the test scores of passing candidates be positively correlated with measures of performance in practice.

Test validation is not to be done in a vacuum. We have outlined three distinct perspectives on credentialing programs. For individual tests and testing programs, more or fewer perspectives may come to bear. Each perspective is important in creating and supporting (or failing to support) validity claims. Diversity of perspective, diversity of opinion, and distinct sources of evidence are all important to validation efforts.

# References

American Educational Research Association, American Psychological Association, & National Council on Measurement in Education (AERA, APA, & NCME) (2014). *Standards for educational and psychological testing*. Washington, DC: American Educational Research Association.

Brennan, R. (2001). *Generalizability theory*. New York: Springer-Verlag.

Brennan, R. (2013). Commentary on "Validating the interpretations and uses of test scores". *Journal of Educational Measurement, 50*, 74–83.

Camilli, G. (2006). Test fairness. In R. Brennan (Ed.), *Educational measurement* (4th ed., pp. 221–256), Westport, CT: American Council on Education and Praeger.

Clauser, B. E., Margolis, M. J., & Case, S. (2006). Testing for licensure and certification in the professions. In R. Brennan (Ed.), *Educational Measurement* (4th ed., pp. 701–731). Westport, CT: American Council on Education and Praeger.

Clauser, B. E., Margolis, M. J., & Clauser, J. C. (2014, October). *Validity issues for technology-enhanced innovative assessments.* Paper presented at the 14th Annual Maryland Assessment Conference, College Park, MD.

Cronbach, L. J. (1971). Test validation. In R. L. Thorndike (Ed.), *Educational measurement* (2nd ed., pp. 443–507). Washington, DC: American Council on Education.

Cronbach, L. J. (1980). Validity on parole: How can we go straight? *New Directions for Testing and Measurement: Measuring Achievement Over a Decade, 5,* 99–108.

Cronbach, L. J. (1988). Five perspectives on validity argument. In H. Wainer & H. Braun (Eds.), *Test validity* (pp. 3–17). Hillsdale, NJ: Lawrence Erlbaum.

Cronbach, L. J. (1989). Construct validation after thirty years. In R. L. Linn (Ed.), *Intelligence: Measurement, theory, and public policy* (pp. 147–171). Urbana, IL: University of Illinois Press.

Cronbach, L. J., & Meehl, P. E. (1955). Construct validity in psychological tests. *Psychological Bulletin, 52,* 281–302.

Crooks, T., Kane, M., & Cohen, A. (1996). Threats to the valid use of assessments. *Assessment in Education, 3,* 265–285.

Dorans, N. J. (2012). The contestant perspective on taking tests: Emanations from the statue within. *Educational Measurement: Issues and Practice, 31*(4), 20–37.

Haertel, E. (2006). Reliability. In R. Brennan (Ed.), *Educational Measurement* (4th ed., pp. 65–110). Westport, CT: American Council on Education and Praeger.

Harik, P., Clauser, B. E., Murray, C., Artman, C., Veneziano, A., & Margolis, M. (2013, April). *Comparison of automated scores derived from independent groups of content experts.* Paper presented at the annual meeting of the National Council on Measurement in Education, San Francisco, CA.

Holland, P. W. (1994). Measurements or contests? Comment on Zwick, Bond, and Allen/Donogue. In *Proceedings of the Social Statistics Section of the American Statistical Association, 27–29.* Alexandria, VA: American Statistical Association.

House, E. R. (1980). *Evaluating with validity.* Beverly Hills, CA: Sage Publications.

Kane, M. (1992). An argument-based approach to validation. *Psychological Bulletin, 112,* 527–535.

Kane, M. (2004). Certification testing as an illustration of argument-based validation. *Measurement: Interdisciplinary Research and Perspectives, 2,* 135–170.

Kane, M. (2006). Validation. In R. Brennan (Ed.), *Educational Measurement* (4th ed., pp. 17–64). Westport, CT: American Council on Education and Praeger.

Kane, M. (2013). Validating the interpretations and uses of test scores. *Journal of Educational Measurement, 50*(1), 1–73.

Kolen, M. (2006). Scaling and norming. In R. Brennan (Ed.), *Educational measurement* (4th ed., pp. 155–220). Westport, CT: American Council on Education and Praeger.

Messick, S. (1989). Validity. In R. L. Linn (Ed.), *Educational measurement* (3rd ed., pp. 13–103). New York: American Council on Education and Macmillan.

Porter, T. (2003). Measurement, objectivity, and trust. *Measurement: Interdisciplinary Research and Perspectives, 1,* 241–255.

Ramineni, C., Harik, P., Margolis, M.J., Clauser, B., Swanson, D.B., & Dillon, G.F. (2007). Sequence effects in the USMLE® Step 2 Clinical Skills examination. *Academic Medicine (RIME Supplement), 82*(10), S101–S104.

Raymond, M. (2001). Job analysis and the specification of content for licensure and certification examinations. *Applied Measurement in Education, 14,* 369–415.

Shepard, L. (1993). Evaluating test validity. In L. Darling-Hammond (Ed.), *Review of research in education* (pp. 405–450). Washington, DC: American Educational Research Association.

Shimberg, B. (1981). Testing for licensure and certification. *American Psychologist, 36,* 1138–1146.

Toulmin, S. (1958). *The uses of argument.* Cambridge, UK: Cambridge University press.

Yen, W., & Fitzpatrick, A. (2006). Item response theory. In R. Brennan (Ed.), *Educational measurement* (4th ed., pp. 111–153). Westport, CT: American Council on Education and Praeger.

# 3 Test Design
## Laying out the Roadmap

*Susan Davis-Becker and Timothy J. Muckle*

### The Importance of Test Design

Organization leaders ready to embark on the development of a credentialing exam are often eager to dive right into the test development process—some are already writing items in their head before they have even fully defined the purpose of the test. Before jumping right in, it is important to engage in careful planning as the design phase creates the foundation for the test development processes. Test design, as described in this chapter, is the process by which key stakeholders make decisions about the plan for the development, administration, and maintenance of the test. Figure 3.1 shows the key phases of the test development process starting with the Design and moving through Development, Delivery, and Documentation. Within the Design phase, the first step (program structure) is the process by which program leaders determine how testing will fit within the larger credentialing process, the number of tests to be developed, how the tests will fit together within the program, and what other guiding parameters will be set at the program level.

After the program structure is defined, the test design focuses on the specifics of the test to be developed, aligns with the program design decisions, and is linked to the overall validity evidence that will support the intended use of test scores (Wendler & Walker, 2006; Wise & Plake, 2016). Not every program takes the time to have such planning discussions. However, these decisions made at the outset of the process will influence how subsequent activities throughout the development cycle are designed around the overall plans and goals for the program. Downing (2006) refers to this step as the development of the "overall plan" and notes that these decisions are ultimately a source of validity evidence for the use of test scores. For example, deciding to provide candidates with multiple levels of feedback on a score report (e.g., total test, content area level) should be considered when you are finalizing the test specifications that will provide the structure and weight of each area of the test. Moreover, a critical component is the documentation of these decisions in a specific plan to move forward with. In addition to being good for communication of decisions, documentation of key information is mandated by professional standards (AERA, APA, & NCME, 2014; NCCA, 2014). In this chapter, we will detail how this process should be conducted, what decisions should be made, the inputs to each, and the impact of each outcome. Each design element relates to one or more of the test development stages shown in Figure 3.1.

### Test Design Process

Programs may approach the process of test design in a number of ways, but here we make some recommendations for the key features that are critical to the success of this process

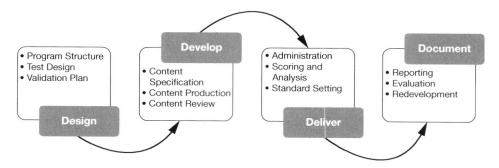

*Figure 3.1* Text Design and Development Process

and the ability to establish well-grounded decisions that will serve as the foundation for the development, administration, and use of the exam. The first question that should be addressed is who to involve in the process. As is described in the next section of this chapter, there are a number of goals but also constraints that should be considered when making each of the critical decisions and therefore, it is important that parties representing all critical factors be a part of the decision-making process.

Several stakeholder groups should be considered as potential participants in the test-design process. The first would be the organizational leaders of the testing program. This group will represent the overall goals for the exam program including the purpose and intended uses, the resources available for development activities (subject matter experts, finances), and other constraints (e.g., time frames). The second group to be included would be subject matter experts (SMEs). In some cases, program leaders can also provide current and relevant subject matter expertise, but if not, it is critical that some of these decisions are made with an understanding of the field and expectations for the job role(s). The third group to be included would be psychometric expertise. Many of the decisions described in the next section have critical psychometric implications and the impact of such should be considered before finalizing any plans. The fourth group would be industry regulators who are responsible for overseeing the licensure of a profession. This group can provide insight into the current state of the licensure aspect of the profession.

There are several options when it comes to executing a test design process. In some cases, program leaders choose to conduct extensive research on each decision to be made, bring all the options to the table, and tackle this task in a focus group-style meeting. This option allows all relevant parties to be focused on designing the test and collaborate with one another to make the best decisions for the program. Another option is to engage in test design through a series of collaborative meetings either in-person or virtually (i.e., via a Web-based meeting tool). This option allows for key stakeholders to be in different locations and flexibility in scheduling and program leaders can focus on one topic during a given meeting, which will allow for staggered preparation and decision making.

The outcome of this process (regardless of how it is conducted), will be a draft test design that outlines the major elements and high-level plans for the new testing program along with a shared understanding among the key stakeholders as to how the test will be developed to focus on the intended uses of scores. The specific decisions to be made throughout this process are reviewed here in this chapter, and the reader will be referred to additional discussion on each topic throughout this volume as well as other key sources. Once the test design is complete, program leaders are encouraged to share this information with their test-development staff as a guiding set of principles for their efforts in developing the test.

## Influences on Test Design

It is assumed at this point in the process that program leaders have already decided on the intended and unintended uses of test scores (see Chapter 2). In addition, the overall program design has been conducted to determine how many exams the program will include (e.g., number of levels [beginner, intermediate, advanced], subspecialties), eligibility requirements, and how the exam results contribute to the credentialing process. Even with this work accomplished, there still remains a number of decisions to be made, which will be reviewed in this chapter. To prepare for making these decisions, program leaders must first review the parameters and constraints that exist, which may limit their options for any given decisions, and identify the organizational/programmatic resources and goals that will contribute to the decision-making process. Here we describe these elements that should be discussed.

### *Purpose/Intended Use*

*What is the Purpose of the Exam?*

Although this first question seems pretty obvious, as a program would not be developed without intent, it is important to document the purpose of the exam, which includes how this exam fits into a credentialing process and why it is being developed. In documenting the purpose, exam designers should address topics such as: what type/level of knowledge and skills the credential will recognize, what need the credential is addressing, how the credential helps with protection of the public, and how the new credential will be different from related/similar credentials in the field. Documentation of this will help maintain the focus throughout the test development process as it ties together the business drivers for the credentialing programs and the foundation for the validity evidence (Standard 4.1, AERA et al., 2014). In Chapter 1, Buckendahl discusses the varying types of credentialing programs and how the purpose of each is shaped and defined.

*Who is the Intended Examinee Population?*

For a credentialing examination, the description of the intended examinee population will likely be a phrase starting with "candidates seeking a credential in _____". Beyond this type of statement, there are several other clarifying parameters that should be documented. For example, the next step may be defining the locations for which this credential will be recognized. If the locations span areas where multiple language are spoken, programs leaders will need to determine if the test will be translated/adapted into other languages. If this is a goal, the test design should include considerations for the translation/adaptation process (ITC, 2005) as well as the specific nuances of each part of the examinee population.

Also as a part of defining the intended examinee population, it is important to specify the eligibility requirements for the test itself. What education, training, and/or experience must candidates possess before they become eligible for testing? By carefully defining who may sit for the test, programs are able to make decisions that will best serve the intent of the program and the target population. Program leaders also need to ensure that all testing groups are considered when designing and developing the test in order to make it as fair as possible for all examinees, including relevant subgroups (Standards 3.0, 3.1, AERA et al., 2014). As a part of this process it is important to estimate the expected annual candidate volume. The size of the testing population will have a substantial impact on a number of the decisions to be made regarding test design and development.

*What is the Intended Use of the Test Scores? What are the Unintended (but likely) Uses of Test Scores?*

The focus of any test-development process should be on building validity evidence to support the intended use of test scores. Therefore, at each step within the test-development process (including test design), program leaders should stop and ask "Are we approaching this process step in a way that will support the intended uses of these test scores?" As such, it is important that the intended uses of scores (and any unintended but likely uses) be clearly defined by the time initial test development begins. Standard 4.0 notes that the goal of appropriate measurement for the intended use should drive design (AERA et al., 2014). Any documentation of intended or unintended uses should be aligned with the targeted purpose of the exam.

*What is the Intended Reporting Scheme?*

Although score reporting is not often thought about until the end of the test development process, it is actually a key factor that should influence some test design decisions and therefore should be a consideration at the outset. Not all decisions may be made at this point; however, leaders should determine if they have any definitive goals in this area and evaluate whether subsequent design decisions should be made to accommodate these goals. First, programs can consider their options for what types of performance information and scores should be reported. Most credentialing exams are focused on reporting simply pass/fail (decision), but others may have reasons to include scores as well, both at the overall level and domain level. Making the decision for what to report should follow directly from and support the defined intended uses of test scores.

Second, many programs are motivated to provide failing candidates with feedback on their performance that helps in preparation for retaking the exam or for informing other future study. Often, this pressure may come after the development of the exam without the preplanning in the design stage. Therefore, even if program leaders are unsure if they want to report such information, test designers are encouraged to evaluate how the development of the exam will result in reliable and meaningful subscores. This feedback often takes the structure of the exam domains (content areas, sections) and requires a particular amount of precision. Therefore, the plans for reporting should be discussed during the domain specification and blueprint development process (see Davis-Becker & Kelley, 2015; Chapter 8, this volume; and Zenisky & Hambleton, 2016, for more about score reporting in credentialing).

### External Input

*What Stakeholder Groups will have an Interest in the Outcome of the Exam?*

For any credentialing program, test results have an impact beyond just the candidates—numerous stakeholder groups exist that have a vested interest in the meaning and use of results. It is important to identify these groups and consider their input and perspective during the design phase. Which groups should have a seat at the table for the design discussions? Which groups should be able to provide input as to their needs? For a given credentialing program, this may include program leaders, SMEs, employers, educators, or even members of the public (see Chapter 1).

*What Goals does the Program have for Accreditation?*

Many credentialing programs have aspirational goals for external accreditation and acknowledgement of adherence to professional standards for test development, administration, and use. In Chapter 10, Fabrey describes many of these opportunities for accreditation. Although many of these accreditation organizations have similar expectations, it is important to determine the goals that a program has for accreditation after the launch of their test and ensure all test design decisions are adhering to the documented expectations for that accreditation group.

### Logistics

*What Resources are Available to Develop and Maintain the Testing Program?*

Developing a meaningful and quality exam takes a substantial amount of resources, both financial and time/effort from program leaders and subject matter experts (among others). Before designing the test-development process, it is important to understand what budgetary or manpower resources are available to assist in the process as this will influence some of the decisions made. For example, a program with a limited budget may only have the resources to conduct two in-person meetings as a part of the test-development process. Therefore, the design of the process would be around getting the most value out of those two in-person meetings knowing that the remainder of the work will have to be conducted virtually. Similarly, resources will influence how an organization plans to use external vendors to support the development of their testing program (e.g., outsourcing psychometric support if not in house, see Roeber & Trent [2016] for a description of how testing services can be contracted).

*What is the Timeline for Development of the Exam?*

Given the multiple steps and the groups that need to be involved in the test-development process, there can be a substantial amount of time between the design phase and when an operational test is ready for launch. Numerous factors can impact this timeframe, including timing of meetings, which stakeholder groups are involved in the development and review processes, technology that must be developed, etc. Therefore, before making any key design decisions, programs should determine if there is a specific timeframe in which all test development must be completed. This may be timed around the expiration of an earlier version of the program, accreditation requirements, or local regulatory requirements/legislation. The timeline and project plan should be developed and circulated to key players for their input and approval.

*What Security Concerns or Risks do we have During the Development and Administration of this Exam?*

Most credentialing programs are under the risk of some types of security threats—whether they come from individual candidates trying to gain an advantage on the exam or an external organization trying to gain inside knowledge to their exam content for their own financial benefit. At the outset of the design phase, programs should determine where their particular security concerns come from (e.g., SMEs, employers, international, segments of the certification constituency, administrations) and design their test development process to minimize the risk of their intellectual property. For example, if a program plans to administer in a foreign country where there is limited protection for their test content, the design may include development of a separate test form for use in this area that is unique from any content administered in other countries (see Chapter 9).

## Design Decisions

With the key parameters and considerations discussed and documented, program leaders can then focus on design decisions of the test itself. Although described below in order as they pertain to the test-development process (see Figure 3.1), each decision is likely influenced by the previous decisions and will influence the subsequent decisions. Therefore, program leaders are advised to review this list to determine if any are fixed based on additional program constraints or previously made decisions (e.g., existing contract with a test administration vendor may influence some decisions about administration or item types). Similarly, the design questions that are presented in this chapter do not dictate a fixed order in which they must be addressed, as one decision may require developers to revisit earlier decisions to ensure that plans are aligned. For example, decisions about test administration (e.g., technology, schedule, delivery locations) may impact features of the content development and review plans (e.g., item types, piloting strategy). The areas of test design and specific questions to be addressed are presented in Figure 3.2 as an advanced organizer. Each of these questions is detailed in the subsequent sections.

### *Domain Specification*

*How is the Domain being Defined?*

From the earlier design questions, the purpose of the exam has been defined, including the intended purpose of the credential, the intended use of test scores, and the targeted examinee population. Before engaging in the job/practice analysis process (see Chapter 4 for details on the process), it is important to have a high-level conversation about the how the "domain" to be measured is being defined.

This includes two types of discussions. The first centers on defining the boundaries of the domain. As an example, imagine that a new credential is being developed in a field where no credential currently exists—test development expert. In situations like this, the boundaries of a field might be a bit blurred. Program leaders may want to be ambitious and cover a wide range of job settings for this new field, including educational assessments, assessment-based certificates, placement exams, employment testing, certification, and licensure testing. In this case, the domain may become too broad to cover with one credential. If this outcome may be anticipated, the parameters (bounds, focus) of the domain should be defined prior to the practice analysis efforts in order to guide that stage in the test development process. In some ways, this step in the process helps to refine the stated purpose of the exam as well as the start of the initial domain definition (Standard 15—NCCA, 2014).

As a related example for an existing program, imagine that an organization has a base credential acknowledging broad expertise in a given field such as a test development

Test Design: Laying out the Roadmap   47

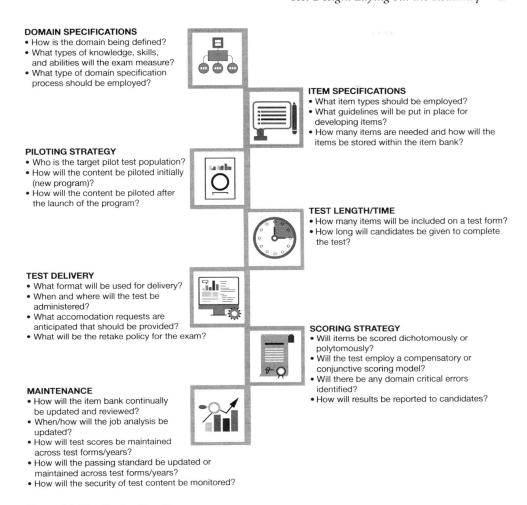

Figure 3.2 Test Design Questions

expert but their next goal is to develop a credential for an emerging specialty where employers are looking for additional acknowledgment of specific knowledge, skills, and abilities (KSAs) such as development of technology-enhanced items. Naturally, some of the KSAs required for the specialty credential would be a part of the base credential exam. The program would need to first define how this new credentialing exam would or would not overlap with the content measured in the base exam. To make these determinations, the program leaders should consider what the purpose and intended use of scores will be for the specialty exam as well as who the examinee population is. Have they all taken the base credential examination? Have they been required to recertify through either retesting or continuing education to ensure they have maintained the KSAs they were required to demonstrate for the base credential? Taken together, these two questions will help program leaders determine what types of claims they want to make about someone who passes the exam and is eligible for the credential. These claims can then help drive the subsequent questions and the domain specification process.

## What Types of Knowledge, Skills, and Abilities will the Exam Measure?

The second part of the domain that must be identified are the types of KSAs that will be tested. For a given credential, this may include both cognitive and physical skills that are part of the job domain. For other credentials, the measurement may be focused on just the cognitive abilities if the goal is determining who is minimally qualified. The judgments made regarding this question will help shape the focus of the job task analysis. Relatedly, this will influence, or could be influenced by, what item types are identified for use. Ideally, programs would be in the position to first determine what they want to measure and then the measurement tools that will best meet their need. In some situations, programs may be constrained by resources or a limited range of item types due to a delivery format that will limit the scope of the domain that they can measure. As an example, to become a licensed crane operator, candidates must pass a written exam as well as a practical exam demonstrating use of a crane. In contrast, an electrical contractor can obtain a license based on a written exam only; there is no requirement to demonstrate the psychomotor ability to physically do electrical work.

## What Type of Domain Specification Process should be Employed?

After the domain boundaries have been defined, the next design decision is to determine how the domain itself may be defined. There are a number of procedural options for doing this—many credentialing programs choose to employ some type of formal job analysis process but others that are restricted by the novelty of a field or the number of identifiable SMEs may select a different approach to defining a job role.

### Item Specifications

## What Item Types should be Employed?

As a part of the test design, program leaders should plan for and define the particulars about the test content (items) that are to be developed. These are sometimes referred to as item specifications (Haladyna & Rodriguez, 2013) or format specifications (AERA et al., 2014). If this part of the design that occurs before any test development, it should be expected that these are revisited and possibly revised after the domain has been specified.

The recommendations from Haladyna and Rodriguez (2013) suggest that there are three process components related to the item development that should be documented. The first is what item types are to be used and why each was selected. Item type selection is a complex decision as there are a number of factors that might be considered. These include:

1. **Item types available within the planned administration format**. The decision about which item types should be used can be influenced by the test delivery strategy (e.g., paper and pencil vs. computer based, one delivery vendor vs. another). Some programs have the flexibility to select their delivery modality once they have set their item types, whereas others are constrained with particular options based on pre-set delivery plans.
2. **Fidelity to the job environment**. Fidelity is a critical concept, particularly in credentialing as this relates to how well the task approximates the target domain. One of the most common criticisms of standardized testing is that such environments do not properly approximate the professional environment. This should be key in selecting

item types (Haladyna & Rodriguez, 2013, also referred to as directness, Lane & Stone, 2006). For some programs, this can be achieved through use of various selected response item types (Sireci & Zenisky, 2016, measuring the same cognitive processes) whereas others find an appropriate level of fidelity requires performance tasks (see Swygert & Williamson, 2016).

3. **Measurement goals**. Through the job task analysis process, the content to be measured by the exam has been specified and these specifications include both the content to be covered as well as the cognitive level at which each will be measured (see Davis & Buckendahl, 2011 for a review on incorporating cognitive demand in credentialing test development). Program leaders are encouraged to think about whether the measurement goals could be achieved through candidates selecting the correct response from a set of options (e.g., multiple choice, multiple select, multiple choice, matching, drag and drop, hot spot), or whether they would need to produce the correct response (e.g., essay, troubleshoot a piece of technology, design a building), or demonstrate a performance (e.g., teach a class, operate a crane, consult with a patient) to achieve the measurement goals (Messick, 1994; Rodriguez, 2002).

4. **Costs**. Many of the new technology-enhanced item types (see Chapter 5) require substantial resources for development, delivery, and scoring. Similar cautions can be made about traditional item types, including essay or other constructed-response items. Programs are encouraged to ensure they understand all the costs associated with a particular item type and then weigh those against the benefit of increased fidelity of the exam.

These four factors should be evaluated and considered together when determining which item types should be used. In some cases, programs have determined that the best strategy is to effectively develop their own item type to maximize the fidelity of their exam (e.g., NCARB developing the vignette tasks, USMLE developing the simulated patient; see Clauser, Margolis & Case, 2006; Clauser, Margolis & Clauser, 2016). For documentation, programs should describe which item types have been selected for use, why each was selected, and how each should be used if there are any restrictions (e.g., constructed response item format is selected to ensure that candidates can communicate their own thoughts in writing).

*What Guidelines will be Put in Place for Developing Items?*

Once item types have been selected for a particular program, it is important to lay out specifications for how these items should be developed and reviewed. This can be thought of as a manual for the test development team that is developed collaboratively between program leaders and those leading the test development efforts (whether internal or external). This documentation should include program-level expectations including:

1. **Item writers**. Most programs employ similar guidelines for selecting and training item writers. These individuals should be SMEs in the field and who have received training on item-writing practices. For planning purposes, it will be important for programs to document the expectations for SMEs, including work experience, credentials, or potential conflicts of interests. In terms of preparation, test designers should document the training to be provided to item writers, including how to understand the domain specifications, appropriate use of item types, item writing guidelines, style

guide, and any item writing tools (e.g., online software, bank). Beyond these requirements, some programs also maintain standards for item writers to remain as part of the program such as frequency of items submitted for review, items accepted for pilot testing, or items accepted for operational use.

2. **Item writing guidelines**. There are a number of sources available that have suggested guidelines for writing appropriate, effective, and clear test items. Programs should identify a set or sets of guidelines for adoption that are followed during the item development and review processes. In addition, there should be a formal orientation for new items writers which includes comprehensive training according to item writing best practices.

3. **Style guide**. Within any professional field, programs must ensure that their exam content is fair, and one way to do that is to be very clear about any terminology or content-specific terms that are used within the exam. This may include adopting a particular set of standards from within the industry, identifying which acronyms are used industry-wide, and limiting the use of any brand names or references. Programs may want to consider sharing this information publically with the candidate population to ensure that they can adequately prepare for the content of the exam.

4. **Use of multimedia**. For a number of programs, incorporating media (e.g., images, video, audio samples) can markedly enhance the fidelity of the measurement. Specifically, skillfully integrated media stimuli can simulate the everyday situations familiar to candidates, in which they would have to gather information based on what they are seeing and make an evaluation or judgments. Testing programs using media exhibits for items will want to avoid "window-dressing," meaning the use of media supplements that are not really necessary to answer the question, but merely make the question more attractive. Window-dressing does not really add any value to the question. Rather, when any media are used, they should be pertinent and necessary for the test taker to actually examine the visual or aural subject matter in order to respond to the question. Incorporation of media in test questions will require specific consideration of the test production (paper booklet) or administration (computer) capabilities. In addition, there may be specific requirements for the use of various media file formats (e.g., .jpeg, .wav, or .mp4) supported by delivery drivers. It is important to evaluate copyright or licensing status, as well as cost, for any media used on the examination. For instance, using collections of images from copyrighted publications (e.g., a digital textbook) may require a license and can be cost-prohibitive. Also, one should not assume that digital assets found through Web searches are automatically fair game for use in items. Web-based images may be tempting to use and easily procurable, and there are a number of open-source, public domain sources for images (e.g., Wikimedia, *Gray's Anatomy*); however, images from sites that are not explicitly public domain may also feature usage restrictions, and should not be used without written permission from the owner of the website on which they are found. With the inherent challenges of paying for licensing or procuring permission to use copyrighted material, testing programs may wish to devote resources to developing their own digital asset libraries. Asking item authors to take pictures from their own practice or working with a contracted illustrator are both cost-effective means of home-growing a bank of images. Obviously, the case for home-growing becomes more complicated the more dynamic the media. The inclusion of video samples in questions can greatly enhance the "realism" of a question, but it also will likely involve great effort and expense in producing and editing. Also, testing programs must verify and ensure that advanced media types (e.g., streaming video)

are in fact supported, to a reasonable degree of quality and clarity, through the chosen delivery engine.

*How Many Items are Needed and How will the Items be Stored within the Item Bank?*

Within the context of building a brand new test "from scratch", item bank needs are primarily driven by anticipated candidate volume. There should be a sufficient number of items approved and ready for testing to support the numbers of candidates that are expected to test. This is true for two reasons. First, there should be an adequate number of items to counteract potential item exposure and resulting compromise. Second, administration of items should be consistent with volume projections, so that a respondent sample may be accumulated, and the items themselves may be analyzed and their statistical performance understood, as soon as possible after their deployment to the field. Thus, a balance must be struck between protecting the items from being seen by too many test takers and allowing enough administrations of items to justify item analyses. Testing programs must make their best efforts to forecast how many test takers will sit for the pilot version of the test, and whether the projected volume is sufficient to yield enough data to conduct meaningful evaluations of individual items and the test as a whole, and to support future test development work.

Programs are encouraged to determine how items will be classified and categorized within the item bank (Vale, 2006). There are several characteristics which are important to document and note including:

1. **Content alignment**. This refers to how items are mapped to the blueprint based on the content the item is designed to measure. In some cases, items are identified as measuring one part of the test blueprint (e.g., objective, KSA) whereas in others, items are intentionally designed to measure multiple areas of the test blueprint.
2. **Cognitive complexity**. Cognitive complexity is a key component of defining the level at which KSAs should be measured. There are different approaches for describing and classifying cognitive complexity, but the majority distinguish among KSAs that are focused on the recall of information (e.g., memory of factors or information), the comprehension of information, and then analysis and/or evaluation skills (see Davis & Buckendahl, 2011). Typically, credentialing programs either identify a targeted cognitive level for each test objective or they create a two-dimensional blueprint where a targeted number of items are identified for each objective, at each cognitive level. Regardless of how the specifications are designed, it is important to track this item-level feature so that test forms can be assembled following the program's expectations for alignment or representation of cognitive levels across the test blueprint.
3. **References**. In addition to an item being approved by SMEs as appropriate, many programs choose to have reference requirement/restrictions regarding the source materials for items. The requirements might be that a program wants to define a set of reference materials that items must be linked to, criteria for reference selection (i.e., published in the past five years), or restrict types of materials as unacceptable references (i.e., proprietary materials that cannot be accessed by the public). It is important to note that items measuring higher levels of cognitive complexity may be difficult to link to a specific reference. In such cases, a program may adopt a practice to allow for reference by committee where the panel of SMEs can sign off on the validity of the item content.

### Piloting Strategy

Testing programs also need to take into account a new test or assessment components will be introduced into the administration field. Despite best efforts to create a quality examination that is representative of the measurement construct of interest, one cannot be sure if the aims of the test have been met until it undergoes actual administration with a representative candidate sample. This process of "trying-out" a new examination is known as *pretesting* or *piloting*.

#### Who is the Target Pilot Test Population?

A sample of test takers must be identified which reflects, as much as possible, the population of individuals who will eventually be eligible to take the examination. This can sometimes be challenging, as there tends to be a self-selection bias in the test takers who first come forward to take a new examination tend to be self-starters, highly motivated, and higher performers than test takers who wait longer to take the examination. Attempts may be made at identifying a random, representative sample, perhaps using other metrics that correspond to test performance (e.g., GPA) ahead of time and conduct the piloting stage by invitation.

#### How will the Content be Piloted Initially (New Program)?

The pilot-testing window, or the time frame for the initial piloting stage, should be set to balance test-taker convenience with the need to collect performance data so that the other test development activities (item analysis, standard setting, rendering pass/fail decision) can be conducted in a timely manner. Most programs have to consider special situations or arrangements for the initial pilot if there is not yet an existing program. Specifically, programs need to consider how they can recruit appropriate examinees and facilitate a pilot-testing event if such a pool does not yet exist. Some programs may choose to have a stand-alone pilot where examinees are recruited for some type of incentive (e.g., gift card) whereas others might conduct an operational pilot test where examinees can earn credit for the exam for the credential.

#### How will the Content be Piloted After the Launch of the Program?

In addition to an initial pilot strategy, future infusion of pilot items onto the test is necessary in order to both "grow" the item bank and to replace items that are lost due to poor performance, over-exposure, or other forms of attrition. Test developers will need to determine first how many pretest (unscored) items will be included on each post-pilot form of the examination, and second, how the items will be administered within the test itself. Generally speaking, it is desirable to seed the experimental questions randomly throughout the test, rather than in stand-alone blocks of items. Random seeding counteracts "order effects," or differential (sometimes detrimental) impact on pretest item performance based on where they appear in the exam—for instance, at the end vs. scored items at the beginning.

If larger numbers of items are available for pretesting (i.e., more than would "fit" into the pretest slots on a single forms of the test), a strategy will need to be developed for piloting new items across forms. The guiding principle for this decision should be the administration of item sets to roughly equivalent groups of candidates. This can be accomplished by randomly dividing among forms or using some metric (such as SME ratings of item difficulty) to achieve the difficulty balance of items across alternate forms. Then, to the extent that possible forms should be randomized among registrants for the examination, another alternative, if it is enabled within the test administration engine, would be to place all available experimental items into a collective "pool" that is available on all forms. In this case, the test driver would randomly select the appropriate number of pretest questions randomly from the experimental pool.

Finally, the introduction of novel item types into an already existing examination raises a number of practical concerns. To what extent should the testing program be "public" about the implementation of the new items? Particularly, should examinees be informed that the new items would initially undergo pilot testing, and that they would not necessarily be scored? It may very well be a concern of the program that telling candidates outright if the pilot stage would lead some candidates not to take the new questions seriously, resulting in unreliable statistical information and problems in the stability of the item's life cycle. Withholding this information, however, seems to fall short of current expectations for transparency. Credentialing programs confronting this dilemma may consider that the likelihood of a certification candidate's "blowing off" any examination question is probably low, whether or not the candidate knows it will count toward the score. This is a complicated issue, and one that testing programs owe due consideration before arriving at a policy.

Another issue related to initial implementation of new formats is the problem of novelty or memory effects. At the heart of this issue is the supposition that (a) any given item may be seen by a substantial proportion of the examinee sample, and (b) examinees are more likely to remember test questions in innovative formats strictly due to their standing apart from MCQ questions. As a result, innovative items may be more susceptible to exposure, examinee sharing, compromise, and piracy. One strategy to counter potential novelty effects is to hold off the implementation of the new item types until a sizable pool of novel items could be developed and field tested. Once a fairly robust collection of items was attained, the probability of any one item being seen by a sizable contingent of examinees is decreased, thus diminishing the problem of overexposure. Also, although novelty effects are a valid concern, some research on the memorability of innovative item types (Harmes & Wendt, 2009) suggests that while examinees may attempt to remember detailed aspects of new questions, this information tends to be inaccurate or unhelpful to answering the question correctly. Obviously, strong non-disclosure policies, while not completely eliminating theft of intellectual property, can help to discourage piracy and to protect the testing sponsor in the event that it happens.

### Test Length/Time

The next important consideration related to test design is the issue of test length. Test developers must balance competing pressures when determining test length: available administration time, desired reliability, adequate coverage of the content domain, cognitive demand and fatigue thresholds in candidates, and item formats, among others. In this section, we discuss separately considerations that should lead to decisions about test length, both in terms of total number of items, and the test time limit.

### How Many Items will be Included on a Test Form?

"The optimum test length is one that is brief enough to be acceptable to those who will use results and accurate enough to support the inferences that will be made on the basis of the test results" (Schmeiser & Welch, 2006, pp. 318–319). A major driver for the length of the test, in terms of numbers of items, is the desired level of reliability of the examination (Wise & Plake 2016). The general rule is that greater quantities of items tend to translate into higher reliability. There are different ways of conceptualizing reliability and several indices are used as metrics for each. Internal consistency reliability references the consistency among items within a test, and measures of this take the form of a correlation (e.g., coefficient alpha, Kuder-Richardson 20), having an effective range of 0 to +1. Decision consistency and decision accuracy (Livingston & Lewis, 1995) refer to the reliability of the decisions that are being made based on test scores either with a parallel form of the exam (decision consistency) or with a perfect form of the test (no error in measurement, decision accuracy). In credentialing, decision consistency and accuracy are often more critically evaluated as the ultimate use of test scores is based on the decision (e.g., pass/fail) rather than the score itself.

The testing program's duty, in part, is to weigh the Type I (false positive) and Type II (false negative) error risk. The higher the false positive risk—the likelihood that a truly unqualified person, or non-master, passes the exam—the higher they should want to set the target for reliability. In other words, the program should lean towards maintaining high reliability in order to minimize the likelihood of misclassifying a candidate as a "master" (certifying a person who "does not really measure up"). Of course, other factors do come into play in order to address this tension between Type I and Type II errors. If of necessity a program needs to lean toward fewer items and lower reliability, upward adjustments could be made to the eventual adopted passing standard on the test to prevent non-proficient candidates from earning the moniker of "certified."

Variance in the candidate population may play a role in determining score reliability. The more homogeneous (similar) a candidate population is, the more difficult it is for the test to make distinctions between candidates. If the reliability of the test is, in part, an indication of the discriminatory power of the test, a more homogeneous test-taker group will result in lower reliability than a more diverse one. This is evident in reliability indices which depend, in part, on variance of true scores, such as Cronbach's alpha (Haertel, 2006), in which variance of scores comprises the denominator. Other factors held equal, this reliability index will decrease as score variance increases. Educational programs that are standardized to comply with accreditation standards may result in a more uniform population of students. In such situations, other factors being equal, a test would have to be longer for a homogeneous population of students/trainees than a more heterogeneous population, in order to achieve the same level of reliability.

Once a requisite level of reliability is agreed upon, several formulaic tools such as Woodcock's Test Construction Nomograph (Woodcock, 1992) or the Spearman-Brown prophecy formula (Haertel, 2006) can be used to determine the appropriate number of items required to attain that level of reliability. Close investigation of these guides for test length reveal somewhat of an oxymoron. Longer tests tend to result in higher precision, however, as one continues to add more and more items to a test, the associated gains in precision with each additional item become less and less. For instance, adding 50 questions to a test may result in an increase in the reliability coefficient from 0.8 to 0.9, but adding 50 more may only increase the reliability from 0.9 to 0.95. Again, testing organizations often have to weigh competing interests, and determine whether gains in precision are really worth the concomitant increases in test length.

While desired levels of reliability are the first consideration in determining test length, testing programs should also consider if the number of questions on the test can adequately sample and assess the breadth of knowledge reflected across the various elements of the content domain. To be sure, it will not be possible to ask every single question or draw off of every possible topic related to a given field. The goal, rather, is to ask a sufficient number of questions, selecting from across the knowledge domain, so that, based on the (admittedly) incomplete sample of questions posed to the examinee, a sound inference may be made regarding the candidate's mastery of the content domain at large.

### How Long will Candidates be Given to Complete the Test?

The testing organization will need to establish time constraints for the test administration. The time limit should be determined taking into account the number of items on the examination, item formats included on the examination, and general level of aptitude of the candidate population. As a rule of thumb, a testing program can assume that one minute per item (multiple choice) will be necessary for 95% of the candidate population to complete the test within the time limit. Of course, item formats involving more cognitive processing will require more time to complete. Items involving numerical computation may take 50% longer than a standard multiple choice item. A single essay item may take 15–20 minutes to complete.

In the case of a brand new test, it would be desirable, once the test is assembled and packaged, to administer the test to a small sample of mock candidates—for instance, program leaders or SMEs who helped to develop the items, in order to get a rough idea of what pace one can reasonably expect real candidates to proceed through the examination. It may be advisable for a testing program to be more lenient in setting the initial time constraints at the time of deploying a brand new test, to assess total test times and item response times across different formats, then fine-tune the time limit to allow for 90–95% of test takers to complete the examination. As a matter or course, testing organizations should continually monitor test times and investigate the prevalence of candidates who fail to complete the test within the time limit, to identify any unintended speededness, and to make adjustments where necessary (Standard 4.14, AERA et al., 2014). There will always be an expectation that a small proportion of candidates will not complete the test within the time. In this case, it is possible to provide time extensions or other special accommodations if warranted.

## Test Delivery

### What Format will be Used for Delivery?

Many different options are available to testing programs for how to administer items in a test. Generally speaking, more advanced test administration modalities, such as computerized adaptive testing (CAT), linear-on-the-fly testing (LOFT), or multistage testing (MST) will not be options until an initial and sizable cohort of items have undergone pilot testing, so that their quality and measurement characteristics are well understood. Therefore, in most instances, a traditional linear fixed-form administration (perhaps using multiple, alternate forms built to the same specifications) will be necessary for a newly deployed examination. Multiple forms will enable the piloting of questions forming the beginnings of an item bank. All alternate forms of an examination must be balanced with respect to content distribution (using the test blueprint) and skill level/difficulty, so that no examinee is disadvantaged from receiving an arbitrarily more/less difficult set of questions than another examinee. Also, alternate forms should have a minimal level of overlap, so that forms may be equated, if desired, at a later time (see Chapter 6).

Item linkages between alternate forms is also a prerequisite for common-item equating—for instance, in analysis using either classical test theory (CTT) or item response theory (IRT) models.

Eventually, the goal is to build a robust bank of items which have passed piloting stage and whose statistical properties are known through item analysis or IRT calibration. Projected candidate volume is a factor at this stage. Test takers are needed in order to collect response data on items and to run item analyses. For classical item analyses, a minimum sample size of 100 exposures is necessary in order to compute stable statistics and to quantitatively evaluate performance (Jones, Smith, & Talley, 2006). For more advanced analytical models, such as three-parameter IRT, upwards of over 1,000 administrations *per item* may be required in order to reliably compute item parameters. Obviously, the anticipated test-taking volume will be a determinant in what type of analysis can be conducted, how quickly items can flow through the piloting stage, and how speedily the item bank can be developed in terms of size. Once the item bank reaches a critical mass, usually at least 500 questions, more advanced administration modalities become possible.

CAT is probably the most advanced form of item administration for traditional item types. The main distinguishing principle of CAT is that items are dynamically selected and administered to an examinee in such a manner such that the difficulty of the items is targeted to the estimated ability of the candidate. Examinees of lower ability, on the whole, receive easier items; higher ability test takers receive more difficult questions. Differences in the average difficulty of questions received between different candidates are accounted for in the estimation of ability using IRT procedures. The main theoretical benefit of CAT is equally precise estimates of aptitude, using fewer number of questions, because time is not "wasted" asking questions that are too easy or too difficult for the candidate. Rather, each test is individualized; each question is selected to be appropriate to each individual candidate's ability.

The goals of CAT—to match quantitative item difficulty/skill level to candidate ability level and to adequately measure examinees across the ability spectrum—necessitate a large, calibrated item bank. The size of the item bank should be sufficient to feature a distribution of item difficulty matched to the ability distribution of the candidate population. Even if the item bank can be "sculpted" to meet this requirement, other parameters must be set before migrating to a CAT administration: rules for starting the examination, content balancing, procedures for estimating ability level of candidates, and rules for when to terminate the administration of items (Bergstrom & Lunz, 1999, Parshall, Spray, Kalohn, & Davey, 2002; van der Linden & Glas, 2000). All these parameters are the focus of extensive study and must be encoded into an adaptive algorithm supported by the selected test delivery engine and vendor.

Programs looking for reduced item exposure, but reluctant or unable to devote the necessary resources to support a full-fledged adaptive test, may consider LOFT (Gibson & Weiner, 1998; Folk & Smith, 2002; Leucht, 2005) as a viable compromise between traditional fixed-forms and CAT. LOFT essentially is a means of dynamically generating many alternate forms of an exam, without all the complicated technical requirements of a CAT. Like CAT, each candidate is presented with a unique set of items which satisfy a predefined set of conditions set forth in the test specifications (i.e., the number of alternate forms is equal to the number of candidates). Usually, the LOFT conditions, at minimum, ensure consistent content representation and difficulty level for all candidates. LOFT can overcome the item exposure problems that often arise as a result of (a) administering a (usually) small number of statically defined forms to a large sample of examinees, and

(b) over-administration of "most-informative items" in CAT. LOFT can also take into account statistical item characteristics (classical or IRT) in balancing form difficulty, and can be programmed to impose equivalent cut-scores.

Multistage testing (MST) is another delivery modality which is gaining traction as an alternative to other options such as CAT and LOFT. MST take on several different forms (Luecht, 2003; Luecht & Nungester, 1998; Wainer & Kiely, 1987), but generally involve grouping items into pre-assembled clusters called "testlets" (Wainer & Kiely, 1987) built to have predefined characteristics. Testlets can be combined progressively and dynamically during test administration in order to optimize measurement properties (e.g., average difficulty or maximum information or reliability), given the characteristics of the test taker.

*When and Where will the Test be Administered?*

Decisions regarding test administration are partly a pre-design consideration/constraint and partly a design decision. There are numerous options for delivery of a credentialing exam (e.g., brick-and-mortar vs. Internet-based, on-demand vs. window vs. event-based). If the delivery plans are set before the test is developed, the plans may represent a constraint with regards to test length (e.g., online proctoring is recommended for no more than XX hours), item types (e.g., the delivery driver may only support some item types), and development of test forms (e.g., windowed testing might suggest the need for a unique form per window). Most computer-based examinations have enabled year-round, on-demand, continuous testing for the sake of examinee convenience. However, there may be very legitimate reasons for offering test administration only in limited testing windows (e.g., two weeks at a time) with defined start and end dates. For instance, a testing program may select tight testing windows in order to control extended exposure of a nascent item bank. Or in the event of a brand new testing program, testing windows can be an effective strategy to collect pilot data, which can be essential for setting baseline performance of a new test, within a reasonable, predictable time frame, rather than have it strung out over several months.

*What Accommodation Requests are Anticipated that Should be Provided?*

Credentialing programs are often faced with numerous accommodation requests from candidates for modifications to the test administration process. Program staff must then determine what accommodations are reasonable to provide in that they do not change the measurement of knowledge, skills, and abilities in the context of determining who is minimally qualified. If able, program leaders should review what accommodations they may anticipate and plan to accommodate and consider this when developing the test design. For example, if administering a test in brick-and-mortar centers that are open for at most 8 hours a day, a program may wish to ensure their test is timed at no more than 3.5 hours in order to accommodate a double time request from a candidate.

*What will be the Retake Policy for the Exam?*

Programs must determine and publish a policy that explains when candidates can retake the exam upon receiving a failing score. From a business perspective, programs want to keep their candidate population engaged and encourage them to focus on additional preparatory activity and their next attempt at the exam. From a test security perspective, programs are concerned about candidates with malicious intent having too much exposure to their operational test content. From a validity standpoint, programs may want to minimize the possibility of a false positive occurring due to continual access to test content. Therefore, it is expected that programs would set some type of reasonable limit either on the waiting period between attempts or the maximum number of attempts within an administration year. The number of times that a candidate can take the exam within a given administration timeframe (e.g., window, year) may influence the number of forms that should be developed.

### *Scoring Strategy*

The scoring process for an exam is not often thought about until after the content is developed and the test is ready for administration. However, professional standards note the importance of a scoring plan aligning with the overall test design and format (Standard 19—NCCA, 2014) so it is important to ensure that the desired scoring plan is understood at the outset of the exam development. As with all the decisions identified in the chapter, the scoring plan design may be constrained by pre-existing parameters, available resources, or other design decisions, which is why this topic was introduced earlier as part of defining the intended use of test scores (thinking about what type of reporting and what level[s] of reporting to provide).

The simplest scoring strategy would be to score all items as correct/incorrect (dichotomous), have all items of equal weight, incorrect responses counted as zero (i.e., no penalty is imposed), and determine pass/fail status based on a total score which represents the number of items answered correctly. However, the nature of the domain, tested content, or potential errors that could be made on the exam may indicate the need for additional parts to the scoring structure.

### *Will Items be Scored Dichotomously or Polytomously?*

One element that can add complexity to scoring is to consider alternative point values for varying levels of performance on an item. Dichotomously scored items are scored as either correct/incorrect (full credit/points or no credit/points) regardless of the number of points that the item is worth. In contrast, polytomously scored items allow candidates to earn partial credit for responses that have some elements of the correct solution. For example, on a short-answer item a candidate may receive partial credit for providing the correct answer but not full credit if they did not fully justify their answer. Many programs choose to score items dichotomously because it is a straightforward approach as compared to polytomous scoring, in which one must define all the ways in which partial credit may be achieved and ensure that score points are consistent across items and item types (e.g., one point represents a comparable amount of work/knowledge). In contrast, other programs choose to allow for polytmous scoring as they feel a minimally qualified candidate would be able to demonstrate some (but maybe not all) of the KSAs required to answer the item correctly. The choice of this more complex scoring strategy may require additional resources dedicated to scoring (e.g., more rater training, more complex algorithm).

### *Will the Test Employ a Compensatory or Conjunctive Scoring Model?*

Typically, the domains as defined for credentialing exams include a number of content areas and a variety of types of KSAs that are being measured. In measuring all of this content knowledge, programs have two choices in terms of overall scoring models (Buckendahl & Davis-Becker, 2011). The first is that they can create a compensatory model whereby the score points earned across the entire test are combined to determine the total test score and the total test score is used to make a decision about the candidate's competency. This is called a *compensatory* model as candidates can compensate for weaknesses in one area with strengths in another area (e.g., cut score is 70 out of 100—a candidate can answer any 70 items correctly to pass the exam). In contrast, there is reason within some programs to create a model where candidates must achieve a minimum level of performance in multiple areas of the exam (e.g., pass/fail is determined based on two or more sets of content). This is a *conjunctive* model as the performance scores are combined to determine the overall decision (e.g., you can only pass the exam if you pass each section individually). This model requires a bit more work during the content specification/blueprint development, standard setting, and score reporting processes, but may provide stakeholders the reassurance that candidates have demonstrated competency in several key areas and that the evaluation of a candidate's knowledge base in each area results in a reliable decision. For example, the Architect Registration Examination is divided into multiple divisions (NCARB, 2015). Candidates must take and pass each division to become eligible for their license. The design of this exam ensures that candidates have demonstrated competency within each of the defined divisions before they are allowed to practice as a licensed architect.

*Will There be any Domain Critical Errors Identified?*

Within some credentialing domains, there are specific KSAs that are considered very critical to being minimally competent. In turn, failing to successfully demonstrate these KSAs on a credentialing examination would indicate that a candidate could pose a risk to the public if granted a credential and allowed to work in this area. These are often described as Domain Critical Errors (DCEs; see Chapter 4). In most cases, when a program identifies the potential for such an error within their testing program, they want to design a scoring system whereby any candidate who makes this type of error will automatically fail the exam. For example, in most dental exams where candidates demonstrate their physical ability to perform certain dental operations, any errors resulting in damage to the patient's mouth (e.g., cheeks, gums) would result in an automatic failure on the exam, regardless of the other indicators of performance. Typically, such extreme scoring designs are only used when an error is such that it cannot be undone (e.g., with money and/or time, damage to human tissue in a dental procedure—tissue will never be fully normal again).

*How will Results be Reported to Candidates?*

Due consideration should be given to the information that is presented to the candidate upon completion of the examination. As mentioned earlier in this chapter, the information provided in score reports should be consistent with, and refrain from going beyond, the primary purpose of the test. This topic is revisited here because at this point in the design process, leaders should be prepared to make many of these decisions in accordance with professional standards. Test takers have a right to accurate, meaningful information related to their test performance, provided the inferences can be supported by the validity argument for the test (Standards 8.7—AERA et al., 2014; Standard 19—NCCA, 2014). Test sponsors must follow due diligence in securing sensitive information and protecting test takers from unauthorized use of test scores (Standards 6.6, 6.16, 8.5—AERA et al., 2014), presenting the information clearly in score reports, providing guidance in interpretation (Standard 6.10—AERA et al., 2014), and delineating appropriate and inappropriate uses of test scores (Standard 9.6, AERA et al., 2014). In situations where scores feature diminished reliability (e.g., domain-level subscores), testing programs have a duty to point this out to test takers, at minimum by a qualitative disclaimer describing limitations in interpreting and using this feedback.

Most credentialing programs plan for providing at least two levels of performance information (to at least failing candidates, if not all), including both an overall measure of performance and then some type of detailed feedback at a more specific level (e.g., domain, content area, section). However, there are numerous options to consider regarding what will be reported to candidates. Is the purpose of the exam to classify examinees into ordinal groups (e.g., pass/fail, certified/not certified, master/non-master, novice/proficient/expert)? If so, the reported results should generally not go too far beyond this purpose. If the purpose of a testing program is to determine certification or licensure status, for instance, the testing program may want to carefully consider the consequences of reporting quantitative score information in addition to pass/fail status. If the purpose of the test is to indicate the position of the test taker on some quantitative continuum (e.g., educational verbal and mathematical aptitude), then the score report should reflect quantitative information.

While reporting both overall scores and subscores is a common practice, especially for failing candidates, this information is often accorded a precision and trustworthiness which is undue, resulting in inappropriate uses and inferences. A case in point is a passing candidate using a high test score on a professional certification examination in order to negotiate a higher salary in his/her job. This is an inappropriate use of the test score, as it likely goes beyond the validity evidence and supported inferences for most credentialing exams. Therefore, testing programs must carefully balance advantages and disadvantages of reporting test performance information which exceeds the primary purpose of the test.

## Maintaining the Test Design

The test design should be considered an active and dynamic plan for developing and administering a credentialing exam. Therefore, although extensive initial planning should take place to discuss each of the identified design influences and decisions, it is important to continually revisit this document during the test development process (Standard 4—NCCA, 2014). Changes may result from additional constraints that are identified that influence design options, identification of KSAs that require specific measurement tools, or the influence of available technology.

Once a test-development program has launched, the test-design document should then be expanded to include test-maintenance decisions. As is well understood, a testing program cannot live forever in its original form; elements will need to be updated and refreshed to address content relevance (validity), security concerns, and stakeholder needs. Therefore, programs should consider questions such as:

- How will the item bank continually be updated and reviewed?
- When/how will the job analysis be updated?
- How will test scores be maintained across test forms/years?
- How will the passing standard be updated or maintained across test forms/years?
- How will the security of test content be monitored?

There are chapters in this volume that address options to answer each of these questions. However, part of the test design process is thinking into the future of the program and making some plans to evaluate the initial design decisions that were made at the outset of the program. Parshall and Guille (2016) discuss strategies for implementing changes to the test design using the *agile* approach, including testing out and implementing changes to the test design. Although it can be challenging to make changes to a program, the evolution of professions and availability of new testing options may outweigh the potential drawback of conducting such evaluations and implementing changes.

## Summary

The test design step is a key fundamental component of developing a testing program that will result in sufficient validity evidence to support the intended use of test scores. It can be challenging to make all these decisions at once and weigh all the options that are available. In this chapter, we have attempted to outline these key decisions for credentialing programs and specific considerations that are a part of each. The final decisions should be made based on what is best for the program, feasible in terms of resources, and ultimately meets professional standards. Wise and Plake (2016) outline how the *Standards* (AERA et al., 2014) express expectations for each of these key topics and the reader is referred here for specific language on each topic. As each decision is made, program leaders are encouraged to engage in thorough documentation of the decision and supporting rationale (Ferrara & Lai, 2016). Defensibility of any part of a testing program comes from not only engaging in best practice supported by professional standards, but the documentation available to describe and support the practice.

Finally, although the test-design process and initial development can be cumbersome, programs are encouraged to revisit the test design and potentially update or refine the design in a way to maintain or increase the fidelity of measurement. For many programs, the initial design decisions will remain the most appropriate, but for others there may be possible updates that would be beneficial.

## References

American Educational Research Association (AERA), American Psychological Association (APA), & National Council on Measurement in Education (NCME) (2014). *Standards for educational and psychological testing*. Washington, DC: American Educational Research Association.

Bergstrom, B. A., & Lunz, M. A. (1999). CAT for certification and licensure. In F. Drasgow & J. B. Olson-Buchanan (Eds.), *Innovations in computerized assessment* (pp. 67–91). Mahwah, NJ: Lawrence Erlbaum.

Buckendahl, C., & Davis-Becker, S. (2011). Setting passing standards for credentialing testing. In G. Cizek (Ed.), *Setting performance standards: Foundations, methods, and innovations* (2nd ed., pp. 48–502). New York: Routledge.

Clauser, B., Margolis, M., & Case, S. (2006). Testing for licensure and certification in the profession. In R. Brennan (Ed.), *Educational measurement* (4th ed., pp. 701–732). Westport, CT: Prager Publishers.

Clauser, B., Margolis, M., & Clauser, J. (2016). Issues in simulation-based assessment. In F. Drasgow (Ed.), *Technology and testing: Improving educational and psychological measurement* (pp. 49–78). New York: Routledge.

Davis, S. L., & Buckendahl, C. W. (2011). Incorporating cognitive demand in credentialing exams. In G. Schraw & D. Robinson (Eds.), *Assessment of higher order thinking skills* (pp. 303–326). Charlotte, NC: Information Age Publishing.

Davis-Becker, S., & Kelley, J. (2015). Score reporting: Where policy meets psychometrics. Washington, DC: Institute for Credentialing Excellence.

Downing, S. (2006). Twelve steps for effective test development. In S. Downing & T. Haladyna (Eds.), *Handbook of test development* (pp. 3–25). Mahwah, NJ: Lawrence Erlbaum.

Ferrara, S., & Lai, E. (2016). Documentation to support test score interpretation and use. In S. Lane, M. Raymond, & T. Haladyna (Eds.), *Handbook of test development* (2nd ed., pp. 603–623). New York: Routledge.

Folk, V. G., & Smith, R. L. (2002). Models for delivery of CBTs. In C. Mills, M. Potenza, J. Fremer, & W. Ward (Eds.), *Computer-based testing: Building the foundation for future assessments* (pp. 41–66). Mahwah, NJ: Lawrence Erlbaum.

Gibson, W. M., & Weiner, J. A. (1998). Generating random parallel test forms using CTT in a computer-based environment. *Journal of Educational Measurement, 35*(4), 297–310.

Haertel, E. H. (2006). Reliability. In R. L. Brennan (Ed.), *Educational measurement* (4th ed., pp. 65–110). Westport, CT: Praeger.

Haladyna, T., & Rodriguez, M. (2013). *Developing and validating test items.* New York: Routledge.

Harmes, C., & Wendt, A. (2009). Memorability of innovative items. *CLEAR Exam Review, Winter 2009*, 16–20.

International Test Commission (ITC) (2005). *International guidelines on test adaptation.* Retrieved from: www.intestcom.org

Jones, P., Smith, R., & Talley, D. (2006). Developing test forms for small-scale achievement testing systems. In S. Downing & T. Haladyna (Eds.), *Handbook of test development* (pp. 487–525). Mahwah, NJ: Lawrence Erlbaum.

Lane, S., & Stone, C. (2006). Performance assessment. In R. Brennan (Ed.), *Educational measurement* (4th ed., pp. 387–432). Westport, CT: Prager Publishers.

Livingston, S. A., & Lewis, C. (1995). Estimating the consistency and accuracy of classifications based on test scores. *Journal of Educational Measurement, 32*(2), 179–197.

Luecht, R. M. (2003, April). *Exposure control using adaptive multistage item bundles.* Paper presented at the Annual Meeting of the National Council on Measurement in Education, Chicago.

Luecht, R. M. (2005). Some useful cost-benefit criteria for evaluating computer-based test delivery models and systems. *Journal of Applied Testing Technology, 7*(2). Retrieved from: www.testpublishers.org/assets/documents/Volum%207%20Some%20useful%20cost%20benefit.pdf

Luecht, R. M., & Nungester, R. J. (1998). Some practical examples of computer adaptive sequential testing. *Journal of Educational Measurement, 35*(3), 229–249.

Messick, S., (1994). The interplay of evidence and consequences and validation of performance assessments. *Educational Researcher, 23*(2), 13–23.

National Commission for Certifying Agencies (2014). *Standards for the accreditation of certification programs.* Washington, DC: Institute for Credentialing Excellence.

National Council for Architectural Registration Boards (2015, July). *Architect registration examination guidelines.* Retrieved from: www.ncarb.org/ARE/~/media/Files/PDF/Guidelines/ARE_Guidelines.pdf.

Parshall, C., & Guille, R. (2016). Managing ongoing changes to the test: Agile strategies for continuous innovation. In F. Drasgow (Ed.), *Technology and testing: Improving educational and psychological measurement* (pp. 1–22). New York: Routledge.

Parshall, C. G., Spray, J. A., Kalohn, J. C., & Davey, T. (2002). *Practical considerations in computer-based testing.* New York: Springer.

Rodriguez, M. (2002). Choosing an item format. In G. Tindal & T. M. Haladyna (Eds.), *Large-scale assessment programs for all students: Validity, technical adequacy, and implementation* (pp. 213–231). Mahwah, NJ: Lawrence Erlbaum Associates.

Roeber, E., & Trent, R. (2016). Contracting for testing services. In S. Lane, M. Raymond, & T. Haladyna (Eds.), *Handbook of test development* (2nd ed., pp. 100–116). New York: Routledge.

Schmeiser, C. B., & Welch, C. J. (2006). Test development. In R. L. Brennan (Ed.), *Educational measurement* (4th ed., pp. 307–353). Washington, DC: American Council on Education.

Sireci, S., & Zenisky, A. (2016). Computerized innovative item formats: Achievement and credentialing. In S. Lane, M. Raymond, & T. Haladyna (Eds.), *Handbook of test development* (2nd ed., pp. 313–334). New York: Routledge.

Swygert, K., & Williamson, D. (2016). Performance tasks in credentialing exams. In S. Lane, M. Raymond, & T. Haladyna (Eds.), *Handbook of test development* (2nd ed., pp. 294–312). New York: Routledge.

Vale, D. (2006). Computerized item banking. In S. Downing & T. Haladyna (Eds.), *Handbook of test development* (2nd ed., pp. 261–285). Mahwah, NJ: Lawrence Erlbaum.

van der Linden, W. J., & Glas, C. A. W. (2000). *Computerized adaptive testing: Theory and practice.* Dordrecht: Kluwer.

Wainer, H., & Kiely, G. L. (1987). Item clusters and computerized adaptive testing: A case for testlets. *Journal of Educational Measurement, 24*(3), 185–201.

Wendler, C., & Walker, M. (2006). Practical issues in designing and maintaining multiple test forms for large-scale programs. In S. Downing & T. Haladyna (Eds.), *Handbook of test development* (2nd ed., pp. 445–468). Mahwah, NJ: Lawrence Erlbaum.

Wise, L., & Plake, B. (2016). Test design and development following the Standards for Educational and Psychological Testing. In S. Lane, M. Raymond, & T. Haladyna (Eds.), *Handbook of test development* (2nd ed., pp. 19–39). New York: Routledge.

Woodcock, R. (1992). Richard Woodcock's test design nomograph. *Rasch Measurement Transactions, 6:3,* 243–244.

Zenisky, A., & Hambleton, R. (2016). A model and good practices for score reporting. In S. Lane, M. Raymond, & T. Haladyna (Eds.), *Handbook of test development* (2nd ed., pp. 585–602). New York: Routledge.

# 4 Specifying the Content of Credentialing Examinations

*Amanda L. Clauser and Mark Raymond*

Credentialing is a broad term that encompasses certification, licensure, and other types of occupational regulation (e.g., registration). The purpose of credentialing, according to the *Standards for Educational and Psychological Testing*, is to "provide the public, including employers and government agencies, with a dependable mechanism for identifying practitioners who have met particular standards" (AERA, APA, & NCME, 2014, p. 175). While credentialing processes for some professions require that applicants meet multiple standards (e.g., experience, education, moral character), most require passing some type of test to establish that individuals have demonstrated the requisite knowledge or skills for participation in the profession.

Given the importance of credentialing tests to the individuals required to take them and to the constituents that rely on them, it is imperative that they are job-related. This relationship is typically established by developing detailed content specifications that have been based on a practice analysis (AERA et al., 2014, p. 182). Practice analysis can inform four key test development activities: 1) defining the knowledge and skills required for successful performance, 2) selecting appropriate methods for assessing knowledge and skills that comprise this domain, 3) designing practice-related assessment tasks, and 4) defining score categories that serve as the basis for feedback to examinees and other users. The outcomes of these activities will determine the structure of the test content specifications.

Content specifications represent a subset of the more general documentation called test specifications.[1] The purpose of content specifications is to articulate the important features of a test, including the knowledge, skills, and abilities (KSAs) to be covered, the format of the assessment tasks, the demands of those tasks (cognitive and otherwise), and the emphasis allocated to each of these areas within the examination. While content specifications are essential tools for test developers, they are also valued by educators, examinees, and other users of test-related information (e.g., licensing agencies). Content specifications, once developed, serve several purposes:

- Provide direction to test-question writers.
- Serve as the basis for classifying test items and managing item inventory.
- Guide test-form assembly to ensure that tests are comparable across different forms and over time.
- Help to ensure that equating blocks and linking items are representative of the entire performance domain.
- Assist candidates, educators, and others in test-preparation efforts.
- Provide candidates and other users (e.g., licensing agencies) with an operational definition of the domain being measured.

- Serve as the basis for subscores or other mechanisms for providing feedback to candidates and other users.
- Provide a vehicle for credentialing organizations to communicate their values (e.g., which competencies are important).
- Document the scope and boundaries of a profession, and how it evolves over time.

Given these multiple audiences and applications, it is all the more important that content specifications are developed carefully.

While content specifications can be formatted in a variety of ways, they typically appear as a list or outline of topics or KSAs to be covered by the test. It has become increasingly common to present content specifications as a two-dimensional framework known as a content-by-process matrix. Content-by-process matrices in educational testing are very common, where the process facet corresponds to cognitive processes such as comprehension, application, and problem solving (Haladyna & Rodriguez, 2013; Millman & Greene, 1989). However, the process facet for credentialing tests commonly corresponds to actual job behaviors or classes of behaviors (e.g., client communications). Figure 4.1 presents a stylized and abstracted version of the content-by-process matrix for

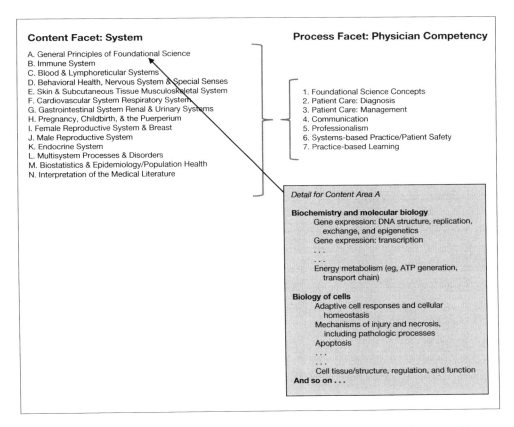

*Figure 4.1* Portion of a Content-by-Process Content Specification for a Physician Licensure Examination (adapted from Federation of State Medical Boards and National Board of Medical Examiners, 2015)

the United States Medical Licensing Examination (USMLE®). The content facet corresponds mostly to human organ systems, while the process facet corresponds to physician task or competency. The portion of the matrix defined by the intersection of B.3, for example, would correspond to test items or assessment tasks that require examinees to manage diseases of the immune system. Variations of the framework presented in Figure 4.1 could be created by adding facets (e.g., cognitive complexity), by nesting rather than crossing facets, or by imposing other changes in layout. This type of framework is particularly flexible and can support a variety of assessment formats.

**Foundations of Practice Analysis**

Practice analysis can be viewed as a specific type of job analysis, of which there are numerous methods ranging from off-the-shelf systems to custom-made surveys and questionnaires (e.g., Wilson, Bennett, Gibson, & Alliger, 2013). Some of the more popular methods include the Job Element Inventory (Harvey, Friedman, Hakel, & Cornelius, 1988), the Position Analysis Questionnaire (McCormick, Jeanneret, & Mecham, 1972), the Fleishman Job Analysis Survey (Caughron, Mumford & Fleishman, 2012), and the O*NET online method, which is associated with the *Dictionary of Occupational Titles* (Dye & Silver, 1999). Most of these methods are applicable to a wide variety of jobs and tend to focus on general human attributes (e.g., verbal reasoning, conscientiousness). They are not particularly suitable for credentialing tests because they lack the detail required to capture occupation-specific KSAs. These methods are intended and designed for other human resource activities such as personnel selection, job design, and benchmarking for compensation. Consequently, those responsible for conducting job analyses for credentialing programs have typically relied on a customized approach to practice analysis that borrows from other methods.

Consistent with other sources, this chapter uses the term "practice analysis" to reflect the emphasis on a comprehensive view of professional responsibilities required for effective practice performance (AERA et al., 2014; Kane, 1997, Knapp & Knapp, 1995; Raymond, 2016; Smith & Hambleton, 1990). The methods included in this chapter are recommended for credentialing examinations because their scope can extend beyond the tasks performed for a particular position to include cognitive and reasoning skills, judgmental demands, and other interpersonal competencies that may be relevant for describing a professional's role. Brain (1991) describes the practical knowledge that professionals should have as the knowledge "which constitutes their capacity to identify a job to be done, to know how to go about doing it, and to recognize when it has been done appropriately" (p. 260). In operational terms, a practice analysis gathers information about what professionals do, as well as about the knowledge, skills, and abilities they employ to perform those tasks successfully. The first part—identifying work activities—is mostly descriptive in nature. The second part—determining the KSAs required for those activities—is inferential in nature and requires the judgments and participation of subject matter experts (SMEs).

The exact approach to practice analysis will be determined by the purpose of the study and the intended use of the results. A practice analysis undertaken to develop a test consisting of multiple-choice questions (MCQs) would likely be different from one intended to inform the design of a performance or skills-based test. Similarly, a practice analysis that focuses exclusively on entry-level practice would be done differently if the results were to be used for assessing continued competence of experienced practitioners.

Table 4.1 identifies several key decisions to be made when planning a study. The decisions in the top part of Table 4.1 pertain to the type and specificity of the information that will be used to describe work. These issues determine the content that make up the practice survey and format of the rating scales. Dunnette (1976) distinguished between task-oriented and person-oriented descriptors, and referred to them as the two worlds of behavioral taxonomies. As previously suggested, task-oriented descriptors tend to be descriptive in nature, while person-oriented descriptors are largely inferential. Task-oriented descriptors focus on the activities and behaviors performed during work. The statement "compose written response to dissatisfied customer" is a task-oriented descriptor. Task-oriented descriptors might also document types of problems that people

*Table 4.1* Key Study Design Decisions for Practice Analysis

| Design Decision | Factors to Consider |
| --- | --- |
| A. Nature of Information for Describing Work | |
| Type of Work Descriptor | *Task-oriented descriptors* document the work activities performed in the actual work setting; can be physical or cognitive activities. *Person-oriented descriptors* require judgments and inferences about the personal characteristics (KSAs or other personal attributes such as knowledge of algebra; verbal reasoning; conscientiousness). |
| Specificity of Work Descriptor | Can range from very detailed to very general statements regarding job activities or personal attributes (e.g., *specific*: interpret ECG strip demonstrating ventricular fibrillation; *general*: diagnose common cardiovascular diseases. Level of detail will influence questionnaire length. |
| Descriptor Attributes (Type of Rating Scales) | Common scales include frequency of task performance; time spent; criticality; consequences if performed incorrectly; difficulty. Many scales can apply to task-oriented or person-oriented descriptors. |
| Design Features of Rating Scales | Scales vary in terms of types of response categories (verbal, numeric), the number of response categories, and whether the categories require relative or absolute judgments (e.g., *relative*: I perform this more often than other activities; *absolute*: I perform this about once per week). |
| B. Source of Information | |
| Sources of Data (Respondents) | Depends on type of data collected and scope of study. Actual practitioners (job incumbents) are usually included in sample. Additional groups may include trainers, supervisor, and clients. The purpose of the credential influences this (e.g., entry-level vs. continued competence). |
| Size and Diversity of Sample | Determined by the size of the profession, purpose of the credential scope of project (e.g., regional vs. international) methods of data collection, variation in specialties or subspecialties), and on type and specificity of the descriptors. |
| Method of Data Collection | Work information typically obtained by administering paper or Internet-based questionnaire. Other methods include direct observation, work diaries, audit of work records, and conducting focus groups with small panels of SMEs. Method depends on type, specificity, and complexity of descriptors. Questionnaires sufficient for eliciting ratings about task performance, while SME focus groups may be effective for complex judgments and inferences. |

encounter and solve in their work, the tools and methods used to solve those problems, and the context within which those problems occur. For example, psychologists encounter certain patient conditions such as depression or anxiety in their work, and a task-oriented questionnaire for psychologists would include a list of such diagnostic conditions (Rosenfeld, Shimberg, & Thornton, 1983).

In contrast, person-oriented approaches to practice analysis focus on the personal qualities required to effectively carry out the job. These qualities may include the KSAs, personality characteristics, and competencies required for successful performance (e.g., conscientiousness, verbal ability, knowledge of calculus). Another design consideration is the level of specificity at which tasks and KSAs are written. Although specificity is desirable, a practice analysis questionnaire consisting of several hundred specific activity statements may yield a low response rate. Conversely, a questionnaire consisting of 20 very general competencies may achieve a good response rate, but the data may come at the expense of clarity of interpretation.

Finally, job descriptors can be rated or judged according to different attributes that form the basis of job analysis rating scales. Task-oriented descriptors lend themselves to ratings regarding the frequency of performance, time spent, and criticality, to name a few attributes. Meanwhile, person-oriented descriptors avail themselves to similar rating scales, including frequency, difficulty of learning, and importance, to name a few possibilities. Raymond (2016) presents a list of 15 different task-oriented and person-oriented ratings scales.

The decisions in the bottom portion of Table 4.1 pertain to the sources of work-related information. Work data are typically collected from individuals knowledgeable about the profession, including practitioners, supervisors, managers, educators, and even customers or clients. It is evident that the source of job-related information will interact with the type of information being sought and its level of specificity, which in turn will influence the method of data collection, the sampling unit, and sample sizes. Some of the more common data-collection methods include observing or interviewing individuals in the profession, which would require a smaller sample of participants, while administering questionnaires or auditing practice records could include a broader sample.

In general, large samples of practitioners are the best source of detailed information for task-oriented descriptors and other concrete judgments. However, small panels of SMEs might be the more effective source for abstract judgments and ratings concerning person-oriented attributes such as the level of knowledge or the degree of conscientiousness required for a job (Kane, 1997; Raymond, 2001). The sometimes ambiguous nature of person-oriented descriptors and their rating scales can benefit from the type of dialogue and interaction afforded by SME focus groups and meetings. A recent meta-analysis of 205 published job analysis reports identifies the differential effects of the design decisions in Table 4.1, and addresses several other important factors (e.g., reliability of ratings) that influence the quality of practice analyses (DuVernet, Dierdorff, & Wilson, 2015).

Until the recent past, it had been common to conduct a practice analysis by gathering input exclusively from small panels of SMEs. Support for this practice came from studies indicating that committee-based practice analyses provided results similar to the results obtained from large-sample surveys (Tannenbaum & Wesley, 1993). However, research also suggests that small groups are susceptible to certain types of social and cognitive biases (Lindell, Clause, Brandt, & Landis, 1998; Morgeson & Campion, 1997), and that this problem is more pronounced when SMEs are asked to rate abstract KSAs and competencies as opposed to observable job activities (Morgeson, Delaney-Klinger, Mayfield, Ferrara, & Campion, 2004). Recognizing the potential limitations of committee-based practice analysis, it is now common for practice analyses to include input from several hundred to several thousand individuals in addition to input from smaller groups of SMEs. Large samples improve the precision of statistical estimates, reduce bias, enhance generalizability of results, and lend credibility to the outcomes of a study. However, SME committees still serve valuable roles by assisting with survey development, interpreting results, and by providing complex judgments such as those related to criticality, importance, and related attributes.

The next section summarizes the more common approaches to practice analysis in a credentialing context. For each approach, we describe its basic features (e.g., task vs. person-oriented), summarize its advantages and disadvantages, and cite studies making use of that method. Although each method represents a distinct approach, it is often the case that any single practice analysis draws on multiple methods, depending on the goals of the project. For example, a practice analysis might consist of a task inventory survey early on, only to be followed up with a cognitive task analysis to identify the KSAs required to perform the most critical or important of the tasks. Or, a critical incidents method might be followed by a survey to quantify the extent to which certain critical incidents actually occur in practice. Consistent with this thinking, we use the term "approaches" rather than "methods" to emphasize that any single practice analysis typically draws on multiple methods.

## Approaches to Practice Analysis

Three methods historically have been popular choices when designing a practice analysis in credentialing; the critical incident technique (Flanagan, 1954) and variants, the task inventory and variants (Newman, Slaughter, & Taranath, 1999), and the professional practice model (LaDuca, 1994). These methods, along with those discussed below, including functional job analysis (Fine & Wiley, 1971), and competency modeling, can be used in combination with other approaches to provide not only a broad view of the requirements for successful professional practice (task orientation) but also describe the knowledge and skills that are required of successful professionals (person orientation). This requires a combination of data-collection methods (including a broad survey and SME review, perhaps). The process of combining methods and developing a data-analysis plan is discussed in the next section.

### *Critical Incident Technique*

The critical incident technique (CIT), introduced by Flanagan (1954) for use in the American military, and adopted by Woolsey (1986), has been used successfully to document anecdotes of "incidents" that have significance in professional practice. Flanagan's original application of this approach invited individuals to describe situations where they felt particularly effective or ineffective, leading to detailed analysis and results reflecting the demands and requirements for military leadership. In other contexts, critical incidents, when collected from a targeted sample of professionals, allow for analysis and documentation of the types of judgments required in the practice setting, as well as the professional's enacted knowledge, skills, and abilities.

The CIT also allows for identification of decision points or situations that may pose challenges or require informed judgment from professionals. As Flanagan suggested, the technique is a tool for collecting situation-specific behavior and experiences. Operationally, the definition of *critical* incidents can vary depending on the profession, but can include incidents that are important to client outcomes and/or those that required a particular intervention on the part of the professional. Similar incidents reported across practice settings/roles can be used to describe the domain of practice.

Critical incident data can be collected via questionnaire as well as through focus groups or interviews depending on the sensitivity of the incidents to be reported and the number of professionals to be sampled. Individuals may be asked to reflect on the incident itself, their approach to handling the situation, the ideal approach to handling the situation, as well as the impact of the incident. This creates a person-oriented design where the professional's KSAs can be matched to the literal demands of practice. This approach may also be task oriented by focusing on what professionals *do* in order to address the critical incidents instead of focusing on the process of problem solving.

The CIT can provide a summary of situations that may be faced by practicing professionals, the tools employed to address those situations, and may provide significant data about elements of practice that occur frequently or are important for client outcomes. The incidents described can be used to guide assessment task development, to complement a task-inventory practice analysis technique (discussed later in this chapter), and also can serve as a guide for individuals writing questions (Raymond, 2001).

A CIT approach should be applied with caution, as it can limit the data collected as part of a practice analysis study; being focused on critical incidents brings the potential for excluding routine elements of practice. The CIT, if applied without a complementary method, can artificially limit the scope of practice provided by the study as day-to-day activities that are not considered to be critical may not be documented even if they exemplify elements of successful practice.

### *Domain Critical Errors*

Domain Critical Errors (DCE) are errors identified as integral to success in professional practice within the tested content—for example, an individual who makes an error during a performance assessment that would prevent their success in practice has made a DCE. Incorporating a DCE approach requires the development of a comprehensive view of incorrect actions and/or judgments that should preclude an individual from moving forward in the process towards a credential. There are several ways to incorporate this approach into a practice analysis. The first is similar to the CIT discussed above and requires surveying a targeted sample of professionals about the demonstrations of knowledge, skills, or decision-making patterns that indicate a *lack* of competence for professional practice. In other words, respondents would define a domain of errors that would be unacceptable for qualified professionals to make and could result in uncorrectable client outcomes or have a negative impact on a professional's standing. These errors then inform the development of assessment tasks and scoring guides or rubrics.

This approach is largely task-oriented, as it requires professionals to identify problematic actions an individual would take. A DCE approach also requires some judgmental review to distinguish between minor errors and the type of uncorrectable action that should be defined as "domain critical." This approach has been applied in several practice analysis studies, including a clinically based dental licensure examination (Buckendahl & Davis-Becker, 2012; Fortune & Cromack, 1995), and the clinical reasoning section of a medical licensure examination (Childs, Dunn, van Barneveld, Jaciw, & McIlroy, 2003).

The second approach uses a DCE technique to review a pre-existing content domain or an examination blueprint to ensure that errors that are considered domain critical are included in the assessment tasks. At this point, there may be an effort to revise the content blueprint or assessment tasks to better incorporate errors that indicate incompetence. DCE techniques can complement other methodologies as a way to describe additional dimensions of practice data. DCE data can be gathered through focus groups, surveys, or SME review depending on the sensitivity of the content domain and the detail requested from participants.

However, like the CIT, the DCE does not easily stand on its own as a practice analysis method given the possibility that errors that are "domain critical" may not adequately cover the scope of day-to-day professional practice. For example, in a profession with significant public safety responsibilities, many errors may be considered domain critical. However, the domain of practice likely requires competence in areas that extend beyond critical missteps. An error or incident-based description of professional practice may not exemplify the typical requirements for professional competence. This challenge can be overcome by including a criticality of error rating scale in a task inventory (discussed next) which provides detailed information about not only domain critical errors but also tasks expected of professionals (Manson, Levine, & Brannick, 2000).

### *Task Inventory*

The task inventory is one of the most common task-oriented methods for defining the content domain for credentialing examinations. Data are collected from a broad sample of individuals using a survey, or questionnaire that outlines tasks or duties, actions, and decision points made by professionals. The questionnaire items can then be rated by a targeted sample of professionals to meet specified needs. For example, a group of early career professionals may rate the frequency with which they perform the included tasks or whether they believe performance of the included tasks is essential for effective practice in the profession. This method has been found to result in relatively reliable and consistent ratings of job responsibilities across survey respondents (Wilson, Harvey, & Macy, 1990).

The task inventory is particularly useful for credentialing purposes as it can be used to identify actions, abilities, and knowledge that is important to successful practice across practice settings. For example, a task inventory for accountants may sample survey respondents from various accounting specialties (forensic, tax, public accounting, etc.) in order to establish competencies that are required across practice contexts. Though some tasks may be more important (or come up more frequently) in some settings or specialties, the task inventory allows for a general overview of the requirements across practice settings. The content drawn from this type of practice analysis can be used to establish discrete tasks that are necessary for establishing minimal competence for entry into the profession. A variant on the task inventory was employed in Acute Care Physical Therapy to develop entry-level acute care competencies and investigate the potential practice domain of Acute Care physical therapy as a subspecialty area (Gorman et al., 2010).

The survey nature of this method allows for broad sampling within the professional population. Surveys are, by their nature, less time-intensive for researchers and participants than focus groups, observations, or in-depth interviews. Gathering a representative sample of survey respondents is also simpler when using a survey tool than an interview, as one can continue distributing surveys until the respondents are representative of the professional population as a whole. Surveys, however, have limitations—for example, describing the cognitive demands and situations requiring professional judgment or decision making is difficult on a task-focused survey. In order to include these aspects of professional practice it may be necessary to supplement a task inventory with additional methods to gather more detailed data about cognitive and judgmental practice demands.

Though the task inventory is relatively efficient and allows for including individuals from a broad sample of practice settings and specialties, it is important to build a reasonable sample and survey instrument to facilitate a high response rate and useful results. For example, including multiple rating scales (frequency, criticality, etc.) in one study may lead to a lower response rate while scales that assess related dimensions of a task (criticality of error and importance of a task, for example) tend to provide redundant and less useful results (Sanchez & Fraser, 1992; Sanchez & Levine, 1989). The task inventory approach can be easily combined with other methods to gather comprehensive practice data along pre-identified dimensions of practice in varying degrees of detail.

### *Functional Job Analysis*

Functional job analysis (FJA), as a practice analysis method, relies on establishing a shared language for describing what workers do. This sounds simplistic but within a profession where tasks differ across individual roles and practice settings, the language used to describe regular professional tasks can carry different meanings from professional to professional (or supervisor to supervisor). In order to develop an understanding of professional demands, this barrier must be overcome. FJA (Fine & Wiley, 1971) breaks down the tasks a professional does into their structure and function based on the action to be performed and the expected results or *what happens* because that task is performed. The distinction between what gets done, or what contributions are made, and the actions taken towards those contributions is a defining characteristic of FJA, and helps to make this method well suited for use in credentialing and other assessments for professionals. Fine & Wiley (1971) suggest that by breaking down a professional role into its component tasks (based on *who* does *what* to what *result*, and relies on which *tools* and *instructions* to do so) a comprehensive description can be developed of what professionals might do across settings (or specialties).

The FJA is particularly useful as a tool to develop a survey for SME review, as the statements can be rated based on several different dimensions at once. SMEs may be called upon to rate the frequency that tasks are required, their importance to competent practice, the level of responsibility or independence required for the task, the skills or knowledge required to complete the task, as well as the task relevance to entry-level performance. Fine & Wiley (1971) suggest several rating dimensions appropriate for FJA, including the relationship of the task to data, people, and things (tools/materials and instructions). This method is thought to provide reliable ratings for skill requirements and differing roles within a profession (see Schmitt & Fine, 1983) and has been used to ensure that the test items are representative of the tasks described, and thus can be useful as a foundation for a credentialing examination.

The FJA has been used in many contexts, including for government agencies (Fine, 1986), and has been adapted to a credentialing context (D'Costa, 1986). The results of an FJA can be used for building task lists that will then be rated and reviewed by SMEs or through a practice survey, and incorporate both person- and task-oriented approaches. For example, an FJA task statement would contain the action performed (task), the tools or requirements to complete the action (KSA and materials), and whether the process used to perform the task requires a professional's judgment or is prescribed (person).

The FJA is similar to the DACUM (or Developing a Curriculum) approach (Adams, 1975; Norton, 1985, 1997) in that both define the tasks performed by professionals and the tools or requirements to complete it successfully. The DACUM approach, like FJA, is well suited for developing training specifications and performance standards, given the detailed results about what professionals *do*. Defining tasks at the required level of detail requires a significant time investment, but the data can be used to guide conversations about the appropriate level of performance required for professional practice. Detailed FJA results are also well suited for designing training materials or performance assessment tasks.

### *Knowledge, Skills, and Abilities Questionnaire*

The foundation of this method, as with the Task Inventory and Functional Job Analysis, is a list of requirements for competent practice. A KSA approach invites professionals or SMEs to rate the knowledge, skills, and abilities that are necessary for competence resulting in a person-oriented approach that is well suited to designing multiple choice examination questions. These KSAs can be gathered from a task list, practice responsibilities (reported by incumbents, supervisors, and educators), reviewing materials (practice records, databases, etc.), job descriptions, or licensure requirements (when applicable). Using one or more of these sources to generate KSAs allows for SMEs to build a model of practice encompassing KSAs as well as tasks and actions that are required for competent practice.

Most credentialing examinations, particularly written tests, don't directly assess an examinee's ability to perform tasks and procedures, but rather assess the knowledge required for successful task performance (Kane, 1982). Some authors advocate what is termed a "linkage exercise" for establishing KSA requirements, whereby SMEs rate the relevance of each KSA for each specific job responsibility (Wilson et al., 2013; Raymond, 2016); these linkage ratings then form the basis of the content specifications. However, fleshing out the link between the KSAs and job responsibilities, and then converting them to a test plan requires a significant investment of SME time. The KSA questionnaire represents a short-cut approach to establishing KSA requirements.

After developing the list of requirements, SMEs can judge, or rate, the KSAs provided in the practice model based on how often the KSA is required and/or how important the KSA is for competent practice. Though frequency and criticality are certainly not the only dimensions on which KSAs can be rated, they are some of the most important for establishing minimal competency and eligibility for a credentialing examination and in turn, can provide compelling evidence for the link between the tested content and competence in the profession (AERA et al., 2014, p. 178). Additionally, the KSAs can be rated on the level of each required for minimal competency. Identifying the necessary level of each KSA to be demonstrated by candidates could guide item writing, content weighting, and assessment task design.

This method has been utilized by the Council on Certified Nurse Anesthetists (Muckle, Apatov, & Plaus, 2009) for several practice analysis studies designed to gather content validity evidence for their certification examination. In combination with details of professional practice (setting, patient population, education, and duties), the survey invited participants to rate the relative importance of knowledge in several content areas and the frequency of tasks/procedures performed.

As credentialing examinations are generally designed to measure the KSAs required for safe and effective practice, this approach allows for a relatively simple translation of practice analysis results to the content domain. This allows for test content specifications to eventually include not only tasks, but the related KSAs required to perform them at the necessary level of competence. It is possible to include KSAs along with tasks on a survey and rate them along similar dimensions (the frequency with which an individual must demonstrate a skill may provide valuable information, for example).

## Professional Performance Model

The professional performance model (PPM, professional performance situation model) approach incorporates KSAs as well as additional descriptors of a profession (for example, practice responsibilities or information like knowledge or tasks specific to a practice context) and has been used as a foundation for several health professions' practice analyses (see LaDuca, 1980, 1994; McGaghie, 1980) including nursing (Hoffart & Woods, 1996). As the practice model is developed, it can be expanded to incorporate different dimensions of practice (for example, practice setting and client issue). As a list of possible client issues is developed for each practice setting (for example a tax question to an accountant practicing independently versus a tax question for a corporate accountant) the practice scenarios can be used to develop KSAs or tasks that are required for effective practice. This approach can be designed as task- or person-oriented, depending on the framing of the KSAs and the design of the data collection instrument.

One of the strengths of the PPM is that it is inductive; the model is developed as a function of the practice analysis study. The general approach of adapting a practice model (based on client issues and practice settings or roles) is useful when translating the practice analysis study findings into test specifications and identifying potential content areas. The inductive approach, though easily applied to test specifications and content, does require a significant investment of time and resources. Gathering a comprehensive view of the professional domain using this approach can require a substantial amount of SME time or extensive surveying to ensure that each practice setting is represented and that a reasonable list of presenting client issues has been developed.

As incorporated by Hoffart and Woods (1996), the PPM proposed for registered nursing has five dimensions: values, professional relationships, patient care delivery model, management approach, and compensation. Within this context a professional domain could be developed that looked at the intersection of presenting issues and KSAs within each dimension—for example, in order to be successful at incorporating a particular management approach in a hospital setting, a nurse would need to have mastered a certain set of KSAs or be prepared to perform a particular set of tasks.

## Cognitive Task Analysis

Cognitive Task Analysis, or CTA, has emerged as a useful approach to practice analysis, particularly for occupations and professions that are more dependent on cognition and judgment and less dependent on physical activities. A task-oriented method, a CTA is designed to yield information specifically about the knowledge, thought processes, and goal structures that are a part of professional performance (Schraagen et al., 2000). Though this is a different conceptualization of "task," it does not develop models of a successful professional's attributes or skills as a person-oriented method might. This approach has been used in designing models for human/computer interaction (John & Kieras, 1994; Whitefield & Hill, 1994) and job knowledge tests and associated training materials (DuBois & Shalin, 1995).

A practice analysis based on CTA can take several forms, but the most general approach involves four steps. The first is developing a detailed list outlining the tasks that professionals do along with the importance and frequency of those tasks. The second is building a model for the conceptual knowledge and cognitive skills employed to perform the task successfully. Tasks may subsequently be grouped based on shared underlying knowledge requirements (step three). After the tasks and knowledge framework have been developed, several techniques can be used to break down the knowledge representations into actual cognitive processes (step four). Schraagen et al. (2000) suggest that structured interviews, carefully analyzed observations, and observations during apprenticeship and teaching are all appropriate fodder for analysis. Once these knowledge representations have been fleshed out, the materials can be used to develop models for the required tasks and identify core cognitive competencies for testing.

Though this approach has not been used as extensively as others for developing test content, it is particularly well suited for professions because it allows for in-depth examination of required problem solving and reasoning tasks. Defining and implementing a CTA approach should be guided by a specific objective statement or plan for the outcomes as there is a significant amount of flexibility in how tasks are defined, how knowledge representations are fleshed out, and how the knowledge data are incorporated into the test blueprint. This is also a challenge for developing content specifications as multiple or overlapping cognitive competencies can be linked to a single action in practice.

*Competency-based Approaches*

Over the past two decades competency modeling has gained prominence as a way for businesses to guide activities related personnel selection, training, and other human resource functions (Shippmann et al., 2000). That influence recently has stretched into the not-for-profit sector, with competency frameworks being promoted by associations and educational organizations in fields such as accounting, engineering, nursing, psychology, veterinary medicine, and other professions.

One example of competency modeling is the CanMEDS framework adopted by the Royal College of Physicians and Surgeons of Canada (RCPSC). That framework describes seven roles required of the competent physician, including medical expert, communicator, collaborator, manager, health advocate, scholar, and professional. Each role is defined and specific competencies are listed under each. The following in an excerpt from the *Health Advocate* role of the CanMEDS framework: "As health advocates, physicians responsibly use their expertise and influence to advance the health and well-being of individual patients, communities, and populations" (Frank et al., 2005, pp. 7–8). This definition is supported by several specific competencies and enabling competencies.

Sample Competency:

- Physicians respond to the health needs of the communities that they serve.

Enabling Competencies:

- Describe the practice communities that they serve.
- Identify opportunities for advocacy, health promotion and disease prevention in the communities they serve and respond appropriately.
- Appreciate the possibility of competing interests between the communities served and other populations.

This very limited sample conveys a key feature of competencies—they are a combination of task-oriented and person-oriented descriptors written at a very general level of abstraction. While the term "competency" lacks a useful agreed upon definition, both proponents and critics acknowledge that a competency is usually a broad statement indicating the behavioral themes that an organization views as core to successful performance (Sanchez & Levine, 2009), and that they represent a combination of job activities as well as the KSAs, motivations, values, and other personal qualities that differentiate superior from average performers (e.g., Shippmann et al., 2000; Spencer, McClelland, & Spencer, 1994).

Sanchez and Levine (2009) highlight several differences between competency modeling and traditional approaches to job analysis, many of which apply to practice analysis. Some of the more notable distinctions are:

- Practice analysis seeks to objectively document work-related behaviors, while competency modeling seeks to influence behaviors. The former is *descriptive*, while the latter is *prescriptive*.
- Practice analysis tends to be *bottom-up*, with workers revealing their daily activities, while competency modeling is more *top-down*, with the organization communicating the behavioral themes that it values and expects to see demonstrated.
- Practice analysis focuses on the *present*, while competency modeling is oriented toward *future* goals.
- Practice analysis describes the *typical* performance of an average or even minimally competent person, while competency modeling usually strives to inspire *maximum* performance.
- The results of practice analysis is a listing of the discrete tasks and KSAs that highlight what makes a profession or specialty different, whereas competency models list behavioral themes that may be common to most jobs and occupations within an organization.

Competency frameworks have a useful role in the evolution of professions. Their popularity can be explained in part by that the everyday language used to describe practice resonates with leadership and membership. By looking forward, competencies can help ensure that job requirements remain current. In contrast, traditional practice analysis relies on the decontextualized language of KSAs that, while rich and informative, is challenging to communicate in a way that seems interesting (Sanchez & Levine, 2009) and may overlook the complex integration of KSAs as applied in real-world settings (cf. LaDuca, 1994).

However, while useful for professions as a whole, competency frameworks have limited utility for designing credentialing tests. They are prone to positive response bias and inflated perceptions of value (e.g., positive response bias) (Morgeson et al., 2004; Lievens, Sanchez & DeCorte, 2004). A second limitation is that competency statements frequently lack the specificity for item writing and, quite frankly, often do not connote measurable skills.[2] Consider the divergent range of items that authors could produce if given instruction to write five questions on a competency such as "appreciate the possibility of competing interests between the communities served and other populations." A third limitation is that single competencies appear to be amalgamations of multiple constructs (Sanchez & Levine, 2009). For example, the competency called "interpersonal and communication skills" likely includes a smattering of personality constructs such as agreeableness and conscientiousness, as well as cognitive skills related to spoken and written language skills.

Finally, while forward-thinking competencies that emphasize superior performance may help organizations advance their missions, the relevance of such competencies to the purpose of licensure—which is to protect the public by ensuring *minimal* competence of entry-level practitioners—is arguable.

It is evident that competency modeling has its benefits. Given its endorsement by businesses and professional associations, it is a practice analysis strategy that test developers in credentialing can't afford to ignore. But it should not be the sole source of information when designing credentialing tests. Research indicates that competency modeling can be a useful job analysis strategy when supplemented by conventional approaches to task analysis (Lievens & Sanchez, 2007; Lievens, Sanchez, & DeCorte, 2004; Sanchez & Levine, 2009).

## Choosing Among Approaches

As seen in the previous section, practice analysis methods can be grouped into those approaches relying primarily on SME input and those that draw on practice data from a broader group of individuals engaged in practice. The ultimate goal of using a practice analysis study to guide the development of a credentialing exam is that the study provides insight about the tasks and responsibilities associated with a range of practice settings and specialties. This allows the examination to encompass KSAs common across practice settings and professional roles. In order to define KSAs and translate practice analysis data into test specifications, many approaches rely on a combination of input from SMEs and current practitioners, educators, and others with knowledge about the domain of practice.

In addition to practical concerns like the availability of resources to design a study and analyze data, as well as the willingness of professionals to participate, the selection of a specific approach should be related to the work requirements of the profession or occupation. In a performance-based occupation, representation of the procedural skills required of professionals may be paramount, while in a setting where success is reliant on an individual's knowledge, it may be more important to assess an individual's mastery of core principles and factual content. A meta-analysis by DuVernet et al. (2015) provides a thorough discussion of the potential impact of study design decisions on the resulting practice analysis data. Though they do not provide specific recommendations, their overall conclusions indicate that matching the selected method to the purpose of the study is important when designing the data-collection model.

The selection of a practice analysis approach should take into consideration the process by which the results are going to be translated into test content specifications. This process generally requires linking the observable behaviors included in the practice analysis to KSAs that are required to perform professional activities (when designing a content-oriented test outline). Typically, when describing a domain of test content, this task requires expert input to review the KSAs and assemble a preliminary content outline that represents the frequency and importance of each to professional practice. This task is well suited to an expert committee. Statistical models can also be used to derive weights for translating a test plan into content specifications. This approach is particularly useful when the practice analysis has resulted in ratings on a list of behaviors or tasks (Kane, 1997).

More complicated content specifications, like those reflecting knowledge *and* behaviors or skills—or those with both a content and process dimension, require a similarly complex translation scheme. As discussed below, this process should add to the evidence linking the study results to the test specifications. The same logic can be applied to support the argument that individuals who pass the examination and earn a credential have been appropriately vetted for entry into the profession.

### Committee-based Methodology

Practice analysis methods that rely heavily on input from expert panels are relatively simple to apply and can provide a definition of practice and test specifications efficiently. However, a method that only includes SME input is inherently limited by design. An expert panel, for example, may not produce test specifications that are representative of the profession (in terms of setting, roles, and responsibilities); the invited group is limited by the scope of their own experience. In addition, a group of experts may have a difficult time creating test specifications that are acceptable to other groups. Since the design process relies heavily on expert judgment, there is little to ensure that their judgment is indeed an accurate representation of the field and may reflect the committee members' beliefs about the profession and exclude other relevant perspectives (Morgeson et al., 2004).

### Survey-based Methodology

Survey-based methods are used to inductively develop a definition and scope of practice based on data provided through a survey, interview, or other data-collection protocol. These data can include not only task frequency and criticality data, but also ratings on the required skills and knowledge for successful practice. These data can be used on their own to develop test specifications, based on commonalities across practitioners and practice settings, as well as to evaluate the test specifications provided by an expert committee.

Task-oriented methods require a significant investment of resources though they tend to be less demanding than a series of SME meetings. The requirements presented by a task-oriented method include survey design, development of rating scales, identifying and contacting appropriate study participants, as well as data analysis to shape the resulting responses into useful descriptions of practice. A survey-based approach can be quite cost effective and can reach a broad swath of professionals in a way that a judgmental method cannot. Creating a useful data-collection instrument, analyzing large amounts of data, and translating the survey results into test specifications can be demanding and labor-intensive activities.

Purely task-oriented methods will rely on eventual support from SMEs in order to develop test specifications from practice analysis data. Reliance solely on SMEs, however, can introduce bias into the exercise (Morgeson & Campion, 1997). This can be mitigated by working with multiple groups of SMEs (panels), and inviting individuals to work independently before coming together for a group discussion. The task-oriented method and the SMEs ideally will complement one another as the study results, and SME panel may provide differing results that provide a more comprehensive view of professional roles and responsibilities than either method alone.

### Process-oriented and Integrated Approaches

Ultimately, test specifications rely on an operational definition of the constructs to be assessed. This means that the test specifications need to encompass not only the knowledge possessed by safe and effective practitioners, but also professional behaviors and demands. Some practice analysis approaches are particularly well suited to identifying processes and incidents where individuals must apply knowledge as well as judgment to a professional problem (the FJA approach as well as Domain Critical Errors, for example).

Translating survey or SME data to content specifications that delineate KSAs related to the tasks or roles of effective practice, as well as the relative weight for each content area or assessment task, is a complex and important task. Levine, Ash, and Bennett (1980) found that the content specifications resulting from four very different practice analysis methods were comparable, prompting the authors to conclude that the process used to translate the job analysis data into test content specifications may be ultimately of greater influence than the selected practice analysis method (Levine et al., 1980). Using a practice analysis method focused on KSAs, professional experience, or necessary professional attributes for the initial practice analysis can simplify this step, as can adopting an integrative framework, such as Principled Test Design.

### *Applications of Principled Test Design (PTD)*

Principled test design is a general term referring to test design approaches like Evidence Centered Design (ECD) (Mislevy, Steinberg, & Almond, 2003) or Assessment Engineering (AE) (Luecht, 2006). Several methods for linking practice analysis results to test specifications have been proposed (see Hughes & Prien, 1989; Landy, 1988; Raymond & Neustel, 2006; Wang, Schnipke, & Witt, 2005), while methods based on PTD explicitly build a link between the constructs included in the assessment, the assessment tasks used to gather information about the constructs, and the inferences to be made from test scores. The use of PTD for building content specifications is logically simple, but when applied to practice analysis data becomes a bit more complex.

Though a thorough discussion of modern test design methodology is not within the scope of this chapter, we suggest Mislevy, Steinberg, and Almond (2003) for a detailed description of ECD methodology. In terms of designing test specifications, ECD provides a useful framework for contextualizing the claims to be made about test scores (and test takers) and working backwards to ensure that the examination design and score use support those claims with validity evidence. In a credentialing context, this means that the claim that an individual who has passed the examination has demonstrated an acceptable level of competence can be supported not only by evidence linking the examination tasks to the tested content, but also the examination content to identified requirements of professional practice.

PTD concepts may be used to organize the claims to be made about individuals that take the test, as well as clarify the supported uses of test scores. Following Tannenbaum, Robustelli, and Baron (2008), practice analysis results can be used to connect the purpose of the examination to the content blueprint; for example, incidents identified during a CIT practice analysis may be important to client outcomes, but if the skills to handle those incidents can be learned after entering practice, they may not need to be represented on the examination. This is an important piece of assembling content specifications, as the purpose of the examination and score use(s) need to be consistent with the demands of professional practice.

The role of expert review in the refinement of practice analysis results can also be defined and guided by PTD. Integrating the knowledge or required tasks identified by a task-oriented approach into a cohesive practice model can be challenging, but the introduction of experts to the task can spur discussion of the relevance and level of mastery required for practice (and thus for inclusion on the examination). This then creates explicit links between not only the KSAs included in the examination but also the level of performance expected from those who earn a credential. SME review can also be a source of evidence to support the tasks selected for the assessment. Thus, each of the selected tasks can be used to provide evidence to support the claim that credentialed individuals have demonstrated the skills and abilities required for practice. As suggested by Tannenbaum et al. (2008), the evidence defined at this point can be used to support the overall claims made based on test scores.

## Evaluating the Study Results

After a practice analysis study has been performed, data have been analyzed, and test content specifications have been drafted, the next step in building a defensible credentialing examination is to evaluate the test specifications. There are many ways to do this, each requiring different strategies from linking work activities from a survey to KSAs reflected on the content specifications (Hughes & Prien, 1989), to building task models, construct maps and other documents set forth by PTD (Luecht, 2006; Raymond & Luecht, 2013; Tannenbaum et al., 2008). Three overarching strategies will be presented here.

In order to relate the constructs being measured to the demands of practice, it is possible to re-create a smaller scale practice analysis study with SMEs or other groups of stakeholders. In this scenario a group of SMEs would review the tested content, either the tasks and blueprint categories or an actual test form, and rate the relevance of each category or item to the constructs to be measured (Messick, 1989). For a credentialing examination this approach would provide evidence that the tested content and assessment approach was relevant to the domain of practice. This approach allows SMEs to determine whether the represented KSAs are relevant to practice, and also if the selected assessment tasks are relevant to practice.

Practice analysis results and test content specifications may also be evaluated by reviewing their alignment with training program curricula, when available, or materials like practice records. Fields like medicine can leverage associated records like hospital admission data or insurance claims to refine the study-defined domain of practice. Curriculum or training materials can also be used for cross-validating content specifications or study results. However, test content will need to evolve along with or ahead of instructional materials which may make it challenging to use them to validate the study results or content specifications. Additionally, SME input can be used to determine if there are gaps in the domain of practice as defined by the practice analysis study or if additional input from records or training materials should be incorporated into the test specifications.

Finally, the domain of practice and study results can be evaluated by reviewing the actual performance and results of the test takers. By sampling from individuals across the performance spectrum on the examination, or the practice records of those who have passed the examination and entered the profession, one can gauge the potential usefulness of the assessment content and tasks. If individuals who have passed are demonstrating the specified KSAs and the examination (based on examinee performance on the specified assessment tasks) is differentiating between those who have demonstrated those KSAs and those who have not, this evidence can be used to support the test content and content specifications. This approach is particularly useful for credentialing examinations designed to protect the public or ensure standard skills across professional settings and specialties, as a professional's weakness in one area may indicate a deficiency in the defined domain of practice.

## In Conclusion

Practice analysis is an important step in defining the scope and depth of content on a credentialing examination. Though there are several ways to go about designing and undertaking a practice analysis study, the most useful approach will be related to the purpose of the credentialing examination. The methods available for practice analysis are quite diverse and will all provide slightly different types of data; it is effective to combine methods and collect data from multiple sources, though collecting data from more than one source without a plan for linking the data to the content specifications can potentially cause more problems than it solves.

In order to select a method and produce useful results, the method and study design need to match the needs of the profession at hand. Ultimately, the results should provide a logical link between what credentialed individuals need to know and be able to do as successful professionals and the content outline of the credentialing examination. Using data from a practice analysis to guide the development of test content specifications provides this link and establishes evidence that the tested content is relevant to professional activities.

## Notes

1. The *Standards* define test specifications as "Documentation of the purpose and intended uses of a test, as well as of the test's content, format, length, psychometric characteristics (of the items and test overall), delivery mode, administration, scoring, and score reporting" (AERA et al., p. 225).
2. All is not lost. Organizations in medicine, for example, are beginning to identify numerous specific milestones (KSAs) associated with each competency.

## References

Adams, R. E. (1975). *DACUM approach to curriculum learning and evaluation in occupation training* (2nd ed.). Yarmouth, Nova Scotia: Nova Scotia NewStarts.

American Educational Research Association, American Psychological Association, & National Council on Measurement in Education (AERA, APA, & NCME) (2014). *Standards for educational and psychological testing.* Washington, DC: American Educational Research Association.

Brain, D. (1991). Practical knowledge and occupational control. *Sociological Forum, 6*(2), 239–268.

Buckendahl, C. W., & Davis-Becker, S. L. (2012). Evaluating the appropriateness and use of domain critical errors. *Practical Assessment, Research & Evaluation, 17*(13). Available online: http://pareonline.net/getvn.asp?v=17&n=13

Caughron, J. J., & Mumford, M. D., & Fleishman, E. A. (2012). The Fleishman job analysis survey: Development, validation, and application. In M. Wilson, W. Bennett, S. G. Gibson, & G. Alliger (Eds.), *The handbook of work analysis: Methods, systems, applications and science of work measurement in organizations* (pp. 231–247). New York: Routledge.

Childs, R. A., Dunn, J. L., van Barneveld, C., Jaciw, A. P., & McIlroy, J. H. (2003). Differential weighting of errors on a test of clinical reasoning skills. *Academic Medicine, 78* (October supplement), S62–S64.

D'Costa, A. (1986). The validity of credentialing examinations. *Evaluation and the Health Professions, 9*, 137–169.

DuBois, D., & Shalin, V. L. (1995). Adapting cognitive methods to real-world objectives: An application to job knowledge testing. In P. D. Nichols, S. F. Chipman, & R. L. Brennan (Eds.), *Cognitively diagnostic assessment* (pp. 189–220). Hillsdale, NJ: Lawrence Erlbaum Associates.

Dunnette, M. D. (1976). Aptitudes, abilities, and skills. *Handbook of industrial and organizational psychology* (pp. 473–520). Chicago: Rand-McNally.

DuVernet, A. M., Dierdorff, E. C., & Wilson, M. A. (2015). Exploring factors that influence work analysis data: A meta-analysis of design choices, purposes, and organizational context. *Journal of Applied Psychology, 100*(5), 1603.

Dye, D., & Silver, M. (1999). The origins of O*NET. In N. G. Peterson, M. D. Mumford, W. C. Borman, P. R. Jeanneret, & E. A. Fleishman (Eds.), *An occupational information system for the 21st century: The development of O*NET* (pp. 9–19). Washington, DC: American Psychological Association.

Federation of State Medical Boards and National Board of Medical Examiners (2015). *USMLE® content outline and from USMLE step 2 clinical knowledge: Content description and general knowledge*. Retrieved from: www.usmle.org/pdfs/step-2-ck/2015_Step2CK_Content.pdf

Fine, S. (1986). Job analysis. In R. A. Berk (Ed.), *Performance assessment: Methods and applications* (pp. 53–81). Baltimore, MD: Johns Hopkins University Press.

Fine, S., & Wiley, W. W. (1971). *An introduction to functional job analysis*. Washington, DC: Upjohn Institute for Employment Research.

Flanagan, J. C. (1954). The critical incident technique. *Psychological Bulletin, 51*, 327–358.

Fortune, J. C., & Cromack, T. R. (1995). Developing and using clinical examinations. In J. C. Impara (Ed.), *Licensure testing: Purposes, procedures, and practices* (pp. 149–165). Lincoln, NE: Buros Institute of Mental Measurements.

Frank, J, R., Jabbour, M., et al. (Eds.) (2005). *Report of the CanMEDS Phase IV Working Groups*. Ottawa: The Royal College of Physicians and Surgeons of Canada.

Gorman, S. L., Hakim, E. W., Johnson, W., Bose, S., Harris, K. S., Crist, M. H., Holtgrefe, K., Ryan, J. M., Simpson, M. S., & Coe, J. B. (2010). Nationwide acute care physical therapist practice analysis identifies knowledge skills, and behaviors that reflect acute care practice. *Physical Therapy, 90*, 1453–1467.

Haladyna, T. M., & Rodriguez, M. C. (2013). *Developing and validating test items*. New York: Routledge.

Harvey, R. J., Friedman, L., Hakel, M. D., & Cornelius, E. T. (1988). Dimensionality of the Job Element Inventory, a simplified worker-oriented job analysis questionnaire. *Journal of Applied Psychology, 73*(4), 639–646.

Hoffart, N., & Woods, C. Q. (1996). Elements of a nursing professional practice model. *Journal of Professional Nursing, 12*(6), 354–364.

Hughes, G. L., & Prien, E. P. (1989). Evaluation of task and job skill linkage judgments used to develop test specifications. *Personnel Psychology, 42*(2), 283–292.

John, B. E., & Kieras, D. E. (1994). The GOMS family of analysis techniques: Tools for design and evaluation (Report CMU-CS-94-181). Pittsburgh, PA: Carnegie Mellon University, School of Computer Science.

Kane, M. T. (1982). The validity of licensure examinations. *American Psychologist, 37*(8), 911–918.

Kane, M. T. (1997). Model-based practice analysis and test specifications. *Applied Measurement in Education, 10*(1), 5–18.

Knapp, J., & Knapp, L. (1995). Practice analysis: Building the foundation for validity. In J. C. Impara (Ed.), *Licensure testing: Purposes, procedures, and practices* (pp. 93–116). Lincoln, NE: Buros Institute of Mental Measurements.

LaDuca, A. (1980). The structure of competence in health professions. *Evaluation and The Health Professions, 3*(3), 253–288.

LaDuca, A. (1994). Validation of professional licensure examinations: Professions theory, test design, and construct validity. *Evaluation and the Health Professions, 17*, 178–197.

Landy, F. J. (1988). Selection procedure development and usage. In S. Gael (Ed.), *The job analysis handbook for business, industry, and government, Vols. I and II* (pp. 271–287). New York: Wiley & Sons.

Levine, E. L., Ash, R. A., & Bennett, N. (1980). Exploratory comparative study of four job analysis methods. *Journal of Applied Psychology, 65*, 524–535.

Lievens, F., & Sanchez, J. I. (2007). Can training improve the quality of inferences made by raters in competency modeling? A quasi-experiment. *Journal of Applied Psychology, 92*(3), 812.

Lievens, F., Sanchez, J. I., & DeCorte, W. (2004). Easing the inferential leap in competency modeling: The effects of task-related information and subject matter expertise. *Personnel Psychology, 75*, 891–904.

Lindell, M. K., Clause, C. S., Brandt, C. J., & Landis, R. S. (1998). Relationship between organizational context and job analysis task ratings. *Journal of Applied Psychology, 83*(5), 769–776.

Luecht, R. M. (2006, May). *Engineering the test: Principled item design to automated test assembly.* Paper presented at the annual meeting of the Society for Industrial and Organizational Psychology, Dallas, TX.

Manson, T. M., Levine, E. L., Brannick, M. T. (2000). The construct validity of task inventory ratings: A multitrait-multimethod analysis. *Human Performance, 13*(1), 1–22.

McCormick, E. J., Jeanneret, P. R., & Mecham, R. C. (1972). A study of job characteristics and job dimensions as based on the Position Analysis Questionnaire (PAQ). *Journal of Applied Psychology, 56*(4), 347.

McGaghie, W. C. (1980). The evaluation of competence: Validity issues in the health professions. *Evaluation and the Health Professions, 3*, 289–320.

Messick, S. (1989). Validity. In R. L. Linn (Ed.), *Educational measurement* (3rd ed., pp. 13–103). New York: American Council on Education and Macmillan.

Millman, J., & Greene, J. (1989). The specification and development of tests of achievement and ability. In R. L. Linn (Ed.), *Educational measurement* (3rd ed., pp. 335–366). New York: American Council on Education & Macmillan.

Mislevy, R. J., Steinberg, L. S., & Almond, R. G. (2003). On the structure of educational assessments. *Measurement: Interdisciplinary Research and Perspectives, 1*, 3–62.

Morgeson, F. P., & Campion, M. A. (1997). Social and cognitive sources of potential inaccuracy in job analysis. *Journal of Applied Psychology, 82*(5), 627.

Morgeson, F. P., Delaney-Klinger, K., Mayfield, M. S., Ferrara, P., & Campion, M. A. (2004). Self-presentation processes in job analysis: A field experiment investigating inflation in abilities, tasks, and competencies. *Journal of Applied Psychology, 89*(4), 674.

Muckle, T. J., Apatov, N. M., & Plaus, K. (2009). A report on the CCNA 2007 professional practice analysis. *American Association of Nurse Anesthetists Journal, 77*(3), 181–189.

Newman, L. S., Slaughter, R. C., & Taranath, S. N. (1999, April). *The selection and use of rating scales in task surveys: A review of current job analysis practice.* Paper presented at the meeting of the National Council on Measurement in Education, Montreal, Canada.

Norton, R. E. (1985). *DACUM handbook.* Columbus, OH: Center on Education and Training for Employment, The Ohio State University.

Norton, R. E. (1997). *DACUM handbook.* Columbus, OH: Center on Education and Training for Employment, The Ohio State University.

Raymond, M. R. (2001). Job analysis and the specification of content for licensure and certification examinations. *Applied Measurement in Education, 14*, 369–415.

Raymond, M. R. (2016). Job analysis, practice analysis and the content of credentialing tests, in S. Lane, M. R. Raymond, & T. M. Haladyna (Eds.), *Handbook of test development* (2nd ed., pp. 144–164). New York: Routledge.

Raymond, M. R., & Luecht, R. L. (2013). Licensure and certification testing. In K.F. Geisinger (Ed.), *APA handbook of testing and assessment in psychology* (pp. 391–414). Washington, DC: American Psychological Association.

Raymond, M. R., & Neustel, S. (2006). Determining the content of credentialing examinations. In S. M. Downing & T. M. Haladyna (Eds.), *Handbook of test development* (pp. 181–223). Mahwah, NJ: Lawrence Erlbaum Associates.

Rosenfeld, M., Shimberg, B., & Thornton, R. F. (1983). *Job analysis of licensed psychologists in the United States and Canada.* Princeton, NJ: Educational Testing Service.

Sanchez, J. I., & Fraser, S. L. (1992). On the choice of scales for task analysis. *Journal of Applied Psychology, 77*, 545–553.

Sanchez, J. I., & Levine, E. L. (1989). Determining important tasks within jobs: A policy-capturing approach, *Journal of Applied Psychology, 74*, 336–342.

Sanchez, J. I., & Levine, E. L. (2009). What is (or should be) the difference between competency modeling and traditional job analysis? *Human Resource Management Review, 19*, 53–63.

Schmitt, N., & Fine, S. A. (1983). Inter-rater reliability of judgements of functional levels and skill requirements of jobs based on written task statements. *Journal of Occupational Psychology, 56*(2), 121–127.

Schraagen, J. C., Ruisseau, J. I., Graff, N., Annett, J., Strub, M. H., Sheppard, C., ... Shute, V. L. (2000). Cognitive task analysis (NATO Research & Technology Organization Technical Report 24). Québec: North Atlantic Treaty Organization.

Shippmann, J. S., Ash, R. A., Batjtsta, M., Carr, L., Eyde, L. J., Hesketh, B., ... Sanchez, J. (2000). The practice of competency modeling. *Personnel Psychology, 53*, 703–739.

Smith, I. L., & Hambleton, R. K. (1990). Content validity studies of licensing examinations. *Educational Measurement: Issues and Practice, 9*(4), 7–10.

Spencer, L. M., McClelland, D. C., & Spencer, S. M. (1994). *Competency assessment methods: History and state of the art*. Boston, MA: Hay/McBer Research Press.

Tannenbaum, R. J., Robustelli, S. L., & Baron, P. A. (2008). Evidence-centered design: A lens through which the process of job analysis may be focused to guide the development of knowledge-based test content specifications. *CLEAR Exam Review, 19*(2), 26–35.

Tannenbaum, R. J., & Wesley, S. (1993). Agreement between committee-based and field-based job analyses: A study in the context of licensure testing. *Journal of Applied Psychology, 78*(6), 975.

Wang, N., Schnipke, D. & Witt, E. A. (2005). Use of knowledge, skill, and ability statements in developing licensure and certification examinations. *Educational Measurement: Issues and Practice, 24*, 15–22. doi: 10.1111/j.1745-3992.2005.00003.x

Whitefield, A., & Hill, B. (1994). Comparative analysis of task analysis products. *Interacting with Computers, 6*(3), 289–309.

Wilson, M. A., Harvey, R. J., Macy, B. A. (1990). Repeating items to estimate the test–retest reliability of task inventory ratings. *Journal of Applied Psychology, 75*(2), 158–163.

Wilson, M. A., Bennett Jr., W., Gibson, S. G., & Alliger, G. M. (Eds.). (2013). *The handbook of work analysis: Methods, systems, applications and science of work measurement in organizations*. New York: Routledge Academic.

Woolsey, L. K. (1986). The critical incident technique: An innovative qualitative method of research. *Canadian Journal of Counselling, 20*(4), 242–254.

# 5 Content Development and Review

*Cynthia G. Parshall and Belinda Brunner*

High-quality test content is a vital component for valid and credible examinations. This chapter addresses content development practices for credentialing examinations, presenting best practices and recognized industry standards. Following these approaches contributes to good quality test items as well as to the validity evidence for examinations. A variety of item types will be presented below, with a focus on the assessment areas where each is most likely to be useful. A framework for developing content for credentialing examinations will be provided.

## Content Development and Validity

Validity is defined by *The Standards for Educational and Psychological Testing* (AERA, APA, & NCME, 2014) as "the degree to which evidence and theory support the interpretations of test scores for proposed uses of tests" (p. 11). The *Standards* also refer to validity as the "most fundamental consideration" in developing examinations. (Chapter 2 in this book provides a comprehensive discussion of validation of credentialing examinations.)

In the case of licensure and certification examinations, the proposed use of the test score is determining readiness to practice a particular profession, and the validation argument focuses on the plausibility of this use by providing evidence supporting it (Kane, 2004). Test scores on credentialing examinations can be viewed in terms of whether candidates have the abilities critical to practice (Kane, 1982). Unlike the norm-referenced tests (NRTs) used in education, which are designed to produce a distribution of scores across the achievement spectrum, certification and licensure tests are almost always designed to produce a clear pass/fail decision. In credentialing, "The focus is on the standards of competence needed for effective performance" (AERA, APA, & NCME, 2014, p. 175).

The content development process is an important component in the collection of evidence to support the validity of the credentialing decisions made through certification and licensure examinations. Key steps in exam validation include delineating the content specification through a job task or practice analysis and then connecting test items to those content specifications.

The job task or practice analysis will typically identify tasks performed by job incumbents as well as the knowledge, skills and abilities (KSAs) needed to successfully perform the tasks. Test blueprints may be based upon the tasks and/or the KSAs. (See Chapter 4 for more information on developing test blueprints through job analysis.) Test items are then written to address the tasks and/or KSAs contained in the test blueprint.

An important consideration in developing test items is the cognitive complexity or demand required to perform the critical professional abilities delineated in the test blueprint. Haladyna and Rodriguez define *cognitive demand* as "the *expected* mental complexity involved when a test item is administered to a *typical* test taker" (emphasis provided in original) (2013, p. 28). This definition recognizes that cognitive demand is a property of the test taker, rather than the test item. For example, a novel situation presented in a test item may be designed to tap higher level thinking skills, but for test takers who have been exposed to the situation before, providing a response may merely require recall.

Cognitive demand has been categorized in different ways, with all the classifications involving some sort of hierarchy. Typically, the hierarchy ranges from declarative knowledge and recall to the application of complex higher order thinking skills. The most well-known classification is Bloom's cognitive taxonomy (Bloom, Engelhart, Furst, Hill, & Krathwohl, 1956), which was later revised by Anderson and Krathwohl (2001).

Credentialing organizations often choose to use a simplified taxonomy with fewer cognitive levels. Some credentialing organizations may adopt cognitive taxonomies that are specific to the particular profession rather than using the generic Bloom's taxonomy. Whatever the taxonomy used, item writers should be encouraged to write test items that are appropriate for the cognitive demand required to perform the critical abilities of the profession.

## A Typical Content Development Cycle

The testing purpose and the exam administration method influence the way in which exam content is developed. For instance, in a pencil-and-paper examination administered in a classroom setting, the entire exam paper may be written by a single author, the course instructor. For modern-day certification and licensure examinations, content development efforts are directed toward placing items into an item bank. An *item bank* is a repository or collection of test items. Items are drawn from the bank for administration according to the appropriate test administration model.

Writing items for inclusion in an item bank means that the unit of development shifts from an examination paper to individual test items. Content development becomes a continuous, cyclical process rather than a periodic activity to create an exam paper or a single test form. Figure 5.1 illustrates a typical content development cycle. The test blueprint provides the operational definition of the test construct and directs all item development activities. In educational testing, the test blueprint may be derived from an analysis of course content, textbooks, syllabi, and similar materials. For professional certification and licensure testing, the test blueprint is frequently derived from conducting a job task or practice analysis (see Chapter 4). The test blueprint is a detailed written plan for a test that typically includes the content or performance areas the test will cover and the weighting for each content area (in terms of either number or percentage of scored items). Item types to be used for each content area may be included. The test blueprint provides direction as to the content and the cognitive demand that is the assessment intent for each test item.

The needs and demands of modern large-scale, high-stakes examination programs typically require the assistance of computer software for several crucial aspects of the test development cycle, including item authoring and item storage. The same software application may be used for both of these purposes or different tools may be used for each.

Item authoring tools aid in workflow management during item development. Using role-based permissions, item authors and writers can perform their content development tasks directly within the item bank, or items may be written through other means and

Content Development and Review 87

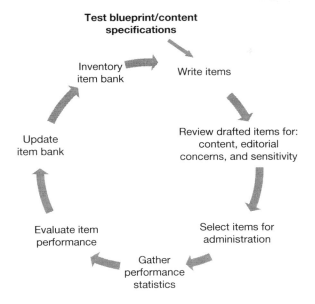

*Figure 5.1* High-level Content Development Process

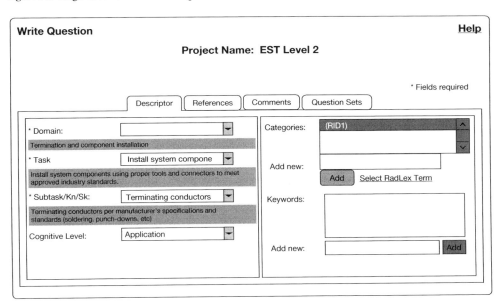

*Figure 5.2* Screenshot of a Stem and Item Metadata Entry Screen from ExamDeveloper™
Copyright 2009-2017 by Pearson Education, Inc. or its affiliate(s). Reprinted with permission.

then imported into the item bank. Numerous item bank applications are available commercially. Figures 5.2 and 5.3 provide examples of item entry screens for writing items directly into an item bank. Standard database features, such as reporting, searching and querying, allow users of the item bank to track items as they move through the development process.

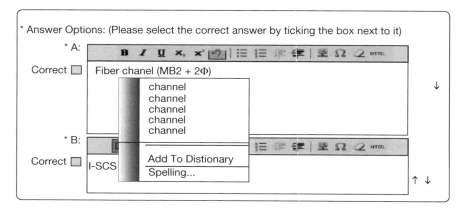

*Figure 5.3* Screenshot of a Response Option Entry Screen from ExamDeveloper™
Copyright 2009-2017 by Pearson Education, Inc. or its affiliate(s). Reprinted with permission.

Computerized item banks, used to store test items, typically have the capability to create the exam structure and select items for inclusion in the examination. A thorough discussion of the elements and uses of a computerized item bank can be found in Vale (2006). A more detailed discussion of each step within the content development process is provided later in this chapter, in the section "The Content Development Process."

## Item Types

One of the most important decisions to be made about an examination program is what item formats, or item types, will most adequately assess the desired test constructs as reflected in the test blueprint. Multiple-choice is still overwhelmingly the most prevalent item format on credentialing examinations (Clauser, Margolis, & Case, 2006). Nevertheless, in part due to computer-based testing (CBT), the number of item formats available is increasing. Licensure and certification programs may use a range of item formats, including performance testing or the computerized simulations.

### *Classifying Item Types*

Items can be classified in a number of different ways (e.g., Rodriguez, 2002). The literature on CBTs frequently refers to "innovative items", or, in the field of educational testing, "technology enhanced items" (e.g., Zenisky & Sireci, 2013). There is no uniform definition of what constitutes an innovative item, though Parshall, Davey, & Pashley (2000) provide an all-inclusive description by stating that an innovative item goes beyond the "discrete, text-based, multiple-choice format." The primary reason for including any innovative item type on an assessment, whether in educational or certification assessments, is to improve the quality of measurement (Huff & Sireci, 2001; Lipner et al., 2010; Parshall & Harmes, 2009; Sireci & Zenisky, 2006; Strain-Seymour, Way, & Dolan, 2009; Wendt, Kenny, & Marks, 2007).

One useful approach to classifying item types is by the degree of response constraint (Bennett, Ward, Rock, & LaHart, 1990; Scalise & Gifford, 2006; Sireci & Zenisky, 2006)—that is, how constrained candidates are in how they respond to test items. For example, in a multiple-choice item, candidates are limited to selecting a response from among the answer options included in the test item.

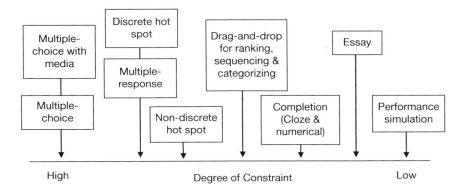

*Figure 5.4* Examples of Item Types Along a Response Constraint Continuum

Figure 5.4 provides a continuum of item types based upon this concept. At the left end of the continuum are item types with a high degree of response constraint, such as multiple-choice. The mid-range of the continuum contains item types with intermediate constraints. These intermediate constraint items include both those with broad utility such as the multiple-response, hot spot, and drag-and-drop, along with more content-specific examples such as editing a passage onscreen, reordering elements in a table, the use of searchable documents, and more. Many of the high and intermediate constraint item types in operational use can be considered variants of multiple-choice (e.g., multiple-response, hot spot). At the right end of the continuum are item types which are open-ended and free form, including the complex open-ended response format of a performance simulation (e.g., Lipner et al., 2010).

### *Development of Items Across the Response Constraint Continuum*

The item types discussed below are representative of the range of assessment formats in use on operational CBTs. Since multiple-choice and its variations are the most commonly used item formats in credentialing examinations, the discussion below concentrates on these formats, along with other item formats capable of being delivered in CBTs. The item types are discussed in, roughly, an order from most to least constrained. Further discussion of item formats used in licensure and certification, including essay and oral examinations, can be found in Clauser et al. (2006) and Haladyna & Rodriguez (2013).

### *Multiple-choice Items*

The multiple-choice item format is useful across an expansive range of content areas, in both educational and professional testing. It is an efficient item type that can usefully contribute to representative sampling of the content domain. Given that construct underrepresentation is a major threat to validity, representativeness in the content sampling process is a significant strength (Downing, 2006).

The multiple-choice format, like every form of assessment, has weaknesses along with its strengths. An important concern, especially in the context of licensure and certification examinations, is simply that knowing is different from performing; the text-based multiple-choice format is not conducive to demonstrations of performance skills (Clauser et al., 2006).

For professions that have a public safety concern, such as medicine, being able to adequately perform appropriate actions in practice is of critical importance. Other criticisms of multiple-choice items include the potential for these items to inappropriately reward test-takers who are "testwise," and a tendency for multiple-choice items to assess trivial facts inconsequential to professional practice. Downing (2006) further asserted that flawed multiple-choice items are more of a problem for small-scale testing programs with limited test development resources. Nevertheless, there is a significant research base on multiple-choice item formats that documents their potential to assess higher-order thinking skills (Martinez, 1999) and to produce results that are highly correlated with "stem equivalent" constructed response items (Rodriguez, 2002). To attain these goals a testing organization needs to train its item writers and apply effective item-writing guidelines.

### Multiple-response Items

The multiple-response item type, which has been used in paper-based tests for many years, is currently enjoying a resurgence in CBTs. Also called multiple-answer, multiple-choice and multiple-correct response, this item type is similar to the multiple-choice item, except that a multiple-response item has more answer options (usually four to eight) and more than one key (usually from two to four).

The multiple-response item type, like the multiple-choice, has broad utility across a variety of content areas. Multiple-response items are attractive to testing programs for the following reasons (Muckle, Becker, & Wu, 2011):

1. They are sufficiently similar to multiple-choice items that item authors can easily learn to use them.
2. They offer promise as a means of expanding content coverage, reducing the influence of guessing, and/or providing alternatives to negatively worded stems.
3. They often exhibit higher item difficulty and discrimination than multiple-choice items.

Because of these advantages, and the long history of multiple-response item use in paper-based tests, there is more psychometric information about this item type than many others currently in use in CBTs (e.g., Bauer, Holzer, Kopp, & Fisher, 2011; Duncan & Milton, 1978; Hess, Johnston, & Lipner, 2013; Hong, Liu, Haynie, Woo, & Gorham, 2012; Hsu, Moss & Khampalkit, 1984; Muckle et al., 2011; Pae, 2014).

Testing organizations need to make two primary decisions when implementing multiple-response items (Muckle et al., 2011). The first of these concerns the instructions that will be given to the candidate for responding to the item. The instructions can either specify the number of correct answer options (for example, "select three") or simply state "select all that apply" (Parshall, Harmes, Davey, & Pashley, 2003). The second decision concerns how these items should be scored, whether dichotomously scored (right/wrong), or using one of a number of polytomous models. Polytomous scoring models allow for partial credit scoring, though they typically require larger testing volumes to be used. These issues are related and they must be addressed conjointly (Muckle et al., 2011). For instance, negative scoring should not be used with instructions that dictate the number of answer options to be chosen, because candidates are forced to pick a set number of responses.

### Items with Graphical or Media Assets

One of the most direct ways of making multiple-choice items more authentic to real-life situations is to include graphical or other media assets in the item. This multiple-choice variation is sometimes referred to by the specific type of media asset included. For example, if a multiple-choice item includes a video, the item type may be called a video item (Parshall & Harmes, 2009). It is more common for the media asset to be included in the item stem, but another approach is to include the assets in the answer options, with the media replacing or being used in addition to text-based answer options (Parshall & Cadle, 2014).

When media are added to multiple-choice items, the range of constructs that can be covered expands into the performance testing arena. For example, Sulaiman and Hamdy (2013) found that the use of clinical videos, along with rich text vignettes, was effective in measuring clinical reasoning and medical decision-making. The ability to assess skills, and not only knowledge, is one of the main justifications for investing in multimedia for use with multiple-choice items. The media assets used in this item type can be artifacts that a professional would see and interact with on the job. For example, in an examination within a medical field, the stem could contain an image of an electrocardiogram reading, an audio clip of heart sounds, or a video of a real patient with a movement disorder or other pathology. Sample video vignettes on the American Board of Psychiatry and Neurology's certification website further illustrates the potential relevance and fidelity of this item type (www.abpn.com/become-certified/information-about-initial-certification-exams/sample-video-vignettes/).

Obtaining high-quality, relevant media for an exam can be challenging. Copyright is a consideration with the use of media from external sources, and it can be expensive to develop media specifically for an examination. In addition, extensive use of media, particularly video, can affect the overall size of the files used to deliver the test to examinees; a larger file size can lead to bandwidth considerations. If an item includes a long video clip, or several other media resources, this could potentially increase the item response time.

### *Hot-spot Items*

Hot-spot items are similar to items with graphical assets, in their ability to measure visual content. In hot-spot items, however, candidates respond by clicking directly on the image itself. This approach has the potential to reduce guessing or cuing, and to support more direct measurement of some content (Parshall & Cadle, 2014).

Hot-spot items can be classified as either *discrete* or *non-discrete*, based on whether regions within the image are clearly defined. For example, an item that prompted candidates to select a particular organ on a diagram of the abdomen would be a discrete hot-spot item, while an item that prompted candidates to indicate a specific pathology on an X-ray would be non-discrete.

A weakness of the hot-spot item type is that they are often written only to require recognition or recall (Parshall & Cadle, 2014). To address this potential problem, item writers can be trained to target higher-order thinking skills with the hot-spot item. For example, candidates could be prompted to interpret some aspect of the image, or required to use the image as they apply a content-relevant principle to a novel situation (Kubiszyn & Borich, 2000). Further discussion of preparing item writers to use the hot spot is provided in Parshall and Harmes (2009).

### *Drag-and-drop Items*

Drag-and-drop items are technologically enhanced selected-response items in which graphic tokens are dragged and dropped onto targets. Drag-and-drop items can be used for several different cognitive tasks, including: to label objects or parts of an object; to sort, prioritize, or sequence a series of answer options; or to match a series of prompts to corresponding answer options (e.g., Parshall, Depascale, & Skinner, 2011). These cognitive purposes give the drag-and-drop item type the potential to provide more direct measurement than multiple-choice items in certain types of content (Parshall & Cadle, 2014).

The testing organization will need to make decisions about the number of tokens and targets to allow within their drag-and-drop items. If many are included, the item could require more testing time than a single-point dichotomous item should support. In that case, the item could be assigned a greater weight, or polytomous scoring could be used.

### *Integrated Item Sets*

Integrated item sets involve the administration of multi-step, integrated tasks or scenarios. These may be called vignettes, case-based items, task-based simulations, or testlets (though this last term may also refer to sets of items that are not integrated). In this assessment structure, a small collection of items are created around a central stimuli or scenario. The stimuli may include graphical assets, such as a graph or diagram, or the stimuli may be entirely text-based, usually a passage of one to a few paragraphs. This approach can be thought of as a shift from an item paradigm to an activity paradigm (Behrens & DiCerbo, 2012).

In education, examples of operational exams that use scenario-based item sets include interactive tasks in the NAEP Science Assessment (Carr, 2013) and the PISA assessment of Scientific Literacy (Steinhauer & Van Groos, 2013). Scenario-based items are becoming increasing popular in credentialing examinations—the American Institute of Certified Public Accountants (AICPA), the Certified Financial Institute (CFI), the National Council of Architectural Registration Boards (NCARB), the National Board of Medical Examiners (NBME), and the Joint Commission on National Dental Examinations (JCNDE) are among the credentialing organizations that use case-based assessments (Haladyna & Rodriguez, 2013).

These item sets offer the potential of greater fidelity to professional practice as the scenarios can be based upon problems or situations encountered in practice. The scenario provides a content-relevant situation for the items, which can address the measurement weakness of decontextualized assessment. However, case-based item sets can be somewhat more challenging to write than stand-alone items. The number of items per stimuli needs to be sufficient to justify the time required for a candidate to read through or analyze the stimuli. Thus, item writers are required to produce multiple items based upon the scenario and the item writers need to be cautious to make sure that the content of one item is not dependent on the content (or a correct response) from another item.

### *Performance Assessments*

Performance assessments "are often complex in nature and generally require the test takers to demonstrate their abilities or skills in settings that closely resemble real-life situations" (AERA, APA, & NCME, 2014, p. 77). Performance assessments provide a means of assessing both the *process* involved in the performance of a task as well as the *product* resulting from it (Lane & Stone, 2006). For example, in a performance assessment of a candidate's ability to take a blood-pressure reading examiners might evaluate the process of taking the reading (e.g., putting the cuff on and inflating it), as well as the accuracy of the result (i.e., the actual reading itself). In other cases, the process and product may not be so easily differentiated, as in public speaking (Fitzpatrick & Morrison, 1971), or a testing organization might elect to evaluate only one component.

Within CBTs, performance tests can sometimes be developed and delivered as computerized simulations. As noted in the Standards (AERA, APA, & NCME, 2014), "Simulations are sometimes a substitute for performance assessments, when actual task performance might be costly or dangerous" (p. 78). In some cases, these computerized simulations can be viewed as highly unconstrained integrated item sets. In these simulations some aspect of the real world is modeled in a much richer and more integrated manner than in simpler case-based scenarios. A wide range of assessment applications can potentially use the approach of a computerized simulation. For example, the Cisco Networking Academies online curriculum and assessments include extensive simulations of computer networks (Behrens, Mislevy, DiCerbo, & Levy, 2012), while "virtual patients" are being used in medical training and assessment (e.g., Gesundheit, et al., 2009). These assessments are typically very specific to the content and context of a given exam program, and they tend to require extensive resources to develop, administer, and score.

### *Considerations in Item-type Selection and Use*

As mentioned previously, item-type selection is an important consideration in developing a credentialing examination. Rarely is only a single item type appropriate to assess the test constructs, so testing organizations are usually presented with options. Item types should be selected based upon which type(s) will provide the best measurement opportunity given the circumstance and considerations for their use, such as how they will be scored.

#### *Scoring*

Scoring decisions should be made early in the content development process before the items themselves are developed. Historically, the scoring of multiple-choice items has generally been straightforward dichotomous scoring—the response is either correct or it is incorrect. Many of the item types discussed above can be implemented with dichotomous scoring, though more elaborate scoring models may be needed for item types with less constrained response options. For these item types, more complex scoring methods may be used to obtain more information from each item. Indeed, one impetus for moving to less constrained, more innovative item types is their increased measurement capacity. For example, partial credit scoring models may be used to award points based upon the degree of response completeness or accuracy (Schmeiser & Welch, 2006). For many high or intermediate constraint items such as the multiple-response, the use of computer-based testing allows for automated scoring even when partial credit scoring is used. In other cases, whether the assessments are delivered on computer or not, the constructed-response items or performance assessments may be scored by human raters using detailed scoring rubrics.

#### *Construct-irrelevant Variance*

Any novel item type has the potential to add construct-irrelevant variance (CIV) for candidates who are unfamiliar with the new item features. CIV occurs when the examination assesses one or more unintended constructs in addition to the construct it was designed to measure (Messick, 1989). When a test item includes CIV, it may cause certain groups of test takers to respond in ways that will *not* provide an accurate interpretation of their knowledge, skills and abilities with regard to the desired test construct. CIV in the context of an alternative item type refers to the possibility that novel aspects of the innovation could interfere with the item's capacity for getting an accurate assessment of ability for certain candidates. To avoid this potential measurement problem, any new assessment type should be thoughtfully designed. The testing organization may wish to conduct usability studies as part of the new item development (e.g., Parshall & Harmes, 2009), along with the careful development of representative tutorials and practice items for the candidate population.

*Accessibility*

Another important consideration when developing a new item type is the potential effect on candidates with disabilities. Attention to principles of *universal design* will often enable the testing organization to design an item type that functions appropriately for the majority of candidates, even without accommodations (Parshall, Brunner, & Bovell, 2016; Thompson, Johnstone, & Thurlow, 2002) For example, a clean user interface for the item, in which all necessary features are provided in a user-friendly manner, and no unnecessary features clutter the interface, will be especially helpful to candidates with visual challenges, while also being valuable to many other candidates. The *Standards* address universal design in the context of a range of potential test adaptations, from modest modifications to alterations that change the construct and produce non-comparable scores (see "Minimizing Construct-Irrelevant Components Through Test Design and Testing Adaptations", AERA, APA, & NCME, 2014, pp. 57–62).

Certain aspects of a new item type may create challenges for candidates with specific disabilities. Increased use of images will create difficulties for candidates with visual challenges and the addition of audio will be problematic for those with hearing disabilities. In many cases, an adaptation can be provided that will not affect the test construct. For example, providing candidates with the ability to magnify images could be very helpful to the majority of the candidates with low vision, while fully maintaining the test construct. On the other hand, whether text descriptions of a heart sound are regarded as comparable to audio recordings of those same sounds may depend on how the construct of auscultation is defined within a given exam program.

There are times when adaptations must be implemented, even though they result in changes to the construct and produce non-comparable scores. A blind candidate can respond to text items that are presented aurally through use of screen reader software like JAWS; however, if the test construct includes interpretation of visual images, no fully comparable adaptation is likely to be possible. In many instances the goal is to design "adaptations [that] change the intended construct to make it accessible … while retaining as much of the original construct as possible" (AERA, APA, & NCME, 2014, p. 59).

## *Item-writing Guidelines*

Item-writing guidelines are consistent rules or instructions that testing organizations, both in education and in professional assessment, typically provide to item writers. The use of appropriate item-writing guidelines is an important and effective tool which helps item writers produce high-quality items. An authoritative taxonomy of multiple-choice rules was provided by Haladyna, Downing, & Rodriguez (2002) (updating Haladyna & Downing, 1989). This taxonomy of item-writing rules was based upon consensus in relevant textbooks, as well as research studies and reviews. Well-established guidelines for the multiple-choice item type have also been documented in Downing (2005), Haladyna (1997), and Haladyna & Rodriguez (2013).

Most testing organizations, in both education and professional testing, produce their own set of item-writing guidelines, including best practices from the field of measurement along with rules that are specific to the organization. An exam program with relatively few candidates may find it easier to use an existing reference; Haladyna (1997) provides an easy-to-read and comprehensive guide on writing guidelines for a variety of item types. Another reference is Case and Swanson (2002) which specifically provides guidelines for writing test questions for the basic and clinical sciences, and that are useful when writing items in other contexts as well.

The majority of the professional literature on item-writing guidelines addresses the multiple-choice item type. These guidelines can be beneficially modified for multiple-choice variants. When item types beyond the multiple-choice format are included on an exam, a valuable additional step is to provide targeted item-writer training and to include item-writing guidelines specific to each additional item type (Parshall & Harmes, 2009).

## The Content Development Process

Developing high-quality test items requires a principled and systematic content development process (see "Standards for Item Development and Review" in the *Standards*, AERA, APA, & NCME, 2014, pp. 87–90). The methods described in the following sections adhere to best practice and industry standards for the development of traditional item types, such as the multiple-choice. Relevant adaptations for less constrained item types are also provided.

### *Selecting Item Writers and Reviewers*

The expertise of item writers is a critical piece of validity evidence (Downing & Haladyna, 1997). Subject matter experts (SMEs) should be selected so that there is a broad scope of knowledge and experience within the item-writing and review panels. In addition to ensuring the appropriate range of knowledge to adequately address the test blueprint, the item-writing and review panels should also reflect the demographics of the profession (e.g., gender, ethnicity, professional affiliations, geographic location, etc.).

SMEs may be selected to perform both item-writing and reviewing tasks, or they may be selected for one of these. It can be more efficient if the same SMEs perform both roles, which could be particularly helpful to small testing programs. However, the final quality of the items may be strengthened when separate groups of writers and reviewers are used.

### *Training*

Subject matter expertise can be thought of as a prerequisite for item writing. Beyond this requirement, new item writers need training in the principles of good item-writing practices. Subject matter knowledge does not necessarily translate into the ability to write good test items; effective item-writing requires training and practice (Downing, 2006). Medical education literature provides support for the importance of training on the quality of test items. Jozefowicz, et al. (2002) analyzed the quality of examinations developed in-house at medical schools and concluded that items written by item writers who had received training were of better quality than those written by untrained faculty. The use of test items that violate evidence-based principles of item writing has also been found to disadvantage some medical students (Downing, 2005; Durning, 2005).

Many testing organizations deliver item-writing training in group item writing and review meetings, whether in person or through webinars. The training should include examination-specific information, such as the test blueprint and specifications, as well as guidelines on the format and style to be used, and item-writing guidelines specific to the particular types of items required (Parshall & Harmes, 2009; Schmeiser & Welch, 2006). New item writers need to see examples of good and bad items (Schedl & Malloy, 2014), along with targeted training opportunities for each item type that the test includes (Parshall & Harmes, 2009). Collegial review of the items that are written during training sessions is also beneficial.

Training of item writers should go beyond mere instruction on good item-writing practices. Instruction should be combined with practice and feedback. Because of the time between writing and actual use of the test items, performance feedback on the actual items written by a specific item writer may prove difficult. However, qualitative feedback gained through the review process can be provided. Item performance statistics can be used in training sessions by showing items with a range of difficulty and discrimination values, along with a discussion of the potential reasons for the variation in item performance.

Novel item formats often require the development of item-writing guidelines and training beyond that required for more traditional item formats. For example, when creating integrated item sets, item writers must create not only the items themselves but also the stimulus upon which the items are based and perhaps artifacts used within the stimulus. This may involve a different skill set focusing more heavily on design and writing (Brunner, Becker & Tagoe, 2016; Brunner, Flatman, Balzan, Wilderspin, & Rimington, 2014). Scoring rubrics may also need to be developed as part of the item-writing process for open-ended response formats and performance-based tasks. Whether the scoring rubrics are applied automatically within a CBT or used by human raters after an exam administration, the item writers will need targeted training to prepare useful rubrics.

### *Item-writing Assignments*

Item authors need direction as to the nature of the items that they should write. To ensure that items are written in areas for which items are needed, a production plan should be created and item writers should be given writing assignments according to the plan (Schmeiser & Welch, 2006). For new tests, the initial item production process will likely need to be a more intensive effort in order to provide a sufficient number of items for the initial administration of the test. Thereafter, item banks are built to support ongoing exam administration, using periodic gap analyses to determine content areas that need replenishing over time. Many testing organizations that use a variety of item types also control the proportion of items of each type that are developed and that are included on each candidate's exam.

### *Item Authoring*

Once item writers have been sufficiently trained and have received their assignments, the item-writing process can begin. For many exam programs, face-to-face item-writing workshops are held periodically throughout the year. These item-writing workshops can also be held using web-conferencing facilities. The face-to-face meetings have the advantages of providing better opportunity for exam program staff to reinforce good item-writing practices and supporting an exchange of ideas among the item writers; the Web-based meetings have the advantages of not incurring travel costs and of being potentially easier to schedule.

In between these group meetings, item writers can work on their own. The item writers may submit items to the test sponsor to be incorporated into the item database, or they may be given remote access to the item bank and write items directly into it. In addition to writing the test item itself, item authors should submit supporting information such as the key (i.e., the correct answer), a reference from an authoritative source for the content contained in the item, and any metadata that will be stored with the item such as the relevant content classification from the test blueprint and the cognitive complexity of the item. Each item format may also have unique fields. For example, an audio item might require information about file type or length, while a hot-spot item will require the item writer to indicate a graphical region on the image in order to identify the key.

### *Item Review*

Three types of review should occur on exam items. *Content* review refers to the review performed by content experts regarding the appropriateness of the item content. *Editorial* review refers to a review to determine if the items have adhered to the exam's style guidelines and if they are free of grammatical and typographical errors. *Sensitivity* review refers to a review to determine if the items are free of judgmental bias. Table 5.1 provides an overview of these three types of review and the desired outcomes that result from them.

### *Content Review*

The underlying concern in content review is relevance (Haladyna, 2004). Messick (1989) advocated that judgments of test-item relevance needed to take into consideration all aspects of the examination process that could potentially affect test performance, including the content specification, the item formats and the response conditions, and the administration conditions and scoring criteria.

Content reviews may be performed during item-review panel meetings or through independent SME review of draft items. As part of the review process, the SME verifies that each item is relevant to competent practice, correctly classified to its content domain,

*Table 5.1* Types of Item Review and their Desired Outcomes

|  | *Content Review* | *Editorial Review* | *Sensitivity Review* |
| --- | --- | --- | --- |
| Key question | Is the item pertinent to current and competent practice? | Does the item conform to style and formatting guidelines? | Does content in the item treat a certain group of test takers in a stereotypical or derogatory manner? |
| Desired outcome | Test items that are relevant to the content specifications and appropriate for the test purpose. | Test items that clearly and accurately present the task statement and potential responses. | Test items that are fair to all groups of test takers. |

and that its cognitive level is correctly specified. Verification of the key is a crucial element in content review, and the reference provided by the item author should be reviewed and confirmed. For constructed response items, including performance-based tests, the content review will need to include the associated scoring rubric. If an assessment includes media (e.g., graphic, audio, video), those elements should also be reviewed. The outcome of the SME review is either approval, recommendation for revision, or rejection of the item.

*Editorial Review*

Editorial review requires a different set of skills from content review. Editorial review of test items is much like the proofreading or editing that occurs for manuscripts written for publication. Items are reviewed by editors for clarity, mechanics (spelling, punctuation, etc.), grammar, and consistency with the examination's style guidelines (Haladyna, 2004).

While it is best to have the editing conducted by someone formally trained or experienced in proofreading and editing, this may not be possible in small credentialing programs. In this case, the role of "editor" should be assigned to someone who checks items against style guidelines. It is important that this review should be performed by someone other than the item writer, as a second set of eyes is often needed. Professional editors are adept at editing text without changing its meaning. However, items should be referred back to content reviewers if there is any question about whether the meaning and intent of the item will be affected by the proposed editorial changes.

Editorial review of item formats that include media will need to include a review of those elements as well. Additional procedures may be needed to verify that the media asset is consistent with the rest of the item. For example, if the item contains an audio clip of a woman's voice, a review step could include verification that the text stem uses feminine pronouns when referring to the clip.

*Sensitivity Review*

The issue of concern during sensitivity review is fairness, and "the driving force" behind the review is validity (Zieky, 2006, p. 363). Sensitivity or fairness reviews primarily address the possibility of bias. More specifically, a sensitivity review is carried out to identify any potential sources of CIV in the test items. As noted previously, CIV interferes with the capability of the test item to provide an accurate interpretation of the candidates' knowledge, skills and abilities. CIV occurs when the examination assesses one or more unintended constructs in addition to the construct it was designed to measure (Messick, 1989).

As Standard 3.2 of the *Standards for Educational and Psychological Testing* (AERA, APA, & NCME, 2014) states: "Test developers are responsible for developing tests that measure the intended construct and for minimizing the potential for tests' being affected by construct-irrelevant characteristics, such as linguistic, communicative, cognitive, cultural, physical, or other characteristics" (p. 64).

Potential sources of construct-irrelevant variance may be cognitive, affective, or physical (ETS, 2009). Cognitive CIV can occur when knowledge or skill unrelated to the test's purpose is needed to provide a correct response to an item. For example, if a sport-specific acronym such as RBI ("runs batted in"), were used on a test of mathematics skills, this would be a source of cognitive CIV since the test item requires knowledge of content irrelevant to the test's purpose. Physical CIV is most likely to affect test takers with disabilities; it occurs when the presentation of the item (for instance, the font used) interferes with test takers' ability to answer the item.

Affective sources of variance may be caused by the inclusion of unnecessary controversial, culturally sensitive, or emotive content. A sensitivity review of affective CIV may differ for educational tests and professional tests. In the case of credentialing examinations, the key determination to be made during a sensitivity review is whether the controversial or emotive content is essential for assessment of the content domain from the test blueprint. For instance, a reading passage on an exam might contain content related to capital punishment, which could be emotionally fraught for some candidates. Nevertheless, an examination in a legal-related profession may need to contain that content.

Since items developed for credentialing examinations are related to job performance, affective sources of variance are typically less of an issue than they may be for educational tests which have less direction with regard to content and context. While larger credentialing organizations may have separate sensitivity review panels, the potential for affective sources of variance is most often addressed, particularly for smaller organizations, through the development of sensitivity guidelines that promote fairness for diverse test-taking populations. For example, the organization may develop guidelines that caution against the use of words or references which are clearly more familiar to certain groups of candidates or that have different meanings for different groups. Item writers should receive training on these guidelines, and the training should provide a discussion of any content areas which may be more susceptible to sensitivity and fairness concerns. The review process should incorporate checks that the sensitivity guidelines have been followed.

## *Field Testing*

No matter how skilled item authors are at item writing and how rigorous the item review process is, some items do not function as intended when they are administered (Wendler & Walker, 2006). To address this situation, field testing items before they are used as operational items is recommended. In field testing, items are administered to members of the examinee population for the purpose of evaluating item performance. Field testing is essential if the examination is computer-administered and scores are to be provided to candidates immediately after exam administration (Parshall, Spray, Kalohn, & Davey, 2002).

Field testing occurs through three methods: beta testing, pre-testing, and independent trialing. *Beta testing* occurs prior to operational testing with a sample of actual test takers. Beta testing is appropriate for computer-based tests which have not been administered before, or when sufficient numbers of items which have item statistics in the item bank are not yet available to produce an examination. In beta testing, scoring is deferred until after the test has been administered to an adequate sampling of candidates and item statistical analyses have been performed. Beta testing can be used for many alternative item formats. Since scoring is deferred initially, even items that require a post-exam human scoring stage can be included in the beta test, though the test as a whole will not be able to transition to immediate scoring even after item statistics have been obtained.

In the *pre-test* approach, items are embedded within an operation exam, either as a contiguous block or seeded throughout the entire examination. Since the embedded pre-test items are being evaluated, they do not contribute toward candidate scores. Candidates are typically told that there are unscored items on the test, along with the reason for this; however, as long as they are unable to identify the pre-test items, their motivation will be consistent across both operational and pre-test items. To help obscure which items are unscored, credentialing examinations are more likely to have the pre-test items seeded throughout the test.

Field testing with embedded pre-test items is most appropriate for credentialing programs when releasing scores to candidates immediately is desired (Jones, Smith, & Talley, 2006). However, this method may be impractical for smaller scale testing programs since it may be difficult to keep up with item development needs, especially in rapidly evolving professions in which the content of items becomes obsolete more quickly (Jones, et al. 2006).

The pre-test method can be used for most of the intermediate constraint item formats. In particular, multiple-choice variants that are dichotomously scored (e.g., multiple-response, video items, hot spots) can be embedded within an operational exam. Testing organizations may decide that a new item type warrants administration as a contiguous block, rather than embedded. In either approach, targeted communication to the candidates about the new item types is recommended. This may include advance notification as well as practice items on the exam tutorial.

*Independent trialing* requires that an examination be developed and administered, separately from the live administration. This separate, independent trialing must use a sample of appropriate test-takers. There are strong challenges in implementing this method of field testing, as it is difficult to obtain a representative and motivated sample of test takers (Wendler & Walker, 2006). Obtaining an appropriate sample may prove especially challenging for smaller scale testing programs (Jones, et al., 2006). For all testing programs, this method imposes an additional administrative burden and associated expenses (Jones, et al., 2006).

For these reasons, independent trialing is typically avoided unless the other field testing methods are not feasible. Nevertheless, in some instances independent trialing may be the only feasible choice such as some innovative items. For example, a scenario-based item set that must be trialed as a block, or a complex performance based test that utilizes special equipment may necessitate independent trialing.

Regardless of the field-test method employed, certain conditions should be met to ensure that the item statistics obtained reflect how the item would perform operationally. (Chapter 8 provides a comprehensive discussion of item analysis.) The field-test examinees should be representative of the candidate population; the sample size used should be sufficient to support the psychometric analyses that will be used; and the field-test examinees should be motivated to do well.

The purpose of field-testing items is to determine which items are of sufficient quality to be used as operational, scored items. The new items are subjected to an analysis of their psychometric properties. Items should not be rejected solely on their statistical properties, but only after review by subject matter experts. The SMEs should consider both the item analysis results and the content of the item. Statistical criteria can be used to determine which items are flagged for review by content experts. Content experts can then decide whether each item should be approved for operational use, rejected, or revised. If the decision is that the item requires revision, then it is sent back through the content development process and trailed again after revision.

## Design Strategies for Content Development of Novel Item Types

The content development methods described above are the standard approach used in preparing item types such as the multiple-choice for credentialing purposes. As noted, item types that are relatively similar to the multiple-choice, especially those with high or intermediate constraints (Figure 5.4), can be developed following the same basic procedures, using only modest adaptations. Nevertheless, any item type that is being developed for the first time by a testing organization, especially those with low constraints, will benefit from a process of careful planning and thoughtful preparation (Parshall & Harmes, 2008).

Alternative item formats may be attractive to testing organizations as a way of increasing the perceived value of their credentials or for brand enhancement. While this may be a secondary advantage to using more innovative item formats, the primary considerations for adopting these formats is increasing the capability to assess the desired test constructs. Implementing alternative item formats is an expensive endeavor, and one that should only be undertaken if they have the potential to add to the information obtained on candidate ability.

One highly valuable step, when a testing organization considers adding new item formats to the exam, is to start with a design stage. In that regard, a framework for designing innovative items that begins with a detailed analysis of the desired test construct can be found in Becker and Brunner (2014). And the use of iterative methods, in which preliminary item type designs are improved through multiple rounds of review and revision, is discussed in Parshall and Harmes (2008).

In this era of continuous computing changes, some testing organizations are beginning to anticipate ongoing, continuous innovation. Item types that were novel a few years ago may be relatively routine now, while new assessment formats can be seen on the horizon. Parshall and Guille (2015) have proposed an approach to strategically manage these ongoing changes that utilizes an *Agile* philosophy (Beck et al., 2001), including an Agile approach to prioritizing the order in which innovations are developed. This flexible approach to development uses "experimental innovation" (Sims, 2011) in which solutions are built over time, as learning occurs.

For further discussion on structured and principled approaches to the entire test-development lifecycle, including design, development, and scoring, see Luecht, 2006; Mislevy, Almond, & Lukas, 2003; and Wilson, 2005. These and other models can be useful guides to a testing organization preparing to implement one or more new item types. Use of a principled, thoughtful approach supports the content development goals of the organization and contributes to the likelihood that the new assessment methods will improve the test as a whole.

## Conclusion

High-quality content is crucial to a successful exam. To achieve this, best practices for content development should be followed. The industry standard procedures for content development were presented in this chapter, along with targeted citations for the reader interested in further discussion of specific topics. As part of the content development process, an organization can elect to use a variety of item types. Each type has strengths and weaknesses, and each is likely to be better suited to measuring certain constructs than others. Aspects of the content development process may need additional attention or modification when novel item types are included.

In all of this wash of details, it is worth remembering the importance of a well-constructed credentialing exam. The critical question in any credentialing exam is "Is an individual proficient enough in the body of knowledge to practice a profession?" Evolving scientific and technological advancements provide new ways of determining the answer to this question, but the question itself remains the same.

## References

American Educational Research Association, American Psychological Association, & National Council on Measurement in Education (AERA, APA, & NCME) (2014). *Standards for educational and psychological testing*. Washington, DC: American Educational Research Association.

Anderson, L., & Krathwohl, D. (2001). *A taxonomy for learning, teaching and assessing: A revision of Bloom's taxonomy of educational objectives.* New York: Longman.

Bauer, D., Holzer, M., Kopp, V., & Fischer, M. R. (2011). Pick-N multiple-choice-exams: A comparison of scoring algorithms. *Advances in Health Sciences Education, 16*(2), 211–221.

Beck, K., M., Beedle, M., van Bennekum, A., Cockburn, A., Cunningham, W., Fowler, M., Grenning, J., Highsmith, J., Hunt, A., Jeffries, R., Kern, J., Marick, B., Martin, R., Mellor, S., Schwaber, K., Sutherland, J. & Thomas, D. (2001). *Manifesto for Agile software development.* Retrieved from: http://agilemanifesto.org

Becker, K. A., & Brunner, B. (2014, April). *Defining the innovative item: Test constructs and item prototypes.* Paper presented at the 76th annual meeting of the National Council on Measurement in Education, Philadelphia, PA.

Behrens, J. T., & DiCerbo, K. E. (2012). *Technological implications for assessment ecosystems: Opportunities for digital technology to advance assessment.* Paper written for the Gordon Commission on the Future of Assessment in Education.

Behrens, J. T., Mislevy, R. J., DiCerbo, K. E., & Levy, R. (2012). An evidence centered design for learning and assessment in the digital world. In M. C. Mayrath, J. Clarke-Midura, & D. Robinson (Eds.), *Technology-based assessments for 21st century skills: Theoretical and practical implications from modern research* (pp. 13–54). Charlotte, NC: Information Age.

Bennett, R. E., Ward, W. C., Rock, D. A., & LaHart, C. M. (1990). *Toward a framework for constructed-response items* (RR-90-7). Princeton, NJ: Educational Testing Service.

Bloom, B. S., Engelhart, M. D., Furst, E. J., Hill, W. H., & Kratwohl, D. R. (1956). *Taxonomy of educational objectives.* New York: Longmans Green.

Brunner, B., Becker, K., & Tagoe, N. (2016). Using technology to assess real-world professional skills: A case study. In Y. Rosen, S. Ferrara, & M. Mosharraf (Eds.), *Handbook of research on technology tools for real-world skill development.* Hershey, PA: IGI Global.

Brunner, B., Flatman, S., Wilderspin, S., & Rimington, H. (2014, September). *Designing innovative learning and assessment programs to achieve employability.* Paper presented at the annual conference of the European Association of Test Publishers. Budapest, Hungary.

Carr, P. (2013, September). *NAEP innovations in action: Implications for the next generation science standards.* Presented at the Invitational Research Symposium on Science Assessment, Washington, DC.

Case, S. M. & Swanson, D. B. (2002). *Constructing written test questions for the basic and clinical sciences* (3rd ed.). Philadelphia, PA: National Board of Medical Examiners. Retrieved from: www.nbme.org/pdf/itemwriting_2003/2003iwgwhole.pdf

Clauser, B. E., Margolis, M. J., & Case, S. M. (2006). Testing for licensure and certification in the professions. In R. L. Brennan (Ed.), *Educational measurement* (4th ed., pp. 701–731).

Downing, S. M. (2005). The effects of violating standard item writing principles on tests and students: The consequences of using flawed test items on achievement examinations in medical education. *Advances in Health Sciences Education, 10,* 133–143.

Downing, S. M. (2006). Selected-response item formats in test development. In S. M. Downing & T. M. Haladyna (Eds.), *Handbook of test development* (pp. 487–525). Mahwah, NJ: Lawrence Erlbaum Associates.

Downing, S. M., & Haladyna, T. M. (1997). Test item development: Validity evidence from quality assurance procedures. *Applied Measurement in Education, 10*(1), 61–82.

Duncan, G. T., & Milton, E. O. (1978). Multiple-answer multiple-choice test items: Responding and scoring through Bayes and Minimax strategies. *Psychometrika, 43*(1), 43–57.

Durning, S. M. (2005). The effects of violating standard item writing principles on tests and students: The consequences of using flawed test items on achievement examinations in medical education. *Advances in Health Sciences Education, 10*(2), 133–143.

Educational Testing Service (ETS) (2009). *ETS guidelines for fairness reviews of assessment.* Princeton, NJ: Author. Retrieved from: www.ets.org/Media/About_ETS/pdf/overview.pdf

Fitzpatrick, R., & Morrision, E. J. (1971). Performance and product evaluation. In R. L. Thorndike (Ed.), *Educational measurement* (2nd ed., pp. 237–270). Washington, DC: American Council on Education.

Gesundheit, N., Brutlag, P., Youngblood, P., Gunning, W. T., Zary, N., & Fors, U. (2009). The use of virtual patients to assess the clinical skills and reasoning of medical students: Initial insights on student acceptance. *Medical Teacher, 31*(8), 739–742.

Haladyna, T. M. (1997). *Writing test items to evaluate higher order thinking.* Boston, MA: Allyn & Bacon.

Haladyna, T. M. (2004). *Developing and validating multiple-choice test items* (3rd ed.). Mahwah, NJ: Lawrence Erlbaum & Associates.

Haladyna, T. M., & Downing, S. M. (1989). A taxonomy of multiple-choice item-writing rules. *Applied Measurement in Education, 1,* 37–50.

Haladyna, T. M., & Rodriguez, M. C. (2013). *Developing and validating test items.* New York: Routledge.

Haladyna, T. M., Downing, S. M., & Rodriguez, M. C. (2002). A review of multiple-choice item-writing guidelines for classroom assessment. *Applied Measurement in Education, 15*(3), 309–334.

Hess, B. J., Johnston, M. M., & Lipner, R. S. (2013). The impact of item format and examinee characteristics on response times. *International Journal of Testing, 13*(4), 295–313.

Hong, J., Liu, J., Haynie, K., Woo, A., Gorham, J. (2012). Comparison between dichotomous and polytomous scoring of innovative items in a large-scale computerized adaptive test. *Educational and Psychological Measurement, 72*(3), 493–509.

Hsu, T., Moss, P. A., Khampalkit, C. (1984). The merits of multiple-answer items as evaluated by using six scoring formulas. *Journal of Experimental Education, 52*(3), 152–158.

Huff, K. L., & Sireci, S. G. (2001). Validity issues in computer-based testing. *Educational Measurement: Issues and Practice, 20,* 16–25.

Jones, P., Smith, R. W., & Talley, D. (2006). Developing test forms for small-scale achievement testing systems. In S. M. Downing & T. M. Haladyna (Eds.), *Handbook of test development* (pp. 487–525). Mahwah, NJ: Lawrence Erlbaum Associates, Publishers.

Josefowicz, R. F., Koeppen, B. M., Case, S., Galbraith, R, Swanson, D., & Glew, H. (2002). The quality of in-house medical school examinations. *Academic Medicine, 77,* 156–161.

Kane, M. (1982). The validity of licensure examinations. *American Psychologist, 37*(8), 911–918.

Kane, M. (2004). Certification test as an illustration of argument-based validation. *Measurement, 2*(3), 135–170.

Kubiszyn, T., & Borich, G. (2000). *Educational testing and measurement: Classroom application and practice* (6th ed.). New York: John Wiley & Sons.

Lane, S., & Stone, C.A. (2006). Performance assessment. In R. L. Brennan (Ed). *Educational Measurement* (4th ed., pp. 386–431). Westport, CT: Praeger.

Lipner, R. S., Messenger, J. C., Kangilaski, R., Baim, D., Holmes, D., Williams, D., King, S. (2010). A technical and cognitive skills evaluation of performance in interventional cardiology procedures using medical simulation. *Simulation in Healthcare, 5*(2), 65–74.

Luecht, R. M. (2006, May). *Engineering the test: From principled item design to automated test assembly.* Paper presented at the annual meeting of the Society for Industrial and Organizational Psychology, Dallas, TX.

Martinez, M. E. (1999). Cognition and the question of test item format. *Educational Psychologist, 34*(4), 207–218.

Messick, S. (1989). Validity. In R. L. Linn (Ed.), *Educational measurement* (3rd ed., pp. 13–104). New York: American Council on Education and Macmillan.

Mislevy, R. J., Almond, R. G., & Lukas, J. F. (2003). *A brief introduction to evidence-centered design.* Retrieved from: www.ets.org/Media/Research/pdf/RR-03-16.pdf

Muckle, T. J., Becker, K. A., & Wu, B. (2011, April). *Investigating the multiple answer multiple-choice item format.* Paper presented at the 2011 annual conference of the National Council on Measurement in Education, New Orleans, LA.

Pae, H. K. (2014). Forced choice or free choice? The role of question formats in predicting speaking and writing skills of nonnative speakers of English. *Educational Assessment, 19*(2), 97–115.

Parshall, C. G., & Cadle, A. W. (2014, March). *How to identify, develop and implement innovative items.* Paper presented at the annual conference of the Association of Test Publishers, Scottsdale, AZ.

Parshall, C. G., & Guille, R. A. (2015). Managing ongoing changes to the test: Agile strategies for continuous innovation. In F. Drasgow (Ed.), *Technology in testing: Measurement issues* (pp. 1–22). New York: Routledge.

Parshall, C. G., & Harmes, J. C. (2008). The design of innovative item types: Targeting constructs, selecting innovations, and refining prototypes. *CLEAR Exam Review, 19*(2), 18–25.

Parshall, C. G., & Harmes, J. C. (2009). Improving the quality of innovative item types: Four tasks for design and development. *Journal of Applied Testing Technology, 10*(1).

Parshall, C. G., Brunner, B., & Bovell, D. (2016, March). *Universal design, accessibility & fairness: Implications for test and item development.* Paper presented at the Association of Test Publishers annual conference, Orlando, FL.

Parshall, C. G., Davey, T., & Pashley, P. (2000). Innovative item types for computerized testing. In W. J. van der Linden & C. A. W. Glas (Eds.), *Computerized Adaptive Testing: Theory and Practice* (pp. 129–148). Norwell, MA: Kluwer Academic Publishers.

Parshall, C. G., Depascale, C., & Skinner, L. (2011, February). *Adapting Parshall and Harmes' six-step model to the integration of alternative item types into a multiple-choice testing program.* Presented at the annual meeting of ATP, Phoenix, AZ.

Parshall, C. G., Harmes, J. C., Davey, T., & Pashley, P. (2003). Innovative items for computerized testing. In W. J. van der Linden & C. A. W. Glas (Eds.), *Computerized adaptive testing: Theory and practice,* Norwell, MA: Kluwer Academic Publishers.

Parshall, C. G., Spray, J. A., Kalohn, J. C., & Davey, T. (2002). *Practical considerations in computer-based testing.* New York: Springer-Verlag.

Rodriguez, M. C. (2002). Choosing an item format. In G. Tindal & T. M. Haladyna (Eds.), *Large-Scale assessment programs for all students: Validity, technical adequacy and implementation* (pp. 213–231). Mahwah, NJ: Lawrence Erlbaum Associates.

Scalise, K., & Gifford, B. (2006). Computer-based assessment in e-learning: A framework for constructing "Intermediate Constraint" questions and tasks for technology platforms. *Journal of Technology, Learning and Assessment, 4*(6). Retrieved from: www.jtla.org

Schedl, M., & Malloy, J. (2014). Writing items and tasks. In A. J. Kunnan (Ed.), *The companion to language assessment, volume II: Approaches and development* (pp. 796–813). Chichester: Wiley-Blackwell.

Schmeiser, C. B., & Welch, C. J. (2006). Test development. In R.L. Brennan (Ed.), *Educational measurement* (4th ed., pp. 307–353). Westport, CT: American Council on Education and Praeger Publishers.

Sims, P. (2011). *Little bets: How breakthrough ideas emerge from small discoveries.* New York: Simon & Schuster.

Sireci, S. G., & Zenisky, A. L. (2006). Innovative item formats in computer-based testing: In pursuit of improved construct representation. In S. M. Downing & T. M. Haladyna (Eds.), *Handbook of test development* (pp. 329–348). Mahwah, NJ: Lawrence Erlbaum Associates.

Steinhauer, E., & Van Groos, J. (2013, September). *Presentation of a Program for International Student Assessment (PISA) science 2015 task variant.* Presented at the Invitational Research Symposium on Science Assessment. Washington, DC.

Strain-Seymour, E., Way, W., & Dolan, R.P. (2009). *Strategies and processes for developing innovative items in large-scale assessments.* Retrieved from: http://images.pearsonassessments.com/images/tmrs/StrategiesandProcessesforDevelopingInnovativeItems.pdf

Sulaiman, N. D., & Hamdy, H. (2013). Assessment of clinical competencies using clinical images and videos "CIVA." *BMC Medical Education, 13*(78).

Thompson, S. J., Johnstone, C. J., & Thurlow, M. L. (2002). *Universal design applied to large scale assessments* (Synthesis Report 44). Minneapolis, MN: University of Minnesota, National Center on Educational Outcomes. Retrieved from: http://education.umn.edu/NCEO/OnlinePubs/Synthesis44.html

Vale, C. D. (2006). Computerized item banking. In S. M. Downing & T. M. Haladyna (Eds.), *Handbook of test development* (pp. 261–285). Mahwah, NJ: Lawrence Erlbaum Associates.

Wendler, C. L., & Walker, M. E. (2006). Practical issues in designing and maintaining multiple test forms for large-scale programs. In S. M. Downing & T. M. Haladyna (Eds.), *Handbook of test development* (pp. 445–467). Mahwah, NJ: Lawrence Erlbaum Associates.

Wendt, A., Kenny, L. E., & Marks, C. (2007). Assessing critical thinking using a talk-aloud protocol. *CLEAR Exam Review, 18*(1), 18–27.

Wilson, M. (2005). *Constructing measures.* Mahwah, NJ: Lawrence Erlbaum Associates.

Zenisky, A. L., & Sireci, S. G. (2013, April). *Innovative items to measure high-order thinking: Development and validity considerations.* Presented at the annual meeting of the NCME, San Francisco, CA.

Zieky, M. T. (2006). Fairness review in assessment. In S. M. Downing & T. M. Haladyna (Eds.), *Handbook of test development* (pp. 359–375). Mahwah, NJ: Lawrence Erlbaum Associates.

# 6 Estimating, Interpreting, and Maintaining the Meaning of Test Scores

*Walter D. Way and Kathleen A. Gialluca*

## Introduction

The policies and practices of credentialing tests have been highlighted throughout this volume, and include the need to establish evidence of validity based on a comprehensive content specification analysis and the test design considerations that are unique to credentialing settings. In this chapter, we will concentrate on those aspects of credentialing tests that relate specifically to estimating, interpreting, and maintaining the meaning of scores and credentialing decisions.

Probably the greatest difference between credentialing tests and tests used for other purposes lies in the way the test scores are interpreted. Credentialing test users and stakeholders are typically not interested in rank-ordering candidates or placing them along some continuum (of knowledge, skill, or ability) from low to high. Rather, they are primarily interested in making a (typically binary) decision as to whether a specific candidate has mastered the requisite knowledge for practicing a profession—i.e., is *minimally competent* and should therefore be *credentialed.*

As noted in the *Standards for Educational and Psychological Testing* (AERA, APA, & NCME, 2014, p. 176):

> Defining the minimum level of knowledge and skill required for credentialing is one of the most important and difficult tasks facing those responsible for credentialing. The validity of the test score interpretations depends on whether the standard for passing makes an appropriate distinction between adequate and inadequate performance.

Because of the binary decisions made based on credentialing test scores, consideration must be given to the tradeoffs associated with a cut score that might be too high (in which case, truly unqualified candidates would be unlikely to pass, but at the cost of having more truly qualified candidates fail as well) or too low (in which case, truly qualified candidates would be unlikely to fail, but at the cost of also having more truly unqualified candidates pass). In general, passing standards must balance the goals of protecting the public interest and maintaining a sufficient pool of qualified practitioners. Verifying the appropriateness of the cut score or scores on a credentialing test is a critical element of the validation process (AERA, APA, & NCME, 2014).

In addition, scores on tests used for credentialing need to be precise in the vicinity of the passing score. They may not need to be as precise for those who clearly pass or clearly fail because it is not important to distinguish among candidates that clearly perform above the passing standard or those that clearly perform below the passing standard. This mastery-based focus provides some opportunity for unique test designs that would not necessarily make sense in other testing contexts. In addition, the mastery-based focus of credentialing tests leads to the use of different statistical indices to document their precision, such as estimates of decision consistency and/or decision accuracy (AERA, APA, & NCME, 2014, Standard 11.14).

Finally, once a passing standard is established, it is necessary to establish mechanisms that can be used to maintain the standard over time. This would be quite easy if the same test form could be used repeatedly over time. However, this is typically not feasible because of test security concerns. Most credentialing programs recognize the need to develop and administer different test forms over time, and utilize test-equating techniques to ensure that candidates taking different test forms across administrations are held to the same performance standard.

This chapter comprises three major sections. In the first section, we discuss techniques and considerations in estimating scores for credentialing tests, both at the level of individual items or tasks as well as the aggregation of items and tasks to produce total scores and/or pass/fail decisions. In the second section, we discuss the interpretation of scores on credentialing tests, which derive primarily from the fundamental and critical process of standard setting. In the third section, we discuss maintaining the meaning of credentialing test scores over time, which depends primarily (but not exclusively) on the techniques of test equating.

Throughout the discussion in this chapter, connections to the decisions related to test design will be made, as the meaning of scores for credentialing tests are inextricably linked to test design and the intended uses of the credentialing test results.

## Estimating Scores for Credentialing Tests

The process of estimating scores for credentialing tests is an outcome of decisions made during the phases of test design, content specifications, and content development, which are discussed in detail in Chapters 3, 4, and 5 of this volume. For example, scoring decisions depend not only upon item formats (e.g., selected-response, short-answer, extended response), but also upon how credit (and potentially partial credit) is assigned. Aggregating over items and tasks to achieve total scores is guided by the content specifications and should be explicitly connected to a job or practice analysis (AERA, APA, & NCME, 2014, Standard 11.13). When tests comprise primarily selected-response items (which is probably the case in most credentialing test applications today), scoring decisions at the individual item level are obvious and well understood. However, the options available for test designs and item formats have expanded significantly through the widespread availability of computer-based testing. As new item types are identified that make use of the available technology, the processes of scoring and item development become much more intertwined.

### *Item- and Task-level Scoring*

To a large degree, scoring of items and tasks depends upon the item types that have been specified during the design and development phase of the credentialing test. These in turn depend upon the purposes and defined content specifications of the test. Selected-response formats, such as multiple-choice items, are suitable for many credentialing test applications. Other credentialing test purposes may be more effectively served by short constructed-response or extended-response formats. Performance assessments are used in a variety of occupational settings, including teacher licensure (Darling-Hammond, 2010), medicine (Norcini & McKinley, 2007), and a variety of workplace tests (cf, Weiner, Schmitt, & Highhouse, 2013). One type of performance assessment often used in credentialing tests is the standardized work sample, in which a specific on-the-job task is presented to the candidate. For example, a teacher candidate may be asked to prepare a lesson plan or be videotaped while delivering an instructional unit to a class. A medical student's ability to make an accurate diagnosis and treatment recommendation may be based on an interview with a "standardized" patient who has been trained to articulate particular symptoms and behaviors.

*Performance Tasks*

Human scoring of performance tasks and other more complex item types depends upon clearly articulated rubrics and qualified and well-trained judges. Documenting that judges are able to carry out the scoring in ways consistent with the construct and measurement goals is an important aspect of score validity (Bejar, 2012; Kane, Crooks, & Cohen, 1999) and specifically addressed in the *Standards* (AERA, APA, & NCME, 2014, Standards 6.8, 6.9). There are a number of quality assurance processes and quality-control procedures that are utilized in human scoring of constructed responses (McClellan, 2010). Quality assurance processes include documentation of overall guidelines to be utilized for a particular assessment, clearly defined scoring rubrics, and a well-articulated scoring design (including length and content of scorer training, the frequency and types of scorer monitoring, roles and responsibilities of various stakeholders, etc.). Scorer training focuses on improving the consistency of scoring and reducing rater bias. Quality control procedures include specific techniques such as rater calibration (assessing and certifying raters before scoring begins), back-reading (having expert scorers rescore samples of scored papers), validity scoring (inserting previously scored papers that represent particular score points into the scoring process) and monitoring statistics (e.g., agreement rates and related statistics for papers scored by two or more raters). Because of the investment of time and resources needed to administer and score performance tasks, their use in credentialing tests should be considered carefully and supported by a strong content or construct validity argument.

*Automated Scoring*

When credentialing tests are administered by computer, one option to save time and expense with written performance tasks is to use automated scoring. Automated essay scoring approaches have been demonstrated to be as reliable as human scoring (Shermis & Burstein, 2003), and a number of automated scoring engines have been shown to reliably score essays that have a specific content basis (Landauer, Latham, & Foltz, 2003), such as would be represented by a particular profession. Most commonly operational automated scoring models are "calibrated" from a sample of human-scored responses. The structure of the calibration sample and associated scores can influence the quality of the calibration and subsequent automated scores, so these factors must be carefully considered. A comprehensive framework for evaluating and using automated scoring was proposed by Williamson, Xi, and Breyer (2012).

There are several examples of focused automated scoring approaches that have been successfully implemented for credentialing programs. Relatively early innovations in this area included simulations that were developed for licensure tests in architecture (Bejar & Braun, 1994), medicine (Clauser, Margolis, Clyman, & Ross, 1997; Melnick & Clauser, 2006) and accounting (Breithaupt, Mills, & Melican, 2006).

*Innovative and Technology-enhanced Items*

Although early innovative assessments in architecture, medicine, and accounting involved years of expensive research and development, the maturation of computer-based testing has made it possible to consider a more widespread use of innovative items and tasks in credentialing tests. There are varied definitions of the term, but it is generally agreed that innovative items are computer-based test items that cannot be easily translated to paper (Parshall, Davey, & Pashley, 2000). A more liberal definition of innovative item suggests some kind of performance or interaction by way of responding or, in some cases, before responding, regardless of whether the resulting response is "constructed" or selected from explicitly available options.

Several researchers have made efforts to classify innovative items. Parshall et al. (2000) proposed a framework in terms of five dimensions: item format, response action, media inclusion, level of interactivity, and scoring method, or algorithm. Scalise and Gifford (2006) described a taxonomy organized along the degree of constraint on the respondent's options for answering or interacting with the assessment item or task. Their taxonomy included 28 example types and 7 categories of ordering involving successively decreasing response constraints ranging from "fully selected" to "fully constructed." Each category of constraint included four representative examples that varied on level of complexity.

Operationally, innovative items can present scoring challenges because item types that are less constrained may not have clear and obvious scoring rules. Efforts in the computer-based assessment field to increase interoperability have led to industry recognized standards for the development and exchange of assessment items. One advantage of these interoperability standards is in providing common structures that can be used across practitioners and vendors to publish, process responses from, and generate scores for different types of computer-based items.

In general, the coming years should see expanded use of innovative items and tasks in credentialing tests. These applications will benefit from recent efforts focused on the use of templates to describe the interaction between a test taker and the item or task presented, the response data that result, and the approach for scoring the responses (Haertel et al., 2012; Parshall & Harmes, 2007). Such templates are designed to encourage efficiency and consistency in the development and scoring of technology-enhanced items.

## Raw Scores: Combining Results from Individual Items and Tasks

For many credentialing tests, total scores are based on a simple sum of the item and task scores. However, differential weighting schemes may sometimes be applied to reflect differential emphasis on specific content. For example, a teacher licensure test that included multiple-choice items and a written extended response item might assign more weight to the essay because of the importance of the task and because it is not feasible to include more than one of these items in the test. In this case, a weighted summed score would provide the basis for the pass/fail decision. Summed scores are usually most appropriate when the content of the test primarily measures a single construct. However, in this case, it is possible that high performance on one sub-area of the test can compensate for low performance on another sub-area.

## IRT-based Scores: Estimating Ability from a Pool of Calibrated Items and Tasks

Most credentialing tests are scored using item-response theory (IRT), which in some applications can result in different scoring weights across items, an approach sometimes referred to as "pattern scoring" (Yen & Candell, 1991). Applications of the two-parameter logistic (2PL), three-parameter logistic (3PL), and/or generalized partial credit (GPC) models can include pattern scoring, although these models can also be used to scale and equate tests based on summed or weighted summed scores. Many credentialing exams utilize the Rasch and Rasch Partial Credit (RPC) models; scoring based on these models is theoretically consistent with summed scoring. Besides differences in supporting pattern versus summed scores, different IRT models also differ in complexity, ease of use, and how well they are able to fit observed test data. For smaller credentialing programs with low candidate volumes, the simpler Rasch model tends to be more attractive because it has been found to be tractable in the presence of small sample sizes (Lord, 1983). All of these IRT models provide the ability to construct pools of calibrated items and tasks once items are administered. Utilizing a pool of calibrated items and tasks supports applications such as pre-equating, linear on-the-fly testing (LOFT), and computerized adaptive testing (CAT).

There are numerous examples of credentialing programs that utilize CAT, which is a form of computer-based testing that utilizes a pool of calibrated items and adapts the selection of items to the candidate ability level. Several of these CAT approaches involved providing different numbers of questions to candidates depending upon a statistical evaluation of performance relative to a cut score (Lewis & Sheehan, 1990; Spray & Reckase, 1994; Zara, 1999). However, most credentialing CAT programs employ fixed-length CAT approaches through which each candidate receives a unique set of items but all candidates see the same number of items. Some of the more recent CAT applications in credentialing have involved multistage adaptive testing (MST; cf. Breithaupt, Zhang, & Hare, 2014). In MST, a short section of items is administered together, and the test adapts by choosing easier or more difficult sections based on the candidate's estimated ability. Although MST places less of an emphasis on minimizing test length as compared to traditional CAT, it is still an efficient adaptive procedure. Because it is more similar to traditional testing, MST can retain valuable traditional testing features such as better controlling the administration of items associated with a common stimulus, the ability to implement comprehensive review of each section before it is to be administered, and providing candidates with options for reviewing and changing previous responses within each section (or "stage") of the test (Hendrickson, 2007; Luecht & Clauser, 2002).

Still another approach to computerized testing that has some similarities to CAT is LOFT (Stocking, Smith, & Swanson, 2000). With LOFT, the computer dynamically selects unique sets of items for each test-taker, each of which meets the same set of content and psychometric specifications.

## Scaled Scores: Combining Scores and Establishing Scaling Transformations

Scoring credentialing tests requires not only rules for combining scores across items and/or tasks to obtain a total score, but in some cases, rules may be needed for combining scores on sections or components into an overall composite. In nominal weighting, scores from multiple sections of a credentialing test are combined into a linear composite using weights that reflect policy judgments about the importance of each component relative to the others. Often, nominal weighting is chosen to increase the contribution of certain sections of a test that are limited in length or number of tasks that are feasible to administer. Nominal weights can be misleading because the variance of the composite score is determined by the variances and covariances of the sections or components in the test. As a result, the true or effective weight of each component may differ from the nominal weighting. In some cases, if mastery of each section of a credentialing test is considered important, a non-compensatory approach to making the pass/fail decision can be selected which would require candidates to achieve a minimum score on each section of the test in order to achieve an overall passing result.

It is important to report the scoring rules and procedures used to combine scores for credentialing tests to test takers before the test is administered (AERA, APA, & NCME, 2014, Standard 11.15). This documentation should be connected to the content specification analysis (see Chapter 4). For most credentialing tests, raw scores or IRT scores are transformed to scale scores to facilitate interpretation. In addition, the use of a scale, in conjunction with equating procedures, allows scores from different forms to be reported on the same scale across administrations. Typically, the range of desired scores is specified and the scores are rounded to integers.

Transformations from raw scores or IRT scores to the scale score metric are usually linear; although curvilinear transformations are certainly possible, they are typically not utilized with credentialing tests. Linear transformations can be fixed at two points; the pass/fail cut score is generally one of those points because it is desirable with a credentialing test to specify a particular value for the pass/fail cut score and to maintain that value across forms and over time.

The type of score used as the basis for setting the scale can affect the variability of the scale. For example, the standard error for scaled scores that are linear transformations of summed scores tends to be higher in the middle of the scale and lower at the ends of the scale. For linear transformations of IRT scores, the opposite tends to be the case—that is, standard errors tend to be lower in the middle of the scale and highest at the ends of the scale.

In making decisions about scale properties for credentialing tests, thought should be given to the scale properties in the vicinity of the pass/fail cut score. Kolen (2006) reviewed a variety of recommendations for determining the number of scale points on the test. Two of the "rules of thumb" could be applied given a test with an estimated reliability of about 0.90. For such a test, an interval of ±3 points around a score on a 60-point scale would include a candidate's true score approximately 68% of the time, and an interval of ±1 points around a score on a 30-point scale would include a candidate's true score approximately 50% of the time. According to Kolen (2006), these rules of thumb were the basis for the original decisions for number of score points on the SAT and ACT tests, respectively, and might be taken into account when establishing a new score scale for a credentialing test.

## Interpreting Scores on Credentialing Tests

As previously stated, the primary interest for users and stakeholders of credentialing tests is whether the candidate is *credential worthy*. This decision is driven (at least in part) by whether the candidate's obtained score on the credentialing test is above or below the cut score for determining pass/fail status. Thus, the key to defensible score interpretations in a credentialing framework lies in the nature of the cut score itself and, especially, in the process used to define it. This process, referred to as *standard setting*, is described below.

## Standard Setting

There are numerous standard setting methods described in the professional literature, although only a few of them enjoy frequent and widespread use in credentialing settings (Smith & Springer, 2009). Only those that are most appropriate for (and most commonly used in) credentialing settings are described below; the reader is referred to Cizek (2012) and Cizek and Bunch (2007) for a more thorough discussion of the topic. The following descriptions of these methods assume that a single cut score is being determined; most of the methods can readily be extended for those cases where it is necessary to separate candidates into more than two categories—e.g., *basic* or *below standard*, *proficient*, *advanced*—though the latter is a situation more likely to be observed in an educational setting than for a credentialing test.

### The Logic of Standard Setting

All standard setting methods share a set of common features and the same underlying logic (cf. Cizek, 2012; Cizek & Bunch, 2007). The basic assumption for the process is that there is some theoretical or underlying continuum of knowledge and skills that appropriately reflects that required for professional practice. Along that continuum, there is a point that distinguishes competence, or sufficient knowledge/skills, from lack of competence or a knowledge/skill level insufficient for safe or competent practice.

We cannot, of course, know for certain what a candidate's true position is on that underlying continuum; the purpose of any test and any observed test score is to estimate that value. The credentialing test, if developed according to best practices and with the credentialing goal clearly in mind, can be inferred to be a valid reflection of that continuum. The goal of standard setting, then, is to determine the point on the observed test-score scale that best maps onto the point on the underlying continuum that separates those who are credential worthy from those who are not. This point on the test-score scale is referred to as the *cut score* (or *cut point*), and candidates who score at or above the cut point are deemed to have passed the exam.

### The General Standard Setting Process

Common to all standard setting methods is a set of judges or subject-matter experts (SMEs) who are familiar with the job or practice requirements for those entering the profession (Loomis, 2012); they may be job incumbents and/or trainers or educators who are typically credentialed themselves. Importantly, SMEs who participate in the standard setting process for credentialing tests should regularly work with (or otherwise be familiar with the characteristics of) individuals in the target population (e.g., entry-level practitioners). Some testing programs make a point to include newly credentialed individuals as part of their panel of judges to ensure that the discussions and process are a realistic reflection of current training, expectations, and practice. This panel of judges is provided training in the standard setting process itself, the purpose of the credential, and the content of the test blueprint. The panel discusses and reaches consensus on what it means to be credential worthy or minimally competent as an entry-level practitioner in their particular profession; this conceptualization of minimal competence drives the rest of the standard setting process.

Depending on the specific standard setting method that is employed, each SME judge is then asked to make judgments regarding individual test items, individual candidates, and/or the candidate population as a whole. The SMEs may then be provided with feedback regarding other SMEs' judgments, the performance of candidates on those items, and/or the impact on the test's passing rate of various cut score decisions. The SME judgments are then combined in some manner, and the final result of the standard setting process is a recommended cut score for the credentialing test.

While this standard setting process is generally the same for credentialing tests as it would be for tests in other domains (K-12 education, for example), the unique features of the credentialing situation may drive differences in the meeting logistics (cf. Buckendahl & Davis-Becker, 2012). Specifically, the SME participants are typically recruited by credentialing programs precisely because they are employed professionals, and it is often difficult for them to commit to an activity that requires time away from work for both the standard setting meeting and the accompanying travel to a face-to-face meeting. Moreover, many credentialing programs are international in scope, so the meeting might also include participants from around the globe. These features can prove daunting for many programs—prohibitively so for technology-focused credentials where content changes rapidly and the test items and cut score may need to be revised every year or two. Consequently, many programs have turned to virtual meetings for their standard setting exercise, requiring them to address additional issues such as test security and how to effectively engage participants who are remote participants in the process (see, for example, Katz & Tannenbaum, 2014).

*Additional Considerations*

The cut-score recommendation is typically provided to a special committee or the Board of Directors of the test-sponsoring organization. The final determination of the test's cut score is, ultimately, a policy decision that appropriately considers, in addition to the results of the standard setting exercise, such factors as candidate normative information, economic pressures, and other profession-specific concerns.

For testing programs that administer conventional linear (i.e., form-based) tests, the standard setting process typically is based on the set of items contained on the individual test form(s). Standards for pool-based tests such as CAT or LOFT are typically based on a sample of items representative of those that might appear on any one candidate's test form.

Programs that maintain a consistent metric for all items and test scores (i.e., those that link all test items onto a common metric, or that equate test scores from year to year—see below), can employ the same IRT-based or scaled cut score on repeated administrations of the exam. The standard setting process needs to be repeated, however—and a new cut score needs to be set—when a new job or practice analysis has been conducted and the test blueprint is revised. For when the test blueprint changes, the underlying knowledge continuum is changed, and the point on that continuum that identifies the credential worthy candidates—and therefore the point on the observed test score scale that determines pass/fail status—may also change. Testing programs that do not maintain a consistent metric or scale for all items and test scores but, instead, "start from scratch" every time a new test form is deployed in the field, should repeat the standard setting process for each test form.

*An Important Caveat*

In all cases, it is important to note that the standard setting process, while defensible when employed thoughtfully and consistently, is necessarily imperfect. Classification errors will always occur: All test scores contain error and are fallible, so some candidates who are truly credential worthy may fail the exam, and some candidates who are not credential worthy may pass the exam. More to the point, different standard setting methods will likely yield different results (i.e., different recommended cut scores), and even the same standard setting method may yield a different result when used a second time with different items and/or a different set of judges.

The different classification errors that are an inevitable part of testing and the standard setting process may not be equally serious. In some situations, the effect of a false-positive error—passing and therefore licensing an incompetent surgeon, for example—may be quite harmful to the public at large, and a higher cut score may be warranted. In other situations, passing a candidate who is not credential worthy may be more acceptable than failing a qualified candidate and thereby denying that person an opportunity for employment—and a lower cut score may be more appropriate in that case.

Hence the earlier statement that the determination of a test's cut score is necessarily a policy decision, with the caveat that the responsible individuals need to be cognizant of the relative impact of classification errors and the fallible nature of test scores and standard setting—in addition to other concerns—when setting the official cut score for the credentialing test. In keeping with Standard 5.21 of the *Standards for Educational and Psychological Testing* (AERA, APA, & NCME, 2014), the rationale and all procedures for establishing the cut score should be clearly and fully documented.

*Angoff and Related Methods*

The most commonly used method for setting a cut score on a credentialing test is the Angoff method or one of its variations (Smith & Springer, 2009). In its original incarnation (Angoff, 1971), SME judges estimate whether the target candidate would answer the item correctly; that candidate would then receive a score of 0 or 1 (for an incorrect or correct response, respectively) on that item (cf. also Impara & Plake, 1997).

More commonly, judges are asked to provide estimates of the probability of the target candidate responding correctly to each item (or, equivalently, the proportion of target candidates who would respond correctly to each item). In its typical "modified" form, two or three rounds of ratings are made by each judge (again, with relevant feedback provided between rounds). The final ratings are averaged across judges; the items' average values are summed to yield the recommended raw cut score.

The Angoff methods are most typically applied to dichotomously scored selected-response item types (e.g., multiple-choice items); the process can also be extended to include item types with multiple-scale points, where the judges are asked to estimate the number of scale points that would be obtained by a target candidate. The method can also readily handle tests that contain a combination of those item types.

The Angoff methods are usually applied to intact test forms. However, they have also been utilized for pool-based exams that are rooted in IRT. In that case, the raw cut score would need to be transformed to the IRT-based theta metric; the IRT-based cut score can then be applied to any subsequent test score that is expressed on that metric, regardless of the specific set of items actually administered to the candidate.

In the Direct Consensus Method proposed by Sireci, Hambleton, and Pitoniak (2004), the test is organized into separate sections by content area, and judges are asked to estimate how many items would be answered correctly in each section by the target candidate. This process can be completed much more quickly and efficiently than can a full Angoff process, and therefore may be particularly appealing to smaller credentialing programs with limited resources. See Plake and Cizek (2012) for a fuller discussion of the various Angoff methods.

*Bookmark Method*

As originally conceived, the Bookmark method (Lewis, Mitzel, & Green, 1996; see also Lewis, Mitzel, Mercado, & Schulz, 2012) was based in item-response theory, and therefore appropriate for those testing programs that use IRT in the test-development process; it has since been extended and used successfully with the *p*-value statistics of Classical Test Theory (cf. Buckendahl, Smith, Impara, and Plake, 2002). For this method, items are printed in a test booklet (ordered easiest to hardest by item difficulty), one item per page. The judges' task is to answer the question, "is it likely that the minimally competent candidate will answer this item correctly?" and then to place a bookmark in the ordered item booklet after the last item for which the rating is "yes" (call it *the bookmarked item*). The recommended cut score for any individual rater is the ability value associated with a specified probability value corresponding to the bookmarked item. The mean of these individual cut scores, averaged across all raters, is taken to be the cut score of the test; this value may be transformed to raw- or scaled-score units.

The Bookmark method can be used for complex, mixed-format assessments. The task is relatively easy for participants to understand and to perform (since, unlike the Angoff methods, it does not require the SMEs to provide difficulty judgments for the individual test items). The method also has the advantage that it is not restricted to use with intact test forms and is therefore appropriate for pool-based CAT and LOFT exams.

*Body of Work*

The Body of Work method (Kingston & Tiemann, 2012) is a method of standard setting that requires judges to make holistic judgments about candidates' performance on a full work sample or exam (rather than on individual items), and is therefore particularly applicable to complex assessments that consist of constructed response or performance-based items or a combination of item formats. While typically used to classify candidates into multiple categories (e.g., *basic*, *proficient*, *advanced*), it can readily be applied to a single cut-off (pass/fail) situation.

**Score Interpretation**

As described above, a cut score is typically defined for a credentialing test so that a candidate who obtains a score at or above the cut (i.e., *passes the test*) can be said to be *credential worthy* or minimally competent to practice in the specified profession. Thus, the focus for score interpretation naturally and rightly shifts from the test-score continuum to the candidate's pass/fail status.

Take, for example, the case of a credentialing exam that is used as part of the process for determining whether the test-taker receives a license to practice medicine. It is important to remember that the entire test-development process was conducted in a manner to support the interpretation of a score as reflecting minimal competence as a physician. The content specifications (or test blueprint) were defined to reflect the scope of knowledges needed to ensure competence at the entry level of practice (in this case, to reflect the knowledge needed to practice medicine safely). As described above, the cut score specifies the level of test performance that reflects minimal competence at this entry level.

Thus, it would *not* be appropriate to expect that a high-scoring candidate would be a higher performing or better physician than a lower-scoring but passing candidate; the test was not designed or developed to predict job performance per se. While the high-scoring candidate may possess a greater level of knowledge than the lower-scoring candidate, the truth of the matter is that both of these candidates passed the test and both of them can be assumed to have the knowledge needed to avoid making costly and deadly errors (i.e., to be minimally competent as entry-level physicians)—which is, ultimately, what the stakeholder public really cares about.

## *Reporting Subscores*

Items on a credentialing test are typically analyzed and calibrated as a single unit and then combined into a single test score; this score, in turn, determines the candidate's final pass/fail status on the test and drives the inference of credential worthiness. The computation and provision of content-area subscores is, therefore, less likely to be driven by the demands of the credentialing process or the sponsoring organization itself than it is by the needs and desires of the candidate population. While a candidate who passes the test is likely to be content to receive a congratulatory message or the word *Pass* printed on a score report, a candidate who fails the test will want to receive more diagnostic information about his/her test performance and, specifically, will want to be provided with a succinct answer to the question "What do I need to study for next time?" The challenge for the test developer is to balance the needs of the candidate population with the realities of the testing paradigm. Additional challenges concern the effectiveness of the actual score reports; these challenges are taken up in more detail in Chapter 8.

Subscores tend to correspond to the content areas enumerated in the test blueprint, though in some cases they may be based on some other combination of test items. But regardless of their derivation, they are necessarily based on a relatively small number of items—and the more granular the desired report, the smaller the number of items used for any particular subscore. So one of the biggest problems with subscores is that the small numbers of items implies a corresponding unreliability of the subscores themselves and, by extension, of the interpretations thereof. Note that this problem cannot be resolved by overlapping the subscales and scoring items on more than one subscale (thereby increasing the number of items scored on each subscale); such an approach would confound the meaning of the individual subscores and thereby diminish the value of the diagnostic information.

The challenges with subscore reports go beyond the small numbers of items, however. In many testing programs, the subscores are not separately equated, nor is a separate standard of performance established for each subscore. Thus, there is no reason to believe that getting four out of five items correct on one subscale means the same thing (in terms of reflecting comparable levels of knowledge) as getting four out of five items correct on another subscale. Moreover, the comparison of performance trends for unequated raw subscores across multiple test forms is problematic.

Some of the problems inherent in raw scores can be resolved when advanced IRT models are used. In this case, separate IRT-based ability estimates can be computed for each separate subscale; given a set of appropriately calibrated and linked item parameters, the IRT-based ability estimates for the different subscales can be interpreted as being on a common metric. But even then, one is left with the question of how to provide meaningful diagnostic feedback to the candidate—specifically, what constitutes "poor" performance at the subscale level? One could assume that the (IRT-based) cut score for the full test applies to each of the subscores, but that assumption is likely not validated and therefore is tenuous at best.

Importantly, any suggestion that subscale results provide valid diagnostic information needs to be accompanied by relevant evidence in support of that claim (cf. Standard 1.15 of the *Standards* (AERA, APA, & NCME, 2014). Feinberg and Wainer (2014) recently provided a simple formula based on the work of Haberman (2008) and Sinharay (2010) that can be used to evaluate whether subscores are adding any value above and beyond the total score for a given test.

## Maintaining the Meaning of Credentialing Test Scores

No testing program can administer a single test form for an indefinite amount of time and across all testing conditions. Multiple test forms may need to be developed and available for failing candidates who take the test more than once; security issues may also demand the use of multiple test forms in a single testing window. Different candidates may need to take the test under different conditions or in different administration modes—on paper versus on a computer, for example. Trends in candidate performance may need to be tracked over long periods of time. In other words, there are numerous situations in which there is a bona fide need for scores to be compared across multiple test forms, multiple testing conditions, and/or across time. Thus, it is imperative that the inferences that are drawn from the test scores can be justified across all these situations.

### *Equating and Linking*

Smaller credentialing programs and programs that administer tests only during specific testing events may have a single test form that is operational at any one time. When tests are administered globally and/or during longer testing windows (from a few days to year-round and on-demand), programs typically deploy multiple forms simultaneously. Whenever it is necessary to compare test scores from one test form to another within a single test administration or across test administrations, it is generally necessary to establish that the forms are comparable and that the desired comparisons are meaningful and support unambiguous conclusions (cf. Standards 5.6 and 5.12). This process is termed *score equating*, and a successful equating process means that the test-taker is not unfairly disadvantaged by being administered a more difficult test form[1]—i.e., that it is a matter of indifference to the test-taker which form he/she is administered (Lord, 1980).[2] In a credentialing framework, successfully equated test forms ensure that the inference of credential worthiness is supported regardless of the specific test form that was administered.

The research on various equating designs and analyses is voluminous and unable to be adequately summarized here; see Kolen and Brennan (2014) for a comprehensive treatment of this subject. As noted by these authors, a variety of data-collection designs and statistical procedures are available for equating scores across multiple test forms, although the extent to which these various equating procedures are successful is largely a function of the specific characteristics of the individual testing program. Importantly, these authors recommend evaluating the effect of equating error on the subsequent test scores, and offer the following caution: "For any of these methods to be used appropriately, the test specifications, the data collected, and the standardization and quality control procedures should be adequate. Otherwise, not equating (or using identity equating) might be the preferred option" (p. 305).

*Data-collection Designs*

For example, the Common (or Anchor) Item and the Random (or Randomly Equivalent) Groups methods of equating are applicable when the testing program deploys multiple forms in the field at any one time. In both these designs, however, the number of candidates required for the equating study increases proportionally with the number of test forms for which the scores need to be equated. Thus, these designs may not be feasible for testing programs with low numbers of test takers.

When the need is to equate scores from different test forms over different administration periods, it is difficult to validate the assumption of equivalent groups in the absence of extra-test information; in that case, group differences in ability are inextricably confounded with differences in the difficulty of the test forms (cf. Standard 5.14 of the *Standards*). It may be for this reason that the Common Items design is frequently used for equating credentialing tests, though its use with groups that have widely varying ability may prove problematic, regardless of the statistical procedures used (Kolen & Brennan, 2014).

Tests containing performance tasks or other constructed response items pose additional hurdles for equating, among them the additional source of error if the tasks are human scored and the possibility of inadequate domain sampling and therefore non-comparable content because of the few numbers of tasks that can be placed on each form. Practical administrative constraints may make it difficult to employ the Single Group design or to justify the assumption of equivalent groups for the Random Groups design; it may not be feasible to construct an appropriately representative set of anchor items to employ the Common Items design. Many testing programs use mixed format tests and use only the multiple-choice items as anchors for Common Item equating; see Kolen and Brennan (2014) for a discussion of the conditions under which that is a viable approach.

*Statistical Equating Methods*

Small-volume testing programs would do well to use the mean and linear equating procedures based in Classical Test Theory—or the Rasch-based IRT methods if appropriate—particularly if the test forms to be equated are of similar difficulty and it is most important to have accurate scores near the mean score (i.e., at a single cut score located near the center of the score distribution). The circle-arc method of equating (Livingston & Kim, 2009; see also Dwyer, 2016) may be of value for some small-volume testing programs.

Large-volume programs have the flexibility to use Classical Test Theory-based equipercentile equating or the more complex (i.e., 3PL) IRT methods, which may provide greater accuracy all along the score scale.

Programs that have IRT-calibrated item pools (where the items are all linked together and scaled to a common metric) are able to pre-equate their test forms and produce a raw-score-to-scaled-score conversion table prior to test administration. This, in turn, allows candidates to receive their score reports (and pass/fail decisions) immediately upon the conclusion of a computer-administered test, enabling tests to be administered in extended testing windows or on an on-demand basis. The availability of calibrated item pools also enables programs to employ CAT and LOFT test designs.

Because the statistical analyses are conducted prior to (and not after) test administration, this paradigm also permits faster score reporting to candidates even with paper-based test forms.

## Comparability Across Modes of Administration

Generally speaking, the requirement for establishing comparability across test administration modes is no different for credentialing tests than it is for tests designed for other purposes (cf. Standards 4.5 and 5.17 in the *Standards*).

Historically, most of the research studies investigating this issue have involved a comparison of scores from paper-based and computer-based administrations. However, many high-stakes credentialing exams are now administered only on computer and only in tightly controlled test centers with comparable (if not identical) computer equipment. In that case, the comparability question becomes moot, particularly if items are calibrated and the cut score has been established using data collected from current computer administrations of the test.

The conventional wisdom states that when there has been careful attention paid to item construction and test layout issues, there is typically little difference in candidate test performance that can be attributed to mode effects (cf. Mead & Drasgow, 1993; Wang, Jiao, Young, Brooks, & Olson, 2007, 2008). It is likely to become even less of a concern in the future, as more testing programs begin to take greater advantage of available technology and employ item types that are not readily implemented on a paper form (e.g., drag-and-drop or more complex interactive item types)—that is, if fewer programs employ paper-based testing at all.

The focus of concern is beginning to shift from a paper-versus-computer comparison to a comparison across a variety of devices (e.g., desktop computer versus tablet). The move to test administration on mobile devices brings with it corresponding comparability concerns and greater implications for test design (Way, Davis, Keng, & Strain-Seymour, 2016). As always, the burden is on the test sponsor to demonstrate that it is immaterial to the candidate (in terms of final test scores) how and where the test is administered.

## Item Bank Maintenance

The issue of item bank maintenance is little different for credentialing tests than it is for tests used for other purposes, particularly where statistical issues are concerned. Ideally, a credentialing test program will have available a large set of operational items whose content and item statistics are current and accurate. The monitoring and maintenance of item content is discussed below; this section will discuss statistics-related issues only.

To facilitate the construction of new forms and the appropriate interpretation of the resulting test scores, programs whose statistical methods are rooted in IRT should, preferably, have a large bank of items that are appropriately calibrated and linked to a common metric. Such an item bank will also support the determination of (raw, scaled, and/or IRT-based) cut scores based on those forms (as discussed earlier).

Ideally, programs that rely on classical methods of test construction and analysis (presumably the smaller programs) would also have a bank of items that have already been pretested and that have the classical item statistics necessary to support the equating of test forms and the determination of cut scores. All sound and mature testing programs systematically pretest newly developed test items (typically embedded within the operational forms) so that the item bank can continually be refreshed with new content that reflects current professional practice.

## Monitoring Appropriateness of Test Content

The case for the validity of credentialing exams (i.e., the inference of credential worthiness) rests on an argument for the appropriateness of the test content. Thus, it becomes critical that item content be up to date, and that the test blueprint be appropriately reflective of current practice.

### *Currency of Item Content*

In practice, the appropriateness of individual test items is (and should be) evaluated regularly. In the case of testing programs that administer intact test forms, each form is typically reviewed by subject matter experts prior to its release to the field. This review is structured, in part, to identify and eliminate any item whose content may no longer reflect current practice. Programs with pool-based tests may need to review an entire operational pool prior to its deployment or, alternatively, institute another process to ensure timely and regular review of the item content.

For all programs, item databases should support search capability and/or sufficiently detailed content tags to permit the ready and immediate identification of items as might be needed—for example, for a medical test when a drug is taken off the market.

### *Job and Domain Analysis*

The test's content specifications (i.e., the test blueprint) are typically updated immediately following the completion of the job or practice analysis (see Chapter 4). Standard 4.24 of the *Standards* (AERA, APA, & NCME, 2014) dictates that test specifications be updated when new research data or testing situations warrant; rule-of-thumb guidelines suggest that a new job analysis be conducted every 3–7 years, depending upon how quickly the nature of the profession itself is changing.

Following the implementation of a new test blueprint, the items themselves should be recoded to reflect any changes in the content area specifications. If an entire content area has been eliminated from the new blueprint (and therefore should not appear on future tests), the corresponding items should be tagged as inactive or otherwise deleted from the operational item database.

## Summary

Tests used for credentialing purposes are designed to determine whether the essential knowledge and skills of a specified domain have been mastered by the candidate. The focus of performance standards is on levels of knowledge and performance necessary for safe and appropriate practice. Because of this, there are unique considerations regarding how scores are obtained and what they mean. This chapter addressed the estimation, interpretation, and maintenance of test scores for credentialing exams.

We began the chapter with a background discussion of the unique features of credentialing tests, focusing on how the purposes and contexts of credentialing testing differ from other testing applications. These differences in purpose and context set the stage for the processes used in scoring credentialing tests and maintaining the meaning of scores across test administrations. The chapter then provided a detailed discussion of options for scoring items and the aggregation of items to credentialing test scores, interpreting the scores in terms of the credentialing process through the critical process of setting and maintaining performance standards, and finally, discussed approaches to maintaining the meaning of scores across administration forms (i.e., equating, scaling, and linking).

Each of these interrelated processes is critical to establishing the fairness and legal defensibility of credentialing exams. Although estimating, interpreting, and maintaining the meaning of test scores on credentialing tests is executed once the tests are developed and administered, it is clear that the proper execution of these processes is inextricably linked to test design, underlying content specifications, and the intended uses of the credentialing test results.

## Notes

1. Note that equating involves adjusting scores for differences in test form difficulty; it is assumed that the test forms are comparable in terms of content (Kolen & Brennan, 2014).
2. An exception to this paradigm may be that of a credentialing program that chooses, instead, to set a new cut score each time a test is administered. Practical considerations aside, it may be difficult under this scenario to ensure that the resulting passing standards reflect the same underlying degree of competence over time.

## References

American Educational Research Association, American Psychological Association, & National Council on Measurement in Education (AERA, APA, & NCME) (2014). *Standards for educational and psychological testing*. Washington, DC: American Educational Research Association.

Angoff, W. H. (1971). Scales, norms, and equivalent scores. In R. L. Thorndike (Ed.), *Educational measurement* (pp. 508–600). Washington, DC: American Council on Education.

Bejar, I. I. (2012). Rater cognition: Implications for validity. *Educational Measurement: Issues and Practice, 31*, 2–9.

Bejar, I. I., & Braun, H. (1994). On the synergy between assessment and instruction: Early lessons from computer-based simulations. *Machine-Mediated Learning, 4*, 5–25.

Breithaupt, K. J., Mills, C. N., & Melican, G. J. (2006). Facing the opportunities of the future. In D. Bartram, & R. K. Hambleton (Eds.), *Computer-based testing and the Internet* (pp. 219–251). Chichester: Wiley & Sons.

Breithaupt, K. J., Zhang, O. Y., & Hare, D. R. (2014). The multistage testing approach to the AICPA Uniform Certified Public Accounting Examinations. In D. Yan, A. A. von Davier, & C. Lewis (Eds.), *Computerized multistage testing: Theory and applications* (pp. 343–354). Boca Raton, FL: Chapman & Hall/CRC.

Buckendahl, C. W., & Davis-Becker, S. L. (2012). Setting passing standards for credentialing programs. In G. J. Cizek (Ed.), *Setting performance standards: Foundations, methods, and innovations* (2nd ed., pp. 485–501). New York: Routledge.

Buckendahl, C. W., Smith, R. W., Impara, J. C., & Plake, B. S. (2002). A comparison of Angoff and Bookmark standard setting methods. *Journal of Educational Measurement, 39*, 253–263.

Cizek, G. J. (Ed.). (2012). *Setting performance standards: Foundations, methods, and innovations* (2nd ed.). New York: Routledge.

Cizek, G. J., & Bunch, M. B. (2007). *Standard setting: A guide to establishing and evaluating performance standards on tests*. Thousand Oaks, CA: Sage.

Clauser, B. E., Margolis, M. J., Clyman, S. G., & Ross, L. P. (1997). Development of automated scoring algorithms for complex performance assessments: A comparison of two approaches. *Journal of Educational Measurement, 34*, 141–161.

Darling-Hammond, L. (2010). *Evaluating teacher effectiveness: How teacher performance assessments can measure and improve teaching.* Center for American Progress. Retrieved from: https://scale.stanford.edu/system/files/teacher_effectiveness.pdf

Dwyer, A. C. (2016). Maintaining equivalent cut scores for small sample test forms. *Journal of Educational Measurement, 53*, 3–22.

Feinberg, R. A., & Wainer, H. (2014). A simple equation to predict a subscore's value. *Educational Measurement: Issues and Practice, 33*, 55–56.

Haberman, S. (2008). When can subscores have value? *Journal of Educational and Behavioral Statistics, 33*, 204–229.

Haertel, G. D., Cheng, B. H., Cameto, R., Fujii, R., Sanford, C., Rutstein, D., & Morrison, K. (2012, May). *Design and development of technology enhanced assessment tasks: Integrating evidence-centered design and universal design for learning frameworks to assess hard to measure science constructs and increase student accessibility.* Paper presented at the ETS Invitational Research Symposium on Technology Enhanced Assessments, Princeton, NJ.

Hendrickson, A. (2007). An NCME instructional module on multi-stage testing. *Educational Measurement: Issues and Practice, 26*, 44–52.

Impara, J. C., & Plake, B. S. (1997). Standard setting: An alternative approach. *Journal of Educational Measurement, 34*, 353–366.

Kane, M., Crooks, T., & Cohen, A. (1999). Validating measures of performance. *Educational Measurement: Issues and Practice, 18*, 5–17.

Katz, I. R., & Tannenbaum, R. J. (2014). Comparison of web-based and face-to-face standard setting using the Angoff method. *Journal of Applied Testing Technology, 15*, 1–17.

Kingston, N. M., & Tiemann, G. C. (2012). Setting performance standards using the body of work method. In G. J. Cizek (Ed.), *Setting performance standards: Foundations, methods, and innovations* (2nd ed.). New York: Routledge.

Kolen, M. J. (2006). Scales and norms. In R. L. Brennan (Ed.), *Educational measurement* (4th ed., pp. 155–186). Westport, CT: American Council on Education/Praeger.

Kolen, M. J., & Brennan, R. L. (2014). *Test equating, scaling, and linking: Methods and practices* (3rd ed.). New York: Springer.

Landauer, T. K., Latham, D., & Foltz, P. W. (2003). Automated scoring and annotation of essays with the Intelligent Essay Assessor. In M. D. Shermis & J. C. Burstein (Eds.), *Automated essay scoring: A cross-disciplinary perspective* (pp. 87–112). Hillsdale, NJ: Lawrence Erlbaum Associates.

Lewis, C., & Sheehan, K. (1990). Using Bayesian decision theory to design a computerized mastery test. *Applied Psychological Measurement, 14*, 367–386.

Lewis, D. M., Mitzel, H. C., & Green, D. R. (1996, June). Standard setting: A bookmark approach. In D. R. Green (Chair), *IRT-based standard setting procedures utilizing behavioral anchoring.* Symposium conducted at the Council of Chief State School Officers National Conference on Large-Scale Assessment, Phoenix, AZ.

Lewis, D. M., Mitzel, H. C., Mercado, R. L., & Schulz, E. M. (2012). The bookmark standard setting procedure. In G. J. Cizek (Ed.), *Setting performance standards: Foundations, methods, and innovations* (2nd ed., pp. 485–501). New York: Routledge.

Livingston, S. A., & Kim, S. (2009). The circle-arc method for equating in small samples. *Journal of Educational Measurement, 46*, 330–343.

Loomis, S. C. (2012). Selecting and training standard setting participants: State of the art policies and procedures. In G. J. Cizek (Ed.), *Setting performance standards: Foundations, methods, and innovations* (2nd ed.). New York: Routledge.

Lord, F. M. (1980). *Applications of item response theory to practical testing problems.* Hillsdale, NJ: Erlbaum.

Lord, F. M. (1983). Small N justifies Rasch model. In D. J. Weiss (Ed.), *New horizons in testing: Latent trait test theory and computerized adaptive testing* (pp. 51–61). New York: Academic Press.

Luecht, R. M., & Clauser, B. (2002). Test models for complex computer-based testing. In C. Mills, M. Potenza, J. Fremer, and W. Ward (Eds.), *Computer-based testing: Building the foundation for future assessments* (pp. 67–88). Mahwah, NJ: Erlbaum.

McClellan, C. (2010, April). *Quality assurance and control of human scoring*. Paper presented at the annual meeting of the National Council on Measurement in Education, Denver, CO.

Mead, A. D., & Drasgow, F. (1993). Equivalence of computerized and paper cognitive ability tests: A meta-analysis. *Psychological Bulletin, 114*, 449–458.

Melnick, D., & Clauser, B. (2006). Computer-based testing for professional licensing and certification of health professionals. In D. Bartram, & R. K. Hambleton (Eds.), *Computer-based testing and the internet* (pp. 163–185). Chichester: Wiley & Sons.

Norcini, J. J., & McKinley, D. W. (2007). Assessment methods in medical education. *Teaching and Teacher Education, 23*, 239–250.

Parshall, C. G., Davey, T., & Pashley, P. (2000). Innovative item types for computerized testing. In W. J. van der Linden & C. A. W. Glas (Eds.), *Computerized adaptive testing: Theory and practice* (pp. 129–148). Netherlands: Kluwer Academic Publishers.

Parshall. C. G., & Harmes, J. C. (2007). *Designing templates based on a taxonomy of innovative items*. In D. J. Weiss (Ed.). Proceedings of the 2007 GMAC conference on computerized adaptive testing. Retrieved from: www.psych.umn.edu/psylabs/CATCentral/

Plake, B. S., & Cizek, G. J. (2012). Variations on a theme: The modified Angoff, extended Angoff, and Yes/No standard setting methods. In G. J. Cizek (Ed.), *Setting performance standards: Foundations, methods, and innovations* (2nd ed., pp. 485–501). New York: Routledge.

Scalise, K., & Gifford, B. (2006). Computer-based assessment in E-learning: A framework for constructing "intermediate constraint" questions and tasks for technology platforms. *Journal of Technology, Learning and Assessment, 4*(6). Retrieved from: http://ejournals.bc.edu/ojs/index.php/jtla/issue/view/192

Shermis, M. D., & Burstein, J. C. (Eds.) (2003). *Automated essay scoring: A cross-disciplinary perspective*. Hillsdale, NJ: Lawrence Erlbaum Associates.

Sinharay, S. (2010). How often do subscores have added value? Results from operational and simulated data. *Journal of Educational Measurement, 47*, 150–174.

Sireci, S. G., Hambleton, R. K., & Pitoniak, M. J. (2004). Setting passing scores on licensure examinations using direct consensus. *CLEAR Exam Review, 15*, 21–25.

Smith, I. L., & Springer, C. C. (2009). Standard setting. In J. Knapp, L. Anderson, & C. Wild (Eds.), *Certification: The ICE Handbook* (2nd ed.). Washington, DC: ICE.

Spray, J. A., & Reckase, M. D. (1994, April). *The selection of test items for decision making with a computer adaptive test*. Paper presented at the national meeting of the National Council on Measurement in Education, New Orleans, LA.

Stocking, M. L., Smith, R., & Swanson, L. (2000). *An investigation of approaches to computerizing the GRE subject tests* (ETS Research Report RR-00-04; GREB-93-08P). Princeton, NJ: Educational Testing Service.

Wang, S., Jiao, H., Young, M. J., Brooks, T. E., & Olson, J. (2007). A meta-analysis of testing mode effects in Grade K–12 mathematics tests. *Educational and Psychological Measurement, 67*, 219–238.

Wang, S., Jiao, H., Young, M. J., Brooks, T. E., & Olson, J. (2008). Comparability of computer-based and paper-and-pencil testing in K-12 reading assessments: A meta-analysis of testing mode effects. *Educational and Psychological Measurement, 68*, 5–24.

Way, W. D., Davis, L. L., Keng, L., & Strain-Seymour, E. (2016). From standardization to personalization: The comparability of scores based on different testing conditions, modes, and devices. In F. Drasgow (Ed.), *Technology and testing: Improving educational and psychological measurement* (pp. 260–284). New York: Routledge.

Weiner, I. B., Schmitt, N. W., & Highhouse, F. (2013). *Handbook of psychology: Industrial and organizational psychology* (Vol. 12). Hoboken, NJ: Wiley.

Williamson, W. M., Xi, X., & Breyer, F. J. (2012). A framework for evaluation and use of automated scoring. *Educational Measurement: Issues and Practice, 31*, 2–13.

Yen, W. M., & Candell, G. L. (1991). Increasing score reliability with item-pattern scoring: An empirical study in five score metrics. *Applied Measurement in Education, 4*, 209–228.

Zara, A. R. (1999). Using computerized adaptive testing to evaluate nurse competence for licensure: Some history and a forward look. *Advanced Health Science Education: Theory and Practice, 4*, 39–48.

# 7 Data and Scale Analysis for Credentialing Examinations

*Richard M. Luecht*

Data analysis serves a critical role in examination processing, from estimating the statistical item characteristics used in test assembly and standard setting through score scale development and maintenance, and score reporting. This chapter provides an overview of the primary analysis steps and types of data used in processing credentialing examinations, together with common scenarios, challenges, and solutions typically encountered in practice. Industry standard data analysis methods are described with examples of how these methods can be implemented in practice for both small- and large-scale applications.

This chapter is organized to cover four relatively broad data analysis steps needed to process most types of credentialing examination programs: 1) data preparation; 2) item analysis; 3) scale analysis; and 4) examinee scoring and reporting. Obviously, these steps will differ in their specific scope and implementation details for different organizations and given the mode of test delivery—for example, paper-and-pencil or computer-based tests—in the types of items or assessment tasks used, and in the way that the score scale(s) are developed and maintained over time.

This chapter also discusses some of the essential quality control systems and procedures for exchanging data across processing systems used by many credentialing test programs, including data cleaning and reconciliation methods for ensuring the integrity of the data inputs. Specific attention will also be paid throughout the chapter to pragmatic issues that impact data and scale analysis for credentialing examination programs (e.g., small-to-moderate sample sizes, somewhat high pass rates, relatively homogeneous populations, and the potential use of performance item types and technology enhanced/enabled item types).

## Data Preparation

The data preparation step involves data extraction, data cleaning and data reformatting procedures—that is, getting the data ready to be analyzed. Most credentialing examination organizations or their vendors are likely to maintain specialized databases to store the detailed information about the items, test forms, examinees, and examinee's responses. Those database forms are usually not convenient for analysis. Instead, one or more data *queries* are executed to extract the data from one or more larger databases. The data resulting from those queries often needs to be further reshaped into formats that can be input to various analytical software programs.

### The Importance of Strong Data Quality Control

Even a relatively small-scale credentialing examination program may require somewhat elaborate processing and quality control systems comprising many operational components, including item and content data management, test assembly and composition, examinee eligibility, registration, scheduling, test delivery, item analysis and key validation, specialized psychometric analyses such as differential item functioning (DIF) analysis, item response theory (IRT) item calibrations and linking studies, statistical equating of the score scales to a common metric, test scoring, and reporting.

Credentialing examinations come in many varieties ranging from knowledge tests using multiple-choice and other selected-response formats to complex performance simulations or work-sample tasks (see Chapters 1 and 3). The examinations may also be administered in either paper-and-pencil or computer-based testing (CBT) formats. The latter raises the possibility of a credentialing examination adopting any of several varieties of test design, including pre-assembled fixed test (PFT) forms, linear-on-the-fly test (LOFT), item-level computerized adaptive testing (CAT), or many types of adaptive multistage testing (MST) designs (Drasgow, Luecht & Bennett, 2006; Folk & Smith, 2002; Luecht & Sireci, 2011; Sands, Waters, & McBride, 1997; Zenisky, Hambleton, & Luecht, 2010).

The choice of test design and test administration/delivery have serious implications for how and when the data are processed, as well as the nature and extent of the data generated. For example, examination programs using paper-and-pencil PFT forms can limit their testing exposure to a small number of testing events each year. A relatively small number of PFT forms can be constructed and administered as intact units and all the data can typically be processed at the same time, following the test administration event. In contrast, LOFT and CAT examinations employ real-time test assembly over an expanded period of time—especially for larger credentialing examination programs that cannot simultaneously accommodate all their examinee population on a limited number of testing dates at CBT sites. The real-time test assembly introduces some rather complex quality control and data-processing challenges (e.g., reconciling the data coming in and periodically processing sparse data from an ongoing stream of data continuously flowing in from CBT sites in multiple locations).

High-quality data analysis begins with ensuring the absolute integrity of the data. Data integrity refers to both the secure storage and transmittal of the data as well as its accuracy given various transformations and reformatting operations. A thorough description of data security, but would include protection of the data sources against unauthorized access or tampering, backups, and data encryption. This chapter focuses on the integrity of data structures.

It may seem counterintuitive to state, but data has no inherent *structure*. Rather, we (data management specialists and psychometricians) can impose structure on the data for various purposes. Some structures are convenient and/or easy to use from a data analysis perspective, but may lack proper data integrity safeguards. Unless the data structures are designed to be robust and constantly checked to ensure the veracity of the data, any subsequent analyses of a particular data set may be wrong or at best, misleading. Two simple scenarios can help illustrate this point.

*Scenario 1*

Suppose that we typically analyze the data for a test using a *person by item (p × i) raw response matrix* where items are represented by columns and examinees are represented by rows. Figure 7.1 shows a rather typical response matrix layout for a relatively short, 20-item test where the selected-response entries (A, B, C, D, or E) might correspond to one-best answer multiple-choice (MC) items. This type of matrix might be used for item analysis (discussed further on). Only the first eight examinee records (rows) are shown in

```
001    CCDAECDDCDCEDCBCBDCC
002    CCDAECDCCDCECCCCDDBC
003    CEEAECECAECABCEACDBC
004     CDAECDDCDCEDCBCBDCC
005    BCBAACEDCBBDEEBCDBBD
006    BEDAECDDCDCEDCBCBDDC
007    DCDAECDECDCEACBC
008    CADAECDDCDCECCBCBDDC
```

*Figure 7.1* A $p \times i$ Raw Response Matrix for a 20-Item MCQ Test

this response matrix. The first three columns provide an assigned examinee number. The raw responses begin in the sixth column.

While we might *assume* that each column of responses corresponds to a particular item, can we be absolutely sure of that? For example, person #004 appears to have omitted item #1 and person #007 appears to have omitted items #17–20. However, what if we had inadvertently moved person #004's responses one position to the right and dropped the response to item #20? And what if person #007 had actually omitted four other items, but we inadvertently eliminated the spaces and left justified the response string? In both cases, we would be analyzing the *wrong* data. The need for continual quality control (QC) and quality assurance (QA) procedures to ensure the integrity of the data cannot be overemphasized, regardless of the stakes of a credentialing program, the number of examinees, or the test length.

*Scenario 2*

A statistical item analysis (IA) is carried out to verify the answer keys for a multiple-choice testing program with two active test forms, Form A and Form B. Some of the same (common) items are used on both forms. The IA is carried out separately for each test form and we discover that item #10 on Form B is miskeyed (e.g., the current keyed answer is "B", but the actual correct answer is "C"). Because of time pressures, we manually change the answer key in the key file used for the IA and rerun our analysis. We send an email to the test development staff to change the answer key in the item database. Everything looks great. But what if item #10 was one of the common items on Form A? The proper procedure would have been to ensure the answer key change in the master item database, regenerate the answer keys (and possibly) the response data, and then rerun the IA.

These two scenarios are not at all uncommon. Without proper QC/QA steps and effective operational policies and procedures in place, data errors will occur. Hopefully, procedures are in place to prevent them where possible and catch the errors before they impact scores or credentialing decisions. There are probably one or two testing organizations that boldly claim to never have data integrity problems. There are two possible explanations for that claim: 1) the testing program's QA and QC procedures are so incredibly thorough that their data error rates mirror those of the best banking institutions processing high-stakes financial transactions; or 2) they never bother to look for errors and just assume that everything is okay.

### *Scoring Evaluators and Measurement Opportunities*

Most people are familiar with how a multiple-choice (MC) item is scored. The examinee's response choice on the item is compared to the stored answer key. If the choice and

126  Richard M. Luecht

answer match, the examinee gets one point; otherwise, no points. However, this same type of scoring does not necessarily generalize to constructed response items, performance-based items, or some of the new classes of technology-enhanced (TE) items emerging to take advantage of computer-based test delivery.

It is helpful to reconceptualize the process of generating scored responses as one of applying *scoring evaluators* to *measurement opportunities* (Luecht, 2005, 2007). A *measurement opportunity* (MO) is merely a selection, an entry, or an action performed by the examinee that we wish to score. Not everything the examinee does necessarily results in a MO. *Scoring evaluators* are procedures, rules or other mechanisms that apply specified evaluative criteria to the MOs to produce an item score. Even human scorers applying a rubric to score essays can be considered scoring evaluators.

MOs tend to fall into broad classes: selected- and constructed-response MOs. Selected-response (SR) MOs include MC responses, binary selections such as true–false or alternate-choice items, and extended matching items that require the examinees to make one or more selections from one or more lists. CBT has further expanded the array of selected-response MOs, adding functional descriptions like *hot-spot* items, *drag-and-drop* items, *build-list-and-reorder* items, and *create-a-tree* items (e.g., Luecht, 2001; Zenisky & Sireci, 2002; Parshall, Harmes, Davey & Pashley, 2010). SR MOs are characterized by providing the examinees with one or more fixed list of options and some type of SR mechanism (e.g., using a pencil to fill in the appropriate "bubble" on a MC answer sheet, clicking on an area of the computer screen to indicate the response choice, dragging appropriate "connectors" to designate various types of relationships between two or more network nodes).

In contrast to SR items, constructed-response (CR) items do not incorporate fixed lists of alternatives or other response choices. Instead, CR MOs usually require the examinee to provide an entry in response to a prompt or otherwise carry out a designated set of actions (e.g. filling in a blank, using a text editor to compose memo, entering values in a spreadsheet). CR items can also employ highly interactive applications that track a series of activities the examinee performs or that yield complex work products. CR MOs can theoretically produce an enormous number of possible responses. It seems convenient to use a formulaic expression to distinguish between the measurement opportunities that collect the response or process data from the examinee and the scoring evaluator that converts the responses to a SR or CR score.

Let $m_i(v_{pi})$ denote the data acquired from examinee $p$ using a particular measurement opportunity collection mechanism(s) for item $i$. Further, let $a_i$ be the answer key, rubric or other scoring evaluator used by a simple pattern match (SPM) scoring evaluator for item $i$. A single answer key scoring evaluator can now be written as

$$y_{pi} = SPM\left[m_i(v_{pi}), a_i\right] \qquad (7.1)$$

Selected-response MOs can directly use this type of pattern-matching scoring evaluator. For example, a typical MC item might have a response-capturing mechanism or measurement opportunity that allows the examinees to select only one answer from the list of five available distractors, A to E. The examinee selects option "D", which happens to be the correct answer. Using Equation 7.1 to represent a simple pattern matching (SPM) algorithm, the scoring rule would resolve to $y_{pi} = 1$ if $m_i(v_{pi}) = $ "D" and $a_i = $ "D" match or $y_{pi} = 0$, otherwise. More complicated scoring rules often require more sophisticated measurement opportunities and scoring evaluators. A moderately complex scoring evaluator may need to resolve rather complex logical comparisons involving conjunctive rules such as $a_i = $ "A or B and NOT(C OR E)", or a set of network node connections such as

$a_i$ = "*connect* ($node_3$,$node_5$; $link_2$) and *connect* ($node_3$,$node_7$; $link_4$) and *connect* ($node_7$,$node_9$; $link_5$)", where the nodes are types of relationship links are treated as discrete objects. When the examinee's response involves multiple selections from the list of options, the number of combinations of MOs and answer data can become very large.

There are numerous and highly sophisticated types of scoring evaluators that can be implemented for CR items. CR scoring evaluators can range from simple matching algorithms that compare the test taker's response to an idealized answer set of responses, including "tolerances" from the idealized responses, or even automated scoring algorithms using linguistic analysis, neural nets or artificial intelligence algorithms and logic (Luecht, 2005). As noted above, human scores using rating rubrics can also be considered to be part of the system of scoring evaluators.

## Scope and Types of Assessment Data

It is easy to underestimate the nature and amount of data to be analyzed for even a relatively small credentialing examination program. Modern data specialists often refer to various unique data components as *entities*. In the world of assessment, the typical entities of interest are the examinees, registrations or sessions, test forms, and items or other assessment tasks. However, there are also more subtle entities to consider. For example, when a particular examinee responds to a particular item, he or she produces a "transaction" that is usually characterized as a raw response. Each of these transactions is likewise an entity from a data perspective.

The concept of an *entity* is extremely useful in data management. Each entity is considered unique from other entities and can be correspondingly distinctively identified in even an enormous collection of data, as long as we retain the entity of every item and examinee. If we consider the earlier example, items were supposedly "identified" by their relative column position in the record. That type of positional identification scheme tends to lack integrity.

Entities are often related to other entities (e.g., belonging to the same class or group such as 50 items uniquely assigned to Form Z04B). Most entity relations fall into one of three classes: 1) hierarchical relationships (usually characterized as "parent–child–cousin" associations); 2) one-to-one relationships by a data field or category reference; or 3) one-to-many relationships (e.g., one examinee to many items). Finally, entities often have various *properties*. For example, Test Form Z04B may have a set of instructions, the number and list of associated items, timing instructions, and other test administration data. Sometimes the entity properties are relevant to data analysis; sometimes not. What is important is to have a clear set of documented structures for all entities, as well as their properties and relations.

In general, there are six types of data entities used to identify various types of credentialing examination data: 1) the examinees; 2) the test forms; 3) any item sets or groups; 4) items and other assessment tasks; 5) item subcomponents such as MCQ distractor options or other scorable responses or identifiable actions—that is, measurement opportunities; and 6) the unique transaction between the examinee and the item and/or item subcomponents—what the examinee provides in response to each task challenge. From an examination processing perspective, the database/information technology jargon used here is less important than understanding and explicitly documenting the types of data needed, the required data structures and the nature of the relationships among the structured data. And perhaps most importantly, there needs to be convenient and high-integrity data queries and export capabilities for extracting and appropriately formatting the data as needed for analysis purposes.

Credentialing examination programs that may be transitioning toward increased use of performance-based tasks and technology-enhanced test items may further need to plan for changes in the nature of the item subcomponents and examinee "transactions". Those will almost certainly become more elaborate, possibly requiring innovative scoring and analysis procedures. As long as robust structures are created for the data, however, the additional complexity associated with more elaborate entities should be relatively straight-forward to manage.

## *Creating Flexible Data Extraction Views for Data Analysis*

A data view is a particular choice of a stylized output format for the data. Well-designed database structures can produce different data views to accommodate multiple analysis and reporting needs. It is important to understand that the data should reside in a primary location—the master or *single-source database*. It is extracted using a carefully designed data view for various purposes. For example, Figure 7.2 shows the behind-the-scenes data table extractions needed to generate a simple person-by-item raw response file.

Consider a rather common scenario where we need to create a data extraction view for analyzing all the raw data for two 50-item forms of a test. Form A is taken by 290 examinees and Form B is taken by 310 examinees. Furthermore, ten of the items are shared (common) between Forms A and B. Under this scenario and depending on the type of analysis we wanted to carry out, we could create two separate $p \times i$ analysis files: a 290 record by 50-item file for Form A and a 310 by 50-item file for Form B. Or we could create one larger 600 by 90-item file that combines the two forms and allows the item data to be combined across forms.

Figure 7.3 shows a "transactional" data extraction view that could accommodate either of those scenarios. Each row in the extracted data table contains the examinee identifier, the item identifier, the sequence in which the item was presented, and the examinee's

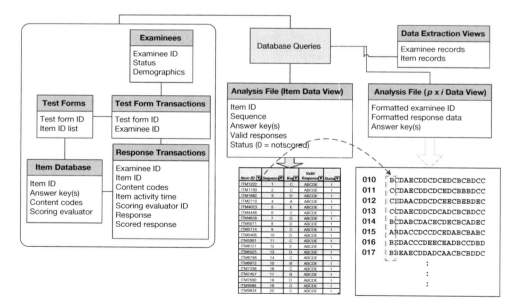

*Figure 7.2* Processing Entities to Produce an Analysis File

| Examinee ID | Item ID | Sequence | Response |
|---|---|---|---|
| PER0001 | ITM0038 | 1 | C |
| PER0001 | ITM0134 | 2 | D |
| PER0001 | ITM0140 | 3 | B |
| PER0001 | ITM0146 | 4 | A |
| PER0001 | ITM9909 | 49 | C |
| PER0001 | ITM9954 | 50 | A |
| PER0290 | ITM0038 | 1 | C |
| PER0290 | ITM0134 | 2 | B |
| PER0290 | ITM0140 | 3 | B |
| PER0290 | ITM0146 | 4 | A |
| PER0290 | ITM9909 | 49 | D |
| PER0290 | ITM9954 | 50 | A |
| PER0291 | ITM0884 | 1 | A |
| PER0291 | ITM1031 | 2 | D |
| PER0291 | ITM1071 | 3 | B |
| PER0291 | ITM1144 | 4 | D |
| PER0291 | ITM9909 | 49 | B |
| PER0291 | ITM9954 | 50 | A |
| PER0600 | ITM0884 | 1 | A |
| PER0600 | ITM1031 | 2 | D |
| PER0600 | ITM1071 | 3 | C |
| PER0600 | ITM1144 | 4 | D |
| PER0600 | ITM9909 | 49 | B |
| PER0600 | ITM9954 | 50 | A |

*Figure 7.3* Item Responses Extracted for 600 Examinees on One of Two 50-Item Forms

response to that item. In its complete form, the data table would have 3,000 records (50 items for each of 600 examinees).

There are alternative formats to Figure 7.3. However, the "normalized" structure in Figure 7.3 is preferred because it is a highly efficient way to store the data (i.e., minimizes redundancy) and explicitly ties the response data, including possible timing data and activities to a particular examinee on a particular item.

However, efficient data storage structures may not always be convenient for analysis purposes. It is therefore important to create standardized, reusable data extraction queries and formats. That way, the input data can be reliably produced for the analysis software. (Note: the same basic data extraction view shown in Figure 7.3 would work equally well for a paper-and-pencil test with fixed item positions or for a computer-based test with randomized item positions. This "data view" would therefore be reusable.)

## Item Analysis

Item analyses (IAs) serve two purposes. One purpose is to validate the answer keys or rubrics. Despite our best efforts to design and write effective test items, problems unanticipated by the item writers can occur. For example, miskeyed item answers or items with a secondary correct answer may be difficult for test developers to catch initially. An IA helps to statistically detect those unanticipated problems, hopefully before final scores or certification decisions are made. Key validation is also relevant in regulated industries where laws may frequently change (e.g., an answer key that was correct during pretesting may become incorrect after pretesting, or another distractor option becomes a second, correct answer key). The second purpose is to provide item difficulty and various other statistical indices that relate to the psychometric quality of the individual test items. These indices can be useful for detecting problematic items that warrant additional review. They can also help item writers and test development staff improve their designs of future items (e.g., perhaps trying to model the stylistic characteristics of items that work well and modifying aspects of specific types of items that do not behave as expected). The statistical indicators obtained from an IA can be uploaded to a statistical item database and used for building test forms in the future or as part of a standard setting exercise where the standard setting panel needs to consider the statistical performance of the individual test items.

## *Typical IA Statistical Indices*

Most IAs are carried out using commercially available or proprietary statistical software. There is also a growing user-base of open-source IA software applications written for the R programming language (e.g., Willse & Shu, 2008).

Two common types of indicators are item difficulty and item discrimination (Allen & Yen, 1979; Crocker & Algina, 1986; Schmeiser & Welch, 2006). Item difficulty is useful for understanding whether the item is at a suitable level of difficulty for the intended purpose of the test. Item discrimination indices are used in answer key validation as well as to evaluate the degree to which the scored item responses on a particular item are related to the examinees' performance on the rest of the test. The term "discrimination" is used to denote appropriate separation of the examinees along the score scale—that is, items that discriminate well do a very good job of helping to distinguish lower and higher performance on the score scale.

Probably the most common statistical item difficulty index used in an IA is the item mean—that is, item difficulty can be represented as a simple average or mean statistic aggregated for each item. Higher averages indicate easier items. Summing over examinees, the item mean can be written as

$$\mu(y_i) \doteq \bar{y}_i = \frac{\sum_{j=1}^{N} y_{ji}}{N_i} \qquad (7.2)$$

where "$\doteq$" implies that the population mean score of interest for item $i$ "is estimated" by the average score computed for a sample of examinees with valid scores ($N_i$). The notational indexing scheme used here $i = 1,\ldots, n$ items and $j = 1,\ldots, N$ examinees. The item means can also be computed "conditionally"—that is, restricting the sample to a subset of the larger group. In a credentialing examination situation, for example, we might want to see how difficult the items are for examinees grouped by level of experience. Conditional means are also useful for computing certain types of "discrimination" indices and for displaying item-level results as a function of total-test performance, as discussed further on.

If the items are scored using a binary scoring evaluator—for example, for common one-best answer multiple-choice or similar selected-response items score such that $y_i = 1$ if examinee gets an item correct, or $y_i = 0$ otherwise—the item mean in Equation 7.1 is mathematically equivalent to the proportion of correct response on item $i$, and is more commonly called a "p-values". For example, if 90% of the examinees get a particular item correct $\bar{y}_i = p_i = .9$; the item considered to be quite easy. If only 30% of the examinees get an item correct, the item p-value of $p_i = .3$ would suggest that the item is very difficult.

An item mean can also be used to denote the difficulty of constructed response items and other items that use multi-point scoring evaluators—often called polytomously scored items, where $y_i = \{0, 1, \ldots, y_i^{[max]}\}$. However, having a maximum number of points greater than one complicates interpretation. Therefore, the item mean for polytomously scored items may be normalized by dividing the mean by the maximum possible points as follows:

$$\mu(y_i) \doteq \bar{y}_i = \frac{\sum_{j=1}^{N_i} y_i}{N_i y_i^{[max]}} \tag{7.3}$$

where $N_i$ is the number of valid responses to item $i$.

If test scores are to vary, it is important that the examinees likewise vary in their responses to the items. The variance of the scores for an item is

$$\sigma^2(y_i) \doteq s_i^2 = \frac{\sum_{j=1}^{N_i}(y_{ij} - \bar{y}_i)^2}{N_i}. \tag{7.4}$$

The square root of the variance is the item standard deviation, $s_i$. If the items use a binary (dichotomous) scoring evaluator, the estimator of the standard deviation simplifies to a function of the item p-value, $s_i = \sqrt{p_i(1-p_i)}$.

Another useful statistic is the item-total correlation. As noted below, there are actually different types of item-total correlations that go by names like point-biserial correlations or biserial correlations. However, despite formulaic differences, the function of these correlations in an IA is essentially to demonstrate the strength of statistical association between performance on each item and scores on the rest of the test.

Correlations are statistical measures of association between pairs of variables that range from −1.0 to +1.0, where values near zero imply little or no [linear] relationship between. Values near +1.0 denote a nearly perfect linear association and values near −1.0 denote a nearly perfect inverse relationship. In testing, we typically want very high correlations between the items. That is, psychometrically speaking, we want items that "hang together." In fact, the overall score scale reliability will tend to increase in direct proportion magnitude of the inter-item correlation and the number of items on the test. (The concept of scale *reliability* is discussed further on.)

However, inter-item correlations are somewhat inconvenient to work with, especially for moderate to long tests because of the sheer number of correlations generated—which, for a k-length test is $[k(k-1)]/2$ unique pairwise correlations. For example, a 25-item test would have 300 unique pairwise correlations to consider. In contrast, most IAs will typically only compute one or two item-total correlations per item.

As the name implies, an item-total correlation is a measure of [linear] association between the responses on a particular item and all other items—*considered* in aggregate as a "total score." The subject item is usually excluded for the total score to prevent artificially inflating the correlation coefficient. Ideally, we would like to see all items having extremely high positive item-total correlations—that is, values near to one. That is not always possible. The nature of the response data and "variance restriction" can deflate a correlation coefficient. For example, easy items with *p*-values (item means, described above) near one, or difficult items with *p*-values nearer to zero, have restricted variation in the responses. For example, if everyone gets an item correct there is *no* variation. In that case, it is relatively easy to show that the correlation will be zero as well.

There are several types of item-total correlations typically used in most IAs. A Pearson product-moment correlation between is probably the most popular. Using our variables and indexes for items and examinees from above, the product-moment correlation between a scored item response at the total score can be written in as

$$r(y_i, \Upsilon) = r_{i,\Upsilon} = \frac{N_i \sum_{j=1}^{N_i} y_{ij} \Upsilon_j - \left(\sum_{j=1}^{N_i} y_{ij}\right)\left(\sum_{j=1}^{N_i} \Upsilon_j\right)}{\sqrt{\left[N_i \sum_{j=1}^{N_i} y_{ij}^2 - \left(\sum_{j=1}^{N_i} y_{ij}\right)^2\right]\left[N_i \sum_{j=1}^{N_i} \Upsilon_j^2 - \left(\sum_{j=1}^{N_i} \Upsilon_j\right)^2\right]}} \tag{7.5}$$

The total-score variable $Y_j$ is simply the sum of the item scores for each examinee. In practice it is important to "correct" the total score by removing the influence of the subject item on the correlation. That is, $\Upsilon_i = \sum_{h \neq i} y_h = \sum_{h=1}^{n} y_h - y_i$. Otherwise, the product-moment correlation will be artificially inflated.

We would like the item-total correlations to be as large as possible, where 1.0 is the maximum possible value. However, because of the variance restriction noted above, easier tests—including many certification tests that tend to pass a large percentage of the examinee population—will have lower item-total correlations, on average. Correlations near zero and especially negative correlations are never acceptable, even if the content of the items is deemed "essential".

When this product-moment correlation is computed between an assumed "continuous" total score and a binary response, it is called a *point-biserial correlation* (and the computational formula also simplifies a bit because of the zero-one item scores). If the binary scored item response is further assumed to be based on a normally distributed variable that is artificially dichotomized by the scoring evaluator, a different type of correlation can be computed called a *biserial correlation* (Allen & Yen, 1979). If the assumptions under their use hold, biserial correlations somewhat correct for the variance restriction noted above for difficulty items with very low *p*-values or easy items with very high *p*-values. In general, biserial correlations are higher in magnitude than point-biserial correlations. Therefore, when biserial correlations are used, it is important to adjust the flagging criterion (discussed in the next section) to a higher value. For example, if items are flagged for review whenever the point-biserials are below 0.10, the corresponding critical flagging value for biserial correlations would need to be at .21 or even higher, depending on the difficulty of the items. (Also note that there is an analog to the biserial correlation called a *polyserial* correlation that can be used for polytomous scores—i.e., scores covering three or more ordered point categories.)

Another useful item discrimination statistic that is very simple to compute (even for small samples) is called the "item discrimination index." First, we need to separate the examinees into three performance groups: lower ($L$), moderate ($M$) and upper ($U$), based on their total scores, $Y_j$. For example, we might assign the lowest one-third of the examinees to group L, the middle third to Group M and the upper one-third to the Group U. The item discrimination index can now be computed as

$$d_i = \frac{\sum_{j \in U} y_{ij} - \sum_{j \in L} y_{ij}}{N_i} = p_{i,U} - p_{i,L} \tag{7.6}$$

Although an item-total correlation is usually preferred to the discrimination index, $d_i$ can also be useful to detect miskeyed items—that is, if the group L performs better than the upper performing group, $d_i$ will be negative and can be used to flag the item (Kelley, 1939).

Table 7.1 shows selected IA results for a 50-item multiple-choice test with five options per item (A to E). The column labels describe each of the item statistics: the item means (p-values), the item standard deviations, the point-biserial correlations, the biserial correlations, the p-values for the examinees scoring in the lower 33% of the total-score distribution (L), the p-values for those scoring in the upper 33%, and the item discrimination index.

Three items are highlighted with shading: items #7, #14, and #44. Item #7 shows a negative point-biserial, indicating that the examinees who perform better overall tend to do worse on this on this item than the lower performing examinees. The biserial correlation and item discrimination index confirm that result. Item #14, in contrast, has a high point-biserial correlation of $r(y_{14}, Y) = .651$ and very high corresponding values of both the item biserial correlation and discrimination index. Finally, item #44 shows relatively low, positive item-total correlations and a modest item discrimination index of $d_{44} = .18$.

One technique to shed additional light on the performance of the items is to graphically plot the item mean scores for examinees divided into five groups, or "quintiles,"

*Table 7.1* IA Results for a 50-Item Multiple-Choice Test

| Item No. | Item Mean | Item SD | $r(y_p, Y)$ | $r(bis)$ | L | U | d |
|---|---|---|---|---|---|---|---|
| 1 | 0.375 | 0.484 | 0.399 | 0.509 | 0.13 | 0.69 | 0.56 |
| 2 | 0.895 | 0.307 | 0.333 | 0.561 | 0.76 | 0.97 | 0.21 |
| 3 | 0.620 | 0.485 | 0.373 | 0.475 | 0.37 | 0.83 | 0.46 |
| 4 | 0.320 | 0.467 | 0.425 | 0.554 | 0.13 | 0.62 | 0.49 |
| 5 | 0.790 | 0.407 | 0.599 | 0.827 | 0.40 | 1.00 | 0.60 |
| 6 | 0.625 | 0.484 | 0.448 | 0.572 | 0.35 | 0.91 | 0.55 |
| 7 | 0.055 | 0.228 | −0.121 | −0.248 | 0.06 | 0.02 | −0.05 |
| : | : | : | : | : | : | : | : |
| 14 | 0.685 | 0.465 | 0.651 | 0.845 | 0.18 | 0.98 | 0.81 |
| : | : | : | : | : | : | : | : |
| 44 | 0.430 | 0.495 | 0.101 | 0.128 | 0.39 | 0.57 | 0.18 |
| : | : | : | : | : | : | : | : |
| 49 | 0.335 | 0.472 | 0.391 | 0.507 | 0.15 | 0.68 | 0.53 |
| 50 | 0.145 | 0.352 | 0.301 | 0.464 | 0.06 | 0.28 | 0.21 |

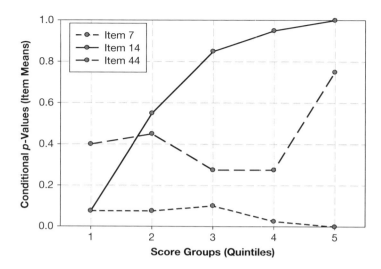

*Figure 7.4* "Quintile" Plots for Three Items

based on their total scores (i.e., the lowest 20%, the next highest 20%, etc.). These are sometimes called "profile plots" or "trace lines", too (e.g., Haladyna, 2004). The item means are then computed and plotted for each group. The grouping variable acts as what is termed a "conditioning" variable. If the item responses follow a pattern expected for a well-discriminating item, the plotted means will systematically increase from the lowest to highest groups.

Figure 7.4 shows the "quintile" plots for the three items highlighted in Table 7.1 (#7, #14 and #44). We can see that Item #14 shows the expected increasing p-value across the five performance groups. In contrast, Item #44, which showed only modest discrimination, seemed to demonstrate decreasing performance, on average, for groups 3 and 4. Performance increased again for group 5, which explains why the discrimination index for Item #44 may have suggested less of a problem than the point-biserial or biserial correlations. Item #7 shows decreasing performance across the highest two score groups, implying that examinees who score the best, overall, did worse on this item than the lowest performing examinees. A key validation analysis, discussed in the next section, is essential to further understand what might be happening with the items, especially an item like #7.

### *Answer Key and Rubric Validation*

It makes little sense to compute test scores and other statistics before verifying that all of the answer keys and/or item-level scoring rubrics are working properly. Despite the best test development and data management efforts, incorrect answer keys or other faulty criteria can be supplied to a scoring evaluator as the "answer." A key validation analysis (KVA) helps to detect those types of anomalies—hopefully before any subsequent processing takes place. Most IA software programs employ various "flagging" criteria as part of the KVA. All flagged items are then sent to subject-matter content experts and test development editors for additional review (Baranowski, 2006). If the item answer key is

*Analysis for Credentialing Examinations* 135

incorrect, appropriate changes are made to the item database and the KVA can be rerun. If there are no apparent problems with the answer key, the item may nonetheless be dropped from scoring as a matter of policy.

Some of the more common flagging criteria used in a typical KVA are:

1. items having negative item-total correlations (point-biserial or biserial correlations);
2. extremely easy items (e.g., $p_i > .95$);
3. extremely difficult items (e.g., $p_i < .25$ for multiple-choice items);
4. items with incorrect MC distractor options that show a positive correlation with the total scores; and/or
5. items with incorrect SR or MC options that are statistically more popular (i.e., have a higher proportion of examinees choosing them) than the correct answer key.

For example, consider the detailed IA results for Item #7 in Figure 7.5. This problematic item would be flagged in multiple ways (see flagging criteria #1, #3, #4 and #5 in the list, above). The negative point-biserial correlation and plot clearly suggest a problem, but not necessarily the nature of the problem. The lower section of the detailed IA results show the statistical characteristics for each of the five possible MC distractors, A to E. (Note that a specialized scoring evaluator is needed for each of the incorrect options to produce the binary scores used in the "distractor analysis.")

The keyed answer is "A", but it should quickly become apparent that option "B" may be the correct answer key for this item. It has a strong, positive point-biserial correlation with total scores, a reasonable *p*-value for a moderately difficult item—see *p*(Total)—and seems to be the most popular distractor. Of course, in practice, we would ask subject matter experts to confirm that "B" was the correct answer, rekey the results and then rerun the entire IA. If "B" was *not* the correct key, this item might have other problems related to the wording, typos, or other issues, and might be dropped from scoring. As demonstrated here, an IA can be extremely useful to ensure that every item is performing well.

Given the increased use of technology enhanced and other novel item types that allow multiple selections and multiple correct answers—with possible partial-credit scoring where some answer patterns of responses are worth more than other patterns—the IA can become quite complex (Luecht, 2005). For example, suppose that a new multiple-selection item—what some have called "pick n" or "P type" items—has 12 possible options and the

| ID Identifier: ITM0007 | Valid N-Size | 200 |
| --- | --- | --- |
| Number of Keys: 1 | No. omitted/invalid | 0 |
| Answer Key(s): A | Item mean (p-value) | 0.0550 |
| Number of Response Options: 5 | Item std. deviation | 0.2280 |
| Response Options: A,B,C,D,E | Item pt. biserial correlation | −0.1210 |
| | Item biserial correlation | −0.2480 |
| | Reliability if deleted | 0.9221 |

| Option | Key | p(Total) | p(Low) | p(High) | r(pt.bis) |
| --- | --- | --- | --- | --- | --- |
| A | ** | 0.055 | 0.364 | 0.091 | −0.121 |
| B | | 0.665 | 0.165 | 0.519 | 0.580 |
| C | | 0.075 | 0.800 | 0.000 | −0.358 |
| D | | 0.060 | 0.583 | 0.167 | −0.127 |
| E | | 0.145 | 0.793 | 0.035 | −0.359 |

*Figure 7.5* Detailed IA Results for Item #7

examinees are required to select exactly three responses. It can be shown that there are 220 possible response combinations, of which only a small number might be considered as correct. Furthermore, partial-credit scores could be used where some in-part correct response selections might receive fewer points than the "best" three answer choices. A potential solution would to accumulate all possible response patterns out of the 220 possible patterns with a minimum frequency—say, more than $min(N_i) \geq 10$. We could then treat those retained response patterns as "distractor patterns" for IA purposes. If the retained patterns are further sorted by the frequency count of respondents, it is relatively easy to see which patterns are most popular and then use the pattern-total score point biserial correlations to evaluate whether any non-keyed response patterns might be considered as alternative, partially or wholly correct answer keys.

## *Item Response Theory (IRT) Item Analysis*

It needs to be recognized from the onset that only a cursory overview of IRT can be presented here. Entire IRT books are available on the topic (see Hambleton & Swaminathan, 1985; Hambleton, Swaminathan & Rogers, 1991; Lord, 1980; Nering & Ostini, 2010; Wilson, 2005; Wright & Stone, 1979). IRT characterizes the item characteristics such as difficulty and discrimination and the examinees' proficiency scores on a common, underlying scale. This approach offers many analytical benefits over classical test theory when it comes to evaluating the statistical quality of items and test forms.

The mathematically simplest IRT model—known as the "Rasch model—represents the probability of the observed response to a particular item as a function of the *difference* between an examinee's proficiency, usually denoted by the Greek letter θ ("theta"), and the item difficulty or location, denoted $\delta_i$. For an item scored using a binary-scoring evaluator, the associated probability is modeled by a relatively simple exponential function:

$$P_i(\theta) = \frac{exp(\theta - \delta_i)}{1 + exp(\theta - \delta_i)} \tag{7.7}$$

When the difference between θ and $\delta_i$ is zero, the probability is exactly $P_i(\theta) = .50$. The proficiency scores usually range from about −4.0 to +4.0, depending on scaling choices made when establishing an IRT-based scale. Easier items tend to have negative item difficulty values and hard items have positive difficulty values.

The examinee proficiency scores, θ, and item difficulty values, $\delta_i$, needed to compute the probability function, $P_i(\theta)$, are numerically estimated from the observed scored-response data (i.e., from the $y_i$ scores generated by the scoring evaluators). For example, Figure 7.6 shows the probability curves for three items from Table 7.1. Under the IRT Rasch model, as proficiency (θ) increases, the probability of a correct response (i.e., $y_i = 1$) also increases. For example, any examinees having proficiency scores of exactly θ = 0.0, would have a probability of about .34 to correctly answer Item #1. In contrast, examinees at that same level of proficiency would have probabilities for Items #2 and 3 of $P_2(\theta = 0.0) = .94$ and $P_3(\theta = 0.0) = .66$. Item #2 is the easiest item of the three with a *p*-value of .895 (see Table 7.1). It is represented by the leftmost curve in Figure 7.6; the probability for Item #2 increases even for relatively low proficiency scores. In contrast, Item #1 is the most difficult of the three items with a *p*-value of .375. The corresponding probability curve is the rightmost curve. Finally, Item #3 is moderately difficult with a *p*-value of .62. Its probability curve therefore falls furthest to the right, implying that a relatively high degree of proficiency is needed to correctly answer that item.

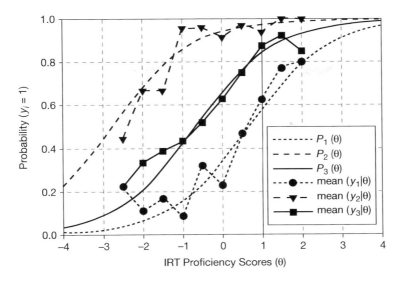

*Figure 7.6* IRT Probability Curves and Conditional Means for Items #1–3

The conditional *p*-values (empirical, conditional item means) for each item are also presented within each of ten equal-sized intervals along the θ scale—similar to what was done to get the "quintiles" shown earlier in Figure 7.4. Here, however, the estimated θ scores were used to group the 200 examinees into the ten intervals. The corresponding conditional *p*-values are plotted as symbols superimposed onto the plot in Figure 7.6 and using the same line style as for the corresponding IRT probability curve (see legend). These plots demonstrate more or less how the IRT model curve is fit to the observed data. If the fit of the Rasch model is reasonable, the smooth curves should track closely to the empirical data. There is one noticeable anomaly. Item #1, the most difficult item, shows a slight upshift in the conditional *p*-value within the lowest proficiency interval. That minor aberrance is likely to be due to guessing on the part of the lowest proficiency examinee—something that the Rasch model does not specifically include in its parameterization.

Since IRT models are fundamentally just regression models with unobserved explanatory variables, it is entirely appropriate to use regression-based diagnostic statistics to evaluate fit between the observed item-response scores and the model based prediction—that is, $\hat{\varepsilon}_{ij} = y_{ij} - \hat{P}_i(\hat{\theta}_j)$. For example, as we saw above in Figure 7.6, Item #1 showed a small amount of misfit between the data and the model within the lowest proficiency interval. Had there been more serious types of misfit, we would need ways to flag the potentially problematic items for additional review. Fortunately, there are a number of powerful statistical methods for evaluating the fit of an IRT model to various types of assessment data, most of which aggregate the residuals in particular ways across examinees for individual items (see IRT reference books, cited earlier).

### *Common Issues in Item Analysis*

There are three fairly common data analysis issues encountered by many credentialing examination programs: 1) small samples; 2) homogeneous populations, and restriction of range/limited "person" information; and 3) definition of a consistent "reference group". These are briefly discussed below as they pertain to IAs.

We need a sufficiently large sample of hopefully high-quality data to carry out a useful IA. For example, although an IA can be carried out with fewer than 50 examinee responses per item, the results will not be very stable—implying that the obtained item statistics could vary substantially if estimated using a different sample of examinees. The small samples sometimes encountered by credentialing agencies therefore may place a severe limitation on the number of examinees available for a given analysis, especially if testing is spread out across an entire year with different examinees taking different test forms. Unfortunately, there is no viable fix to the problem of small samples. While there is a fairly comprehensive literature base on small-sample statistical estimation techniques, most of these studies either use simulated data generated from convenient, well-behaved distribution functions (e.g., a "normal" distribution) or small samples randomly selected from larger samples. The results from such small-sample studies will only generalize to actual credentialing examination settings if the same sampling assumptions hold for the real data.

The second issue, restriction of range, is a well-known statistical phenomenon that can be manifested as possibly severe limits on the spread or variance of particular variables of interest. There are two ways in which restriction of range can impact IAs. The first involves the actual design of the test, especially if the credentialing decision (cut score) tends to affect only the lower or upper region of the score scale. For example, suppose that 90% of the candidates tend to pass a particular credentialing examination. In that case, optimal test design would call for building the tests comprised primarily of easy items to maximize the precision at the 10th percentile of the total score distribution (Luecht, 2006, 2015). That optimal design strategy, however, will impact the item variance (Equation 7.5). That is, the estimated item variance tends to be systematically lower for very easy and very difficult items. In addition, the associated item-total score correlations will likely be lower as well. When compared to academic achievement or college entrance tests, the items on a credentialing examination may sometimes appear to have lower item quality, when in fact the test is optimally designed for making the pass/fail decision.

Homogeneous populations of candidates can further compound the restriction of range problem. Homogeneous populations are characterized as being statistically similar to each other—in this case, resulting because of self-selection into a profession, similar training, and/or common eligibility pathways. The potential range of total scores may therefore be restricted. Any restriction of the variance of a variable will tend also to suppress the correlation of that variable with other variables. Although there are "corrections" for variance restrictions, it becomes risky to naively apply them with small to moderate-sized samples.

The final issue refers to the use of a "reference group" for purposes of creating the examinee sample used in IAs and other types of analyses. A reference group is a designated subset of the larger population of test takers and can be useful to help maintain reasonable consistency of the sampling used in IAs and other data analyses over time. For example, the reference group might be defined as the all first-time test takers who graduated from an accredited training program. Only the reference group examinees are included in the IA. Operationally, the specification of a reference group for purpose of item analysis and some types of scaling studies is merely a concrete definition of the target population and avoids making arbitrary analysis exclusion rules that might vary over time. All examinees will receive scores, but the quality assurance aspects of the IA will be carried out only using the reference group. This type of definition is a matter of policy, but it is an important policy to consider that can help in evaluating IA results.

## Other Special Issues in Item Analysis

There are two important, additional issues in item analysis. The first involves item analysis for technology enhanced items (TEIs) and performance-assessment tasks (PATs). The second issue involves implementing item analysis for computerized adaptive tests and multistage tests.

The development of an effective system of scoring evaluators greatly simplifies item analysis, regardless of the type of items or assessment tasks involved. As noted earlier, a scoring evaluator turns almost any measurement opportunity (MO) into a Boolean or binary value that can then be assigned a designated number of points. Each measurement opportunity can therefore be analyzed using the same types of item statistics (means, standard deviations and item-total correlations) as demonstrated earlier for multiple-choice (MC) items. One caution is warranted, however. When new item types are included to measure "something else"—that is, skills or applied knowledge not tapped by more traditional MC items—it is important to identify the appropriate total score scale with which to correlate the responses (i.e., the Y variable in Equation 7.5). A total-score comprised of both the MC and new item types can easily favor items that are measuring the same trait as the MC items, especially when the MC items proportionally out-number the new types of items.

A principal challenge is to identify the *intended*, valid scale or subscale with which to correlate the points on the new items. For example, suppose that we have a mixed-format test comprising MC items to measure the concept and topical knowledge component and some number of work-based simulations that measure applied quantitative skills. We would not expect the latter simulations to correlate perfectly with knowledge trait measured by the MC items. For the IA, we would therefore need to specify an appropriate score scale to use as Y variable when computing the item-total correlations for the simulation items. This would likely be a special composite score involving a designated subset of MC items that are developed to assess the same [new] knowledge and skills as the TEIs or PATs, rather than relying on the total test score using all items.

Computerized-adaptive tests (CATs) and multi-stage tests (MSTs) target the difficulty of the test to the examinees' apparent proficiency (Luecht, 2014, 2016; van der Linden & Glas, 2010). Carrying out an item analyses for adaptive tests is therefore complicated by the fact that examinees at different levels of proficiency are administered differentially difficult test forms. In fact, the near-perfect CAT will tailor the difficulty of each test so that every examinee gets about 50% of the items correct. The implication is that there is little or no variation in total scores, rendering as almost useless any descriptive item statistics or item-total correlations from a traditional IA—that is, if every CAT or MST examinee has the same raw total score, Y, Equation 7.5 will produce an item-total correlation of zero for all items.

The solution in this case is to compute a score that takes the item difficulty into account. IRT-based proficiency score estimates can be used in that context and substituted for the more typical number-correct total score for purposes of computing the item-total correlations. Estimated expected *p*-values can be computed by approximating an integral of Equation 7.7 (or another IRT model of choice), with assumed population density weights for the proficiency scores, $\theta$. For example, if we assume that the ability of the examinees is "normal" with a mean of zero and standard deviation of one, the weights for integration can be computed from a relatively well-known Gaussian density

140  Richard M. Luecht

$h(\theta_k) = (2\pi\sigma^2)^{-1/2}\exp\{-.5[(\theta_k-\mu)^2/\sigma^2\}$ at $k=1,\ldots,K$ points along the $\theta$ scale. The expected p-value can then be approximated as $p_i = \sum_{k=1}^{k} h(\theta_k) P_i(\theta_k)$.

IRT-based model fit statistics and graphics similar to Figure 7.6 are also useful as part of an IA for CAT and MST examinations. The point is that traditional IA methods may not work because of the adaptive nature of the tests and alternative approaches are needed (Luecht, 2005).

### Use of Item Statistics in Test Construction

Classical item or IRT statistics estimated from operational field tests or from embedded pilot testing of new items can be an effective way to improve test construction. Statistical targets can be developed for purposes of building new test forms as a function of the item statistics. If every new test form is constructed using the *same* statistical targets and content specifications, the forms will be near parallel and may reduce the amount of statistical equating needed.

A simple example can help illustrate how the item statistics relate to statistical raw-score targets. Suppose that we want to build several forms of a multiple-choice (MC) test, each with a specified mean and standard deviation. First, we can use the fact that a raw-score mean can be expressed as the sum of the item means (p-values for MC items), $\mu(Y) = \Sigma p_i$. Conveniently, the standard deviation can be expressed as the sum of the product of the item standard deviations and the point biserial correlations, $\sigma(Y) = \Sigma s_i r_{i,Y}$, where $s_i = [p_i(1-p_i)]^{1/2}$ for MC items. This latter expression is sometimes called the "reliability index" (Gulliksen, 1950). The item mean, $p_i$, and item reliability index, $s_i r_{i,Y}$, are therefore said to be additive, respectively, in the mean and standard deviation.

Now suppose that we have an item bank with 200 MC items. There are three content areas: BP = basic principles; QM = quantitative methods; and AP = applications. The means, standard deviations, minimum and maximum values of the estimated item p-values and point-biserial correlations are shown in Table 7.2. The counts of items within each of the three content areas are shown in the right-most columns of the table.

Now suppose that we need to build two near-parallel forms of a 50-item test, each with a mean of 35.0 points and a standard deviation of 10.0 points. We furthermore want content distributions for each form to be exactly 15 BP items, 10 QM items and 25 AP items. Although this type of problem can be solved using manual trial and error, there are mathematically sophisticated algorithms and search heuristics that can often effectively build numerous simultaneous forms to exacting and sometimes very complex specifications in seconds (Luecht, 1998, 2000; van der Linden, 2000, 2005). For example, this particular problem actually has $10^{21.49}$ possible solutions—an enormous number of possibilities. Using an ATA solver called CTT-ATT (Luecht, 2014), the two forms were

*Table 7.2* Summary of 200 MC Items: Item Statistics and Content Counts

| Statistics | p-Values | Pt. Biserial Correlations | Content | Count |
|---|---|---|---|---|
| Mean | 0.591 | 0.398 | BP | 67 |
| SD | 0.099 | 0.050 | QM | 47 |
| Minimum | 0.250 | 0.271 | AP | 86 |
| Maximum | 0.832 | 0.523 | Total | 200 |

*Table 7.3* Form-level Statistics

| Test Form and Scale Statistics | Form #1 | Form #2 |
|---|---|---|
| Item Count | 50 | 50 |
| Mean | 30.0215 | 30.0159 |
| Std. Deviation | 9.993 | 10.024 |
| Reliability (α) | 0.899 | 0.899 |
| BP Item Count | 15 | 15 |
| QM Item Count | 10 | 10 |
| AP Item Count | 25 | 25 |

constructed in .05 seconds. Table 7.3 shows the observed score means, standard deviations and the test score reliability—a statistic discussed in the next section.

However, we can solve the problem by realizing that the raw score mean is equal to sum of the item means (*p*-values). Therefore, we can specify the test assembly problem as minimize:

$$\sum_{i=1}^{200} x_i p_i - 35.0 \tag{7.8}$$

subject to:

$$\sum_{i=1}^{200} x_i A_i = 15 \tag{7.9}$$

$$\sum_{i=1}^{200} x_i B_i = 10 \tag{7.10}$$

$$\sum_{i=1}^{200} x_i C_i = 25 \tag{7.11}$$

$$\sum_{i=1}^{200} x_i = 50 \tag{7.12}$$

and $x_i \in \{0, 1\}$ (i.e., $x_i$ is binary). $\tag{7.13}$

The key to solving this type of problem using a mathematical "solver" (i.e., optimization software) is to specify the binary decision variables, $x_i$. If selected for the test form, $x_i = 1$, otherwise, $x_i = 0$. Since the decision variables are multiplied times each item value, $p_i$, $A_i$, $B_i$, and $C_i$, only the selected variables count in the summations. Using a sample item bank of 200 items and these specifications, a "solver" available in commercial spreadsheet software using an evolutionary algorithm was able to find a feasible solution to exact specifications in about 10 seconds. The point is that having the item statistics available makes it entirely possible to create test forms with designated properties such as a mean score and standard deviation of scores.

## Building and Maintaining a Score Scale

The purpose of most score scales is to help interpret the apparent performance of the examinees within a domain of interest (Peterson, et al., 1989). Most credentialing examinations maintain at least one primary scale for which numerical results are reported, and quite probably a "pass/fail" decision based on an established cut score on the reported scale. Building and maintaining *the* score scale are perhaps the most important aspects of data analysis. Some of the policy and practical issues related to selecting and implementing score scales are included in Chapter 7.

There are three types of score scales that are used for most credentialing examinations: 1) non-equated raw score scales; 2) equated raw-score scales; and 3) IRT-based score scales. Each requires somewhat different data analysis procedures and there are definitely differences with respect to score-scale maintenance and reuse of a cut score over test forms and time.

A non-equated score scale merely reports the total point or percent-correct scores for every test form. The total points score is simply the sum of the item points—that is, $Y = \Sigma y_i$. A percent-correct score multiplies the raw score times 100 and divides by the maximum number of points, $\% \ correct = 100 \cdot Y/Y^{[max]}$. Other mathematical transformations of the raw scores are sometimes employed. Some transformation examples include linear transformations such as $U = \alpha + \beta\left[(Y - \bar{Y})/s_Y\right]$, percentile equivalents computed for a *reference* or standardization sample of examinees, or normal score equivalents (i.e., $z$-score-based percentiles). As discussed in Chapter 7, it is extremely important to understand that performance on one non-equated test form is *not* directly comparable to performance on another non-equated test form—even if the test forms are randomly assigned to the examinees. Declaring the forms to be randomly equivalent as a matter of policy is not acceptable. As discussed earlier (see Use of Item Statistics in Test Assembly, p. 140), it is possible to construct all the test forms to be statistically and content-parallel. However, that requires clear evidence that the scores are exchangeable across the forms.

In general, a separate cut score must be set for each non-equated test form. Some have referred to this process of setting form-specific cut scores using standard setting as "judgmental equating" since the subject-matter experts ideally will take the differential difficulty of the test forms into account when setting each cut scores. Certainly, one of the biggest technical mistakes that organizations can make would be to *assume* that all constructed test forms are equally difficult and reliable, and that scores are exchangeable across forms. Equally problematic would be the use of a fixed cut score on non-equated test form such as "70% correct."

Equated score scales are built by first establishing one test form as a "base form" and then equating new, subsequent forms to that base-form scale. Additional transformations can be applied, once scores on the new forms are equated to the base scale. If all the active test forms can be randomly assigned to examinees within a reasonably short testing period or "window"—including the base form or a previously equated form—we can assume that any differences between the examinees are due to differences in the test forms. As an example, two random groups each take a different 100-item test form. Group 1 has a mean score of 72.5 on Form A and Group 2 has a mean score of 76.0 on Form B. Because of the random assignment of forms to examinees, we can assume that the two groups are randomly equivalent in proficiency and that the difference between the means is because Form B is easier than Form A by 3.5 points, on average. We might therefore subtract 3.5 points from all the examinees who take Form B to "equate" their scores to the Form A (baseline) score scale.

Note that this "random group" assumption seldom holds for different years and almost certainly does not hold for examinees taking a credentialing examination at different times of the year. For example, some professional credentialing examinations have different test administrations at the end of an academic year to accommodate the examinees who complete their degree or certificate program. Other test administrations in the fall or winter months may accommodate test retakers or others on a non-standard training or academic schedule. To claim that these groups taking the test at different times of the year are equivalent is usually inappropriate from an equating perspective. The same is true for new test forms administered each year.

There are test score equating methods for non-equivalent groups. Those methods are somewhat technically complex and require using common test items on all the test forms administered to the non-equivalent groups. The common items serve the basis for statistically linking the groups to equate new test forms to the base scale. Kolen and Brennan (2014) provide an excellent overview of random groups and non-equivalent group equating methods and issues.

IRT-based score scales are becoming extremely popular for many credentialing tests. Using IRT, the proficiency scores—denoted as $\theta$—are estimated using the examinees' response data and the calibrated item statistics (see Item Response Theory (IRT) Item Analysis, p. 136). As long as all of the item statistics are calibrated to the common item bank scale, any scores estimated for the examinees are automatically equated to the same scale. The IRT-equated scores can be used interchangeably—within reason—for complex adaptive tests where different examinees may get test forms that differ substantially in difficulty from one another. Therefore, a primary advantage of using IRT is that a single $\theta$ scale can be developed and maintained for an entire bank of test items, without needing to specifically equate test forms to one another.

New items can be statistically linked to this same scale using a process known as a "linking calibration." The statistical IRT item parameter estimates can be further improved over time by various estimation stabilization procedures to corresponding improve the quality of the item bank scale. The IRT calibration and linking process provides an alternative to random groups or non-equivalent groups equating of raw scores. Any test forms comprising the IRT-calibrated items can then be used for scoring. IRT automatically equates the difficulty of the test forms to the same underlying scale.

A final advantage of using IRT-based score scales in a credentialing context is that the cut score can be determined once using an appropriate standard setting methodology and then maintained via the IRT $\theta$ scale over several years. This can significantly reduce costs and the potential logistical complications of setting standards every year or every time that new test forms are generated.

## *Classical Test Theory Analysis of Score Scale Quality*

Scale analysis and on-going scale maintenance are probably the most complicated aspects of data analysis for credentialing examinations. As suggested above, score scales can range from simple number-correct or percent-correct raw-score scales to rather sophisticated scales developed and maintained using mathematically complex statistical test score equating procedures or item response theory (IRT).

Two of the critical features of any score scale are its reliability and validity evidence. Reliability relates to the precision or accuracy of the scores along the scale. All scores contain some amount of measurement or estimation error. Various reliability functions help estimate the amount of error—including decision consistency in a credentialing examination context. Validity refers to the degree to which interpretations of the scores— such as pass/fail decisions on a credentialing examination—are credibly supported by the scaling practices employed and other evidence about the entire process of building, administering, scoring and reporting scores. The *Standards for Educational and Psychological Testing* (AERA, APA, NCME, 2014) provide rather comprehensive discussions of reliability and validity—also see Kane (2006) and Haertel (2006).

From a data analysis perspective, reliability and validity refer to how measurement errors are conceptualized, quantified, and managed relative to the score scale. Reliability refers to the accuracy of the scores and treats errors are observational measurement or estimation errors in the scores relative to some "true score." Under classical test theory (CTT), the measurement errors remain after we take the large-sample average or expectation of the observed scores—that is, $E_j = Y_j - T_j$, where $T_j = \mu(Y_j)$. $T_j$ is called the "true" score—that is, the examinee's score that would result from retesting the examinee a very large number of times. A reliability coefficient is used to represent the precision of scores along the scale. This type of coefficient is computed as the ratio of the variance of the [estimated] error variance to the observed-score variance. One of the most commonly reported reliability coefficients is "alpha" or α (Cronbach, 1951):

$$r^2(Y,T) = \hat{\alpha} = \left(\frac{n}{n-1}\right)\left[1 - \frac{\sum_{i=1}^{n} s^2(y_i)}{s^2(Y)}\right] \quad (7.14)$$

where $s^2(y_i)$ is the estimated item variance (see Equation 7.5) and $s^2(Y)$ is the estimated total-score variance. Most high-quality IA software packages and even many statistical analysis software programs provide estimates of α. Values over 0.85 are usually considered "reasonable." Values over 0.9 are considered "very good" and values over 0.95 are considered "excellent." Test length indirectly impacts the reliability coefficient. A convenient mechanism for estimating the impact of test length on reliability is called the Spearman-Brown formula:

$$r^2(Y',T) = \frac{kr^2(Y,T)}{1+(k-1)r^2(Y,T)} \quad (7.15)$$

where $k$ is the ratio of the new-to-old test length (Allen & Yen, 1979). For example, if our 60-item test demonstrated mediocre reliability of 0.8, we could evaluate the likely impact of increasing the test length by 40 items, i.e., for $k = (60 + 40)/60 = 1.667$. Substituting those values into Equation 7.15 would suggest that our change in test length could increase the reliability to about 0.87.

Some credentialing examinations have only moderate scale reliability coefficients but may still be considered to be excellent tests, especially if the test is sufficiently long to sample all of the relevant professional domain content covered in the examination's qualification claims. It may be the case that a moderate reliability coefficient results not from quality issues, but from an almost unavoidable problem related to statistical item variance restrictions. For example, when the items are purposefully written to an average level of difficulty meant to maximize the precision of decision accuracy relative to a cut score on the scale (see Common Issues in Item Analysis, p. 137) and when the cut score is well away from the mean of population distribution of scores, a reliability coefficient like α will be depressed. In fact, only very long credentialing examinations may actually demonstrate what most measurement professionals would consider as "very good" to "excellent" reliability (e.g., over .95). That is, a credentialing test with only moderately good reliability may still yield highly accurate pass/fail decisions that reflect the primary purpose of the scale.

Practitioners sometimes confuse decision accuracy with decision consistency. Decision consistency occurs when two observers (or instruments) evaluating the same individual's performance come to the same decision such as issuing a credential. Decision accuracy assumes that we know the true or appropriate decision (e.g., whether the candidate really is qualified or not). In that case, there are two potential faulty decision outcomes: 1) passing or credentialing an individual who is *not* qualified (a false–positive error) or 2) failing or not credentialing an individual who *is* qualified (a false–negative error). High-decision accuracy implies that, in aggregate, false–positive and false–negative errors are minimized. However, actually estimating decision accuracy is mathematically quite complex and often requires some strong assumptions. Nonetheless, there are several statistical methods for evaluating classification accuracy (see Hanson & Brennan, 1990; Lee, Hanson, & Brennan, 2002; Livingston & Lewis, 1995). Luecht (2015) also presents some IRT-based analytical methods for evaluating decision accuracy.

## IRT Scale Quality Analyses

When IRT is used, a type of virtual scale resides in the calibrated item statistics—that is, performance or proficiency relative to the underlying scale, θ, is inferred from knowing the estimated (i.e., calibrated) item statistics and the examinee's observed item response data. Any combination of items can theoretically be used as long as they are calibrated to the same underlying scale.

IRT scale quality analysis amounts to evaluating some relatively strong assumptions. For example, one of the more typical assumptions of IRT is that the underlying proficiency trait, θ, is unidimensional. Given the multifaceted content covered by many credentialing examinations, it may seem implausible that a single proficiency underlies the examinees' performance on every item. Nonetheless, it remains an important assumption to meet in order to use IRT. As noted earlier, it is common to evaluate data-model fit as an omnibus approach to addressing dimensionality as well as other types of violations of fundamental IRT assumptions. For example, if we square and aggregate the data-IRT model-based residuals presented earlier—i.e., aggregating $\hat{\varepsilon}_{ij}^2 = \left[ y_{ij} - \hat{P}_i(\hat{\theta}_j) \right]^2$ by items, we can detect those items with the highest magnitudes of aggregate residual as possibly not fitting the IRT model of choice. We can similarly aggregate the residuals for individual examinees or groups of examinees to evaluate data-model fit for "persons." Most of the popular IRT software provides convenient tabular listings and graphical fit plots that can be used to detect potentially problematic items or individuals for whom the IRT-based scale does not appear to be functioning well. In those cases, more in-depth analyses are needed to determine an appropriate solution. Simply using IRT without verifying that the model-of-choice fits the empirical data reasonably well is irresponsible and could have serious ramifications.

If the data fit the model of choice, IRT offers some very convenient and powerful ways to evaluate the quality of the scale. One of the primary tools for scale quality analysis is called a test information function (TIF). The mathematical form of the TIF will change as a function of the IRT calibration model chosen (see, for example, Hambleton & Swaminathan, 1985). Nonetheless, generally speaking, the TIF provides a way to concretely quantify and graphically display the precision of the scores at specific points along the IRT score scale, θ.

Figure 7.7 shows the TIFs for two 100-item tests. One important feature of the plot is the vertical solid line denoting a credentialing cut score at a value of $\theta_{cut} = -1.28$. One test is an achievement test with good precision where the concentration of examinees is highest (referring to the long dashes, – –, that peak just past the zero point on the scale). This achievement test would also demonstrate a very good scale reliability coefficient of

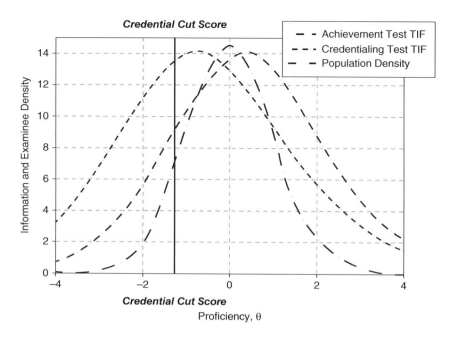

*Figure 7.7* Test Information Functions for Two Tests with the Population Score Density and Cut Score Shown

about .93, assuming that the population of examinee scores is normally distributed with a mean of zero and standard deviation of one—as indicated by the dash-dot-dot patterned lines (–···–) in Figure 7.7. The final line plot, which comprises short dashed lines (--), shows the TIF for a credentialing examination designed to provide peak precision nearer to the cut score. This test would also provide good scale reliability of about .92. However, the credentialing test would be about 50% more precise near the cut score. This design strategy could be shown to significantly improve decision accuracy when compared to the achievement test, for example.

The use of IRT information functions has revolutionized testing by providing test design and assembly strategies for targeting measurement precision (the peak of the TIF) where it is more needed (van der Linden, 2005; Luecht, 2006, 2015). Whereas a reliability coefficient only rather globally indicates the precision of the scale—principally indicating the precision of the scale where there is the highest concentration of scores—an IRT TIF will allow credentialing examination test developers to place the peak precision in the region of the cut scores (or anywhere else). In this sense, IRT can be highly proactive in planning for intended scale properties such as locating the measurement precision where it is most needed.

IRT-based scale analysis can also include systematic evaluation of the "person" fit along the scale for particular groups of examinees (e.g., demographically determined subgroups, non-traditional examinees who may have taken alternative pathways to become eligible for certification). The earlier discussion of IRT data-model fit included a brief overview of residual statistics such as $\hat{\varepsilon}_{ij} = y_{ij} - \hat{P}_i(\hat{\theta}_j)$, referring to the previous section in this chapter subtitled Item Response Theory (IRT) Item Analysis (p. 136). If the IRT model does a plausible

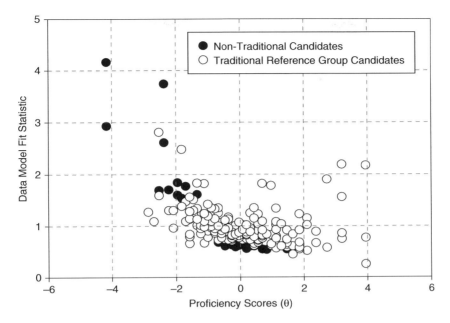

*Figure 7.8* Conditional IRT Person Fit for Traditional and Non-traditional Examinees

job of explaining the scored response data, the residuals show systematic departures from expected values.

Figure 7.8 shows an example of a conditional person-fit plot for two groups of examinees. In this example, the (lower proficiency) non-traditional candidates appear to be misfitting the calibrated items more so than the reference group examinees. Further investigation might be warranted to determine if this fit anomaly is merely random misfit by a small number of non-traditional examinees—possibly because of lax eligibility requirements—or if the misfit is symptomatic of potential test score validity problems.

Examining the fit for examinees merely requires "creatively aggregating" the residuals for individual examinees. Most IRT calibration packages provide one or more "person fit" indicators that can be conveniently displayed as a function of overall estimated proficiency, $\theta$, to evaluate any systematic patterns of examinees exhibiting relative large magnitudes of misfit.

### *Other Quality Control Steps in Scale Analysis*

There are numerous other important score scale quality control analyses and indicators that can and should be evaluated. Some examples include: 1) correlations between content-based subscores—that is, consistency of the subscore correlations over time; 2) comparisons of the current score distributions for "known" samples to their past performance distributions; and 3) computer simulations or analytical methods to evaluate potential impact (e.g., potential pass/fail rates under the proposed scaling).

## Reporting Scores

Most credentialing examination programs maintain multiple "score scales." The official scale is usually an IRT $\theta$ scale or a CTT equated raw score scale. The underlying official score scales maintains the pass/fail cut score derived from standard setting as well as other key interpretations (e.g., means and standard deviations for an established reference group such as first-time test taker). However, non-technical score consumers often find it difficult to understand IRT θ scales or equated score scales. Thus, the official scores may need to be transformed to some other convenient and easy-to-understand scale before they are reported to credentialing examination candidates.

## Types of Score Scale Transformations

A pass/fail decision is actually a scale transformation to a binary score scale (0 = fail and 1 = pass). In addition, there are five other basic types of score transformations possible (also see Allen & Yen, 197; Anastasi, 1986; Crocker & Algina, 1986; Kolen & Brennan, 2014): 1) percentile rank transformations; 2) standardizing transformations; 3) linear transformations; 4) error variance equalizing transformations; and (5) IRT-based expected percent-correct score transformations. These are briefly described below.

Percentiles are used to compare the credentialing candidates' performance to an established normative group—typically called a "reference group." The designation of the reference group is a policy decision. For example, the credentialing board authorized to make such decisions might designate the reference group as "all eligible first-time takers from accredited training programs that took the examination this year." Percentile ranks are defined as the percentage of examinees falling at or below a particular score (e.g., Anastasi, 1986; Crocker & Algina, 1986).

If we let $f(Y_j)$ denote the frequency (count) of examinees attaining a score of Y, and $F(Y-1)$ represent the cumulative frequency of examinees scoring one point below Y, the percentile rank can be computed as:

$$P(y \leq Y) = \left[\frac{f(Y) + 0.5}{F(Y-1)}\right] 100 \quad (7.16)$$

A standardizing transformation recenters and rescales the units of the score scale relative to a defined reference group. The recentering step resets the mean of the scale relative to the mean score of the reference group, $\mu(Y_{rg})$. The rescaling step then divides the recentered values relative to the standard deviation of scores for the reference group, $\sigma(Y_{rg})$. These two steps can be combined to compute a simple a z-score:

$$z_{rg} = \frac{Y - \mu(Y_{rg})}{\sigma(Y_{rg})} \quad (7.17)$$

Standardizing transformations are effectively linear transformations of the scale. On the transformed scale, the mean and standard deviation of the reference group are, respectively, zero and one. Those standardized scores can further be linearly transformed to a different scale, as described below. Normalized percentiles are sometimes also reported by determining the area at or below $z_{rg}$, using the well-known cumulative normal distribution.

Linear transformations require two constants: a slope denoted A and an intercept term denoted B. The linear transformation uses the simple formula:

$$Y^* = A \cdot Y + B \quad (7.18)$$

Extreme scores may be further truncated to "lowest obtainable scale scores" (LOSS) and "highest obtainable scale scores" (HOSS) values. For example, if we wish to apply a linear transformation of IRT θ score estimates to a scale where the reference group has a mean of 150 and standard deviation of 15, we can combine the standardizing and linear transformations ($A = 15$, $B = 150$) as follows,

$$Y^* = 15 \left[ \frac{\hat{\theta} - \hat{\mu}(\hat{\theta}_{rg})}{\hat{\sigma}(\hat{\theta}_{rg})} \right] + 150 \qquad (7.19)$$
$$= 15 \cdot z_{rg} + 150$$

where the carets ("^") denoted estimated quantities. If we set the LOSS at 100 and the HOSS at 200, any scores below or above those values would be set to the corresponding LOSS and HOSS.

Error variance equalizing transformations are sometimes used to non-linearly transform the official scores to a reported scale where the conditional measurement error variances are more equal across the score scale. This type of mathematical transformation allows for the measurement precision to be interpreted consistently across the scale. A typical error variance transformation applied to percent- or proportion-correct scores is an arcsine transformation (see Kolen & Brennan, 2014).

An IRT-based expected percent-correct score[1] (EPC) is a non-linear transformation that is essentially a prediction of how well an examinee with an estimated θ score would be expected to perform on the well-chosen reference test form (RTF)—that is, a set of carefully chosen test items with estimated (calibrated) item characteristics represented by the item response function for a particular IRT model of choice. Given the calibrated item response functions for the RTF, an EPC can be formally computed as:

$$EPC = ROUND_{int} \left\{ 100 \left[ \frac{1}{U^{max}} \sum_{i=1}^{n} \sum_{k=0}^{x_i} u_{ik} P_{ik}(\hat{\theta}) \right] \right\} \qquad (7.20)$$

where $P_{ik}$ is the category response probability for an observed item score, $u_{ik}$ are the possible score points on each item and $U^{max}$ denotes the maximum score points on the RTF. This same formula therefore works for most IRT models for dichotomous and polytomous data.

There are some distinct advantages of the EPC metric. First, it has the "look-and-feel" of a percent-correct scale and is intuitively understood by the examinees and most other score users. Second, mathematically speaking, the guaranteed LOSS and HOSS values are 0 and 100, respectively—no truncation of the score distribution is needed. Third, the non-linear EPC transformation can be shown to reduce the magnitude of IRT-based conditional error variances near the tails of the θ scale—similar the arcsine transformation discussed above. Finally, if based on the examinees' total test IRT scores on a credentialing examination, the candidates' predicted performance on content-based subsets of items within the RTF can provide useful feedback to the examinees—especially failing examinees—while avoiding the typical lowered reliability of so-called "diagnostic" subscores.

### *Quality Control of Score Reporting*

As emphasized throughout this chapter, data quality control (QC) needs to be a top priority for any credentialing examination program. QC further needs to extend beyond reusing scoring scripts and/or running scoring software that has been used in the past, and it certainly goes beyond merely setting up a protocol of personnel sign-offs on processing steps and data exchanges. Routine and non-routine double- and triple-checks should be carried out by auditors or evaluators to look for anomalies before any score reports are produced. Samples of score reports should likewise be checked against source records to ensure that reported scores are correct for all examinees.

## Final Comments

Ideally, this chapter has served to emphasize the extremely important role of high-quality data analysis of the entire credentialing examination enterprise: from test assembly and standard setting through score scale development and maintenance, and score reporting. Many specific data procedures were provided, with an emphasis on practical credentialing examination scenarios. Perhaps most importantly, this chapter stressed the absolute need for adopting flexible data management systems and strong quality controls throughout the data analysis process, regardless of the size and stakes of the examination program.

## Note

1. An EPC is a special case of what previous IRT literature has called a "domain score" (Lord, 1980).

## References

Allen, M, J., & Yen, W. M. (1979). *Introduction to measurement theory*. Monterey, CA: Brooks/Cole Publishing.

American Educational Research Association, American Psychological Association, & National Council on Measurement in Education (AERA, APA, NCME) (2014). *Standards for educational and psychological testing*. Washington, DC: American Educational Research Association.

Anastasi, A. (1986). *Psychological testing* (6th ed.). New York: Macmillan Publishing Company.

Baranowski, R. A. (2006). Item editing and editorial review. In S. M. Downing & T. M. Haladyna (Eds.), *Handbook of test development* (pp. 349–357). Mahwah, NJ: Erlbaum.

Crocker, L., & Algina, J. (1986). *Introduction to classical and modern test theory*. New York: Harcourt Brace Jovanovich College Publishers.

Cronbach, L. (1951). Coefficient alpha and the internal structure of tests. *Psychometrika, 16*(3), 297–334.

Drasgow, F., Luecht, R. M., & Bennett, R. (2006). Technology and testing. In R. L. Brennan (Ed.), *Educational measurement* (4th edition, pp. 471–515). Washington, DC: American Council on Education and Praeger.

Folk, V. G., & Smith, R. L. (2002). Models for delivery of CBTs. In C. N. Mills, M. T. Potenza, J. J. Fremer, & W. C. Ward (Eds.), *Computer-based testing: Building the foundation for future assessments* (pp. 41–66). Mahwah, NJ: Lawrence Erlbaum Associates.

Gulliksen, H. (1950). *Theory of mental tests*. New York: John Wiley & Sons.

Haertel, E. (2006). Reliability. In R. L. Brennan (Ed.), *Educational measurement* (4th ed., pp. 65–110). Washington, DC: American Council on Education/Praeger.

Haladyna, T. M. (2004). *Developing and validating multiple-choice test items* (3rd ed.). Mahwah, NJ: Lawrence Erlbaum Associates.

Hambleton, R. K., & Swaminathan, H. R. (1985). *Item response theory: Principles and applications*. Hingham, MA: Kluwer.

Hambleton, R. K., Swaminathan, H., & Rogers, H. J. (1991). *Fundamentals of item response theory*. Newbury Park, CA: Sage Publications.

Hanson, B. A., & Brennan, R. L. (1990). An investigation of classification consistency indexes estimated under alternative strong true score models. *Journal of Educational Measurement, 27*, 345–359.

Kane, M. T. (2006). Validity. In R. L. Brennan (Ed.), *Educational measurement* (4th ed., pp.17–64). Washington, DC: American Council on Education/Praeger.

Kelley, T. L. (1939). Selection of upper and lower groups for the validation of test items. *Journal of Educational Psychology, 30*, 17–24.

Kolen, M. J., & Brennan, R. L. (2014). *Test equating, scaling, and linking: Methods and practices* (3rd ed.). New York: Springer.

Lee, W., Hanson, B. A., & Brennan, R. L. (2002). Estimating consistency and accuracy indices for multiple classifications. *Applied Psychological Measurement, 26*, 412–432.

Livingston, S. A., & Lewis, C. (1995). Estimating the consistency and accuracy of classifications based on test scores. *Journal of Educational Measurement, 32*, 179–197.

Lord, F. M. (1980). *Applications of item response theory to practical testing problems*. Hillsdale, NJ: Erlbaum.

Luecht, R. M. (1998). Computer-assisted test assembly using optimization heuristics. *Applied Psychological Measurement, 22*, 224–336.

Luecht, R. M. (2000, April). *Implementing the computer-adaptive sequential testing (CAST) framework to mass produce high quality computer-adaptive and mastery tests*. Symposium paper presented at the Annual Meeting of the National Council on Measurement in Education, New Orleans, LA.

Luecht, R. M. (2001, April). *Capturing, codifying, and scoring complex data for innovative, computer-based items*. Paper presented at the Annual Meeting of the National Council on Measurement in Education, Seattle, WA.

Luecht, R. M. (2005). Item analysis. In B. Everitt & D. Howell (Eds.), *Encyclopedia of statistics in behavioral science* (pp. 1–9). Chichester: John Wiley & Sons. Retrieved from: http://onlinelibrary.wiley.com/doi/10.1002/0470013192.bsa318/pdf

Luecht, R. M. (2006). Designing tests for pass/fail decisions using IRT. In S. Downing & T. Haladyna (Eds.), *Handbook of test development* (pp. 575–596). Mahwah, NJ: Lawrence Erlbaum and Associates.

Luecht, R. M. (2007). Using information from multiple-choice distractors to enhance cognitive-diagnostic score reporting. In J. P. Leighton & M. J. Gierl (Eds.), *Cognitive diagnostic assessment for education: theory and applications* (pp. 319–340). London: Cambridge University Press.

Luecht, R. M. (2014). Computerized adaptive multistage design considerations and operational issues (pp. 69–83). In D. Yan, A. A. von Davier, & C. Lewis (Eds.), *Computerized multistage testing: Theory and applications*. London: CRC Press/Taylor & Francis.

Luecht, R. M. (2015). Applications of item response theory: Item and test information functions for designing and building mastery and criterion-referenced tests. In S. Lane, T. Haladyna, & M. Raymond (Eds.), *Handbook of test development,* (2nd ed., pp. 485–506). New York: Taylor & Francis/Routledge.

Luecht, R. M. (2016). Computer-adaptive testing. In B. Everitt & D. Howell (Eds.), *Encyclopedia of statistics in behavioral science* (pp. 1–10). Chichester: John Wiley & Sons, Ltd. Retrieved from: http://onlinelibrary.wiley.com/book/10.1002/0470013192.stat06405.pdf

Luecht, R. L., & Sireci, S. (2011). *A review of models for computer-based testing*. Research report 2011–2012. New York: The College Board.

Nering, M., & Ostini, R. (2010). *Handbook of polytomous item response models*. New York: Routledge.

Parshall, C. G., Harmes, J. C., Davey, T., & Pashley, P. (2010). Innovative items for computerized testing. In W. J. van der Linden & C. A. W. Glas (Eds.), *Computerized adaptive testing: Theory and practice* (2nd ed., pp. 215–230). Norwell, MA: Kluwer Academic Publishers.

Petersen, N. S., Kolen, M. J., & Hoover, H. D. (1989). Scaling, norming and equating. In R. L. Linn (Ed.), *Educational measurement* (3rd ed., pp. 221–262). New York: Macmillan.

Sands, W. A., Waters, B. K., & McBride, J. R. (Eds.) (1997). *Computerized adaptive testing: From inquiry to operation*. Washington, DC: American Psychological Association.

Schmeiser, C. B., & Welch, C. J. (2006). Test development. In R. L. Brennan (Ed.), *Educational measurement* (4th ed., pp. 307–354). Washington, DC: American Council on Education/Praeger.

van der Linden, W. J. (2000). Constrained adaptive testing with shadow tests. In W. J. van der Linden & C. A. W. Glas (Eds.), *Computer adaptive testing: Theory and practice* (pp. 27–52). Boston, MA: Kluwer.

van der Linden, W. J. (2005). *Linear models for optimal test design*. New York: Springer.

van der Linden, W. J., & Glas, C. A. W. (Eds.) (2010). *Elements of adaptive testing*. New York: Springer.

Willse, J. T., & Shu, Z. (2008). *CTT: Classical test theory functions*. Retrieved from: http://CRAN.R-project.org/package=CTT. Version 1.0

Wilson, M. (2005). *Constructing measures: An item response modeling approach*. Mahwah, NJ: Lawrence Erlbaum Associates.

Wright, B., & Stone, M. (1979). *Best test design*. Chicago: Mesa Press.

Zenisky, A., Hambleton, R. J., & Luecht, R. M. (2010). Multistage Testing: Issues, Designs, and Research. In W. J. van der Linden & C. A. W. Glas (Eds.), *Elements of adaptive testing* (pp. 355–372). New York: Springer.

Zenisky, A. L., & Sireci, S. G. (2002). Technological innovations in large-scale assessment. *Applied Measurement in Education*, 15(4), 337–362.

# 8 Communication with Candidates and Other Stakeholders

*Ellen R. Julian and Brian Bontempo*

## Introduction

Certification[1] involves a collaboration among many players—the aspiring professionals (the candidates), their educators and future employers, their professions as represented by the credentialing programs and subject-matter experts, any relevant regulatory agencies, the developers of the certification examinations, and the public. An effective, routine flow of information helps keep the process smooth. When problems occur, good crisis communication can save the day.

This chapter will be broadly inclusive in its scope, defining as "communication" topics as diverse as documentation, score reports, and marketing. Both the content and mode of communication will be addressed as we follow candidates from being potential applicants through the process of gaining certification and then on to becoming the subject-matter experts (SMEs) on whom we rely, from first-time item-writers to members of the Board of Directors who vote on our raises. Special attention will be paid to that most important communication, the test results.

## Communication

Knowing what information people need and when they need it is only half the battle. The credentialing program must provide the information repeatedly and in a variety of formats, balancing succinctness with thoroughness, readability with accuracy, and availability with timeliness. The wrong information must never go out, and information that does go out must speak to both the typical situation and also to the exceptions. It must give people enough time to act, but not so much time that they procrastinate and forget to do so. Much of the communication needs to be automated, but it should feel personal and leave individuals satisfied that they've been treated fairly. Impartiality and protection of confidentiality need to be constantly considered by asking whether any proposed communication might compromise either goal.

Merely providing information is not sufficient. Being able to say, "We told them," may help in a court of law, but it is not sufficient to make the system function smoothly. The recipients must actually understand and act on much of the information credentialing bodies are trying to communicate. Everyone's job is easier when the process is clear and understood. Communication with candidates and other stakeholders is so critical that the new AERA, APA, and NCME *Standards for Educational and Psychological Testing* (2014) references it explicitly and repeatedly, using strong language.

Applicants need to understand the big picture before they start the certification adventure, arguably even before they begin their professional education. They also need precise

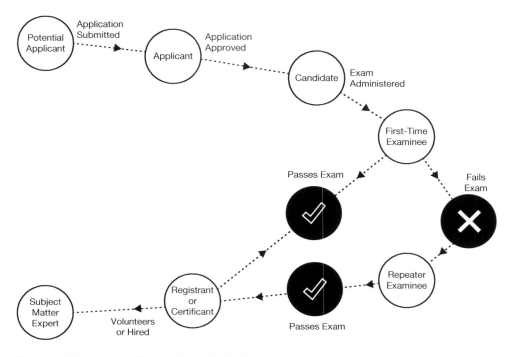

*Figure 8.1* Terminology Changes Through the Certification Process

details and good communication about their progress through the process. They need to know what to expect and what is expected of them.

First is a definition of terms (see Figure 8.1). Generally, applicants or prospective applicants are individuals who are thinking about certification. Once they start the process, they are candidates. When they sign up and sit for an exam, they become examinees. Those who pass the test and all other certification requirements become credential holders (or registrants or certificants) who may, if the credentialing organization has communicated well with them, become volunteers.

## Communicating with Potential Applicants

Often in the domain of the Marketing Department, the public's perceived value of the certification is crucial to the success of a certification program. When the public (as individuals, employers, or regulators) requires certification of its providers, certification offers a start to a respected and rewarding career. If the same marketing materials that highlight the importance of the credential to the public also attract prospective applicants, so much the better. The credentialing program is not just promoting a test and a credential—it is promoting a profession and a community.

If the certification requires a targeted education, information about educational programs also needs to be provided. If graduates of only some (e.g., accredited) educational programs can be candidates for the credential, this must be made explicit and information about relevant accreditations must be provided.

For a certification examination, if the credentialing organization, or one of its partners, offers educational courses related to its certification examinations, care must be taken in developing the courses' publicity material not to state or imply that taking the courses improves one's chances on the test. Providing any opportunity or advantage to students of one course that is not available to all may be viewed as a failure of impartiality. Assessment-based certificates, in contrast, may combine both education and examination.

## Communicating with Applicants

The credentialing program's call center is the voice its applicants hear, and its website is the face they see. Good design can reduce applicant frustration and requests for individual attention, and it can enhance an applicant's chances of success. For a website, the challenge is balancing completeness with convenience. For a call center, it's balancing efficiency and personalization.

Certification programs' websites are often dense and difficult to navigate, born of a fear of leaving out important information or created by staff members trained in the mechanics, but not the art, of creating websites. Programs should match the reading level and accessibility of the website to those required on the job. If vision is not required for certification, the website should be accessible to the visually-impaired applicant. If hearing is not required, text-based modes of communication for the hearing impaired should be supplied. If the examinations are being offered in multiple languages, instructions (and results) should be provided in all languages as well.

"What's going to be on the test?" is the most common concern of applicants, often closely followed by "How much is it going to cost?" and "What do I have to do first?" Answering those three basic questions covers the foundational obligation of a testing program and of the certifying body that sponsors it.

Once in the educational program, applicants' minds will naturally turn to the examination portion of the credential. They will be preparing for the examination as they pursue their education. The credentialing organization should help them make sure they're ready. Making the content outline easily available is a good start. Any task statements or lists of knowledge, skills, and abilities (KSAs) built to support the outline should be readily accessible by anyone studying, or helping others prepare, for the test. Documenting the process of content-outline development is important, as is translating the outline into easily understood prose and all relevant languages. How was it determined what the test will cover and in what proportions? Was this done by a survey of practitioners or a collection of experts? How often is the content outline updated?

Applicants need to know what sort of examination they will be confronting. Will the test be on computer or on paper? Will it be timed? Are all the challenges multiple-choice questions, or will examinees need to write or demonstrate something? Are practice tests available? Is there a correction for guessing? What kind of scores will be produced? When and how will applicants get their test results?

### *Candidate Handbook*

Paper application booklets and candidate handbooks/bulletins are disappearing, and websites have become the primary source of information about certification programs. Candidate handbooks and application materials may be viewed by examinees as essentially a contract, and these materials will surely be introduced as evidence if examinees feel they have been misled. The publicly available information about the test and test day needs to be complete, accurate, specific, and easily found.

Topics that should be included in the handbook (whether paper or online) include:

- Eligibility requirements, including prerequisites in education and experience.
- Certification requirements, number of tests, sample timelines.
- How to request accommodations to the test or testing environment.
- Fees and refund policies.
- Test specifications and example items.
- Registration and scheduling instructions, and timing information.
- Test-center locations and parking instructions.
- Test administration rules.
- Candidate agreements: Nondisclosure, cooperation with any investigation.
- Test security procedures and verifications, including any statistical techniques used to evaluate the validity of suspect scores and what will happen if there is evidence of a problem.
- Score scales and diagnostic information provided.
- Score reporting process and timeline.
- How to complain or challenge a test score.
- Quality assurance measures.
- About the test: Test-development processes, historical passing rates.
- Compliance/discipline requirements and processes.
- Recertification or Maintenance of Certification requirements.
- Information on how to contact the credentialing organization.

If it is not easy to get the information from the credentialing body, applicants will obtain it elsewhere. Information must be easy to find and understand, or people will rely on their teachers or review courses for it.

If the prep courses or educators seem to be providing bad information, channeling the correct information through them is a good option. It is imperative, however, that the same information is available, preferably without request, to anyone interested. Educators can serve as conduits of positive or negative information to their students. What they say about the test in their classrooms is key to how the examinees will experience it. Engaging the educators as active participants in the certification process helps ensure that the same communication is flowing to the students from all directions.

It should be made clear what education and experience are required of a successful applicant and how these must be documented. Certification typically requires a mix of education, experience, and assessment. A test cannot measure everything, so some aspects of competence assurance are delegated to the schools. Because schools cannot be assumed to provide practical experience, some level of work experience, whether measured by time or events, is often required. Neither educators nor employers can be assumed to be unbiased, hence the need for the test.

As with information about test content, descriptions of the registration process are usually online. Performing a trial walk as a new applicant through the website information is advisable, making sure that each step is always simple to determine and to find. The website should be as universally designed as possible, so no one's disabilities could get in the way of learning about the certification. Universal design makes things easier for everyone (Usability First, 2014).

## Lost and Confused Applicants

The first, and perhaps only, individual human contact an applicant may have with the testing organization may be with its help desk, whether for problems with the website or with the application. The help desk is the public face of the organization.

The people who answer the phones and chats should be articulate, well informed, caring, and accurate. They must be well prepared with all the information they need to do their jobs effectively, and they should be taught conflict resolution skills. Remember, applicants don't call unless they're having a problem, even if it's just their own inability to read what they were sent. If they get the help they need from the program, they will think better of the entire organization.

How much help can be automated before alienating people? Certainly, automatic and secure password help should be provided, for instance. Applicants should not have to call for that. In contrast, people don't want to listen to a computer-generated voice explain things they already know. When it gets complicated, the applicant needs to be able to reach an appropriate person—a technical one for website problems and an administrative one for process needs.

## Accommodations Requests

Applicants with special needs may request testing accommodations to allow them to demonstrate their knowledge, skills, and abilities, rather than any irrelevant limitations. Many of these applicants will already have experience dealing with testing accommodations, and others may be new to the concept. Some may have had frustrating experiences with other testing agencies and might start the current interaction already angry. The credentialing program needs to have thoughtfully constructed accommodations policies in place that protect the validity of the typical use of its test scores, while eliminating any irrelevant barriers for persons with disabilities. It must apply these policies consistently and fairly; and it must document and communicate its decisions in a timely, compassionate, and understandable manner.

The credentialing body may need to communicate with some applicants in different manners than it does with the majority. Its website certainly needs to be accommodations-friendly and Section 508 compliant (U. S. General Services Administration, 2016). The organization should think about screen readers when designing the layout for instruction books. It must be conscious of deaf applicants when designing the call center. It needs to consider what accommodations examinees might need when selecting the test administration method and vendor. A specialist can help with such issues.

## Test Difficulty

Summary data for the several previous testing cycles should be offered. Do yearly statistics make sense for the examination program? If testing only happens a couple of times a year, it might make more sense to show statistics for the separate administrations, especially if candidate performance has consistent patterns across administrations, perhaps highest right after graduation time. Annual statistics might not be sufficient, because those can feel awfully old by late in the following year.

Consideration should be given to separating results for first-time takers from those of repeaters, if the examinee volume is large enough. The more reliable the test is, the lower the passing rate of those who have already once demonstrated that they are not yet competent. Including them in passing rate calculations may make it appear that the passing rates are fluctuating, when all that is actually changing is the proportion of retakers. The retakers might not even need to be mentioned explicitly, if the total group and first-time takers are reported.

### *Communicating About Test Day*

Applicants who have successfully registered for a test are voracious consumers of any information they can get about the test. What will the environment be like? Should they bring a sweater? Water? Can they go to the restroom? For many, the content of the test fades behind a fog of worried anticipation. The testing organization should give applicants lots of information and make certain all rules are clear and repeated to prevent gossip that there are hidden "gotchas" at the test sites. Previous examinees are the best ambassadors.

Rules for test day must be communicated clearly, since retests are (at best) costly and distressing for all involved. The testing organization should make sure new examinees understand what they can bring into the testing situation and what the rules are for being late.

If scores aren't reported at the test site, information about how and when to get scores needs to be prominently featured on any receipt or letter given out at the test site—that's one piece of paper most people will not lose. The credentialing body must beware of server overloads when scores all become available at a certain, advertised time. It must make sure the score reports are informative and have additional interpretive information available online. Because providing test results is such an important form of communication, it gets its own section.

## Communicating with Examinees

### *Reporting Test Results*

Test results reports, depictions of an examinee's performance on a credentialing examination or a set of credentialing examinations are important and widely used communications made by credentialing programs. Therefore, they must be accurate and effective.

Since one size does not fit all, certification programs are encouraged to invest resources in the development and evaluation of their test results reports. The commentary on Standard 6.10 suggests that programs conduct research on their test results reports, perhaps including field testing and focus groups as part of the research methodology (Allalouf, 2007; Hambleton & Slater, 1997; Trout & Hyde, 2006). Organizations interested in more information about the process for developing test results reports are directed to Hambleton and Zenisky (2012).

This section explores the design and development of test results reports. The following topics will be addressed:

- Test results report content.
- Providing test results reports.
- Helping with interpretation.

Before beginning, it is important to note that there is a difference between communicating test results themselves and communicating them via a test results report. Some credentialing programs communicate test results to some stakeholders such as hiring mangers or regulators by transmitting the test results electronically. Depending on the program, the test results user(s), and the agreement made between the candidates and the credentialing program, the test results may be transmitted with or without test results reports.

For credentialing programs, the intended user of a test results report is typically the examinee. Examinees may choose to share their test results report with peers, recruiters, supervisors, regulators, or educators. Bontempo and Wilson (2013) identified two types of test results report users: newbies and junkies. Newbies want to know what actions they should take based on their test results. In contrast, junkies want more explanation, information, and data. Satisfying the needs of both types of users is a continual challenge.

Another challenge is building a report that satisfies two opposing objectives. Some view a test results report as a technical report that documents the scientific outcomes of the examination experiment. Others view a test results report as a summary of the "Game Day" performance of the examinee. The contrast between the two perspectives is stark. Testing scientists wish to only report information in which valid inferences can be made, whereas the journalist is more concerned with documenting and publicizing the actual events as they occurred. Although both perspectives are valid, the *Standards* are grounded in the science of psychometrics, so fair deference should be paid to that perspective.

*Test Results Report Content*

The contents of test results reports vary from minimalistic and simple to verbose and complicated depending on the specifications of the credentialing examination, the competency of the candidates, and the level of transparency of the credentialing program. Although credentialing programs may choose to include a great deal more, effective test results reports *must* contain the following essential information:

- The name and/or identifying information of the candidate to which the report pertains.
- The name of the credentialing examination(s) being reported.
- The date and location in which the candidate was administered the credentialing examination(s) being reported.
- The test results.
- Directions for interpreting the test results.

In addition, the *Standards* indicate that the following listed information be provided to candidates. Since this information directly pertains to questions or actions that candidates may have/take while using their test results reports, credentialing programs are encouraged to provide this information or links to it on the test results reports themselves.

- An explanation of the scoring process (Standard 6.8).
- An explanation of the quality control process (Standard 6.9).
- An explanation of who has been provided with or has access to the test results (Standard 8.5).
- An explanation of how to challenge a test result (Standard 9.17).
- An explanation of retake policies (Standard 9.18).
- An explanation of the next steps in the credentialing process.
- The rights and responsibilities of credential holders.

*Types of Test Results*

In designing a test results report, a credentialing body is likely to spend some time deciding which type of test results to include. Since there are many different flavors of test results, it is important to define some terms before proceeding.

- An *outcome* is a classification of a candidate's performance into a meaningful category. The outcome of most credentialing examinations is to classify an examinee into the pass or fail category. As a result, the outcome is commonly referred to as a "pass/fail outcome." Outcomes are also called decisions or classifications.
- The *Standards* define a *score* to be, "Any specific number resulting from the assessment of an individual, such as a raw score, a scale score, an estimate of a latent variable, … a course grade, or a rating." For credentialing, course grades are synonymous with outcomes and are distinctively different than scores. Therefore, for credentialing, a truncated definition is proposed: A score is "any specific number resulting from the assessment of an individual, such as a raw score, a scale score, an estimate of a latent variable, or a rating." In order to differentiate scores from subscores, sometimes the term "overall score" is used instead of the term "score."
- A *subscore* is a numeric description of the performance of a candidate on a subset of items about a similar topic, typically a section of the test blueprint.
- A *rank* is a numeric description of the position of the candidate's performance relative to the performance of other examinees within a meaningful group.
- Credentialing programs are advised to consider that passing and failing examinees use test results reports differently. Failing candidates are interested in diagnostic feedback about their performance that they can use to help prepare for subsequent attempts. Although passing candidates may also have an interest in diagnostic information, they are more likely to use a test results report to communicate their achievement to others. Because of these differences, most credentialing programs produce different types of test results reports for passing and failing examinees.

OUTCOMES

Generally speaking, the purpose of a credentialing examination program is to assess knowledge, skills, and abilities in a specified job or practice domain, and to award a credential to candidates who meet or exceed a specified threshold of performance. To be clear, the purpose of a credentialing examination is not to provide diagnostic feedback to candidates. The current version of the *Standards* does not indicate whether or not credentialing programs should provide diagnostic feedback to candidates. Therefore, the most conservative approach to reporting test results is to report only the outcome—generally "pass" or "fail"—to the candidate.

SCORES

Although the conservative approach is acceptable, candidates are very interested in their test performance and arguably have a right to more information about it. If a credentialing program wishes to provide additional information, the most common choice is the overall test score. Although the reporting of a test score may seem benign, many high-performing candidates would like to report their score to hiring managers or the public as a way to suggest that they are more competent than those with lower scores. This use of overall test scores can be problematic since the measurement error, especially for extreme scores, may be large enough to render small score differences completely meaningless. Since it is likely that overall test scores will be misused by some passing candidates, most credentialing programs opt to provide total scores solely to failing candidates.

Scores can be classified as raw scores (including percent-correct scores) or scaled scores (including latent-trait estimates). Scaled scores may be created as a result of the psychometric scaling and equating process or through a mathematical transformation of the raw scores. Equated scaled scores are optimal since they are directly comparable across test forms of different difficulty, providing for objective comparisons between examinees regardless of when they test or which test form they completed. Although non-equated scaled scores derived from mathematical transformations may not be objectively comparable, programs using them appropriately succeed in providing scores in a unit that is free of any preconceived notions, such as 70% being an often misperceived passing standard for examinations.

Programs should be prepared for pundits who are skeptical of the scaling process itself and for decriers who argue that scaling is a layer of unnecessary abstraction that distorts the true performance of a candidate. Programs should be prepared to provide a variety of responses to these concerns based on the mathematical competency of the challengers.

If the scale mimics another common scale such as the SAT scale or percentage-correct scores, then candidates may incorrectly infer that it is similar. In addition, negative values or larger numbers can have unintended psychological impacts; and regardless of the instruction provided, larger numeric differences can be perceived as larger actual differences.

SUBSCORES

For credentialing programs, subscores are fraught with issues, primarily because credentialing examinations are designed to provide accurate outcomes rather than accurate subscores. As a result, subscores are often imprecise. This creates a dilemma for credentialing programs. If a program decides not to provide subscores, then the program has not provided enough useful diagnostic information to candidates. If a program decides to provide subscores, then it must expend resources preventing the misuse of that information. This dilemma is especially troublesome when the error associated with one topic is much larger than the error for the others, often the situation in credentialing tests where the test blueprint percentage of one topic is much smaller than the others. Psychometrics would suggest that the imprecise subscore should not be reported at all. However, many candidates would argue that it is not fair to hold back useful subscores for all the other topics when only one topic is troublesome.

Leucht (2003) and Haberman and Sinharay (2010) provide some innovative statistical strategies to increase the precision of subscores for mastery tests such as credentialing examinations. Although many of these strategies are sophisticated and unproven, they provide evidence that psychometrics may yield more useful subscores in the future. Even if this is true, the computational complexity of the new models may render these approaches untenable. Moreover, it is unlikely that credentialing bodies will be able to successfully communicate to examinees how these methods function.

The communication of subscore information on test results reports can be tricky. Even with the clearest of instructions, examinees will find creative ways of combining subscores that suggest that they have passed an examination despite the fact that their overall scores are below the passing standard. One way to steer many examinees away from this behavior is to provide the number of items that were administered from each topic. Smart examinees can infer that poor performance in a large area might result in a failing outcome despite passing performance in a handful of smaller areas. Clear instructions also help.

*Providing Test Results Reports*

In addition to deciding what to report, credentialing organizations must also decide how to provide test results reports. This includes when to provide the test results reports, the way in which test results reports will be transferred to candidates, and the format of the test results reports.

TIMING

Test results reports may be provided immediately following the test administration or some time following that. Examinees typically want their test results as soon as possible. Many on-demand, computer-based credentialing programs provide test results immediately. On the other hand, some programs conduct quality-control analyses before delivering test results reports. This advisable practice allows time for test administration irregularities, including potential breaches in test security, to be identified and investigated. Some groups provide *preliminary* test results immediately, which are followed by *official* test results reports at a later date. Although this may require more resources to create and maintain, it satisfies the examinees' desire for immediate results while also allowing the program time to ensure quality. The additional time also creates a window where the credentialing program can conduct more sophisticated normative analyses that can be included in the test results reports.

DELIVERY METHOD

Credentialing programs transfer test results reports to candidates in traditional and tech-savvy ways. If the results are provided immediately following the test administration, the test administrator will likely print out the test results report and give it to the examinee on site. This method is the most likely to reach the examinee. Many organizations provide electronic test results reports in the form of an email or a notification within an authenticated website. With today's technology, the authenticated website option is desirable because it's faster, provides more flexibility in the format and, for tech-savvy programs, opens up the possibility for real-time normative feedback. Some programs send test results reports in the mail. Although this option may be slower, it may be convenient if additional credential materials such as certificates, membership cards, or pins can be included in the mailer. Regardless of which option is chosen, the security of the information must be maintained and the identity of the recipient must be authenticated.

*Format*

The format of test results reports varies as much as the content. The format of the communication and style of the text should follow the recommendations provided for other formal candidate communications discussed elsewhere in this chapter. In addition, it is important to consider the format in which the test results themselves are conveyed within a test results report. Credentialing programs can convey test results by embedding them in the text, conveying them in a table, or rendering them in another type of data visualization such as a graph. Each of these will be discussed below.

Some programs choose to report test results within the text of a paragraph. This method is commonly used by programs reporting nothing beyond the outcome and overall score. Programs selecting this method often use graphic design techniques, such as increasing the font size, to bring attention to the test results. Although this practice is a good one, it is wise not to draw too much attention to the test results. That's because candidates who read the report quickly may ingest only the test results and skip all of the other important information.

Tables and graphs are examples of data visualizations. Bontempo (2014a) provides an overview of the theory of data visualization and its application to testing, including test results reports. The insights provided in that article are summarized below.

Tables are a useful way of communicating information when the exact values are important (Few, 2004). As a result, tables are well suited for reporting test results. Tables are also useful for reporting multiple variables concurrently, especially when the units of measurement differ (Few, 2004). Therefore, test results reports that contains many disparate pieces of numeric information such as overall score, rank, total test administration time, and the number of items, which are all on different scales, may benefit from the inclusion of a table.

Graphs, in contrast, are a useful way of communicating information when the relationship between variables is important. This relationship is usually communicated through the shape of the graph. Despite their effectiveness, a recent survey of over 100 certification programs accredited by the National Commission for Certifying Agencies (NCCA) found that none of these programs used graphs in their test results reports (Bontempo, 2014b). Although NCCA-accredited certification programs represent a subset of the credentialing industry, this finding suggests that tables are currently common; graphs are not. Given the current state of technology, credentialing programs are encouraged to begin using graphs to communicate subscore information. By doing so, the relationship between subscores can be illuminated, which helps candidates identify their strengths and weaknesses.

Although it is beyond the scope of this chapter to provide details about the design of effective graphs (see Bontempo, 2014c for more), a few guiding principles may help.

- The size of the effect in the data should be equal to the size of the effect in the visualization (Tufte, 1983).
- Do not use innovative chart types unless the traditional chart types fail to convey the information.
- Use attributes to highlight similarities or differences (Few, 2004).

Since each way of formatting test results has its strengths, one solution could never work for all credentialing programs. Therefore, credentialing programs are encouraged to consider the options and choose an appropriate format or, perhaps, more than one. For example, a single test results report may contain a table with the overall score information and a graph with subscore information.

### Helping with Interpretation

Since helping candidates to pass the examination is not the primary mission of a credentialing program, resources are not always allocated for providing useful test results reports or helping the candidates to interpret them. Although this is understandable, it opposes the *Standards* and the ideas presented in this section.

Standard 6.10 and 11.1 indicate that testing programs are responsible for developing and communicating appropriate interpretations of test scores for specific uses. The commentary on Standard 6.10 suggests that programs should also guide candidates away from misinterpretation or misuse of the scores. This section will provide some insight into how to build a test results report that will prevent score misuse and help candidates interpret the information.

The following interpretive information is useful to failing candidates, and credentialing organizations should consider including it on their test results reports.

- Comparative Information
- Measurement Error
- Test Taking Behavior
- Recommended Action
- Technical Explanation

The literacy and analytic skills of the candidates will largely impact the utility of each piece of interpretive information. Reports created for low literacy users should highlight recommended action and downplay the technical details including measurement error. In contrast, candidates with strong analytic skills should be provided with all of the technical information so that they can develop their own recommendations.

*Comparative Information*

Comparative information provides context for the score(s) and helps candidates to develop meaning from their performance data. Comparison points can be criterion- or norm-referenced, although the most useful reports contain both. The most important criterion-referenced point is the passing standard ("cutscore") for this discussion. The distance that a candidate's score is from the cutscore is of primary interest to a candidate and commonly an appropriate way to interpret a test score.

Some programs choose to classify failing candidates' performance and provide them with text such as "Far from passing" or "Near the cutscore." This practice is effective for audiences with low mathematical and/or analytical skills since it removes the need for the candidate to use measurement error to interpret the score. It is also commonly used by programs that have complicated scale scores such as Item Response Theory estimates (e.g., 1.11 logits), which may intimidate or confuse candidates. One challenge in implementing this strategy is determining how many categories to use and where to draw the boundaries between the categories. Credentialing programs should use the test's measurement error in determining the range. And the range should never be less than four times the size of the measurement error, since a smaller error band would yield classifications that are different than the true classification for more than 5% of the candidates with scores directly in the middle of the category.[2]

Another way of reporting a candidate's distance from the passing standard is to report the numeric values of the candidate's score and the cutscore. It is also advisable to provide the numeric difference between these two values. This quantifies how much a candidate needs to improve in order to pass.

Although certification programs do not commonly use graphs to report scores, they could use a simple bar graph or thermometer to effectively convey the relationship between the candidate's overall score and the cutscore. The area in-between could be highlighted to bring attention to the amount of improvement needed to pass the examination.

Normative comparisons also help candidates interpret their performance. The most common form of normative feedback is the passing rate. Although credentialing program volunteers and staff members are very interested in the *passing* rate, failing candidates are more interested in the *failing* rate since it tells them how many folks are like them.

Failing candidates are also very interested in comparing their score to the scores of others. This is often expressed as a rank, percentile rank, or categorization such as a quartile, quintile, or decile. Similar to the overall score, normative information can be reported by embedding it in the text, providing it in a table, or visually rendering it using a graph.

As with the overall score, a simple bar chart or thermometer can effectively convey the percentile rank of the candidate as well as a hypothetical student right at the cutscore, also known as the borderline minimally-competent candidate. The difference between these two percentile ranks is important because it indicates the percentage of candidates that a failing candidate needs to "hop over" in order to pass the examination. Despite its importance to candidates, this difference is rarely reported.

Credentialing organizations wishing to avoid reporting numeric values may find it desirable to convey the percentile rank as a histogram. Histograms display the data as an uncommon two-dimensional shape. The science of perception has found that it is difficult for humans to perceive the size of differences in two dimensions (Few, 2004), and histograms can sometimes provide misleading information when the bin size is not selected carefully (Jacoby, 1997). To interpret a histogram also requires knowledge of basic statistics. Given these considerations, histograms are not recommended for use on score reports unless the applicable target population has a firm grasp of their meaning. Instead, programs may find it beneficial to use linear visualizations such as the bar charts suggested earlier.

One important consideration in providing normative information is the definition of a candidate's peers. Since statistics work better with larger, more stable samples, credentialing bodies often compare a candidate's performance to the global or national sample. Typically, candidates are new to the profession and have little understanding of the national or international group of candidates. Therefore, global norms have limited utility to them. For the candidates, a more useful comparison group is their educational program or workgroup. Candidates' intimate knowledge of the individuals in their local group allows them to interpret the percentile ranks as, "I need to improve enough to be as competent as Jimmy or Sally" (other candidates in their class). Since local and global comparison groups satisfy two different objectives—utility and stability—providing normative feedback for both comparison groups may be beneficial. On the other hand, interpreting normative information can be challenging enough for candidates without the added complexity of multiple comparison groups.

Although normative information is useful to candidates, it can be easily misunderstood unless it accompanies criterion-referenced information. Take, for example, a candidate who was only one question short of passing. The percentage of candidates receiving the same score may be quite high—say, 30%. If only the percentile ranks were provided, then the candidate might falsely think that she is very far from the passing standard.

Although it is uncommon for a program to provide normative information about subscore performance, this can help with interpretation. By providing the percentile ranks associated with subscores, candidates can quickly see how their strengths and weaknesses compare to the strengths and weaknesses of others. Areas where candidates are weakest when compared to the performance of others are likely to receive more attention than other weak areas. In uncommonly weak areas, candidates may have missed something that their peers understood, so a review of the content might help. On the other hand, poor performance in commonly weak areas may suggest that some additional learning resources are needed.

*Measurement Error*

The commentary on Standard 6.10 indicates that score precision should be provided on test results reports. The challenge for most organizations is finding a way to provide this in a manner so that candidates can understand it and use it. Providing the numeric value for measurement error may be appropriate for candidates with advanced analytic skills. Providing a visual representation of error is advisable for candidates with low analytic ability.

Although Tukey's original box plot (1977) depicted the boundaries of quartiles, some programs have modified it to represent the confidence interval around a candidate's score. This approach works well for both scores and subscores since performance in the different topics can be visually compared quite easily.

Figure 8.2 is a section of the test results report provided by the Federation of State Boards of Physical Therapy for the National Physical Therapy Examination. This section provides a set of visualizations that highlight a candidate's scale score and subscores, the "retake range" (the 68% confidence interval) around each score, the 95% confidence interval, and the passing standard (600). Colors perhaps (red, yellow, and green) are particularly useful in helping identify areas of strength and weakness.

The size of subscore error is troublesome when helping candidates interpret a test results report. Sometimes, the 95% confidence interval around a subscore is so large that it covers 25%, 50%, or maybe 75% of the scale score range. This typically happens when the number of items within a topic is small. Many certification programs dodge this by adjusting the size of the confidence interval (e.g., 50% or 68%). This practice is somewhat haphazard since these alternative confidence intervals are not commonly used in statistics and suggest that the scores may be too imprecise. On the other hand, proper disclaimers can promote appropriate interpretation of the valuable information contained in subscores.

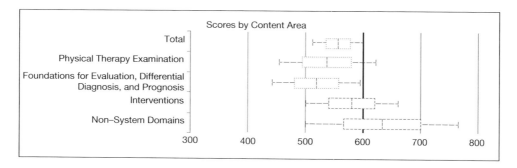

*Figure 8.2* Using Color to Show Content-area Performance Relative to Cut Score: red (shown here as a dotted line '...'); yellow (shown here as a double dashed line '---'); green (shown here as a long dashed line '–––')

Consistent with Standards 2.3 to 2.5, it is vital to provide instructions about the measurement error. These should include how the error was calculated, how the confidence interval was created, the size of the confidence interval, and the meaning of it. It is advisable to use simple phrases like "retake range" that make it is easier for non-technical audiences to grasp these concepts.

*Test Taking Behavior*

Candidates are also curious about their test taking behavior. Providing the total test administration time or the number of incomplete items can help a candidate to monitor and adjust the speed at which questions need to be completed. This information is even more useful if it is calculated by section or topic.

A candidate map provides a detailed, play-by-play picture of a candidate's test event. A candidate map might contain the following information: the item score (0/1 for dichotomous items), the interim or current overall score, the topic area assigned to the item, and the item response time (also known as the latency). Candidate maps are useful in identifying if a candidate had trouble getting warmed up or if and when fatigue may have set in. This information can be used to identify how long a candidate should spend taking the practice questions and when a candidate should take a break. They are particularly illuminating for adaptive exams since they illustrate the power of the algorithm to hone in on the performance of a candidate. An example of a candidate map is shown in Figure 8.3.

*Recommended Action*

Regardless of whether or not candidates have a shallow or deep understanding of their performance, they inevitably want to know what they need to study. A good test results report should provide this information to the extent that the test itself will allow it.

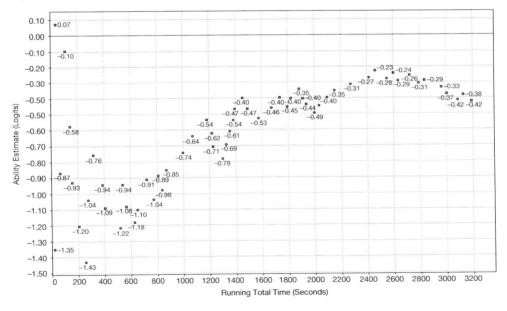

*Figure 8.3* Candidate Map for Adaptive Test

A word cloud is an excellent way to provide a quick response. In it, the name of each topic is displayed in randomized space where the size of the font used for each topic varies based on the candidate's performance for that topic. It may be particularly useful to vary the size of the font based on the inverse in performance, which makes the weak areas stand out. Word clouds and their cousin bubble charts provide the big picture quickly, so they work best for populations with limited analytic skills. Despite their attractiveness, the size of a topic is expressed in only height and width, which are also related to the number of characters. Therefore, it is sometimes difficult to perceive the differences between topics of similar size. Categorizing topic performance by shading or color can help with this, as in Figure 8.4.

After candidates have interpreted the visual or numeric information, they often become curious about the content within each topic. In other words, they become interested in identifying the subtopics or concepts that they should learn or review. Although this information can be obtained from the test blueprint, candidates often forget about this document or struggle to make accurate links between the report and the blueprint. Credentialing programs can do a great deal to assist failing candidates by embedding links to the detailed test blueprint in the test results report itself.

Candidates are also curious to know the amount of information that they need to learn or review for each concept within a topic. One useful way to accomplish this is to identify the concepts that are found in the items near the cutscore. Ben Wright developed a visualization, now called a Wright Map (Wilson & Draney, 2000), that enables a candidate to see the concepts of the items arranged according to difficulty. Despite the attractiveness of this technique, credentialing programs are not likely to be able to provide this information since the content domain of most credentialing programs is not stable enough nor is the item bank large enough to accurately discern the differences in the difficulty of concepts within a particular topic.

*Technical Explanation*

Credentialing organizations should provide an explanation of how the information on the test results report was calculated. Details about the scoring or rating process are necessary as well as the strategies used to calculate subscores, measurement error, and the classification of performance into a category. When these explanations are too sophisticated for the candidates, credentialing programs should provide a high-level explanation on the test results report and a more detailed explanation upon request or on the organization's website.

*Figure 8.4* Word Cloud Emphasizing Areas that Need Additional Studying

Programs are encouraged to provide the technical information about the credentialing examination along with the technical information about the test results report. This facilitates a connection between the examination and the results, and promotes continuity in the communication of the program's technical information.

In summary, test results reports are one of the most important communications that a credentialing program will make. It is imperative that programs spend the time and resources needed to design and develop the best reports possible. Although the majority of time and resources should be spent on the content and format, programs cannot forget about the timing and delivery. Programs are urged to include comparative information, measurement error, test taking behavior, recommended actions, and a technical explanation in order to help users interpret the test results reports while meeting the *Standards*.

## *Reporting the Performance of Groups*

Credentialing bodies may find it beneficial to communicate the performance of groups of candidates to their stakeholders. In fact, some credentialing organizations may find it necessary to report the performance of the group of candidates within each governmental jurisdiction (i.e., state or province). Others may find that national regulatory bodies use this information to accredit education/training programs. And there may be some organizations that opt to report on the employees in a company or division. In addition to providing a service that is directly beneficial to the groups receiving the reports, this service advances the profession, creates goodwill among the stakeholders, and demonstrates the openness and transparency of the credentialing organization.

Before beginning to design and develop group performance reports, credentialing programs are advised to review their candidate agreements for limitations pertaining to the provision of scores. Generally speaking, most candidate agreements allow candidates' test results to be shared in aggregate form as long as the privacy and confidentiality of all examinees is protected. Credentialing programs are advised to especially watch out for small groups. If there are only a few students in a group, then the aggregate performance can approximate the performance of the individuals in that group. This has the potential to violate the privacy of the group's individuals and should be avoided at all costs.

Although Standard 6.16 indicates that programs must ensure that the privacy and confidentiality of test results and the associated reports be maintained, there are certain instances where it is permissible and appropriate to provide the individual test scores of a group of examinees, such as when scores are reported to a regulatory body. If the candidate agreement permits a credentialing program to share the performance of individual candidates, in these instances, credentialing programs are directed to the prior section on test results reporting for more information.

Those programs that are interested in reporting on the aggregate performance of a group may find it useful to consider the same issues that were discussed in the section on test results reporting. Programs are encouraged to move beyond simply reporting the passing rate for the group. For example, group performance reports can include the distribution of scores and subscores or a summary of the distribution(s) expressed as the mean (or median), standard deviation, min and max. This information can provide very meaningful insight into the competency of the group as well as the strengths and weaknesses of the group. This is particularly helpful to educational programs that can use this information as part of their curriculum and program evaluation.

One consideration that is specific to group reports is the reporting period. For tests given during a single testing window, the reporting period may be synonymous with the test date or range of test dates. For continuous testing programs, the reporting period needs to be defined. The best reports are ones that have a long enough reporting period to provide stable, confidential results while short enough to capture meaningful differences. Most credentialing programs have a predictable cycle to their candidates. The best candidates often test in the late spring or early summer, immediately following the traditional academic calendar graduation. For these programs, the worst candidates tend to test in the winter. Credentialing organizations are encouraged to get to know their program's cycle before determining an appropriate reporting period. This ensures that these predictable fluctuations are included in a single reporting period or explained as part of the section on interpretation.

Even if the privacy and confidentiality of the individuals in a small group can be maintained, some groups may be too small for the performance information to be of use. The appropriate minimum group size depends on the specifications of the certification examination and the statistical methods used for aggregation. Therefore, programs are advised to seek consultation from statisticians and psychometricians before deciding on a minimum size.

Ultimately, group performance reports can be a very meaningful way of communicating to important stakeholders who don't normally connect with a credentialing organization. Therefore, programs are advised to invest resources into the design and development of these reports.

### Challenges and Appeals

For those individuals who do not pass, they often believe it is because of an error in the testing process; and testing programs are required by the *Standards* (AERA, APA, & NCME, 2014, and accreditation bodies) to provide the ability for examinees to challenge an exam result they believe to be erroneous. Standard 8.12 (p. 137) states: "In educational and credentialing testing programs, a test taker is entitled to fair treatment and a reasonable resolution process, appropriate to the particular circumstances, regarding … challenges issued by the test taker regarding accuracies of the scoring or scoring key."

A general "rescore" can be offered if the computation of the score is challenged, an item challenge can single out a specific test item believed to be flawed, or a rater's ruling may be appealed. Communication with examinees who challenge their exam can be tricky, in part because the challenging examinees have received a result they do not wish to believe is true. Their emotions are high and negative; they want it to be someone else's fault; and they hope that, with this challenge, they can erase the embarrassment of having failed and avoid having to retake the exam.

Communicating with those who challenge test questions, scoring, or administration requires a delicate blend of transparency, empathy, research, persuasion, timeliness, and legal care. The degree of need for a record of precisely what was said will determine the best mode of communication. It may require a certified letter with delivery confirmation, or a phone call may suffice. Email is useful, although not completely reliable or secure.

### Angry Applicants

People who are not happy with their credentialing progress will often threaten to call a lawyer. Sometimes, but fortunately less frequently, lawyers will write. Applicants might want the prerequisites changed or their application speeded up. Perhaps the credentialing program even made a mistake in processing their application. Applicants might want accommodations they've been denied or to have certain exceptions made. Some requests are reasonable, so by all means, these should be promptly addressed to make people happy to the extent it doesn't give an unfair advantage. Requestors should be treated with respect and their wishes truly acknowledged. It's important for credentialing bodies to find a way to solve a problem, even if it's not with the solution originally suggested by the applicant.

To some extent, humane policies can replace the need for individual exceptions. A clear policy on what "comfort aids" are allowed will be more efficient and equitable than allowing them only for those who know how to "work the system." If reading speed isn't part of what is being measured, the credentialing program could be generous with time allotments for everyone. If private rooms are available and secure, people should be instructed on how to request them. Extra breaks might not be permitted, but maybe allowing a water bottle at the testing station could be.

The more people are given what they need, the less their lawyers will get involved. However, it is inevitable that something will go wrong. Maybe someone had a bad experience and had to retake the test. Possibly the computer ate a response record, or an incorrect score was initially reported. The credentialing organization messed up and the examinee is angry. Or, sometimes people just attack the test, making outrageous claims about it with absolute conviction and threats of injunctions and investigations.

The credentialing organization's response matters. First, it must ask, "Is there any truth to the claims?" If there is, the organization must acknowledge it clearly, quickly, and respectfully; then move the conversation on to what's been done about it and what's being done to ensure it never happens again. What is key is for the credentialing body to remain calm. No one should hit the "Send" button with a red face. It's wise to have legal counsel review anything that could be brought into court, which is mostly everything. If not each individual response, the general response templates need to be reviewed by both counsel and a good editor. Responses to complaints should be personalized. Limitations need to be set on who can send emails to applicants. Above all, promises that can't be kept must not be made.

If the challenge is a general rant in a public forum, the best response may be none at all. However, if it is a specific charge or criticism from a credible-appearing source, getting out in front of it might be better. The credentialing organization should acknowledge the problem, put it in the context of the body's history and mission, and control the conversation. Consideration might be given to working with a public relations firm that specializes in helping organizations write those tough responses (Covello, 2003).

Social media management and search engine optimization are necessary for making good use of online opportunities for communication with all audiences. These endeavors should be made an important part of someone's job, boundaries on content must be clarified, and no plan should begin unless the means and will to sustain it are available. Fortunately, most social media losses are missed opportunities, but the examples of sins of commission are scary. Most often, it is people's temper or libido affecting their judgment. No one should overreact if a staff member makes a mistake. Time passes quickly online, and folks will move on.

## Communicating with Subject-Matter Experts

After passing the examination and all other requirements for certification, an applicant/candidate/examinee becomes a potential subject-matter expert (SME). Whether the SMEs are paid or volunteer, they represent an indispensable resource for test development. Volunteers may require more nurturing than paid experts, but communication with both will be an essential part of the certification program's communication plan.

Volunteers have become the lifeblood of many certification organizations by providing their time and expertise to "give back" and help make the profession stronger. At the onset, organizations should start talking about volunteering to applicants for certification, encouraging them to think of it as a natural extension of the process they are undergoing. Once applicants have become certified, it's time for them to start thinking about volunteering. Their contributions are often on the critical pathway to project completion, and yet credentialing organizations have a lot less control over them than the organizations do over paid SMEs, staff, or vendors. For this reason, many larger associations have SMEs on staff or pay their item writers. As some students later return to the educational system as teachers, this approach provides SMEs with another possible career path.

### Recruiting Volunteers

This chapter can't address the complexities of making people want to volunteer their time and work for the credentialing body, but it is important to acknowledge that recruiting volunteers may require as much marketing skill and investment as recruiting applicants. With volunteers, however, the association must find non-financial motivators that inspire volunteers to complete their assignments as agreed. Communication is a big part of that. Making volunteers feel a responsibility towards the organization and the project requires that they have a relationship with the organization. Credentialing programs must reach out and find out what motivates people. Maybe opportunities to rub elbows with leaders in the field? Making friends with others doing the same work they do? Paying it forward to the next generation? Getting an all-expenses-paid trip with an extra day for sightseeing?

The volunteers' tasks must be defined clearly. As with every job, volunteering well requires understanding what needs to be done. Communicating the tasks to be accomplished with enough context to show where the volunteers fit into the big picture, but not so much that they get distracted or confused, keeps morale and production high. Credentialing organizations must take care to acknowledge volunteers' contributions as publicly as possible and find ways to express how their work is appreciated.

### Working with Remote Volunteers

When testing was a provincial task, the testing program could bring its SMEs together in a conference room for the several days it might require to complete their tasks. Now that testing is often a global activity, new challenges have arisen. When the SMEs are in seven different time zones, even a conference call can be hard. Individual assignments, such as remote item writing, can be easily distributed with the right software tools, but group processes are more difficult.

Asynchronous remote item review has been developed by most of the major item banking systems, but many testing programs end up bringing groups together anyway because the SMEs want that in-person networking experience. Remote standard setting, especially the essential first step of building a group consensus on the detailed description of the minimally competent examinee (Livingston & Zieky, 1982; Cizek, 2001), remains a challenge.

### Talking to Groups

Learning how to run an effective meeting remotely, whether by telephone or with video, increases morale and efficiency for staff and external partners. SMEs, vendors, and clients do work independently, reporting in on a timeline often through a conference call or video meeting. Vendors and clients develop work plans, each at their own desk in a different city/country. Facilitating group remote work is challenging and essential.

Anyone who is uncomfortable speaking in front of groups of volunteers probably doesn't want to make a big report to the Board of Directors either. Both the organization and the individual benefit from people's efforts to become a more effective public speaker, in both scripted and group-discussion situations. Individuals struggling with public speaking should be encouraged to take a class, join a club, practice.

When running the meeting, whether remotely or face-to-face, certification program staff should make sure that goals are clear from the start, all the necessary players are there, and any decisions to be made are clearly defined. People must be kept on topic and on time, background noise dealt with expeditiously, and it should be made certain that everyone who should speak, does speak. Representatives should start on time, but provide a short warm-up period for small talk, technical adjustments, and allowing latecomers to join. It's amiable to announce at the start that the meeting will end a few minutes early so people can be on time for their next meeting. Decisions and next steps must be documented.

For best practices on communicating with volunteers, the archives of the associations serving the credentialing community can be referenced. For instance, The Center for Association Leadership (ASAE, www.asaecenter.org) has many model and sample documents available online, as do the Institute for Credentialing Excellence (ICE, www.credentialingexcellence.org) and the Council for Licensure, Regulation, and Enforcement (CLEAR, www.clearhq.org).

**Crisis Communication**

Have a plan. Every "Best Practices" list for crisis communications starts with: "Have a plan and follow it." That is true whether the crisis is a national emergency, a local power outage, or a copy of a test appearing online. Working with a communication expert at this planning stage may avoid the need to hire one in a hurry later. Key decision-makers should be notified early and kept posted on developments. They, not front-line staff, will need to determine the best approach for the organization. It's the organization's role to facilitate the decision-makers' communications with each other.

The credentialing body must coordinate responses, making sure that anyone who talks to the press, the complainant, or a lawyer is thoroughly prepared. The organization should also provide talking points, laying out the facts as it sees them. Telling the truth, and telling it quickly, is paramount. Acknowledging any harm that has been done, and apologizing if needed, is also of the utmost importance. The credentialing body can then put things in the context of the greater good that the organization does and focus on how things will be better in the future.

A good reference for reducing the chances of a reporter, or a lawyer, surprising a spokesperson with an unexpected question is a list of "77 Questions Commonly Asked by Journalists During a Crisis" (Covello, 2005). While developed for health officers, the questions will be asked in any crisis situation.

**Documentation**

Documentation gets its own chapter, Chapter 7, in the new *Standards*. Accreditors require copious amounts of documentation, and proper documentation can avert many challenges and accusations. Sloppy or missing documentation creates problems. The *Standards* state repeatedly that "evidence should be provided" and "described clearly" (cf. 6.2, 6.8, 6.8, 6.13). In fact, in the beginning, it says, "The process of developing educational and psychological tests should begin with a statement of the purpose(s) of the test, the intended users and uses, the construct or content domain to be measured, and the intended examinee population" (p. 76). As specifics, the *Standards* lists "test manuals, technical manuals, user's guides, research reports, specimen sets, examination kits, directions for test administrators and scorers, or preview materials for test takers" as documents that "are evaluated on the basis of their completeness, accuracy, currency, and clarity" (p. 123). These documents will have different audiences and will be created by a variety of authors. A central system for maintaining and updating this plethora of documents is crucial. In fact, maintaining a good documentation system is such a massive task that there are international standards just for it (ISO 9001, 2015). Maintaining a consistent strategy for documentation across areas is crucial, making organization and retrieval easier, as well as the next accreditation review.

Policies and procedures are communications too—communications with staff and possibly lawyers. It is important for policies and procedures to be complete, accurate, current, and clear, Accredited or not, it's worth the trouble to document procedures. When things (inevitably) go wrong, mistakes get made, or a new wrinkle appears, if documented procedures have been followed, the defense will be much more straightforward. While people can argue that the procedures need improvement, if procedures were followed, it's much harder for individuals to attribute the error to a personal attack. In addition, "continuous quality improvement" initiatives require baseline documentation. Good documentation is not just for a crisis or exception. It is needed in order to coherently improve the process year after year.

### Using the Sources of Influence to Communicate

Whether communicating with staff, contractors, volunteers, credential holders, examinees, educators, or the press, credentialing organizations need to become sensitized to the sources of influence that are being wielded. Cialdini's (2006) Six Universal Principles of Influence are:

1. **Reciprocity:** When given something, people want to give something in return.
2. **Scarcity:** Scarce things seem more attractive.
3. **Authority:** People tend to believe what authorities say.
4. **Consistency:** People want to be consistent with their previous choices and statements.
5. **Liking:** People are more inclined to do things for those they like.
6. **Consensus:** People want to know what others have done.

When one learns to use these tools, others will say "yes" more often. When one learns to recognize when others are using them, it becomes easier to say "no" to others' influence.

Here's a tongue-in-cheek blurb for recruiting volunteer SMEs that uses all six types of influence:

> The CEO and President of the Board of Directors (authority) hope you enjoyed your last all-expenses-paid trip to our city (reciprocity)! They hope you will continue acting on your commitment to our mission (consistency) by acting now to claim one of the few remaining spots (scarcity) on our next test-review panel. Everyone's doing it (consensus)! Your friends (liking) are signing up and need your help.

## Information Privacy and Confidentiality

So far, discussion has been mainly about enhancing information flow. Some data, however, must not leave the organization. Applicants necessarily provide sensitive personally identifiable information (PII), putting an enormous responsibility on the credentialing body. Standards 6.14 and 6.16 require a credentialing body to develop and use privacy and confidentiality procedures for storing, retaining, and sharing PII.

Opportunities for unintentionally divulging confidential information are legion:

- Group emails with everyone's email addresses showing.
- Compliance or discipline-hearing materials leaking.
- Data files containing PII and even test scores maliciously or accidentally divulged.
- Paper files discarded carelessly.
- Email or paper mail sent to the wrong person.
- A volunteer downloaded items for review.
- Medical images submitted by an item writer with PII of patients included.
- Data files provided to other companies for analysis go astray.
- Malicious break-ins to the credentialing program's or a vendor's data systems.

It's imperative for credentialing programs to work with staff, volunteers, and vendors to create a culture of high security. Investing in high-quality protective technology that is easy to use, and requiring training on it for new staff and volunteers, will prevent many of the leaks that are caused by people working around cumbersome systems.

Caution must be taken when summarizing the performance of groups. Each group should have a sufficient number of members (typically three or five is the minimum) so that an individual's performance cannot be revealed through reverse engineering.

Privacy laws vary by state and country. The credentialing body is responsible for abiding by the privacy laws of the location of testing, not the location of its headquarters. Many countries are stricter than the United States, particularly about information leaving the country. Programs are recommended to consult with legal counsel regarding these specific issues in the areas they serve.

### "Do not Contact" Requests

The credentialing program needs to stay current with laws that restrict contacting persons on mailing lists and on how individuals can ask to be removed from those lists. Regulations vary across countries; but, if possible, be clear to people that, even if they have asked to be removed from the mailing list, any "transactional and relationship communications" will continue to be sent. If they need to be contacted about dues, for instance, their "unsubscribe" from the newsletter will not preclude it. The "primary purpose" of the communication determines how it is treated by the rules. The title line, in particular, must reference the ongoing relationship or transaction to assure that it will not be treated as commercial. Some commercial information can be in the communication, however.

Below are the rules as to how to comply with the USA's CAN-SPAM laws (Bureau of Consumer Protection, 2014). While these laws may not apply to transactional communications, most offer good guidance for all emails.

1. Don't use false or misleading header information.
2. Don't use deceptive subject lines.

3. Identify the message as an ad (if it is one).
4. Tell recipients where you're located.
5. Tell recipients how to opt out of receiving future email.
6. Honor opt-out requests promptly.
7. Monitor what others are doing on your behalf.

For more information, see the Federal Trade Commission's Website: www.business.ftc.gov.

## Conclusion

This chapter has defined "communication" very broadly, covering everything from marketing to technical reports, the call center, recruiting volunteers, and talking to the press. It includes communication with SMEs because of their essential role in the quality of a test and the life of the certification organization. A theme throughout the *Standards* and this chapter is the provision of complete, accurate, and accessible information to the persons striving for the credential, and to those who make decisions based on it. Credentialing organizations must be forthright about the characteristics of the tests, documenting and sharing information about test development and performance.

Credentialing programs should provide as much feedback as the data can support to those who need to study more and return to take the test again, along with an indication of the scores' precision. Graphics can communicate test performance with less potential for misuse than numerical scores; and pictures can be especially useful as a way of showing, rather than describing, the precision of different scores.

Programs need to be especially careful with people's privacy and their data's security. If something goes wrong, the best action is to admit it, fix it, apologize, and move on. The certification organization needs to build a lifetime relationship with its people by keeping them informed about their progress through the system, first as applicants, then as examinees, and finally as the subject-matter experts who help build the credentialing process for the next generation.

## Notes

1. Although the term "certification" is used throughout this chapter, many of the practices described and recommendations made are applicable to both certification and licensure programs.
2. As determined by creating a two-tailed 95% confidence interval around the score in the middle of the category.

## References

Allalouf, A. (2007). An NCME instructional module on quality control procedures in the scoring, equating, and reporting of test scores. *Educational Measurement: Issues and Practice, 26*(1), 36–46.

American Educational Research Association, American Psychological Association, National Council on Measurement in Education (AERA, APA, & NCME) (2014). *Standards for educational and psychological testing*. Washington, DC: American Educational Research Association.

Bontempo, B. (2014). Technology and testing. *CLEAR Exam Review, 24*(1), 8–12.

Bontempo, B. (2014a). An Introduction to data visualization for testing. *CLEAR Exam Review, 24*(1), 8–12.

Bontempo, B. (2014b). *The use of data visualization in testing reports.* A paper presented at the 9th Conference of the International Test Commission, San Sebastian, Spain.

Bontempo, B. (2014c). Designing effective data visualizations for testing. *CLEAR Exam Review, 24*(2), 9–14.

Bontempo, B., & Wilson, D. (2013). *Innovating reports with data visualization.* Workshop presented at the 2014 Annual ATP Innovations in Testing Conference, Scottsdale, AZ.

Bureau of Consumer Protection Business Center (2014). *CAN-SPAM Act: A compliance guide for business.* Retrieved from: www.business.ftc.gov/documents/bus61-can-spam-act-compliance-guide-business

Cialdini, R. (2006). *Influence: The psychology of persuasion.* New York: Harper Business.

Cizek, G. J. (Ed.) (2001). *Setting performance standards.* Mahwah, NJ: Lawrence Erlbaum Associates.

Covello, V. T. (2003). *Keeping your head in a crisis: Responding to communication challenges posed by bio-terrorism and emerging infectious diseases.* Association of State and Territorial Health Officers (ASTHO). Retrieved from: www.dshs.state.tx.us/riskcomm/documents/77_Questions.pdf

Covello, V. T. (2005). Risk communication. In H. Frumkin (Ed.), *Environmental health: From local to global* (pp. 988–1009). New York: Jossey Bass/John Wiley & Sons.

Few, S. (2004). *Show me the numbers: Designing tables and graphs to enlighten.* Analytics Press: Oakland, CA.

Haberman, S., & Sinharay, S. (2010). Reporting of Subscores Using Multidimensional Item Response Theory. *Psychometrika. 75*(2), 209–227.

Hambleton, R., & Zenisky, A. (2012). Developing test score reports that work: The process and best practices for effective communication. *Educational Measurement: Issues and Practice, 31*(2), 21–26.

Hambleton, R. K., & Slater, S. (1997). *Are NAEP executive summary reports understandable to policy makers and educators?* (CSE Technical Report 430). Los Angeles, CA: National Center for Research on Evaluation, Standards, and Student Teaching.

International Standards Organization (ISO) (2015). *International standard ISO 9001 Quality management systems.* Retrieved from: www.iso.org/

Jacoby, W. (1997). *Statistical graphics for univariate and bivariate data.* Thousand Oaks, CA: Sage Publications.

Lievens, F., & Motowidlo, S. J. (2016). Situational judgment tests: From measures of situational judgment to measures of general domain knowledge. *Industrial and Organizational Psychology: Perspectives on Science and Practice, 9*(1), 3–22.

Livingston, S. A., & Zieky, M. J. (1982). *Passing scores: A manual for setting standards of performance on educational and occupational tests.* Princeton, NJ: ETS.

Luecht, R. (2003). Applications of multidimensional diagnostic scoring for certification and licensure tests. Paper presented at the annual meeting of the National Council on Measurement in Education, Chicago.

Trout, D. L., & Hyde, B. (2006). *Developing score reports for statewide assessments that are valued and used: Feedback from K–12 stakeholders.* Paper presented at the Annual Meeting of the American Educational Research Association, San Francisco, CA.

Tufte, E. (1983). *The visual display of quantitative information.* Cheshire, CT: Graphics Press.

Tukey, J. W. (1977). *Exploratory data analysis.* Reading, PA: Addison-Wesley Publishing Company.

U. S. General Services Administration, Office of Governmentwide Policy, Office of Information, Integrity, & Access. (2016). *GSA Government-wide section 508 accessibility program.* Retrieved from: www.section508.gov

Usability First (2014). *Principles of accessible and universal design.* Retrieved from: www.usabilityfirst.com/about-usability/accessibility/principles-of-accessible-and-universal-design

Wilson, M., & Draney, K. (2000). *Standard mapping: A technique for setting standards and maintaining them over time.* Paper in an invited symposium: "Models and analyses for combining and calibrating items of different types over time" at the International Conference on Measurement and Multivariate Analysis, Banff, Canada.

# 9 Security Issues in Professional Certification/Licensure Testing

*James A. Wollack and Gregory J. Cizek*

In addition to occurrences of cheating that have always been witnessed in testing contexts where there are substantial consequences for individuals, the phenomenon of organized and professional cheating has arisen more recently as one of the unintended consequences of credentialing programs in which examination requirements often play a prominent role in licensure or certification decisions. The high costs and heightened stakes of these assessments can place tremendous pressure on examinees to succeed, especially in situations where those examinees were required to devote considerable time and incur thousands of dollars of debt just to get the opportunity to attempt to obtain a credential. This pressure has created a market for resources to help examinees be successful. The combination of increased testing volumes and technological advances have prompted some individuals to realize that helping others succeed on tests through any means possible can be a lucrative enterprise.

Over the past decade, there has been a consistent stream of reports of cheating on tests in licensure/certification settings. The problem is evident across a wide variety of disciplines, including health-related fields such as among physicians (Hobson, 2010), physical therapists (Abella, 2010), radiologists (Zamost, Griffin, & Ansari, 2012), and pharmacists (Smydo, 2003) and careers/professions including teachers (Sainz, 2012), the military (Botelho, 2014; Sisk, 2014), information technology (Foster & Zervos, 2006; Maynes, 2009; Mitchell, 2014), crane operators (Kugler, 2008), law enforcement (Lyons, 2015), and lawyers (Beck, 2012), to name a few.

The testing industry has responded to increased cheating threats with new test development and delivery formats that are more resistant to cheating (Impara & Foster, 2006), improved policies and procedures to deal more effectively with cheating and potential cheating incidents (Case & Donahue, 2013; Fitzgerald & Mulkey, 2013; Harris & Schoenig, 2013), and a wave of new research, highlighted by the launch in 2012 of the annual Conference on the Statistical Detection of Potential Test Fraud (which, in 2014 was renamed the Conference on Test Security).

Test security is a paramount concern in a variety of contexts. There are some commonalities—but many differences—in test security concerns that arise, for example, in testing for competence in licensure contexts, testing to assess achievement in educational contexts, and testing to inform hiring decisions in employment contexts. In this chapter, our focus is limited to test security concerns in credentialing contexts. The focus of this chapter is also primarily on test security in the context of computer-based testing (CBT). Although we recognize that some credentialing organizations deliver paper-based tests—indeed, to some extent there might always be a need for paper-based tests for Braille versions or other special considerations—we also recognize the clear shift toward a computer-based mode of test administration. In addition, whereas security issues specific to paper-and-pencil testing are discussed elsewhere in the literature (Cohen & Wollack, 2006; Fremer & Ferrara, 2013; Wollack & Case, 2016), those relating to CBT are less prevalent. Thus, the primary emphasis of this chapter will be on security planning for CBT programs.

## The Credentialing Context

In many areas covered by licensure or certification, a test is often used as one component in the credentialing process. Test security is a heightened concern when a license or other certification is necessary for practice in occupations where risks to public health, safety, psychological or financial well-being exist, or when other serious harms can occur from non-competent practice. In such occupations, requirements in addition to test performance may include a specified amount of supervised practice, completion of a prescribed program of studies, attainment of a specified GPA, or other educational requirements. Although it is possible that any requirements may be circumvented, the testing component of credentialing programs is often the most challenging and visible aspect when candidate knowledge, skill, or ability must be assured.

Thus, although it is certainly important to ensure the integrity of program completion records, GPA requirements, and so on, the integrity of a credentialing process that includes an examination component must involve addressing test security. To that end, the following portions of this section present a validity perspective on test security, discuss the case for security planning, provide an outline of the major components of a comprehensive security plan, and explore the practical issue of budgeting for test security.

### Test Security: A Validity Concern

Concern for test security is frequently—but too narrowly—couched as a concern about preventing, detecting, and responding to cheating. Surely cheating is a concern; Cizek has defined cheating as "any action taken before, during, or after the administration of a test or assignment, that is intended to gain an unfair advantage or produce inaccurate results" (2012b, p. 16). However, attention to test security is best considered to be a concern much broader than dealing with cheating; test security is most appropriately considered as subsumed under the broader psychometric umbrella of validity (Cizek & Wollack, 2017).

Validity has been called "the most fundamental consideration in developing and evaluating tests" (AERA, APA, & NCME, 2014, p. 11). In somewhat technical terms, Cizek has defined validity as "the degree to which scores on an appropriately administered instrument support inferences about variation in the characteristic the instrument was developed to measure" (2012a, p. 35). Or, put more simply, validity refers to the extent to which test scores can be interpreted to mean what they are intended to mean.

An example may help to illustrate. Suppose that a candidate takes a computer-based dental board examination to determine his or her preparation to care for patients. Further suppose that the test-taker scored sufficiently high on the test such that the candidate passed the examination and was thereby labeled as competent for safe and effective entry-level practice. To be sure, we cannot know for certain if the examinee is truly competent; even the best licensure or certification test is only a sample of knowledge, skill, or ability taken at a single point in time and conclusions about competence must necessarily be cautious. In psychometric terms, these conclusions are called *inferences* because an informed judgment about the examinee's more global status must be made based on the smaller sample of behavior. Good tests are designed to support strong, confident inferences—that is, we want tests that allow us, with great confidence, to make claims about proficiency or competence or whatever characteristic it is that we are trying to measure.

There is, of course, a link between the scores that examinees receive on tests and the desired inferences. Low scores suggest inferences of ill-preparation, non-mastery, or incompetence in a specified area; higher scores suggest inferences of greater mastery, more skill, acceptable levels of competence, and so on. To the extent that the body of theoretical and empirical evidence supports the conclusion that those inferences are defensible, test scores are said to have greater validity than scores on tests where the available evidence is weak, absent, or contested. In short, test scores are considered to have validity when the interpretations, conclusions, actions—or *inferences*—we make based on those scores are well supported by evidence that they are good, correct, or accurate.

A number of features of test development, administration, and scoring contribute to that body of evidence in support of valid test score interpretations. The *Standards* (AERA, APA, & NCME, 2014) mention several sources; Cizek (2012a, 2016) has described others. For example, inferences about a prospective dentist's ability to think critically about information supplied by a patient may be supported by (a) the results of a job analysis indicating that such behavior was engaged in frequently in the practice of dentistry, and that it was critical to successful patient outcomes—this kind of validity support is called "evidence based on test content" (p. 14) in the *Standards*—and (b) results of a think-aloud protocol that illuminated the cognitions a candidate uses to conceptualize a problem—this kind of validity support is called "evidence based on response process" (p. 15) by the *Standards*.

Just as there are sources of evidence that can support claims about the validity of test scores, there are also many factors that can weaken the confidence we can have in a given test score. For example, if the aspiring dentist's computer monitor exhibits flickering, making it difficult to clearly see dental pathology on displayed radiographs, then the accuracy of any inference based on that test score is threatened.

In short, although there are diverse lenses through which test security concerns might be viewed (e.g., ethical, statistical, and social), it is safe to say that cheating represents a threat to the valid interpretation of a test score. When cheating takes place—whether in the form of copying from another test taker, collusion, prior access to secure test materials, inappropriate manipulation of answer documents, or any other form—the resulting test scores are not likely to be an accurate measurement of an examinee's true level of knowledge, skill, or ability. Regardless of the other lenses applied, concerns about test security are rightly viewed as a psychometric concern about the validity or "interpretive accuracy" of test scores. The failure to design and implement adequate security policies and procedures or breaches of test security at any point in the testing process can result in a test score that cannot be interpreted as intended, typically indicating a greater level of knowledge or skill than that score would otherwise signify.

## The Need for Security Planning

From a validity perspective, it follows that security planning and implementation are essential to support a test's intended score inferences. And, although the need for security planning may seem obvious, a heightened focus on security planning is a relatively recent development. There are at least three reasons beyond an interest in reducing threats to accurate score interpretations that a comprehensive security plan is needed.

First, threats to test security are omnipresent. Whenever there are important consequences associated with test performance, there will be constant challenges to test security, and it is likely that any entity offering a credential to candidates who pass a testing requirement will experience attempts to compromise the security of the test in any testing cycle. Indeed, the consequences associated with test performance ensure that test security will continue to be a concern. For example, within the U.S., it has been observed that access to occupations is increasingly licensed and regulated, and advancement within occupations is increasingly accompanied by credentialing requirements (Collins, 1979), where credentials play a greater gatekeeping role with regard to entry into and progress within a vocation. A *credential* refers to a formal "attestation of qualification or competence issued to an individual by a third party (such as an educational institution or an industry or occupational certifying organization) with the relevant authority or assumed competence to issue such a credential" (U.S. Department of Labor, 2010, p. 5). It has been an explicit policy goal that the U.S. should lead the world in the percentage of Americans with post-secondary degrees and/or industry-recognized certificates and credentials by 2020" (U.S. Department of Labor, 2010, p. 1). Overall, as credentialing requirements are increasingly mandated and regulate entrance to and advancement within a profession, test security will be an increasing concern.

In addition to the stakes associated with test performance, the increasing frequency of cheating appears to reflect sociological trends: One public policy researcher has opined that America is becoming a "cheating culture" (Callahan, 2004). However, the prevalence of cheating is not limited to the United States: a regular feature called "Cheating in the News" on the website of a prominent test security company chronicles cheating news stories from around the world and across diverse professional and educational contexts (see www.caveon.com/citn/).

Second, test security provides protection. Strong test security policies and procedures provide protection in two important ways. For one, test security helps promote the accuracy and meaningfulness of test scores. In most licensure and certification contexts, testing requirements are part of overall credentialing systems that have as their primary goal protection of the public from incompetent or ineffective practice. Tests that are developed, administered, and scored under secure conditions help ensure that the scores on such tests can be interpreted with respect to that goal. For another, test security helps maintain the integrity of a credential and, by extension, the reputation of the organization sponsoring the credential. In some cases, public protection may not be a major concern; instead, a credentialing examination program might serve primarily to signal advanced training or experience in a field. These score interpretations are important also, and it is typically of great interest to sponsoring organizations to ensure that the recognition associated with acquisition of its credential is deserved.

Third, test security doesn't happen by itself. Without comprehensive security planning, it is unlikely that common threats to a testing program will be prevented, and many instances of cheating may go entirely unnoticed. Further, the specialized expertise required to engage in test security planning is unique. Licensure and certification organization staff members may have extensive training and experience in meeting planning, association management, psychometrics, information technology, and so on, but even specialists in these fields are rarely exposed to in-depth training in test security and are often not well versed in common threats to security or how to prevent them. Thus, test security planning should be addressed as a separate, thoughtful activity in credentialing programs, ideally by those with strong grounding and experience in the area.

## Establishing a Test Security Budget

While security planning is essential—and will be the focus of this chapter—it is of little consequence if the program lacks the resources necessary to implement the plan. Therefore, programs must have a test security budget that allows for prevention and detection strategies to be performed, thorough misconduct investigations to be conducted, and contingency plans to be invoked to mitigate potential damage resulting from a breach. Fitzgerald and Mulkey (2013) identify four components to a test security budget: 1) security personnel and training; 2) candidate misconduct; 3) exam monitoring and analysis; and 4) infrastructure upgrades.

The security personnel component refers to the hiring of a Director of Test Security to oversee all security operations, and the drafting and implementation of a test security plan. It is often valuable for the Director to have a background in either law, law enforcement, or psychometrics, but regardless of the individual's training, it is critical that there is a single individual who is immersed in security issues and is chiefly responsible for ensuring that the program's security policies and practices comply with best practices. In addition, direct costs of training testing staff and subcontractors on the organization's security policies are subsumed under this budget category.

The candidate misconduct budget is intended to cover the various costs associated with investigating a suspected breach. This includes the costs of collecting and analyzing evidence of wrongdoing and associated legal fees. Offering free retests for examinees suspected of misconduct and legal fees for creating a Candidate Agreement are important expenditures that must be accounted for somewhere in a test security budget; Fitzgerald and Mulkey (2013) recommend absorbing those costs within the candidate misconduct component. We would add that the expense of registering the copyright with the U.S. Copyright Office should also be covered under the misconduct budget. Although copyright protection is afforded to the test publisher immediately upon creating the test, according to federal law, registering the copyright is essential to an organization's ability to sue for copyright infringement and to collect legal fees and damages (Semko & Hunt, 2013).

Exam monitoring and analysis covers costs for any analyses to detect potential test fraud. This includes costs associated with identifying contaminated examinees and items, and includes the budget for statistical and routine monitoring approaches, such as patrolling the Web for compromised items. In addition, some funds must be allocated for either replacing compromised items in the item bank or invoking an alternate, emergency testing process to be used until the breach is contained.

Finally, many prevention and detection strategies require significant costs to improve the testing infrastructure, such as remodeling buildings to help better control and monitor access to secure testing materials, acquisition of improved biometric equipment for purposes of authenticating candidates, and software upgrades to allow more cheat-resistant item delivery models to be used.

A test security budget can be a significant expenditure, and an organization beginning to take security more seriously may not be able to immediately fund all desired activities. However, in keeping with the philosophy that a chain is only as strong as its weakest link, it is important to recognize that securing a testing program requires a comprehensive, diverse, multifaceted approach and that inadequate security in any phase of the process can severely compromise the integrity of the entire program. Furthermore, as most programs that have encountered a significant breach will attest, it is much more economical and resistant to legal challenge when security planning is conducted well before the breach itself (Schoenig, Rhodes, & Eyob, 2013).

## A Comprehensive Test Security Plan

A comprehensive test security plan addresses four primary points at which threats to test security are likely to occur: 1) during test development; 2) in item/test delivery; 3) during test administration; and 4) in scoring and reporting of results. In the following sections of this chapter, the unique security concerns at each of these four junctures will be identified and described, with recommendations provided for addressing them.

### *Security During Test Development*

In conjunction with their test development efforts, organizations that sponsor a credentialing examination typically develop a *Candidate Guide, Test Handbook,* or similar documentation. These resources provide examinees with information to help familiarize them with the examination, as well as important guidelines and procedures related to test eligibility, registration, administration, and score reporting. A *Candidate Guide* is often the first exposure a potential examinee will have to the requirements of the testing program, and it is at this first exposure that the first information regarding examinees' rights and responsibilities related to testing should be communicated. A number of good resources exist that spell out these obligations, including the *Rights and Responsibilities of Test Takers* (Joint Committee on Testing Practices, 2000) and portions of the *Standards for Educational and Psychological Testing* (AERA, APA, & NCME, 2014).

Because the *Candidate Guide* is likely an examinee's first formal exposure to his or her responsibilities related to test security, it is important that the document provides examinees with a clear explication of their obligations, examples of permissible and impermissible testing behaviors, and, ideally, a test security agreement form that all candidates are required to sign in order to be permitted to register for the test. Such a form would define cheating, list specific prohibited behaviors, state the obligation of examinees to avoid engaging in such behaviors, and describe the penalties for violations of the security agreement, including possible score cancelation, license suspension, inability to retest for a fixed period, legal action, or other sanctions. A sample test security agreement form used in a health-professions credentialing program is provided in Appendix A.

A detailed *Candidate Guide* should also provide sufficient information to potential examinees about all relevant and appropriate examination characteristics. This might include, for example, specific information on:

- test length, including the number and format of questions or tasks, testing time allowed;
- test structure or "blueprints," including specification of sub-areas to be tested, number of testing sessions, policies on scheduled and unscheduled breaks, etc.;
- test mode, including specialized information related to computer administration;
- test weighting and scoring, including the relative contribution of sub-areas to total score, as well as policies on retesting and score expiration;
- permissible and impermissible items during test administration;
- appropriate identification or documentation to authenticate the candidate at the test site and verify his/her credentials to sit for the exam.

In situations where it is feasible, it may be desirable to provide a Web-based or other tutorial to help candidates become familiar with any computer platform or unique applications that they will be using. Because mystery can motivate misbehavior, it is also desirable to provide candidates with samples of non-secure test items, tasks, and scoring rubrics. In addition to demonstrating transparency and limiting the potential impact of construct-irrelevant variance on their scores, such materials can help diminish the attractiveness to candidates of engaging in commercial test preparation activities that may—intentionally or inadvertently—expose candidates to secure test materials.

In addition to developing a *Candidate Guide* to formally acquaint examinees with their rights and responsibilities, it is desirable for credentialing organizations also to make security obligations known to those who work on the testing program, such as program staff, volunteers, subcontractors, and subject matter experts (SMEs) who develop or review items, approve test forms, or in other roles have access to test content that should be securely maintained. Such personnel should be informed, for example, that the materials they will be developing, reviewing, or evaluating must be handled or maintained according to specified security procedures, must not be used for any other purpose, and must not be disclosed, distributed, or duplicated. A sample non-disclosure agreement is provided in Appendix B.

Notifying candidates, testing staff, employees, and vendors about security protocol and consequences for violations of those policies is critical, in terms of communication of expectations and prevention of violations, as well as opportunities for legal action and compensation in the event of a violation. However, credentialing organizations must also take a more active role in protecting the security of their test content during the test development (or, more generally, pre-administration) process.

Although the focus of this chapter is on computer-administered tests, we note that paper-based test forms present a major threat to the security of a testing program because each page that falls into the wrong hands includes verbatim copies of live test items. Yet, with each test administration involving potentially hundreds of thousands of pages, each having been handled by examinees, test supervisors, proctors, and shipping personnel, recognizing the problem and identifying the source represents the proverbial needle in the haystack problem.

Fortunately, the migration of the overwhelming majority of credentialing exams to CBT has largely addressed the security concerns related to printed test content being shared with the masses during test administration. However, for many programs, much of the test development process, including item writing and review, remains paper-based. An increasing number of software solutions exist to facilitate online item development and review, with security features such as the ability to assign specific roles to different individuals, tracking of individuals who have accessed various items, and the inability to print or download local copies of items. Because of both the functionality and increased security features these systems offer, utilization of paperless environments during test development is quickly becoming a recognized best practice (Scicchitano & Meade, 2013).

To the extent that it is unavoidable to use some paper throughout test development, it is important that adequate security provisions are put in place. Hard copies of any testing materials should be kept in locked cabinets within a restricted access space. Only those individuals whose job responsibilities require access to those archived materials should receive the security clearance to enter this space. Entry into the secure storage area should be logged, as should chain of custody should materials need to be removed from the area. Any individual who will have access to these materials should be required to sign a test security agreement. All checked-out materials should be returned to the secure storage area immediately after they are no longer being used.

In addition, paper-based programs must have agreements in place with any external vendors or partners, such as test printers, typesetters and copyeditors, shipping vendors, and test administration sites with clear policies about how to securely handle and maintain electronic files, as well as any paper-based materials. Testing materials must be sent to vendors using secure electronic file transfer, by hand delivery, or in double-sealed packages (with a unique, tamper-proof seal over the inner-most package) by overnight shipping with a signed return receipt. Each printed test booklet should be marked with a unique identifier (e.g., serial number) to assist in inventorying and reconciling all returned materials. Vendors must agree to destroy any excess pages either by cross-shredding or burning.

Lest we give the impression that stolen paper-based materials are the only mechanism by which secure test information becomes compromised, it is equally critical that organizations maintain the security of their electronic files. As with paper-based testing programs, procedures must be in place to limit in-person access to the systems storing the secure materials. However, with electronic files, special attention must also be given to restricting unauthorized remote access. Scicchitano and Meade (2013) provide a thorough description of best practices surrounding physical security and the protection of intellectual property through limiting access, both in-person and electronic. Files, computers, and servers with secure test materials should not only be in secure, access-controlled spaces, but should themselves be set up with a variety of security precautions, including firewalls, virus detection software, intrusion detection software, strong passwords (which should be changed at least every 90 days, Scicchitano & Meade, 2013, p. 154) and disabling or monitoring of external ports. Sensitive data should be encrypted, particularly when in transit (such as when test files are sent electronically to a print or test delivery vendor), and data should be backed up regularly (e.g., daily) to an offsite facility.

### *Security in Item/Test Delivery*

Credentialing assessment programs vary widely with regard to the logistics surrounding examination delivery. Program features such as test format, item types, administration schedules, and item usage offer different security advantages and limitations, and the selection of the administrative conditions usually constitutes a balancing act between considerations for security, testing volume, the need for candidates to access the test, and the desires of stakeholders (e.g., candidates, constituencies, Board of Directors, etc.).

### *Testing Modality*

All tests are administered in one of three basic testing modalities: paper and pencil, CBT, or Internet-based testing (IBT). As mentioned earlier, very few credentialing programs are administered exclusively on paper, and good resources exist relating to security issues in paper-based testing contexts. Hence, our focus in this chapter is on technology-based tests, which include both CBT and IBT. CBT and IBT are quite similar in many regards, namely, in both cases, the exams are delivered to examinees through a computer platform.

There are two primary differences between CBT and IBT. In CBT, examinations are either loaded onto local servers at the testing center or are pre-loaded onto the testing computers and delivered to candidates through a desktop application that locks candidate access to all other applications such as the Internet, other programs, special keystroke functions (e.g. copy/paste/toggle open programs), and peripheral devices. In contrast, in IBT, examinations are stored on a remote server and are delivered over the Internet through a password-protected website. The second major difference between the two modalities is that IBT exams have historically not been proctored, whereas CBT exams are required to be proctored in real-time (Association of Test Publishers [ATP], 2013). There are undoubtedly assessment delivery mechanisms or contexts for which live proctoring is unnecessary; however, professional credentialing is not one of those. Nevertheless, with the emergence of live online proctoring technologies and the expansion of test center networks (e.g., the Consortium of College Testing Centers), IBT (with live proctoring) has become a viable option for many credentialing programs as well.

*Examination Delivery Models*

Tests also vary with respect to the examination delivery model, with programs choosing from between adaptive, non-adaptive (including both fixed form and linear-on-the-fly testing), or hybrid models, such as multistage tests, in which candidates each take several fixed-form testlets, with the difficulty of the particular testlets being administered determined based on an adaptive algorithm. These different delivery models have been described extensively elsewhere (e.g., ATP, 2013; Folk & Smith, 2002; Hambleton, 1993; Yan, von Davier, & Lewis, 2014); consequently, the present discussion will focus exclusively on the security issues related to each.

Non-adaptive testing is the most straightforward of the delivery models. In general, it does not require as extensive an item pool as adaptive testing, and can be implemented in programs with smaller testing volumes. In non-adaptive testing, multiple fixed forms are built to content specification and any two examinees receiving the same form will see the exact same collection of items. As a result, candidates who are seated next to each other during a test administration should be assigned different forms to prevent answer copying, and controls should be in place to ensure that candidates who retest are administered an alternate form. Exposure of items (i.e, the number of candidates administered a particular item) is controlled indirectly, through manipulating the number of live forms relative to the size of the candidate pool. The most secure variant of multiple fixed forms involves the administration of single-use or one-off forms that are administered for a single test date, after which the items are retired, except, perhaps, for a small handful necessary for equating or item bank maintenance. If used items are not automatically retired, item banks should be sufficiently robust so that new forms can be developed that overlap minimally with the forms they are replacing.

From a security perspective, non-adaptive testing is not without its disadvantages. They are generally somewhat longer than adaptive tests (Stocking, 1994; Weiss, 1982), so item harvesters have greater potential to access large numbers of items. Also, in the event that a non-adaptive test form is compromised in its entirety, individuals with preknowledge who are fortunate enough to be assigned the compromised form will be administered 100% of the compromised items.

In adaptive testing, all candidates receive a unique test (built to the same content specifications), customized to optimize both the precision of the estimate of the candidate's trait level and the utilization of the items in the test bank. Adaptive tests provide many security advantages. By presenting each candidate with different items, answer copying is essentially eliminated as a concern. Candidates taking a computerized adaptive test (CAT) are presented with fewer items. This, combined with the fact that CATs often utilize test banks that expose many more items than do non-adaptive tests, means that examinees who share item content following an examination (either as part of a deliberate harvesting effort or just in casual debriefing with friends) have less opportunity to compromise a large proportion of operational items. Still, CATs are plenty vulnerable to organized item-harvesting efforts, as the test preparation company, Stanley H. Kaplan, demonstrated in 1994 when it reproduced a large proportion of the GRE test bank by asking 22 employees to memorize questions while taking the exam (Way & Robin, 2016). To the extent that items are compromised or the candidates are allowed to retest, CATs provide a more elegant solution for explicitly controlling the amount of item overlap across test forms (Chen & Lei, 2005; Davey & Nering, 2002; Way, Steffen, & Anderson, 2002). Furthermore, in theory, CAT algorithms are inherently self-correcting for any unexpected responses. Because CATs work by adjusting the difficulty level of each subsequent item based on the most recent trait estimate, candidates answering items correctly due to preknowledge will immediately be faced with a series of harder questions. Unless candidates have preknowledge to an unusually large proportion of the test bank, it is likely that many of these will be items about which they have no prior knowledge, allowing the trait estimate to revert towards its expected value.

At the same time, although theoretically CATs should be able to correct for unexpected responses, their ability to do so completely is premised on the notion that items will continue to be administered to examinees until the latent trait score is estimated with sufficient precision. In practice, this is rarely the case. Because of the need to treat candidates equitably and effectively manage seat availability at the testing centers, CATs are most frequently administered as fixed-length tests, which limits, to some extent, their ability to fully correct for unusual responses. This has the added effect of making CATs somewhat longer than may be necessary, to ensure that the test is suitably precise, regardless of the candidate's level of proficiency.

One significant risk with CATs is that the pool of potential items administered to any one candidate is much larger than the number of items actually administered to that person; but because the test administration engine requires constant access to that pool during the test, the entire underlying item bank must exist on a single server. Hence, should those servers become compromised, it may be possible for entire test banks to become compromised. To address this concern, ATP (2013) recommends dividing the bank into item pools which are rotated and sampled for any particular administration, thus mitigating the risk of the entire test bank becoming compromised.

As might be expected of a hybrid model, a multistage test delivery system offers a combination of advantages and disadvantages relative to item-adaptive and non-adaptive tests. Multistage tests require somewhat larger item pools and sample sizes than non-adaptive tests, but far fewer than are required with fully adaptive tests. Item exposure and test overlap are generally controlled through manipulating the number of testlets available for each ability group at each stage, with the number of testlets available being influenced by the proportion of candidates expected to filter into each ability group. Whereas controlling item re-exposure to a candidate upon retesting is challenging in a CAT environment, it is relatively straightforward to constrain the delivery system not to administer testlets that candidates have seen previously.

One unique security advantage that multistage tests have over non-adaptive and fully adaptive tests is that the design of multistage tests appears well suited to detect unusual answer similarity between candidates, as might be expected in cases of answer copying, collusion, or preknowledge. Because each candidate who receives the same testlet will see the exact same items, but each test consists of several randomly selected testlets, candidates who share items and are suspected of colluding are also expected to have a large number of unique items for which colluding would not be possible. Unfortunately, to date, very little cheating detection research has been done within the multistage testing context (see, e.g., Lewis, Lee, & von Davier, 2014; Lee, Lewis, & von Davier, 2014).

However, item-sharing arrangements within multistage testing would seem ideally suited for a variety of detection methods, including answer similarity and change-score methods.

*Scheduling Testing*

Another important consideration in promoting security related to test delivery is the scheduling of the test administration. In the recent past, many high-stakes tests—particularly those in licensure and certification areas—were scheduled to be administered on a fixed schedule, ranging from only once per calendar year to, in many cases, three or four fixed test dates throughout the year. With the proliferation of CBT, several options are available for scheduling, and flexibility in scheduling has increased, although with increased flexibility has come increased security risk.

Fixed date testing allows for control of both item and form exposure. In many cases, depending on the fixed date schedule, it also affords opportunities for data analytics to identify potential security concerns before another form of a test is administered. When one or more single, fixed dates are established for test administration across a calendar year, there are also limited (or no) opportunities for examinees to exchange information about test questions or other secure content such as case scenarios, graphics or other stimulus materials, although programs that test across multiple time zones must remain alert to the possibility of individuals testing early sharing content with those testing later in the day in a different time zone.

Increasingly, however, a test is not administered on one or more fixed dates, but during intervals in which the test may be accessed by examinees. These intervals are often referred to as *testing windows* and may extend from several days to a few months in duration. Testing windows are typically established to address some other practical testing concern, or to improve access and convenience for examinees. For example, a board might offer its credentialing examination during two-week windows three times per year, with the number of administrations per year corresponding to graduation milestones from training programs or allowing failing examinees a timely opportunity to retake the examination, and the two-week windows established to compensate for peak examinee volumes during those program milestones (and, perhaps, as a negotiated way of keeping test administration cost per examinee as low as feasible).

The tradeoff for these conveniences and efficiencies is a less secure test administration compared to fixed date testing. The time zone cheating threat discussed earlier for fixed date testing becomes a much more serious concern the longer the period over which test administration is spread because of the increased opportunity for examinees testing early in a testing window to disclose secure test content to examinees testing later in the window. This was the concern in a Florida court case in which examinees shared test content during the test window (Maupin v. National Board of Podiatric Medical Examiners, 2003) where not only was test content shared improperly, but there it was alleged that examinees implemented a system of scheduling whereby more able test takers would take the examination early in the test window for the purpose of being able to pass along information about test content and answers to weaker examinees who tested later in the window.

An extension of test-window scheduling is what has been called "continuous" or "on-demand" testing. Under these approaches, examinees are permitted to arrange a test administration at any time during the year when a testing center space is available. Of course, security concerns raised by interval scheduling as illustrated earlier are exacerbated when a continuous testing system is implemented by a board or agency. When deciding on examination scheduling, it is recommended that the testing board or agency consider the narrowest possible testing window—a window that balances the most reasonable access to the credentialing process for examinees while affording the entity the greatest protection against score invalidity.

*Item Banking and Item Usage*

In conjunction with test delivery scheduling, the characteristics of an assessment program's item bank and computerized test delivery algorithms can play a significant role in test security. Regarding item banks, one recommendation is clear: the depth of an item pool is one of the most critical requirements for minimizing threats to score validity when tests are administered via computer.

The goal of a CAT is to administer items to examinees that are highly informative at the examinee's estimated proficiency level. However, for all candidates at any particular proficiency level, the same subset of items will be the most informative. Furthermore, items that are highly informative at one proficiency level also tend to be informative at nearby proficiency levels. Therefore, whereas selecting items based entirely on a maximum information criterion allows full realization of the potential advantages of a CAT (i.e., a test that is as efficient as possible in terms of testing time and that optimizes the precision of examinees' proficiency estimations), it also results in dramatic overuse of the best, most informative items in the bank. In specialized fields where the examinee population is fairly homogeneous in ability—as is true in many credentialing settings—this often results in candidates taking exams that share many items in common and are not nearly as customized as intended. This effect can be even more pronounced when a CAT algorithm must also meet additional important test form specifications, such as subdomain coverage, patient/client attributes in case-based items, complexity guidelines for scenarios or reading passages, item format requirements, or other considerations.

Finally, an additional strain on an item bank occurs when an examination includes items with graphics, charts, images, patient descriptions, or other stimulus information that may be highly memorable. Even if items related to these stimulus materials are not initially administered to a large number of examinees, their uniqueness makes them highly susceptible to being recalled and discussed following a test administration. And because many such stimuli are associated with several items that might accompany the stimulus, a compromised stimulus is cause for concern with regard to all its associated items, even those that have yet to be administered to any examinees.

At least three recommendations should be considered to address these concerns. For one, item bank development should focus item generation goals around two objectives. First, precision of the proficiency estimates across the entire candidate pool is maximized when the distribution of item difficulties matches the ability distribution of the examinee population. It is obviously a needless expenditure of important resources to develop items or tasks that may rarely—or ever—be administered to examinees. In addition, item pools should have ample high-discrimination items in the vicinity of the cutscore. This practice will increase information at the cutscore and will improve the likelihood of correctly classifying those examinees for whom Type I and Type II errors are most likely.

Second, rather than selecting items based entirely on maximum information, item selection algorithms should be utilized that control for item exposure, test overlap (i.e., the proportion of items that are common between two exams), and ensure greater utilization of items in the test bank. In general, selection algorithms vary with regard to whether item exposure is explicitly modeled through a conditional selection process, or not explicitly modeled, but controlled through a randomization or stratification process. Research has shown that selection methods based predominantly on randomization work relatively less well than the other two categories of methods with respect to both limiting item over-exposure and greater utilization of the item bank. Stratification methods work well at utilizing the bank and controlling average exposure rates; however, individual items with overly high exposure rates can occur. Item selection approaches that explicitly model individual item exposure rates appear to work better than randomization or stratification methods in that regard (Cohen & Wollack, 2006). In addition to using a procedure to limit the maximum number of individual item exposures, testing programs should consider maximum exposures for stimuli such as images, scenarios, passages, and so on. Additional information on item selection algorithms in CAT is provided by Georgiadou, Triantafillou, and Economides (2007), who have provided a comprehensive review on the topic.

Finally, CBT programs should include monitoring for possible over-exposure of items or tasks. Such monitoring might consist of tracking response latencies (i.e., the amount of time examinees are taking to respond to test items) and item drift (i.e., changes in item difficulty over time), particularly across a testing window and over forms that include overlapping items. One of the security advantages of CBT over paper-based programs is the ability to replace live items quickly, in the event that evidence of item compromise exists, and credentialing assessment programs should be actively collecting and analyzing data that would alert them to situations in which such action might be necessary.

### *Secure Item Delivery Designs*

Although best practices for developing high-quality test items have remained relatively unchanged for decades (Haladyna & Rodriguez, 2013; Wesman, 1971), threats to test security have recently caused conventional item-writing practices to be re-examined. Impara and Foster (2006) argue that common strategies such as minimizing the reading load and the amount of extraneous text, writing items with only a single correct answer, and using a fixed (and logical) order for item alternatives result in items that are more easily memorized. Instead, they recommend developing and administering test items with security principles in mind, including randomizing items and item alternatives, developing multiple item variants that measure the same concept but introduce subtle changes that result in different correct answers, and developing item contexts that are less memorable. Foster (2013) also suggested that items are written in ways that are less recognizable to those with preknowledge. For example, items can be developed so that certain parts of the item that are irrelevant to the content of the question (e.g., the name of the person mentioned, an activity the person is engaged in, etc.) can be treated as random variables so that they are different every time the item is administered.

Another approach that safeguards against item harvesting and item preknowledge when administering tests is to use a delivery strategy that exposes less item content. The most straightforward approach of this type would be to impose rules that limit the delivery of operational items to only those candidates for whom the pass/fail decision has not yet been made. Once it can be determined that, based on the candidate's previous responses, it is highly unlikely (if not impossible) for that candidate to pass or fail the exam, there is no reason to continue to administer that candidate live items. If the particular program is using a stopping rule that allows for candidates to take tests of different lengths, the examination can simply be stopped at this point. If test lengths are required to be the same across candidates, live items can be replaced with non-secure (i.e., decoy) items. Implementation of this approach requires that candidates should not be allowed to review and change responses to previous items; hence, it is best suited for adaptive tests or non-adaptive tests that are taken in sections, and for which candidates are prohibited from returning to items in a previous section.

A more sophisticated approach to dealing with the threat of preknowledge is to adopt an item design that is specifically designed to address that concern. Foster and Miller (2009) introduced the discrete option multiple choice (DOMC), which presents item alternatives to the candidate one at a time and in random order (along with the item stem) until the candidate indicates that a particular item choice is correct or passes on the actual correct answer, at which point the remaining item choices are not shown. This has the advantages of limiting exposure to the entire item, even for items that are presented, and limiting candidates' ability to recognize the item as one for which they have preknowledge. Though much more research is needed, particularly with regard to potential effects on test equating, decision consistency, and test fairness, early research on the item statistics, factor structure, and fairness of these items has found them to be comparable psychometrically to their more traditional multiple-choice counterparts (Kingston, Tiemann, Miller, & Foster, 2012).

One test delivery design that has been proposed to address security concerns is item pool flooding. The premise of item pool flooding is that many candidates are obtaining preknowledge of live test items using what are sometimes called "braindumps." Braindumps are websites that catalogue and collect memorized or stolen live test items. Such sites often provide a forum for recent test takers to document everything they can remember about test questions so that it is possible for future candidates to largely reconstruct the item bank and obtain preknowledge that will lead to a fraudulently high score.

There are several different variations of item pool flooding. In the first, testing programs release to braindump sites many decoy items—items that look much like live items, but, in fact, are not—thereby diluting the pool of compromised items and making it less effective for candidates. As the number of items at braindumps grows, attempts to memorize the entire set will cause cognitive overload and will result in a lower number of live items that are actually memorized. A second form of item pool flooding involves the program releasing items to the braindump that assess completely different content, in hopes that candidates will recognize that the information they have received is of no value and will opt for actual studying rather than relying on the braindump information. The final variant of item pool flooding is reserved for programs with extremely large item banks. Under this model, the organization actually releases the entire live pool of items. The assumptions underlying this third option are that the bank approximates the universe of possible questions, that no one could possibly memorize the entire bank, and that memorizing enough items to make a difference necessarily coincides with a legitimate knowledge gain. The primary security advantage in this last strategy is that it essentially eliminates braindumps and test preparation companies altogether, which might foster some legitimate learning gains and increase fairness issues across candidates.

Item pool flooding has been used by a small number of programs within both credentialing and admissions testing. Graduate Management Admissions Council publishes its entire bank of several hundred essay prompts, from which examinees are administered just one. Since 2009, the National Dental Examining Board of Canada (NDEB) has released an item bank including both active and retired items (Buckendahl & Gerrow, 2016). The original released bank included approximately 7,000 multiple choice items; item keys were not provided for the items. At their website (https://ndeb-bned.ca/en/accredited/written-examination) the NDEB gives a disclaimer that items within the released bank may not be representative of the exam blueprints and that the item content may not be representative of any particular test form. They are forthcoming with the fact that items may have been retired for various reasons and that the bank may also include some question formats that are no longer in operational use. They also make no claims that all operational items will be drawn from the released item banks.

Research on the impact of item pool flooding is very limited. In an experiment to evaluate the impact of disclosure of GRE essay prompts, Powers and Fowles (1998) found no statistical differences in performance between those with preknowledge of the essay prompts and those without preknowledge. However, it is worth noting that this study was done as part of a lab experiment rather than during an operational GRE; hence, although participants reported having spent some time thinking about the topics that they received beforehand, the stakes associated with their essay scores were not parallel to those in a live testing situation. In conducting an evaluation of the NDEB item flooding practices, Buckendahl and Gerrow (2016) found that releasing the item bank did not appear to change item performance. However, due to a number of other programmatic changes that happened concurrent with the release of the item pools, they were unable to conclusively determine the impact of flooding on pass rates and the validity of test score inferences.

The intended outcomes from item pool flooding are laudable. However, realization of those outcomes requires making assumptions about the number of items able to be recalled and the potential impact such preknowledge may have on one's proficiency estimate. As discussed by Buckendahl and Gerrow (2016), the effectiveness of flooding is contingent upon the number of items released relative to the number of items on an operational test form, the stakes of the program, the administration practices, and the process by which new test forms are assembled and released. In considering the potential impact, it is important to recall that candidates in the vicinity of the cutscore do not require an especially large benefit from preknowledge in order to significantly improve their chances of passing the test. Although flooding braindumps or released item pools with misinformation or too much information may have some merits, it is also an extremely risky exercise and should be done with caution. Independent of other measures, we believe that item pool flooding is an inadequate preventive strategy that fails to adequately safeguard against unqualified candidates passing the exam; hence, programs utilizing this approach must continue to implement other prevention and detection strategies as well.

### *Security During Test Administration*

Security during test administration actually begins well before the actual administration with the processes in place to ensure that the examinees who register to take an examination are qualified to do so. Licensure and certification boards routinely have in place criteria that must be met for a candidate to be eligible to sit for a credentialing examination. These policies should be clearly articulated, disseminated to potential examinees, and routinely monitored for compliance.

There may be several elements that qualify a potential examinee as eligible. For example, there may be age, residency, or citizenship requirements. Eligibility criteria might also include a specified GPA, the successful completion of an accredited training or degree program, supervised internship, clinical or practicum hours, other educational requirements, or official recommendations for candidacy. Test-related eligibility requirements might include completion of a practice test, review and acceptance of non-disclosure, test integrity, and test administration conduct provisions, submission of a photograph, signature, or other proof of identity. Finally, a potential test taker would ordinarily *not* be eligible to sit for an examination if he or she had previously passed the test or, if having previously failed, exceeded the number of examination attempts within a specified time period, failed to complete any required remedial activities, or had been disqualified from candidacy because of previous ethical or professional misconduct or disciplinary action. Overall, regardless of the specific eligibility requirements, the entity responsible for oversight of the testing program should have procedures and record keeping in place to ensure that only eligible candidates can be registered to take its examination.

It is recommended that credentialing organizations should establish testing policies that ensure their tests will be delivered only in a professional test administration setting. For example, professional testing centers may be owned and/or managed by the test provider or by a third party, such as by independent, for-profit organizations or university testing centers that serve not only their students' testing needs, but those of the larger community as well. Professional testing centers are those that are dedicated entirely to test administration, strictly follow the standardized administration guidelines established by the program, are committed to maintain the security of the exams and test-related information, and adopt practices that preserve the validity of test score interpretations. Professional testing centers employ full-time test center administrators who are responsible for overall management of the center, including hiring and training of proctors, developing and implementing a test security plan and procedures to protect the integrity of the testing programs and the rights of candidates, and maintenance of all equipment to ensure that exam delivery, registration, score reporting, audio/video, and biometric machinery is functioning as intended. Professional testing centers are also careful about managing potential conflicts of interest, ensuring that their proctors undergo background checks, are not involved in test preparation or candidate advocacy activities, and do not have personal or status relationships (e.g., friends, relatives, employers, etc.) with candidates (ATP & National College Testing Association [NCTA], 2015).

*Candidate Check-in*

The process of admitting only verified, eligible candidates into the testing room is of obvious importance. This is the testing program's final opportunity to prevent a candidate who is intending to cheat from gaining access to the test content. Therefore, the purpose of check-in is to verify the authenticity and eligibility of the candidates, provide candidates with information on misconduct and disallowed behaviors, and ensure that no one enters the testing room with prohibited materials.

Candidates should be required to show a valid government-issued identification (ID), including both a photograph and signature. The name on the ID must exactly match the name on the testing roster, as should any other information (e.g., birthdate) appearing both on the ID and the test roster. The candidate should be asked to sign the test roster, and the signature and the candidate's image must be checked for comparability against the signature and photograph on the ID. If candidates submitted a photograph at the time of registration and the photo is included on the test roster, that should also be checked for consistency with other pictures. Candidates should be asked to provide a secondary form of ID in the event that a proctor is not sufficiently confident that the individual appearing is the same as the candidate approved to test.

Because of the subjectivity involved in signature matching or comparing photos to a person, and because a candidate's physical features can change dramatically in a short period of time (e.g., hairstyles, facial hair, hair color, etc.), best practice is to capture some biometric information for all candidates prior to their testing. Although fingerprinting is the least expensive and most commonly implemented biometric device at testing centers, it is somewhat less reliable than other biometric measures. Fingerprint scanners have a tendency to get dirty, which can cause failures to capture suitable images. They are also much slower than other technologies at performing 1:N matching, in which the scanned image for the candidate is compared against all others in the database to discover, for example, that the identity of a candidate checking in after a break is different from that of the candidate testing before the break, or that the same candidate has previously registered under a different identity. They also have higher false–positive rates (Iridian Technologies, n.d.). Consequently, the best use of fingerprint technology is to image capture fingerprints for purposes of providing a secondary identification check, in the event that a follow-up investigation is necessary. In contrast, iris scans and palm vein scans are considerably more accurate and can be run quickly in a 1:N search environment. Whether biometrics are being used for real-time identification/verification or merely for data capture purposes, the biometric scan should occur each time a candidate enters or re-enters the testing room.

Testing centers should have a secure storage area in which candidates can lock their personal belongings. One of the advantages of a technology-based test is that resources and utilities needed to complete the test (e.g., dictionaries, calculators, magnification) can be built into the system. Hence, candidates should not need to carry anything into the testing room, although some programs do permit candidates to carry in certain items. One item that candidates may be allowed to carry in is something on which to write—for example, for purposes of setting up and solving mathematical equations. Even in these situations, candidates should not be allowed to bring their own materials into the testing room. Best practice is to assign each candidate a whiteboard, marker, and eraser for their use during the test. If candidates are given scratch paper, each piece should be marked with a unique candidate identifier. Ideally, each piece of scratch paper is colored or marked to make it easily distinguishable from the admission ticket, as well as from any unauthorized scratch paper the candidate may have brought in. Testing staff should note how many pieces were given to each candidate, and all distributed sheets should be collected by testing staff before the candidate is excused. The testing center should have an established procedure for securely destroying any scratch paper collected after the exam.

During check-in, candidates should be informed about prohibited items (including clothing, such as hoodies, hats, and sunglasses) and instructed to place in their locker anything that cannot be taken into the testing room, with explicit directions to power off all electronic devices. Proctors must visually inspect each candidate before he or she enters the testing room. Candidates should be asked to turn their pockets inside out to verify that they do not contain notes, cell phones, or other prohibited objects. Similarly, proctors should ask to inspect any clothing or wearable accessory that they feel is suspicious or capable of concealing prohibited items, including jackets, watches, and large jewelry items. Items such as clothing worn for religious purposes may be visually examined; however, it may be necessary for the inspection to be done in a private space by an individual who is the same gender as the candidate.

Once the candidate has completed all necessary paperwork and the security protocol, the proctor may show the candidate to his or her seat. Candidates should not be permitted to select their own seats. If a seating chart is provided by the test sponsor, the candidate should sit in the assigned seat. If a seating chart is not provided, seats should be assigned randomly to candidates. Candidates should never be assigned to seats alphabetically, so as to provide a layer of protection against relatives working together during the test, acquaintances formed because of alphabetization in a different (e.g., instructional) context, and so on.

## Proctoring During the Exam

Perhaps no mechanism is more effective in maintaining test security and deterring cheating during the administration of an examination than conscientious monitoring of examinees taking the test. Monitoring may be conducted by human proctors, in person or remotely, or via various technological solutions such as video and audio recording.

The role of a proctor requires specialized training. Proctors must be familiar not only with test administration procedures, but also able to identify possible threats to test security, and be skilled at observing, recording, and responding to potential cheating situations according to the guidelines and procedures authorized by the test sponsor. Proctors must monitor candidates throughout the entire exam, paying particular attention to examinee's eyes, hands, and immediate surrounding area. Most credentialing assessment programs require that proctors perform a physical walk-through of the testing center approximately every 10 minutes to look for prohibited materials and to remind candidates that they are being actively monitored. When suspicious activity is observed, if possible, proctors should have another proctor observe and confirm the behavior before intervention is contemplated.

It is important at this point to restate that the concern about test security is, primarily, a concern about test score validity. To that end, human proctors can serve many functions that can aid in obtaining fair, dependable, and efficient estimates of examinees' true levels of knowledge and skill. Although proctors are often seen more as guardians to prevent misbehavior, they can serve other functions that contribute to accurate test results. For example, proctors can help ensure that examinees have clean, comfortable, and conducive testing conditions and are not distracted in the test environment. Effective proctors can aid examinees with questions about the examination equipment or procedures, including assistance with technology such as computer monitors, headphones, and test delivery or response input complications that can arise.

Of course, proctors also play an important security role merely by providing a noticeable presence in a testing location. Proctors also enhance test security by ensuring adherence to designated seating chart locations and test timing, by being observant and active during a testing session, and by noting examinee behaviors that can signal copying, collusion, inappropriate access to proscribed resources, test material harvesting, or other suspicious activity. Proctors can, using discretion to avoid disturbing other examinees, notify an examinee during a test that he or she should avoid engaging in such activities or, if judged to be a serious concern, suspend the test administration for an examinee; in all cases, the proctor should make notes of their observations, interactions, and interventions. Such observation notes—sometimes called *irregularity reports*—can provide important substantiating evidence if other sources of evidence such as statistical detection methods suggest that an examinee may have engaged in cheating. Any unusual events that occur during testing—including, but not limited to those involving potential misconduct—should be documented in detail, including information on what exactly occurred, who was involved, when it occurred, where it occurred, how it was identified, and who observed the behavior.

Finally, because it is possible that they might actually collude with examinees to circumvent test security protocols, proctors should be carefully screened, selected, and trained for this role and should themselves be monitored to ensure that they are conducting their duties appropriately. Two such approaches to monitoring proctors are audits and secret shopping. In an audit, the testing sponsor sends an employee to a particular test site for the purposes of monitoring and evaluating the testing staff's adherence to the standardization guidelines and security protocol. In secret shopping, testing companies hire actors to masquerade as testing candidates, either for the purposes of monitoring the administrative behaviors or to engage in various acts of misconduct to evaluate the proctors' attentiveness and adequacy of response. It is recommended that, several times per year, testing programs should randomly select some test centers for audits and secret shopping; however, it is also recommended that specific test centers are targeted for closer monitoring if there is reason to question the center's security and administration practices. Among other resources, readers interested in more extensive information on the responsibilities, selection, training, and evaluation of test proctors may wish to consult *Proctoring Best Practices* (ATP & NCTA, 2015).

*Maintaining Security During Breaks*

Most credentialing examination administrations provide examinees with some opportunity to take a break, either a scheduled break during which the testing clock stops, or an unscheduled break during which the clock continues to run. Because testing can be a long and arduous experience both cognitively and physically, offering candidates a break is an important step toward fair and valid test scores in that it helps examinees demonstrate their true level on the measured construct throughout the entire test. At the same time, if not properly managed, breaks present an opportunity for candidates to discuss test content (with each other or with others outside the test environment), to change places with one another, to access prohibited materials from their storage lockers or other individuals, or to engage in other actions that threaten test security and score validity.

Accordingly, breaks must be carefully managed. Candidates must follow the testing program's process for going on break. This usually involves either logging out of the exam or setting the computer on the break screen. Candidates must be formally checked out on break by testing staff. This may include showing ID, signing a log book, and returning any materials that were issued to the candidate. Candidates should be given instructions outlining expected break behavior, and should be informed that deviations from expected break behavior, including taking unusually long or frequent breaks, will result in an irregularity report. Generally, candidates are allowed to access their locker for purposes of getting food/drink, taking medication, or retrieving a permissible article of clothing, but they should not be allowed access to a mobile device, textbooks, or writing implements. Candidates are often allowed to speak quietly with other candidates, provided they are not discussing test content. Candidates should be informed about the locations of acceptable break areas. In the event that a testing center does not have a designated break area, examinees on break should be limited to staying in the area immediately surrounding the testing center. This area, including bathrooms, should be monitored closely during breaks to make sure that candidates adhere to the break-time security policies.

At the conclusion of a break, candidates must be checked back in prior to restarting their exam. The process for checking a candidate back in after break is similar to the process for checking a candidate in at the beginning of the exam: candidates' identities should be reauthenticated, they should be asked to turn their pockets inside out, and they should be visually inspected for any items that the proctor feels warrant closer monitoring.

## Security in Scoring and Reporting Test Results

Once an examination administration has concluded, the security focus shifts from prevention to detection and investigation. Statistical detection methods are not typically helpful to substantiate eyewitness accounts of candidates using prohibited materials, such as cheat sheets or cell phones; however, they are invaluable in corroborating observational evidence of many cheating behaviors for which evidence is more circumstantial. In addition, because certain types of cheating are very difficult or impossible to detect with proctors (e.g., preknowledge), many credentialing assessment programs routinely perform a number of statistical analyses to identify aberrant test behavior that is consistent with a cheating hypothesis.

### Cheating Detection

There are five types of cheating that are potentially detectable through statistical analysis. These include collusion, preknowledge, item harvesting, answer copying, and test tampering—although the latter two types of cheating are typically not major security concerns in licensure and certification testing contexts. As explained previously in this chapter, answer copying is a relatively small problem in credentialing settings, particularly when candidates taking adaptive tests see different items and, in computer-based, non-adaptive situations, when item orders are scrambled or alternate forms are administered to neighboring examinees. For credentialing examinations, test tampering is also not a significant concern because tests are typically delivered in professional test centers where test administrators are not stakeholders in the way that educators are in K-12 testing contexts. Furthermore, under CBT, test data are submitted automatically to the test sponsor upon completion of the test, so administrators are not afforded the opportunity to change candidates' answers. Consequently, in credentialing settings, statistical detection methods are used to identify evidence of collusion, preknowledge, and item harvesting.

Collusion refers to two or more individuals working together during the administration of an examination, possibly using a communication device. Although collusion is a different cheating mechanism than preknowledge, collusion and preknowledge are often indistinguishable at the level of item responses. Consequently, many of the same categories of methods are used to detect both. Several good sources exist summarizing methods for preknowledge or collusion detection (see Belov, 2016; Eckerly, 2017); unfortunately, few empirical studies exist that make statistical comparisons across different methodologies.

Answer similarity analysis (Maynes, 2014; van der Linden & Sotaridona, 2006) is a particularly effective strategy for identifying pairs of examinees who share an unusual number of item responses in common. However, in preknowledge and collusion situations, common item responses are shared among larger groups of individuals. Wollack and Maynes (2017) have introduced an approach which applies cluster analysis to similarity data to identify groups of individuals with unusual amounts of similarity.

Another approach to both collusion and preknowledge detection involves examining changes in performance level (measured on the latent trait metric) between sets of items that are potentially compromised and those that are unlikely to be compromised (Belov, 2016). For example, if one is examining collusion, it might be worthwhile to compare, for each examinee in the group, the score for items that are common across examinees with the score based on items that are unique. If the hypothesis is preknowledge, two additional item set comparisons may be of interest: operational vs. pilot items and items known to be compromised and those believed to be secure. This method has the advantage of being intuitive and straightforward to compute, and Belov found it to be among the best at correctly classifying examinees. A conceptually similar approach is applied in retesting situations in which a candidate's score is compared to their score from the previous exam for signs of unusual growth.

Person-fit is another methodological approach that has been applied to detect collusion and preknowledge. Although person-fit has the potential to detect these types of misconduct, non-model fitting behavior is observed for reasons other than cheating. Further, the lack of specificity in the person-fit hypothesis results in it being an underpowered and generally unhelpful approach to detecting collusion and cheating. In a large study comparing many person-fit measures, Karabatsos (2003) found that $H^T$ (Sijtsma, 1986) and $D(\theta)$ (Trabin & Weiss, 1983) were clearly the most effective person-fit measures to detect cheating behaviors; however, across all the types of aberrance simulated, cheating was among the two types of anomalous behavior for which person-fit performed the least well.

Three aspects of preknowledge distinguish it from collusion. First, with preknowledge, candidates are expected to perform better on any items for which they have preknowledge. Second, it is reasonable to expect that candidates will respond more quickly to items for which they have memorized answers. Finally, in collusion, one never knows the specific items on which candidates worked together; however, in a preknowledge setting, it is occasionally possible to discover items that are compromised because they are posted on the Web, being illegally sold/distributed as test preparation materials, etc. These three unique aspects of preknowledge have led to a variety of other detection methods.

Two special cases of the score-differencing approach described above exist when preknowledge is suspected. In the Trojan Horse method (Maynes, 2009), several easy items are released (e.g., to a braindump website), but are marked with the incorrect key. These items are then embedded in live tests as unscored items. Candidates producing low scores on these items relative to their score on all scored items provides evidence of preknowledge. Maynes has shown that this method can be very powerful, even with a fairly small number of Trojan Horse items. The method does have a limitation in that it assumes candidates will always utilize the false key. Because these are easy items, candidates may recognize that they are miskeyed and answer them correctly, thereby reducing the likelihood that these candidates would be discovered for having preknowledge on any other items. Another special case of a score differencing approach involves the use of mixture item response models to identify groups of candidates whose performance differs across two sets of items, one believed to be compromised and one believed to be secure (Eckerly, Babcock, & Wollack, 2015; Shu, Henson, & Luecht, 2013).

Item preknowledge is expected to affect more than candidates' item responses. It is also expected that examinees with preknowledge might have unusual response time patterns. In particular, it is reasonable to hypothesize that examinees with preknowledge would respond much more quickly to items for which they have memorized answers than they would to items they must solve or reason through. Consequently, van der Linden and colleagues (van der Linden & Guo, 2008; van der Linden & van Krimpen-Stoop, 2003) have developed statistical models to detect preknowledge based on irregular person-specific response time parameters. These methods have shown promise in simulations; however, our limited knowledge about the effect of preknowledge on response time suggests that more research in this area is warranted.

One of the most promising preknowledge detection methods was recently developed by Belov (2014; 2017). Using information theory and combinatorial optimization, Belov's approach not only addresses the problem of identifying examinees with preknowledge, but also identifies the sets of compromised items in a way that allows for different groups of individuals to have prior access to different collections of items. This approach is more computationally demanding than other approaches and must be studied further under a variety of typical preknowledge situations to understand its appropriateness for operational use. Nonetheless, it appears to be the most realistic of the different approaches in terms of the assumptions the testing program must make about how preknowledge manifests itself in practice.

The other major category of cheating for which statistical analysis may assist in detection is item harvesting. Whereas a wide array of statistical options exist for detecting preknowledge and collusion, the literature on detection methods for item harvesting is barren. The primary detection challenge is that we do not yet understand what item and response time patterns to expect of an item harvester, due to the different mechanisms used to harvest items. It seems reasonable to assume that item harvesters will exhibit peculiar response time patterns, although those patterns may be markedly different. For example, examinees attempting to memorize items might be expected to spend unusually long times on items, whereas candidates taking pictures of items might spend unusually little time. Furthermore, little is known about the response accuracy of the typical harvester. The mere fact that item harvesters may not ultimately be concerned with the score they receive should not presuppose that they will randomly fill in answers to questions, even when they may know the answers.

Taken together, these factors suggest that there is probably not a one-size-fits-all approach to detecting item harvesting. Instead, the best approach is to identify item response and response time profiles that are not plausibly explained by behavior other than item harvesting. For example, candidates with many unusually long response times, many unusually short times (including 0 seconds), and few items with typical response times would seem to be suspicious, particularly if coupled with a random guessing pattern across all items. This is definitely an area where statistical approaches hold promise, but where substantial research is needed. In the meantime, vigilant proctoring remains the best alternative to detect item harvesting.

Not all detection strategies following an examination administration involve statistical analysis. It is important for programs to utilize additional techniques to identify cheating that may have occurred during the exam. One of the easiest and most fruitful strategies is to set up a security hotline. This may take the form of either a 24/7 toll-free phone number where callers can leave a recorded message, or a Web form on which a possible security breach can be reported. In either case, individuals should be asked to be as detailed as possible and should have the option of remaining anonymous. Another effective non-statistical approach is Web monitoring. Following the exam, it is important for testing personnel to maintain an active Web and social media presence (under an alias) to make sure that candidates are not using blog sites, chat rooms, or social media to share test content or describe cheating activities in which they participated. Importantly, this detection approach following an examination administration can also be an effective cheating *prevention* strategy for future examination administrations.

*Using Statistical Detection Methods Operationally*

Buss and Novick (1980) asserted that "statistical methods of detection should generally not be the sole basis for a judgment that an examinee cheated (or that an examinee's scores are sufficiently questionable to justify non-reporting) in the absence of corroboration from other types of evidence" (p. 62). All too often, this statement has been taken to mean that statistical evidence alone is insufficient for sustaining an allegation of cheating or as the basis for prompting additional investigation; it should be used only to trigger an investigation or, perhaps, as a tool to help convince the subject of the investigation to be more forthcoming with information. The conventional wisdom has been that, absent a smoking gun, probabilistic information should not be used as the basis for a sanction.

Because statistical methods for detecting cheating on tests—as well as technologies to assist in covertly obtaining a fraudulent test score—have evolved considerably in the decades since Buss and Novick made their recommendation, we believe that the time has come to put this notion to rest, or at least to clarify what is meant by "in the absence of corroboration from other types of evidence." Just as it is unlikely that a credentialing organization would take action against a candidate based solely on the significance level of a single test statistic, it is equally untenable to insist upon irrefutable, first-hand evidence; such a standard is above that which is used to convict even the most serious criminals.

Standard 8.11 of the *Standards for Educational and Psychological Testing* (AERA, APA, & NCME, 2014) requires that credentialing assessment programs conduct an investigation prior to sanctioning an examinee for suspected misconduct. For many types of cheating, direct evidence of cheating will not exist. However, multiple pieces of other evidence may exist, and this evidence may be quite compelling. For example, suppose a group of candidates was identified statistically as having unusual response similarity and, upon conducting further investigation, it was discovered that they all received their degree from the same institution, attended the same test preparation classes, lived in the same region, and were all Facebook friends. This collection of evidence is still probabilistic in nature and the circumstances just described might also be interpreted as legitimate explanations for the response similarity. Nonetheless, taken together, this collection of evidence would ordinarily cast doubt over the appropriateness of these candidates' test scores.

Now suppose that this group that was first identified based on unusual similarity was subsequently flagged by another statistical analysis, such as one comparing performance on operational and pilot sections or performance on a subset of items known to be compromised with items believed to be secure. These individuals exhibited irregular response time patterns, with unusually short times on those items for which there were shared responses. They also showed unusually large gain scores between their previous and current administrations, and were flagged by a person-fit measure as having an overall response pattern that is not well predicted by the model. In this case—*and even if the investigation described previously revealed no additional evidence of misconduct and no clear connection between these individuals*—it is our belief that enough statistical evidence exists to question the validity of these individuals' scores and to warrant canceling their scores and perhaps more severe sanctions.

Finally, suppose instead that these candidates weren't flagged by six different methods, but by only two, each based on well-researched methods with demonstrated abilities to control the false–positive rate, that the probabilities associated with both were in the order of 1 in 10 billion, and the posterior probability of cheating (Skorupski & Wainer, 2017), which takes into account not only the extremity of the test statistic and the false–positive rate, but also the base rate of cheating in the general population, is one in a million. Would this not also constitute enough evidence to question the validity of the scores? By extension, it is not difficult for us to imagine a similar conclusion based only on a single statistic, provided that statistic has been properly vetted and accepted by the research community and the degree of aberrance is clearly extreme.

Of course, it seems obvious that the circumstances under which greater reliance on quantitative methods would be appropriate are related to the severity of concern regarding the *failure* to detect cheating. In the case of credentialing, the sponsoring organizations are obliged to both protect the public from incompetent practice and to protect the integrity of the profession. With this in mind, it is their responsibility to withhold certification when credible evidence exists to suggest that a particular test score may not represent the individual's true level on the construct being measured. Extreme probabilistic information, whether purely statistical or a combination of both quantitative and qualitative evidence, helps shift the burden of proof onto the candidate to provide a reasonable explanation for the anomalous results. Barring a reasonable explanation, statistical evidence alone may be sufficient for purposes of canceling a score or withholding a credential (Cizek & Wollack, 2017; Weinstein, 2017; Wollack & Cizek, 2017).

*Responding to Cheating*

Nearly all instances of potential misconduct should be investigated. Following the administration of an examination, the test security team should review all the information available related to a potential cheating incident and make a determination about whether to move forward with an investigation. Security investigations may be triggered on the basis of a proctor's irregularity report, information received from a third party, such as the security hotline, data analytics, biometrics, or any other credible source. Organizations frequently allow at least a couple of weeks following a test administration before reporting official scores, so as to allow these potential misconduct triggers to be identified. Once a decision is made to move forward with an investigation, any suspicious scores that have not yet been reported should be held, pending the outcome of the investigation. This is not to suggest that unofficial scores cannot be immediately reported to candidates as soon as they submit their test. In the event that scores have already been reported and the individual in question received a passing score, the organization must make a decision about whether the charges warrant temporarily suspending the individual's credential.

The investigation itself must be comprehensive and should seek as many sources of evidence as possible—including potentially disconfirming evidence. Individuals under investigation should also be given the opportunity to speak in their defense and address any concerns about potential misconduct. Once all the evidence is gathered, it must be reviewed and evaluated in its entirety, weighing evidence in both directions to arrive at a decision about appropriate action. What constitutes "appropriate action" will vary across programs, but assuming it is determined that some sanction is necessary, it typically ranges from failing to report a score to a lifetime ban from retesting or denial/revocation of one's credential. It might also include other provisions such as a required waiting period before retesting, ethics training, additional coursework, etc. Most important is that the investigation must strictly follow the program's prescribed policies regarding security investigations. The U.S. Circuit Court of Appeals has twice made rulings on testing company's rights surrounding score cancelation and, in both cases, has given wide latitude to programs provided they are following their stated policies and acting in good faith (Semko & Hunt, 2013).

As noted earlier, security investigations should proceed as validity investigations, and in reaching its decision, the test sponsor should be considering whether sufficient evidence exists to question the interpretive accuracy of the test scores. We note that it is unnecessary that an individual is involved or intended to be involved in cheating in order to have his or her score held or canceled. Organizations need only credible evidence that the score cannot accurately be interpreted as intended.

During a security investigation or during routine post-examination Web monitoring, the test sponsor may discover copyrighted test-related information on the Internet. Test providers should respond immediately to any such discoveries by emailing the site host with a cease-and-desist letter. To facilitate a swift response, a template for this letter should be developed as part of the organization's test security plan. According to Case and Donahue (2013), this letter should indicate that the materials are copyrighted and that the test publisher is the holder of that copyright, identify specifically the material that is illegally posted along with the date and time of the posting, and request that the material be removed immediately. In the event that the Internet site host is unresponsive, or if the program is seeking legal action, including damages, it will be necessary to enlist the assistance of attorneys. Semko and Hunt (2013) provide a detailed discussion of the legal issues involved in responding to a copyright infringement case.

Finally, although it is understandable that a credentialing organization may be disinclined to make information about security breaches publicly available out of concern that stakeholders will lose confidence in the test results, it is important to recognize that the mere act of taking action against candidates and copyright infringers can serve as a powerful deterrent. Many individuals will refrain from engaging in misconduct if they recognize that there is a real threat of legal action. Consequently, it is generally regarded as best practice for the organization to broadly disseminate information related to security breaches that are adjudicated in the program's favor.

## Conclusions

The problem of cheating on tests and concerns about integrity of test scores has been well documented in diverse testing contexts. However, concerns about cheating and test score integrity are heightened in the context of credentialing examinations where a comprehensive test often serves as a gatekeeper to practicing in a field for which candidates have invested many years and tens of thousands of dollars, and for which incompetent practice presents a tangible risk to the public health and safety or psychological and financial well-being.

In this chapter, we have focused on the test security risks inherent in credentialing programs, advancing the notion that test security is a crucial component of test validity, and that efforts to deter, prevent, detect and respond to security breaches should be approached in the name of improving the usability and interpretations of resulting test scores. We hope that this compilation of best practices, research-based recommendations, and experience-based advice is helpful to those charged with the integrity of licensure and certification testing programs.

At the same time, we recognize that all the work done to date by researchers, practitioners, and credentialing entities will not address the cheating threats that will surely develop in the coming years. Just as so-called "next-generation" assessments and advances in testing technologies will provide fairer, more efficient, more accurate, and more comprehensive assessment of candidates' knowledge and skills, so too will newly developing cheating methods present emerging challenges to security and integrity in testing. To that end, it is our intention that the content of this chapter serves not only to address contemporary test security concerns, but also stimulates on-going research, development, and attention to the important issues faced by licensure and certification bodies related to the integrity of the credentials they are responsible for awarding.

## APPENDIX 9A: SAMPLE EXAMINEE TEST SECURITY AGREEMENT

Before you continue with the examination registration, you must agree to the following statements. If you do not agree to these terms you will not be permitted to register.

### Test Taker Authenticity

*I certify that I am the person who will be taking the [EXAM NAME] and that my sole purpose for taking the [EXAM NAME] is because I am seeking licensure in a U. S. jurisdiction.*

### [EXAM NAME] Ownership

*I am aware that all [EXAM NAME] test materials, including my answers, are the property of the [Test Sponsor].*

### [EXAM NAME] Security

*I understand that the [EXAM NAME] is a confidential and secure examination, protected by U.S. and international copyright and trade secret laws.*

*I also understand that I am contractually obligated to keep all [EXAM NAME] content confidential, by virtue of this Security Agreement I am entering into with [TEST SPONSOR].*

### Prohibited Acts

*I understand and agree that the following things are examples of prohibited acts and that this list is not inclusive of every potential prohibited act.*

*I agree that I will not:*

- *disclose or discuss [EXAM NAME] content with anyone verbally, in writing, or through any other method of communication including on the Internet, through email accounts, or through any social media;*
- *bring any materials or devices into the testing room or attempt to remove any items from the testing room;*
- *copy, memorize, record, or otherwise attempt to retain or recreate examination content including questions, concepts, topics, graphics, and images;*
- *assist anyone to copy, memorize, record, otherwise retain, recreate, or reconstruct the content for any purpose;*
- *share answers to questions;*
- *study from information derived from any item listed above.*

### Obligation to Cooperate

*I recognize that I may be asked in the future to respond to questions, provide information or documents, or otherwise participate in an investigation of an exam security matter related to the [EXAM NAME]. Failure to fully cooperate in an investigation may be considered a breach of my obligations under this Security Agreement.*

## Consequences for Non-Compliance

*I understand that [TEST SPONSOR] has the right to take action against me if I breach this agreement, any of the terms and conditions specified in the Candidate Handbook or Testing Center Regulations, if I fail to comply with reasonable requests from Test Center Administrators or [TEST SPONSOR] staff, or if any of my actions may reasonably be construed to misrepresent myself, jeopardize the security of the [EXAM NAME], or call the validity of [EXAM NAME] scores into question. These actions may include one or more of the following:*

- *The Test Administrator may immediately dismiss me from the test session.*
- *My exam may not be scored, my scores may be canceled, without a refund, and the jurisdiction receiving my scores may be informed of the reason for the cancellation.*
- *The institution where I received my educational training may be informed of actions taken against me.*
- *I may be temporarily suspended or permanently banned from taking the [EXAM NAME].*
- *I may face a lawsuit that may result in my receiving court-enforced penalties.*
- *I may have to pay a monetary penalty.*
- *I may face criminal prosecution.*
- *Disciplinary action may be taken against me by a jurisdiction licensing authority (state board).*

## [TEST SPONSOR] Authority

*[TEST SPONSOR] is the final authority that determines whether I have the privilege of taking the [EXAM NAME], whether an examination is scored, or whether the score from my examination is provided or transferred to any entity or licensing jurisdiction.*

## Attestation

*I have read, understand, and agree to the foregoing statements.*

In order to safeguard the public welfare and the integrity of the [EXAM NAME], [TEST SPONSOR] reserves the right to prohibit any person from taking the [EXAM NAME] who has not accepted the terms and conditions of the foregoing Security Agreement.

**Note**: Modified with permission from the Federation of State Boards of Physical Therapy (2016a).

## APPENDIX 9B: SAMPLE NON-DISCLOSURE AGREEMENT

This agreement shall be effective with respect to the [Exam Name], owned by the [Test Sponsor]. The security and integrity of the licensure examinations, including all examination questions, must be fully protected at all times. All persons involved in item-writing, item-review, test construction, passing score determination or otherwise exposed to any examination item must understand, sign and agree to security conditions. Those conditions include, but are not limited to, the following.

Each licensure examination and all examination items are protected under **Federal Copyright Law**. Items and examinations may not be copied, stored, transmitted or disseminated by any means or for any purpose without the prior, express, written permission of the [Test Sponsor]. For the purposes of this Agreement, an "item" shall be defined as a full multiple choice question and answer pairing.

Current, past and future examinations and examination items are protected under **Federal Copyright Law** and may not be used for research, examination preparation activity, review by any individual or for any other purpose without the prior, express, written permission of [Test Sponsor].

Anyone who has access to the [Exam Name] will agree not to be employed by an exam preparation entity, publish an exam preparation document, or offer a course related to the [Exam Name] and shall not be a candidate for licensure for a period of five years after said access.

I understand and acknowledge that each examination and all of its contents are highly confidential and proprietary to the [Test Sponsor], and that any copying, distribution or disclosure in any manner of any of its contents or any other breach of confidentiality would render the examination unusable and/or severely compromise the purpose for which the examination is being administered.

In exchange for good and valuable consideration, the receipt of which is hereby acknowledged, I agree that: (i) I will not copy or permit the copying of any examination or item for any purpose; (ii) I will not distribute or discuss any of the questions, answers or other contents of an examination with any individual or potential candidate, nor with any organization or agency at any time for any purpose; (iii) I will take all steps necessary to comply with the forgoing conditions; and (iv) while an examination is in my possession, I will store it in a secure place, in a safe or locked file cabinet or other enclosure, and will remove it only for the purpose of my inspecting it, and then only for as long as such actual inspection requires. I also agree that if I am an item writer and use paper to develop my items prior to entry into the electronic Item Entry and Review System, I will shred all paper copies of the items that I have written immediately on submitting the items. If I utilize a computer to generate the items on a template, I will ensure that the items cannot be accessed by others and will delete the item from all forms of digital or analog memory once the item has been submitted.

I understand that my compliance with all of the conditions of this letter is of the utmost importance, and that any breach or failure to comply with any of the covenants and promises set forth herein will cause substantial damage. My signature below indicates my acceptance of this Agreement.

Signature: _____  Date: _____

Please print your name:

**Note**: Modified with permission from the Federation of State Boards of Physical Therapy (2016b).

## References

Abella, J. (2010, July 19). Physical therapy grads from RP barred from taking US exams. *GMA Network*. Retrieved from: www.gmanetwork.com

American Educational Research Association, American Psychological Association, & National Council on Measurement in Education (AERA, APA, & NCME) (2014). *Standards for educational and psychological testing.* Washington, DC: American Psychological Association.

Association of Test Publishers (ATP) (2013). *Assessment security options: Considerations by delivery channel and assessment model.* Washington, DC: Author.

Association of Test Publishers & National College Testing Association (ATP & NCTA) (2015). *Proctoring best practices.* Washington, DC: Author.

Beck, J. (2012, January 2). New York court upholds ruling that woman cheated on bar exam. *IC Inside Scoop.* Retrieved from: www.insidecounsel.com

Belov, D. I. (2014). Detecting item preknowledge in computerized adaptive testing using information theory and combinatorial optimization. *Journal of Computerized Adaptive Testing, 2*(3), 37–58.

Belov, D. I. (2016). Comparing the performance of eight item preknowledge detection statistics. *Applied Psychological Measurement, 40,* 83–97.

Belov, D. I. (2017). Identification of item preknowledge by the methods of information theory and combinatorial optimization. In G. J. Cizek & J. A. Wollack (Eds.), *Handbook of quantitative methods for detecting cheating on tests* (pp. 164–176). New York: Routledge.

Botelho, G. (2014, March 27). 9 Air Force commanders fired from jobs over nuclear missile test cheating. *CNN.* Retrieved from: www.cnn.com

Buckendahl, C. W., & Gerrow, J. D. (2016). Evaluating the Impact of Releasing an Item Pool on a Test's Empirical Characteristics. *Journal of Dental Education, 80*(10), 1253–1260.

Buss, W. G., & Novick, M. R. (1980). The detection of cheating on standardized tests: Statistical and legal analysis. *Journal of Law & Education, 9*(1), 1–64.

Callahan, D. (2004). *The cheating culture: Why more Americans are doing wrong to get ahead.* Orlando, FL: Harcourt.

Case, S. M., & Donahue, B. E. (2013). Security-related communications. In J. A. Wollack & J. J. Fremer (Eds.), *Handbook of test security* (pp. 221–236). New York: Routledge.

Chen, S.-Y. & Lei, P. -W. (2005). Controlling item exposure and test overlap in computerized adaptive testing. *Applied Psychological Measurement, 29*(3), 204–217.

Cizek, G. J. (2012a). Defining and distinguishing validity: Interpretations of score meaning and justifications of test use. *Psychological Methods, 17*(1), 31–43.

Cizek, G. J. (2012b, April). *Ensuring the integrity of test scores: Shared responsibilities.* Paper presented at the annual meeting of the American Educational Research Association, Vancouver, British Columbia.

Cizek, G. J. (2016). Validating test score meaning and defending test score use: different aims, different methods. *Assessment in Education: Principles, Policy & Practice, 23*(2), 212–225. DOI: 10.1080/0969594X.2015.1063479.

Cizek, G. J., & Wollack, J. A. (2017). Exploring cheating on tests: The context, the concern, and the challenge. In G. J. Cizek & J. A. Wollack (Eds.), *Handbook of quantitative methods for detecting cheating on tests* (pp. 3–19). New York: Routledge.

Cohen, A. S., & Wollack, J. A. (2006). Test administration, security, scoring, and reporting. In R. L. Brennan (Ed.), *Educational measurement* (4th ed., pp. 355–386). Westport, CT: American Council on Education/Praeger.

Collins, R. (1979). *The credential society.* New York: Academic.

Davey, T., & Nering, M. (2002). Controlling item exposure and maintaining item security. In C. N. Mills, M. T. Potenza, J. J. Fremer, & W. C. Ward (Eds.), *Computer-based testing: Building the foundation for future assessments* (pp. 165–191), Mahwah, NJ: Lawrence Erlbaum Associates.

Eckerly, C. A. (2017). Detecting preknowledge and item compromise: Understanding the status quo. In G. J. Cizek & J. A. Wollack (Eds.), *Handbook of quantitative methods for detecting cheating on tests* (pp. 101–123). New York: Routledge.

Eckerly, C. A., Babcock, B., & Wollack, J. A. (2015, April). *Preknowledge detection using a scale-purified deterministic gated IRT model.* Paper presented at the annual meeting of the National Conference on Measurement in Education, Chicago, IL.

Federation of State Boards of Physical Therapy (2016a). *NPTE security agreement and general terms of use.* Retrieved from: www.fsbpt.org/SecondaryPages/ExamCandidates/NPTESecurityAgreement.aspx

Federation of State Boards of Physical Therapy (2016b). *National Physical Therapy Examinations item writer and development committees confidentiality agreement.* Alexandria, VA: Author.

Fitzgerald, C. T., & Mulkey, J. R. (2013). Security planning, training, and monitoring. In J. A. Wollack & J. J. Fremer (Eds.), *Handbook of test security* (pp. 127–146). New York: Routledge.

Folk, V. G., & Smith, R. L. (2002). Models for delivery of CBTs. In C. N. Mills, M. T. Potenza, J. J. Fremer, & W. C. Ward (Eds.), *Computer-based testing: Building the foundation for future assessments,* (pp. 41–66). Mahwah, NJ: Erlbaum.

Foster, D. (2013). Security issues in technology-based testing. In J. A. Wollack & J. J. Fremer (Eds.), *Handbook of test security* (pp. 39–83). New York: Routledge.

Foster, D. F., & Miller, H. L., Jr. (2009). A new format for multiple-choice testing: Discreet option multiple-choice. Results from early studies. *Psychology Science Quarterly, 51*(4), 355–369.

Foster, F. F., & Zervos, C. (2006, February). *The big heist: Internet braindump sites.* Poster presented at Innovations in Testing, the annual conference for the Association of Test Publishers, Orlando, FL.

Fremer, J. J., & Ferrara, S. (2013). Security in large-scale paper and pencil testing. In J. A. Wollack & J. J. Fremer (Eds.), *Handbook of test security* (pp. 17–37). New York: Routledge.

Georgiadou, E., Triantafillou, E., & Economides, A. A. (2007). A review of item exposure control strategies for computerized adaptive testing developed from 1983 to 2005. *The Journal of Technology, Learning, and Assessment, 5*(8). Retrieved from: http://ejournals.bc.edu/ojs/index.php/jtla/article/view/1647/1482

Haladyna, T. M., & Rodriguez, M. C. (2013). *Developing and validating test items.* New York: Taylor & Francis.

Hambleton, R. K. (1993). Principles and selected applications of item response theory. In R. L. Linn (Ed.), *Educational Measurement* (3rd ed., pp. 147–200). New York: American Council on Education/Macmillan.

Harris, D. J., & Schoenig, R. R. W. (2013). Conducting investigations of misconduct. In J. A. Wollack & J. J. Fremer (Eds.), *Handbook of test security* (pp. 201–219). New York: Routledge.

Hobson, K. (2010, June 9). Medical board says MDs cheated. *The Wall Street Journal.* Retrieved from: http://online.wsj.com/article/SB10001424052748704256604575294712195930970.html

Impara, J. C., & Foster, D. (2006). Item and test development strategies to minimize test fraud. In S. M. Downing & T. M. Haladyna (Eds.), *Handbook of test development* (pp. 91–114). Mahwah, NJ: Erlbaum.

Iridian Technologies (n.d.). *Biometric comparison guide.* Retrieved from: https://epic.org/privacy/surveillance/spotlight/1005/irid_guide.pdf

Joint Committee on Testing Practices. (2000). *Rights and responsibilities of test takers: Guidelines and expectations.* Washington, DC: American Psychological Association.

Karabatsos, G. (2003). Comparing the aberrant response detection of thirty-six person-fit statistics. *Applied Measurement in Education, 16*(4), 277–298.

Kingston, N. M., Tiemann, G. C., Miller, Jr., H. L., & Foster, D. (2012). An analysis of the discrete-option multiple-choice item type. *Psychological Test and Assessment Modeling, 54,* 3–19.

Kugler, S. (2008, June 9). Senior NYC crane inspector accused of corruption. *Insurance Journal.* Retrieved from: www.insurancejournal.com

Lee, Y.-H., Lewis, C., & von Davier, A. A. (2014). Test security and quality control for multistage tests. In D. Yan, A. A. von Davier, & C. Lewis (Eds.), *Computerized multistage testing: Theory and applications* (pp. 285–300). Boca Raton, FL: CRC Press.

Lewis, C., Lee, Y.-H., & von Davier, A. A. (2014). Test security for multistage tests: A quality control perspective. In. N. M. Kingston & A. K. Clark (Eds.), *Test fraud: Statistical detection and methodology* (pp. 230–238). New York: Routledge.

Lyons, B. J. (2015, January 17). Cheating scandal fouls State Police test. *Times Union.* Retrieved from: www.timesunion.com

*Maupin v. National Board of Podiatric Medical Examiners* (2003). No. 03-20011-CIV (S.D. Fla.).
Maynes, D. (2009). Caveon speaks out on IT exam security: The last five years. Retrieved from: http://caveon.com/articles/it_exam_security.htm
Maynes, D. (2014). Detection of non-independent test taking by similarity analysis. In N. M. Kingston & A. K. Clark (Eds.), *Test fraud: Statistical detection and methodology* (pp. 53–80). New York: Routledge.
Mitchell, R. L. (2014, June 19). Pirates, cheats, and IT certs. *Computerworld*. Retrieved from: www.computerworld.com
Powers, D. E., & Fowles, M. E. (1998). Effects of preexamination disclosure of essay topics. *Applied Measurement in Education, 11*(2), 139–157.
Sainz, A. (2012, November 25). Cheating scandal: Feds say teachers hired stand-in to take their certification tests. *NBC News*. Retrieved from: http://usnews.nbcnews.com/_news/2012/11/25/15430647-cheating-scandal-feds-say-teachers-hired-stand-in-to-take-their-certification-tests?lite
Schoenig, R., Rhodes, A., & Eyob, D. (2013, February). *Developing your test security plan.* Presentation at the annual conference of the Association of Test Publishers, Ft. Lauderdale, FL.
Scicchitano, A. R., & Meade, R. D. (2013). Physical security at test centers and the testing company. In J. A. Wollack & J. J. Fremer (Eds.), *Handbook of test security* (pp. 147–171). New York: Routledge.
Semko, J. A., & Hunt, R. (2013). Legal matters in test security. In J. A. Wollack & J. J. Fremer (Eds.), *Handbook of test security* (pp. 237–258). New York: Routledge.
Shu, Z., Henson, R., & Luecht, R. (2013). Using deterministic, gated item response theory model to detect test cheating due to item comprise. *Psychometrika, 78*, 481–497.
Sijtsma, K. (1986). A coefficient of deviant response patterns. *Kwantitative Methoden, 7*, 131–145.
Sisk, R. (2014, February 5). Navy nuclear cheating scandal grows to 30 sailors. *Military.com News*. Retrieved from: www.military.com
Skorupski, W. P., & Wainer, H. (2017). The case for Bayesian methods when investigating test fraud. In G. J. Cizek & J. A. Wollack (Eds.) *Handbook of quantitative methods for detecting cheating on tests* (pp. 346–357). New York: Routledge.
Smydo, J. (2003, August 3). Health fields fight cheating on tests. *Pittsburgh Post-Gazette*. Retrieved from: www.post-gazette.com
Stocking, M. L. (1994). *Three practical issues for modern adaptive testing item pools* (Research Report No. RR-94-5). Princeton, NJ: Educational Testing Service.
Trabin, T. E., & Weiss, D. J. (1983). The person response curve: Fit of individuals to item response theory models. In D. J. Weiss (Ed.), *New horizons in testing*. New York: Academic.
United States Department of Labor. (2010, December 15). *Training and employment guidance letter, No. 15–10.* Washington, DC: Author.
van der Linden, W. J., & Guo, F. (2008). Bayesian procedures for identifying aberrant response-time patterns in adaptive testing. *Psychometrika, 73*, 365–384.
van der Linden, W. J., & Sotaridona, L. S. (2006). Detecting answer copying when the regular response process follows a known response model. *Journal of Educational and Behavioral Statistics, 31*(3), 283–304.
van der Linden, W. J., & van Krimpen-Stoop, E. M. L. A. (2003). Using response times to detect aberrant response patterns in computerized adaptive testing. *Psychometrika, 68*, 251–265.
Way, W. D., & Robin, F. (2016). The history of computer-based testing. In C. S. Wells & M. Faulkner-Bond (Eds.), *Educational measurement: From foundations to future* (pp. 185–207). New York: Guilford.
Way, W. D., Steffen, M., & Anderson G. S. (2002). Developing, maintaining, and renewing the item inventory to support CBT. In C. N. Mills, M. T. Potenza, J. J. Fremer, & W. C. Ward (Eds.). *Computer-based testing: Building the foundation for future assessments,* (pp. 143–164). Mahwah, NJ: Erlbaum.
Weinstein, M. (2017). When numbers are not enough: Collection and use of collateral evidence to assess the ethics and professionalism of examinees suspected of test fraud. In G. J. Cizek & J. A. Wollack (Eds.), *Handbook of quantitative methods for detecting cheating on tests* (pp. 358–369). New York: Routledge.

Weiss, D. J. (1982). Improving measurement quality and efficiency with adaptive testing. *Applied Psychological Measurement*, 6(4), 473–492.

Wesman, A. G. (1971). Writing the test item. In R. L. Thorndike (Ed.), *Educational Measurement* (2nd ed., pp. 81–129). Washington, DC: American Council on Education.

Wollack, J. A., & Case, S. M. (2016). Maintaining fairness through test administration. In N. J. Dorans & L. L. Cook (Eds.), *Fairness in educational assessment and measurement* (pp. 33–53). New York: Routledge.

Wollack, J. A., & Cizek, G. J. (2017). The future of quantitative methods for detecting cheating: conclusions, cautions, and recommendations. In G. J. Cizek & J. A. Wollack (Eds.), *Handbook of quantitative methods for detecting cheating on tests* (pp. 390–399). New York: Routledge.

Wollack, J. A., & Maynes, D. D. (2017). Detection of test collusion using item response theory. In G. J. Cizek & J. A. Wollack (Eds.), *Handbook of quantitative methods for detecting cheating on tests* (pp. 124–150). New York: Routledge.

Yan, D., van Davier, A. A., & Lewis, C. (Eds.). (2014). *Computerized multistage testing: Theory and applications*. Boca Raton, FL: CRC Press.

Zamost, S., Griffin, D., & Ansari, A. (2012, January 13). Exclusive: Doctors cheated on exams. *CNN*. Retrieved from: www.cnn.com/2012/01/13/health/prescription-for-cheating/index.html

# 10 Using Standards to Evaluate Credentialing Programs

*Lawrence J. Fabrey*

The process of evaluation involves determining the value of something on the basis of judgments. We make judgments every day, and the examples are endless. Judgments can range from subjective and arbitrary to objective and systematic; a primary purpose of this chapter is to highlight the latter end of that range. Judgments that are objective and systematic can only truly be made when there is the possibility of comparison to criteria—that is, some set of guidelines or standards. This chapter describes the most relevant standards and the processes by which credentialing organizations may choose to be evaluated in relation to those standards, with a focus on external sources of evaluation and an emphasis on the psychometric aspects of a credentialing program—that is, a program intended for certification or licensure of individuals in a profession or occupation.

## Brief History of Selected Standards

### AERA, APA, and NCME Standards for Educational and Psychological Testing

Psychometricians who work with credentialing organizations may have a preference as to which standards apply best for the programs with which they work, but there is likely general agreement that the most authoritative and comprehensive standards to guide psychometric practice are those promulgated by the American Educational Research Association, the American Psychological Association, and the National Council on Measurement in Education (AERA, APA, & NCME). These three professional organizations collaborated on a document called *Standards for Educational and Psychological Tests and Manuals*, which was published in 1966. Preceding that time, *Technical Recommendations for Psychological Tests and Diagnostic Techniques* had been developed and published by the APA in 1954. Also, in 1955, *Technical Recommendations for Achievement Tests* was published by the National Education Association, as a joint project of the AERA and the NCME, which at that time was called the National Council on Measurement Used in Education (NCMUE).

Because the three organizations have collaborated on revised versions since 1966, the standards are sometimes referred to as the joint technical standards, or sometimes just the *Standards*. The title of the four versions published since 1966 has remained the same as the first edition jointly sponsored by the three organizations: *Standards for Educational and Psychological Testing*. In each instance, there was a formal agreement among the three organizations, representation from each, and one organization was selected to publish the document. Updated editions have been published in 1974, 1985, 1999, and 2014. While all three organizations played an active role in each update, the first three were published by APA and the most recent two versions by AERA, on behalf of the other organizations.

Creation of the 2014 edition of the *Standards* required nearly ten years. A new edition of virtually any professional publication intends to provide more clarity, better communication, and a more effective structure. In addition to these goals, there were other areas of attention addressed by this edition—namely, accountability issues, fairness and accessibility for examinees, expansion of testing in the workplace, and the importance of the many technology changes impacting testing since 1999.

The 2014 *Standards* includes three major parts—namely: 1) Foundations, 2) Operations, and 3) Testing Applications. Basic principles associated with validity, reliability, and fairness are addressed within the three chapters of the first part. The six chapters within Operations deal with applications related to creating, delivering, and scoring a test, as well as the rights and responsibilities of test takers and users. Also included is a chapter on documentation, which is discussed at some length later in this chapter. While the first two major parts are intended to apply to any testing situation, the Testing Applications part is more specific—namely, psychological testing and assessment, workplace testing and credentialing, educational testing and assessment, as well as the use of tests for program evaluation, policy studies, and accountability. Each of the thirteen chapters begins with background, which describes some of the context that may be needed to help interpret the standards. In addition, the standards within each chapter are organized by clusters. For example, the 25 standards related to validity in Chapter 1 are organized into three clusters.

There are many relevant aspects of the first two parts that apply to credentialing examinations and Chapter 11, Workplace Testing and Credentialing, will certainly apply. More specifically, the third cluster in that chapter includes four standards that are somewhat unique to credentialing examinations. Those four standards relate to identifying the content domain of interest, estimating decision consistency, establishing scoring rules and procedures, and ensuring the appropriateness of the passing score. These concepts are covered in other chapters of this book, and also discussed briefly later in this chapter, in the context of comparing these standards to others.

## *National Commission for Certifying Agencies (NCCA) Standards for the Accreditation of Certification Programs*

The origin of the National Commission for Certifying Agencies (NCCA) dates back to 1977, when the National Commission for Health Certifying Agencies (NCHCA) was created by the United States Congress with a federal grant. The original charge was to develop standards for high-quality allied health certification programs and to develop an accreditation mechanism related to those standards. After approximately ten years, the scope of the NCHCA was broadened and two organizations were created: 1) the NCCA to continue the accreditation of healthcare as well as other certification programs, and 2) the National Organization for Competency Assurance (NOCA), a membership association for certification organizations that was intended to provide educational and technical information related to certification. In an attempt to more accurately reflect the mission of advancing credentialing, NOCA became the Institute for Credentialing Excellence (ICE) in 2009. NCCA remains an independent and separately governed accreditation organization affiliated with the ICE.

The *Standards for the Accreditation of Certification Programs* has been updated twice since 1977. One of the significant changes made in the version approved in 2002 was a change in the scope of the resulting accreditation mechanism. The original version focused on accreditation of a certification organization. However, recognizing that organizations could have multiple programs with various intents and procedures, the 2002 version began to focus on accreditation of individual certification programs. The NCCA's *Standards for the Accreditation of Certification Programs* (ICE, 2014a) has always been intended to be consistent with the AERA, APA, and NCME *Standards for Educational and Psychological Testing.*

NCCA accreditation can be considered to be a status or a process (2014, Preamble). The process involves submitting an online application and an application fee. The application process requires a description and extensive documentation related to each standard, which is reviewed for compliance by the NCCA Commissioners, including administrators, psychometricians, and at least one public member. When a program has achieved accreditation, this status shows any interested party that the program has met each and every one of the standards. Since accreditation requires renewal every five years, applicants, candidates, certificants, and other stakeholder groups will know that the program continues to be in compliance with the most current version of the standards. In addition, accredited programs must complete an annual report that helps to document ongoing compliance.

The 2014 edition of the NCCA standards includes 24 distinct standards related to the purpose of the program, governance, policies and procedures, the process for creating and scoring the examination(s), recertification, and a commitment to maintaining compliance with the standards. To achieve or renew accreditation by the NCCA, the certification program must provide satisfactory documentation related to each essential element underlying each standard, a total of 87 essential elements. The standards document includes commentary related to the standards and essential elements. The commentary statements are intended to clarify aspects of the intent of the standards, and to help credentialing organizations understand and interpret the standards and essential elements. In addition, the commentary is intended to provide examples of good practices that may not specifically be required by the standards or essential elements, as well as to provide suggestions about the documentation that can help demonstrate compliance with the standards. As organizations begin submitting applications for accreditation of a program, beginning in 2016 for this edition of the standards, the NCCA Commissioners will continue to evaluate compliance with each standard and essential element, and the commentary will continue to be advisory in nature.

Each of the NCCA standards has traditionally been considered to be either administrative or psychometric, but with the 2014 version it is slightly more difficult to make that distinction. For example, standards related to security (standard 12), panel composition (13), maintaining certification (22), and quality assurance (23) include significant administrative and psychometric features. The standards that are more strictly psychometric include those related to job analysis (14), examination specifications (15), examination development (16), standard setting (17), examination administration (18), scoring and score reporting (19), reliability (20), and examination score equating (21). As with the previous version of the NCCA standards, validity is not identified as a separate standard, rather components in support of validity are addressed throughout various psychometric standards.

### International Standard ISO/IEC 17024

The full title of International Standard ISO/IEC 17024 is *Conformity assessment—General requirements for bodies operating certification of persons.* The first version of this standard was developed and published in 2003 by the International Organization for Standardization

(ISO) and the International Electrotechnical Commission (IEC), the two groups that promulgate standardization worldwide. The American National Standards Institute (ANSI) is the representative from the United States for ISO and IEC. ANSI was founded in 1918 to represent the US on international standardization issues. The international standard on conformity assessment is therefore sometimes referred to as ANSI/ISO/IEC 17024.

Governmental and non-governmental organizations participate in the activities of ISO and IEC through technical committees. International Standard ISO/IEC 17024 was updated in 2012 through the work of the ISO Committee on conformity assessment (CASCO), and ANSI was the representative from the United States on the ISO CASCO. Following the development process, the updated ISO/IEC 17024 was approved by the international members of ISO and IEC.

Application for accreditation through ANSI involves an extensive review of the requirements of ISO/IEC 17024 by thoroughly trained reviewers. In addition to the review of the application completed by the applicant, the ANSI review process includes an onsite visit.

The structure of ISO/IEC 17024 includes seven overall requirements, with a total of 31 specific requirements, some of which also include further definition and detail. Overall requirements related to general considerations (requirement 4), structure (5), resources (6), records and information management (7), and the management system (10) could be considered to be primarily administrative. Requirements related to the certification scheme (8) and the certification process (9) are both administrative and psychometric. The psychometric requirements are not extensive and detailed, but address the same considerations as other standards—that is, job analysis, examination design and development, standard setting, administration, scoring, comparability, and reliability. Similar to the NCCA standards, validity is not identified as a separate requirement, rather components in support of validity are addressed throughout.

More details about the psychometric requirements are described in the ANSI document entitled *Guidance on Psychometric Requirements for ANSI Accreditation* (ANSI, 2009). The intent of this document is exactly what the title suggests, to provide guidance about how to comply with the psychometric aspects of ISO/IEC 17024. In some respects, this document serves the same purpose of the NCCA commentary or the background of each chapter of the AERA, APA, and NCME standards. Four major sections are included, which address development of the assessment, as well as administration, scoring, and reporting. The guidance identifies some general methodologies, analyses, and procedures, but is not intended to be prescriptive. Perhaps the closest this guidance document comes to being prescriptive is a brief description of the minimum statistical analyses that should be conducted, and that an analysis should be completed at least annually.

### *Other Standards for Psychometrics*

The AERA, APA, and NCME *Standards for Educational and Psychological Testing* have been described here as the most authoritative, and the NCCA *Standards for the Accreditation of Certification Programs* and *International Standard* ISO/IEC 17024 are most relevant to credentialing programs, but other standards may apply to specific types of credentialing programs. Five of these specialty area standards are highlighted in this chapter—namely, those intended for certificate programs, nursing specialty certification programs, real- estate licensure programs, and two guidelines that could apply if a credentialing examination is used for selection or promotion in and employment setting.

There are several ways to distinguish between a certification program and an assessment-based certificate program, and that distinction is well documented (e.g., ICE, 2010). However, the key difference is focus; the focus of a certification program is assessment and the focus of a certificate program is on education or training. As a further description, an assessment-based certificate program includes an examination or other form of assessment, which can be distinguished from certificate programs that only provide confirmation of attendance or participation related to a specific area of education or training, without assessment.

ICE 1100:2010(E) – *Standard for Assessment-Based Certificate Programs* was approved in 2009 by ANSI as an American National Standard. This standard is designed for organizations that wish to document the quality of their assessment-based certificate programs. There are seven main sections within this standard, which address many of the same components that are covered by the previously noted standards for certification of persons, in addition to requirements related to development, delivery, and maintenance of education or training. Section 7 addresses psychometric considerations for the assessment process. Of note is that the ICE 1100 standard acknowledges that slightly different interpretations may be made depending on consequences associated with completion of the program—that is: "A job/practice analysis shall be conducted for high-stakes certificate programs when their scope is sufficiently broad to support such a study" (ICE 1100, 7.5). In 2012, ICE launched an accreditation program for assessment-based certificate programs based on ICE 1100, known as ACAP Accreditation.

The Accreditation Board for Specialty Nursing Certification (ABSNC) is known as the only accrediting body specifically for nursing certification. The accrediting body affiliated with the American Board of Nursing Specialties (ABNS), ABSNC was previously known as the ABNS Accreditation Council. ABNS was founded in 1991, and the ABSNC standards were developed and implemented soon thereafter. The ABSNC reviews the standards annually, and they have been updated periodically. One of the most recent changes, in 2012, was to expand the program to provide accreditation services for certification programs for members of the nursing team who are not registered nurses.

A review team is selected to conduct the primary review of applications for ABSNC accreditation. The team includes nursing leaders (staff or a volunteer affiliated with a nursing specialty organization) and either a volunteer psychometrician or the ABSNC lead psychometrician. Documentation is required to demonstrate compliance with each of the 18 standards. The structure of these standards includes a discussion of the rationale for each standard, which provides background and context for the standard. The rationale is followed by criteria, which typically provides a fairly brief statement about what must be documented related to the standard. Details about the required documentation follow the criteria. The psychometric standards are similar to those noted previously in relation to other standards, and address validity (standard 7), test development (8), reliability (9), test administration (10), test security (11), and passing scores (12).

The Association of Real Estate License Law Officials (ARELLO®) created *Guidelines for Accreditation,* which were first used to accredit a real-estate licensure examination program in 1992. These *Guidelines,* and a companion document called the *Generally Accepted Principles of Examination Development* are intended to be consistent with the AERA, APA, and NCME *Standards,* and, unlike the previously noted accreditation standards, the ARELLO® guidelines focus on the examination rather than the entire program. The purpose of the Examination Accreditation Program is to help reassure real-estate licensing entities about the validity and defensibility of the licensing examinations, which in turn should help promote reciprocity among the jurisdictions.

Another unique aspect of the ARELLO® program is that in addition to a psychometric review, a content review is conducted. This content review is conducted by one of more members of the accreditation committee, or another subject matter expert selected by the committee, and feedback about content is provided back to the applicant. A total of fifteen guidelines cover the expected range of psychometric activities needed for a credentialing examination. As with other standards, the first guideline addresses the need for examination specifications based on a job analysis. Also similar to others, there is a specific guideline identifying the need for a criterion-related passing point study. Other standards include guidelines pertaining to item writing, review, pretesting, and banking, as well as ongoing development, generation, review, publication, and delivery of the examinations. Finally, two guidelines address maintenance and retrieval of data, as well as security.

Most individuals involved with credentialing organizations realize that the examinations are not designed for purposes other than to issue a license or grant certification. However, there are occasions in which a credentialing examination may be used for other purposes—for example, for selection or promotion in an employment setting. While these alternative uses can lead to greater demand for the credential, psychometricians working with credentialing programs should be sure to advise the programs about limitations of the interpretations to be made based on the examination results. In general, it is advisable to make the intent of their credentialing process clear—that is, to grant certification or issue a license.

The *Uniform Guidelines on Employee Selection Procedures* (EEOC, 1978) were primarily intended to help employers and other organizations evaluate the proper use of examinations and other procedures that are used to select or promote employees, and to encourage these entities to use valid selection procedures. It is not clear whether credentialing examinations would be covered by these guidelines; some phrases in the guidelines suggest they could, but others appear to indicate they would not cover voluntary certification examinations. These guidelines are generally discussed from a legal perspective because they have been used in court cases, and since the focus of this chapter is psychometrics, further discussion is not included. However, credentialing organizations should be aware of the existence of these guidelines.

While the EEOC guidelines are sometimes considered to be more from a legal perspective than from a psychometric perspective, the *Principles for the Validation and Use of Personnel Selection Procedures* (SIOP, 2003) help to describe best psychometric practices related to personnel selection. These practices may include hiring, placement, promotion, and other decisions or actions in the employment arena. Now in the fourth edition, the *Principles* document was updated to keep pace with developments in theory and research related to employment testing since the previous version (1987), and to maintain congruence with the 1999 version of the AERA, APA, and NCME standards. The *Principles* document is a publication of the Society for Industrial and Organizational Psychology (SIOP, a division of the American Psychological Association) and represents SIOP's official position. An extensive discussion of the *Principles* is not included here, but the document is worthy of mention because it offers some different perspectives on validation procedures that may be relevant for credentialing examinations.

## Use of the Standards

Because objective judgments can only be made when there is the possibility of comparison to criteria, any of the standards discussed previously could be used as the criteria for evaluation. Someone involved with a credentialing organization likely has some level of familiarity with one or more of the standards discussed, and in some instances, the selection of which set of standards or guidelines to use for an evaluation is clear. Once the distinction is made about whether the intent of a program is for assessment or education and training, the choice can be narrowed down to ACAP accreditation *versus* either NCCA or ANSI/ISO/IEC 17024. For a real-estate licensing entity, the ARELLO® accreditation program is the clear choice. As expected, many nursing specialty organizations choose ABSNC accreditation. A total of 63 programs, sponsored by 21 certification organizations, held accreditation through ABSNC in 2015. At that same time, more than 75 programs sponsored by 15 nursing certification organizations held NCCA accreditation. Some of these nursing specialty programs were dually accredited by both ABSNC and NCCA, including those of the nursing specialty organization with the most certification programs, the American Nurses Credentialing Center (ANCC).

Regardless of which set of standards may be considered for evaluation of a credentialing program, one of the first issues to address is the purpose of the evaluation. Any of the standards can be used for an organizational self-evaluation, and one of the purposes of this chapter is to encourage that self-evaluation. The background for each chapter within the AERA, APA, and NCME standards and the commentary related to each of the NCCA standards can be particularly useful for this purpose. A credentialing organization likely has some psychometric consultation; to be able to communicate effectively with the psychometrician, credentialing organization leaders may want to review these sources as background.

A self-evaluation is clearly the first way to start any review of a credentialing program, but the self-evaluation will certainly have limitations. Through self-evaluation, a credentialing program may gain insights into ways to enhance the credibility of the program. In the words of a long-time certification executive, "Any structured review of a certification organization and its certification programs will identify opportunities to improve . . . organized reviews will lead to excellence" (Brauer, 2011, p. 183). Therefore, a self-evaluation can be of benefit to an organization simply for the sake of identifying potential areas for improvement.

The next step beyond a self-evaluation could be a structured, organized review, which could be conducted at various levels of formality. The potential value of a second opinion is unquestioned in healthcare, and while the focus is clearly different for a credentialing organization, the principle of seeking a second opinion remains the same. At the least formal level, a university professor could help with the evaluation. Some graduate school programs will specifically use a title that includes the word "psychometrics," "measurement," or "evaluation," while some programs will be referred to as "educational," "industrial/organizational," or "quantitative" psychology. Contacting these programs could lead to a consultative arrangement with a faculty member, who might use one or more sets of standards as a guide. As a note of caution, however, credentialing organizations should be aware that it is rare for graduate programs to include much emphasis on psychometrics as applied to credentialing examinations in their curriculum.

An example of a formal variation of this type of a structured, organized review can be provided by the Buros Center for Testing, which is an independent organization within the University of Nebraska–Lincoln. The Buros Center was established in 1994, more than 50 years after Oscar Buros published the first *Mental Measurements Yearbook*. Creation of the Buros Center led to an expansion of services that led to creation of a division that conducts audits of proprietary testing programs, first known as the Buros Institute for Assessment, Consultation and Outreach (BIACO) and presently named Psychometric Consulting. Psychometricians with Buros's Psychometric Consulting unit use their own Buros Standards for Proprietary Testing, which are based on the AERA, APA, and NCME *Standards* as well the *Guidelines for Computer-Based Testing* (International Test Commission, 2005). This formal evaluation uses two stages—an audit of processes and procedures, and then a focused evaluation of specific examinations, if desired.

Other formal evaluations are available through any of a number of testing agencies that provide services to credentialing organizations, ranging from full service management of virtually every aspect of a credentialing program to short-term consultation related to the standards. In considering a consultative relationship, the credentialing organization should decide on goals related to the arrangement and the scope of services. Testing agencies employ psychometricians who are very familiar with the various standards, but understandably have greater expertise with the psychometric standards, and less experience working with the administrative standards. If the goal of the credentialing organization is to seek accreditation, the first step should be to conduct their own self-evaluation, as discussed previously. Most organizational leaders will be able to have a good grasp of general areas of strengths and weaknesses, and will be able to identify those when seeking proposals from psychometric consultants. Just like a second opinion can be of value when reassessing a self-evaluation, seeking proposals from more than one testing agency will provide the organization with options to consider. In rare instances, it may be necessary for a credentialing organization to work with more than one agency to meet all the organization's evaluation needs.

A credentialing program might seek an independent audit or submit to an accreditation review simply for the purpose of their own quality improvement, but it is clear that most programs want to use the accreditation status for promotional purposes. There is no formal accreditation process for compliance with the AERA, APA, and NCME standards, so a program that wanted to promote that they met those standards would have difficult time doing so. One reason there is no formal accreditation is that the AERA, APA, and NCME (2014) standards require judgment about applicability as suggested by these statements in the Introduction:

> Depending on the context and purpose of test development or use, some standards will be more salient than others.
> However, all standards are important in the contexts to which they apply.
> Each standard should be carefully considered to determine its applicability to the testing contexts under consideration.
>
> (p. 5)

Therefore, any attempt to accredit a program according to the AERA, APA, and NCME standards would likely be associated with so many caveats as to be impractical. The program could make a claim, but would have difficulty documenting fully tangible evidence. On the other hand, full accreditation by NCCA or ANSI, for example, can be eminently useful for promotional and marketing purposes. Organizations that achieve these accreditations frequently issue press releases and display the accreditation logo prominently. In essence, the thinking is that through quality improvement, the organization is also able to provide reassurance to applicants, candidates, certificants, employers, and other potential stakeholders in the public that the program has value.

The previous discussion seems to suggest there are two primary reasons for seeking accreditation: improved quality and marketing. Brauer (2011) provided a more refined description, as he identified five benefits of certification accreditation:

1. Identifying opportunities for improvement.
2. Increased value for certificants.
3. Increased value for other stakeholders.
4. Marketing edge.
5. Beating the competition.

(p. 185–186)

While each of these potential benefits can be distinctly described, it appears to come down to the basic idea that improving quality improves value. The improvement in value then can lead to other advantages.

Unfortunately, there is no control over either the use of the word "certified" or the development of certification programs. Any entity can start a program, even when a program or programs exist in a closely related role, profession, or occupation. And, regardless of the characteristics of a program, participants can claim to be certified. Furthermore, a program can display a trademark symbol or register an acronym, which may impress naive members of the public who may think a ™ or ® provides an indication of quality. However, accreditation can help inform the public about the quality underlying a program. Having an accredited program informs stakeholders that the programs' certificants have met rigorous standards.

Although accreditation is intended to be voluntary, the potential benefits of accreditation are so compelling that some organizations find accreditation to be essential. An additional reason for this importance is the value that governmental and non-governmental agencies have placed on accredited certification programs. One example of this is the Magnet Recognition Program®, a recognition program sponsored by the American Nurses Credentialing Center, which is intended to promote high-quality care within healthcare organizations. The evaluation process for the Magnet Recognition Program® considers certification of nurses as an important characteristic, and while not required, accreditation by the NCCA and/or the ABSNC leads to automatic acceptance of the certification as meeting the required features. Many nursing specialty certification organizations have attributed increases in candidate volume in the early 21st century to the Magnet Recognition Program®.

Another example of a strong incentive for accreditation of a certification program was the approval of Public Law 106–50, sometimes known as the Montgomery GI Bill, which led to creation of "uniform guidelines and standards for professional certification of members of the armed services to aid in their efficient and orderly transition to civilian occupations and professions and to remove barriers in the areas of licensure and certification" (PL 106–50, 1999). There have also been instances in which accreditation has become required for recognition of certification status within a state—for example, to be recognized by the California Department of Health Care Services, alcohol and other drug counselors must be certified by a program accredited by the NCCA. Knapp and Kendzel (2009) wrote: "referencing of accreditation standards in legislation has increased over the last several years . . . the *NCCA Standards* and/or accreditation were referenced as a requirement in 20 US State regulations/codes" (p. 370), and they predicted that this is a trend that would likely continue. An example of a continuation of the trend is Senate bill S.2341, introduced in 2014 to authorize reimbursement for professional credentials. The importance of certification, and especially certification that meets the high standards associated with accreditation, does seem to continue to gain momentum.

## Intent Behind Selected Standards and Applying for Accreditation

The AERA, APA, and NCME (2014) *Standards for Educational and Psychological Testing* are intended "to promote sound testing practices and to provide a basis for evaluating the quality of those practices" and "to provide criteria for the development and evaluation of tests and testing practices and to provide guidelines for assessing the validity of interpretations of test scores for the intended test uses" (p. 1). As noted previously, there is no official accreditation mechanism for these standards; rather, they are to be used to provide guidance to psychometricians and other professionals working with examinations. The influence of these standards is pervasive; many credentialing organizations claim to comply, many requests for proposals for testing services specify compliance, and it is likely that many proposals from testing agencies will assert that their procedures are in compliance with these standards. It is only logical that these standards are considered the most authoritative and comprehensive standards to guide psychometric practice.

The AERA, APA, and NCME standards have limitations, which are described in the introduction as a "legal disclaimer" (p. 1) where there are five specific cautions about potential "misinterpretations, misapplications, and misuses" (p. 7). One caution is that the field of psychometrics is rapidly evolving, even though the periodicity of revision of the standards has slowed; this latest revision took 15 years. Other cautions relate to the importance of using professional judgment in interpreting and applying the standards. Also, the standards are not intended to be prescriptive, and when particular procedures are suggested, the "phrase 'or generally accepted equivalent' should always be understood" (p. 7). Lastly, in contrast to the statement about the pervasiveness of the standards, this caution is offered: "Claims by test developers or test users that a test ... satisfies or follows the standards ... should be made with care ... claims without supporting evidence should not be made" (p. 7).

Most of the standards and accreditation programs noted in this chapter make reference to the AERA, APA, and NCME standards, and typically indicate that the intent is to be consistent with those standards. As an international standard, it is logical that ISO/IEC 17024 does not appear to claim consistency with the AERA, APA, and NCME standards. However, while there may be some minor differences, the requirements and guidance related to ISO/IEC 17024 appear to be quite consistent with the overall intent of applicable AERA, APA, and NCME standards. Some of the differences among the various sets of standards are subtle, and the evidence that could be offered to support compliance with accreditation requirements may differ. It would be impossible in this chapter to summarize all the similarities and differences among these several sets of standards, especially when the most authorization and comprehensive standards document is over 200 pages. However, there are a few similarities and differences, both in the standards and in the documentation used for accreditation, which have been considered to be worth noting in this chapter. The previous discussion focused on the history and structure of eight different sets of standards that apply to psychometrics. What follows is a discussion of what can be referred to as the links in the chain of evidence used to support the validity of the examination results, along with some observations about the documentation related to those standards that might be evaluated for audit or accreditation.

### Job Analysis

The foundation for collecting evidence of validity for a credentialing examination is typically a job analysis, which may be called by different names, but regardless of whether the organization calls the study a job analysis, practice analysis, task analysis, or role delineation study, this can be considered to be the first link in the chain of evidence. Not a great deal of attention is paid to the importance of a job analysis in the AERA, APA, and NCME standards and ISO/IEC 17024. In the former, job analysis is only indirectly mentioned in the validity chapter, and in the standards for credentialing, standard 11.13 describes the importance of having a rational basis for establishing the content domain that is to be covered by the test. The comment for that standard starts with: "Typically, some form of job or practice analysis provides the basis for defining the content domain" (AERA, APA, & NCME, 2014, p. 182). ISO/IEC 17024 indicates that a job and task description must be a part of a certification scheme, and that a job analysis must be conducted and updated; and that documentation is required in support of this study. The ANSI guidance document expands on this somewhat, indicating that the validation investigation (i.e., job analysis) should identify the knowledge and tasks needed across a sampling of practitioners, regardless of some of their other key demographic characteristics.

Regarding job analysis, other standards (i.e., NCCA, ABSNC, and ARELLO®) are somewhat more specific, even indicating that the frequency with which a job analysis should generally be conducted is every five years. While this time frame may not be an absolute requirement, the consequences of not complying may be difficult to predict. Throughout the remainder of this chapter, the importance of documentation is a recurring theme. In this instance, all standards suggest the need for documentation; the NCCA standards describe the general content of a report as an essential element: "The report of the job analysis must describe the methods, results, and outcomes of the job analysis study, including supporting documentation for each element and sufficient information to justify the study's findings and conclusions" (standard 14, essential element B) and suggestions for details to include in the report are included in seven bulleted items in the commentary. The ABSNC standards go somewhat beyond this, with requirements in the application to submit considerably more information in the job analysis report or within other sources of documentation. Some of this prescriptiveness could be the result of this accreditation process being intended for a more homogeneous group of credentialing programs—that is, for nursing specialty certification or members of the nursing team. Not surprisingly, the SIOP principles extend beyond collecting validity evidence based on content through a job analysis. Those principles also cover evidence based on relationships between scores and other variables, the internal structure of the test, response processes, and the consequences of decisions, similar to the sources of evidence addressed in the AERA, APA, and NCME standards.

The careful development of examination specifications is a critical component of the examination design and development process, and in the case of a credentialing examination, the specifications are generally a direct result of the job analysis study. Some of the documentation related to the specifications may remain confidential, but all standards suggest that at least some information related to content and the testing method be made available to candidates. Historically, examination specifications were often thought to be a simple outline of content, but the contemporary view of examination specifications is more comprehensive than that. A structured process for designing an examination is identified by Reid, Raymond, and Zara (2009), and they emphasize the importance of documentation:

> Creating documentation may be the least exciting step in examination development so it may be tempting to procrastinate . . . needs to be given a high priority in the project management plan . . . developed as the process moves forward rather than created after the fact.

(p. 152–153)

The importance of creating well-documented examination specifications as a part of examination design is embodied in the 2014 NCCA standards. The previous version of the NCCA standards did not specifically identify examination specifications as a standard; rather, it had been simply assumed as a result of the job analysis study leading to an appropriately designed examination development process. Now, the 2014 examination specification standard (15) specifically identifies that the examination specifications must address how the examination is designed and the ways in which the examination is to be used. The guidance document for ANSI and ISO/IEC standard 9.3.1 similarly identifies the importance of the overall design of the examination, as well as the distribution and job-relatedness of content, as being important characteristics of the examination specifications that will help ensure comparability of the interpretations to be made based on assessment results.

*Examination Content Development*

Item writing is addressed only briefly within the two most broadly relevant accreditation programs for credentialing organizations. The examination process requirement within ISO/IEC 17024 notes that evaluation of competence of an individual may be accomplished by any of a variety of formats—for example, "written, oral, practical, observational or other reliable and objective means" (9.3.1). The ANSI guidance document provides further clarification—that is, that the "components (e.g., items) must be directly related to the skills required for overall competence" (4.3). The document indicates that a multiple-choice item format provides efficient measurement of knowledge, but demonstration of competence for a physical skill would be more effectively assessed with a performance test. The NCCA standards state that a "systematic item development plan must be developed and followed" (standard 16, essential element A), and the commentary for standard 16 also identifies that different formats may be applicable and the first two steps of the examination development process involves training of subject matter experts (SMEs) and developing items.

Perhaps because of the focus on a particular area of subject matter, the ARELLO® guidelines provide considerably more detail regarding item writing. These guidelines provide recommendations about SMEs and their training, as do the NCCA and ABSNC standards. However, the ARELLO® guidelines further specify that the training must address principles that are consistent with the ARELLO® accreditation committee's (2011) *Basic Item Writing Principles,* a detailed document that provides general guidance as well as considerations unique to real-estate licensing examinations.

Standards related to examination development follow a similar trend identified in the previous discussion. The International Standard ISO/IEC 17024 is more general than other standards, identifying broad issues rather than providing detail about procedures. The guidance document does not provide much more detail, other than reinforcing the importance of following the specifications document, and ensuring a thorough content and technical review. The NCCA standards provide a similar level of detail, and the three essential elements associated with standard 16 add unique requirements related to translating examinations into another language and the use of subjectively scored items—that is, those scored by raters. While these two special cases are highlighted, the emphasis of the standard is on ensuring comparability of the assessment and fairness to candidates.

## Standard Setting

Accreditation by any of the mechanisms described in this chapter require a process that is consistent with AERA, APA, and NCME (2014) standard 11.16 for establishing a passing score:

> The level of performance required for passing a credentialing test should depend on the knowledge and skills necessary for credential-worthy performance in the occupation or profession and should not be adjusted to control the number or proportion of persons passing the test.
>
> (p. 182)

This suggests that completion of a criterion-referenced standard setting process to establish the passing standard, or cut score, is required. And while all accreditation program standards are consistent with this requirement, there are some interesting differences that are worthy of note.

Methods for establishing a passing standard are not addressed specifically in ISO/IEC 17024, but several requirements suggest criterion-referenced passing points. First, requirement 9.2.3 indicates the assessment must be "verified with documented evidence to confirm the competence of the candidate." Other requirements address the "validity of the fail/pass decision" (9.3.1), and that "information gathered during the certification process shall be sufficient for the certification body to make a decision on certification" (9.4.1). The situation is clarified further in the guidance document, which indicates "The process for establishing the passing standard should comply with established psychometricand governmental/legal guidelines. Most importantly, the passing standard should be determined using a criterion-referenced technique based upon determining a standard applied to all candidates" (4.5 pass-fail standard(s)). What is unique is the reference to the governmental/legal guidelines, which is also mentioned in the ARELLO® guidelines, but only to make the point that "passing scores set merely by statute, rule, or policy are not defensible in the absence of a professional acceptable study of the level of performance that should be required of entry-level practitioners" (11. Passing Score). While they do not use the term "criterion-referenced standard setting," NCCA accreditation standard 17 describes the same process: "perform and document a standard setting study that relates performance on the examination to proficiency" (Standard 17). This standard includes three essential elements, and very extensive commentary related to recommendations for the methodology of a standard setting study. And to re-emphasize the previously made point about the importance of documentation, commentary about suggested evidence to document compliance with standard 17 would be a report that addresses at least a dozen different aspects of the study. As noted previously in this chapter, the commentary statements are intended to provide clarity or to provide examples of good practices, and suggestions about the documentation that can help demonstrate compliance with the standards. The ABSNC standards do not provide quite as much information about the performance and documentation of a passing point study, but an important difference is the documentation noted in relation to standard 12 includes specifically required aspects of documentation, rather than being suggestive of best practices.

For a psychometrician, the discussion of passing standards logically leads to examination score equating—that is, a way to ensure that the same level of performance leads to the same result. The purpose of equating can be summarized by this comment in relation to AERA, APA, and NCME standard 11.16: "When there are alternate forms of a test, the cut score should refer to the same level of performance for all forms" (p. 182). All the accreditation programs have requirements for ensuring equivalence of results, sometimes very specifically requiring statistical equating procedures. The most comprehensive requirements related to equating appear in the NCCA standards, with standard 21 and the four related essential elements. This standard is not prescriptive in that it does not identify a specific method or methods that must be used for equating. Rather, the emphasis is on the use of statistical evidence of comparability and ensuring fairness for all candidates. Other standards used for accreditation do not have the detail of NCCA standard 21, but they do share the essential principle of ensuring fairness for all candidates.

*Administration, Security, and Score Reporting*

Establishing and maintaining an appropriate passing standard is sometimes considered to be the last link in the chain of evidence used to support the validity of the examination results. However, validity can be threatened by lack of appropriate procedures for examination administration, security, and score reporting. Running the risk of sounding repetitive, these three issues are addressed by all the standards, ranging from simple to more complex.

Within ISO/IEC 17024, the simple requirement for this is 9.3.3: "Criteria for conditions for administering examinations shall be established, documented and monitored." The guidance document expands on that considerably, with eleven specific aspects of security that should be addressed related to administration of the examinations. This level of detail still does not approach what is included in the NCCA standards.

Standards related to administration and security were included in the previous version of the NCCA standards, but the 2014 edition includes an extensive description of four essential elements related to examination administration (standard 18) and two essential elements related to security (standard 12). The essential elements related to standard 18 are among the lengthiest in the NCCA standards, presumably because of the increased importance of ensuring "that all candidates take the examination under comparable conditions, safeguard the confidentiality of examinations, and address security at every stage of the process" (standard 18) and the complexity of doing so. Security standard 12 relates to aspects of security independent of the administration, and the point to be made by including this in the same discussion is that any threat to security, whether while the candidates are interacting with the examination or at any other point in the certification process, can undermine the validity of the examination results, including certification decisions.

Score reporting may seem out of place in the context of the discussion of administration and security, although with the continuing increase in the use of computer-based testing comes the continuing increase in the availability of results for candidates immediately upon completion of the examination. The implications for examination design and development that should be considered in response to this desire for instantaneous reporting are well beyond the scope of this chapter. Mentioning the long-developing change in administration formats from paper to computer is intended to illustrate the need to continue to monitor the standards and their interpretations. It is a given that change will continue, but the principles underlying the standards should remain constant.

To return to the discussion about the most authoritative and comprehensive standards, it is interesting to note that the AERA, APA, and NCME standards focus more on standardization of test administration than on security. And those standards bring together the interrelationship of test administration to scoring and reporting, which is another reason they are discussed together in this section. AERA, APA, and NCME standard 6.0 states:

> To support useful interpretations of score results, assessment instruments should have established procedures for administration, scoring, reporting, and interpretation. Those responsible . . . should have sufficient training. . . . Adherence to the established procedures should be monitored, and any material errors should be documented . . .
> (p. 114)

The importance of documentation is a recurring theme in the discussion of the intent behind some aspects of the standards and applying for accreditation, so it is fitting that this last note about documentation ends that discussion.

## A Comparison of the Standards

What are the overall similarities and differences among the standards used for accreditation? This chapter has attempted to highlight a few specific similarities and subtle differences, but a summary would not be complete without a brief discussion of some overall observations. Focusing first on the comparison between NCCA standards and ISO/IEC 17024, there is generally great similarity in intent. Both indicate the importance of documentation related to each of the links in the chain of evidence to support the validity of the examination results. The NCCA standards, through the commentary, typically offer more information about how to provide that documentation than do ISO/IEC 17024 and the ANSI guidance document. Focusing on the psychometric standards, the probability would be high that an organization found to be in compliance with one set of standards would likely be found in compliance with the other. Of course, there could be exceptions, and one potential area of exception could be an assessment based on an oral, practical, or observational examination that is found in compliance with ISO/IEC 17024 might have difficulty achieving NCCA accreditation. The NCCA standards use the word "examination" to refer to any type of assessment, but the vast majority of NCCA-accredited programs use multiple-choice items as the form of assessment of candidates.

As a practical matter, some organizations have programs that are accredited by both ANSI and NCCA. To help facilitate the process for dual accreditation, ICE has announced plans to begin accrediting using ISO 17024. The 2013–2014 Annual Report for ICE indicated these plans: "In expectation of offering ISO 17024 accreditation in 2015, ICE will build on the pilot program conducted in 2014 . . . allow certification programs already accredited by NCCA to add accreditation to ISO 17024 through ICE" (ICE, 2014b, p. 2). As noted by this statement, this new program is limited to only those programs already holding NCCA accreditation who want to seek accreditation under ISO 17024. The success of the pilot program tends to reinforce the assertion that an organization found in compliance with one set of standards would likely be found in compliance with the other.

How does ICE 1100:2010(E), the *Standard for Assessment-Based Certificate Programs*, relate to either the NCCA standards or ISO/IEC 17024? The obvious difference is that ICE 1100 is intended for assessment-based certificate programs, whereas the other two are intended for voluntary certification of individuals using an estimate of competency using an examination. Beyond that, the psychometric requirements of ICE 1100 are similar, but likely somewhat less rigorous than the other standards, especially if the certificate is not considered to be "high stakes." A curious similarity is that ICE 1100 was developed by the same organization that developed the NCCA standards, but was approved in 2009 by ANSI as an American National Standard on March 25, 2009.

While revisions of both standards have led to some differences, the ABSNC and NCCA standards have many similarities. One difference is the target practitioner, and therefore the target credentialing body. With ABSNC as the only accrediting body specifically for nursing certification, the target could be considered to be a subset of the wide-range of credentialing organizations that might, and do, seek NCCA accreditation. With the change in 2012 to expand the ABSNC program to provide accreditation services for certification programs, for non-RN members of the nursing team that difference may be minimized. Because of the focus on the credentialing of registered nurses, some aspects of the ABSNC standards are focused on considerations unique to nursing, such as the scope of the nursing specialty and research on the body of knowledge for the specialty.

The ARELLO® guidelines are inherently different in that the focus is on examinations for real-estate licensing. However, there are many similarities with the psychometric requirements of any of the other accreditation standards. The fundamental reason there are so many similarities among all the standards for accreditation is that they are ultimately designed to be consistent with the AERA, APA, and NCME standards.

A brief discussion of some of the similarities and differences of the actual process for seeking accreditation may be in order. It has already been noted that only one accreditation requires a site visit—the ANSI accreditation for ISO/IEC 17024. However, the 2014 NCCA standards includes as commentary for standard 24: "The Commission reserves the right to investigate (whether onsite, virtually, or through a third party) if questions arise about the integrity of the information submitted or concerns are raised about compliance to any of the NCCA standards, whether during the initial application review or throughout the five-year accreditation cycle". As noted previously, the NCCA standards commentary is subject to change at any time, but this new provision takes away one of the differences that had been noted previously.

The review processes are similar for all accreditation mechanisms—they all depend on the use of knowledgeable individuals to review the documentation and come to agreement on a decision related to accreditation. The accreditation mechanisms all have in place opportunities to either accredit or deny accreditation, and generally have a provision to allow gathering of more definitive information that can be used by the reviewers to reach an ultimate decision to accredit or deny. The number of reviewers can vary with the different accreditation mechanisms, and the number of reviewers and how they are selected can vary over time for any particular accreditation process.

There is a fee paid by any organization seeking accreditation, and each accrediting body has established a fee schedule that can change over time. The cost of accreditation can be an important consideration, and the cost not only includes the fee paid, but also the time investment, which can be substantial. Another feature that is common to any accreditation is that payment of the fee does not ensure accreditation; the credentialing organization must provide the documentation to be found in compliance.

The reader may be looking for the answer to the question: "Which accreditation process is best for my organization?" Well, unfortunately, the answer to that question can best be provided in the context of the old joke: "If you ask two psychometricians about anything, you can be sure to get at least three opinions, one of which will likely begin with 'it depends.'" Sometimes the answer to the question about which process is best will be fairly easy, but an organization might want to read and consider various standards and types of accreditation. As noted, while a real-estate licensing examination provider could theoretically seek accreditation from NCCA or ANSI, the ARELLO® accreditation is the logical choice. Nursing specialty organizations often seek ABSNC accreditation, but accreditation from NCCA or ANSI might also be considered. The decision goes back to making a judgment about the value of one or more accreditations.

**Summary**

One of the goals for this chapter has been to encourage organizations to seek accreditation to promote the high quality of their programs. The first question an organization should ask is about the value of accreditation for their organization. Some compelling arguments were offered about the general value of accreditation, and those could be viewed from a variety of perspectives. Whether motivated by a perceived threat from a potential competitor or simply to provide reassurance about the quality of the program for the organization, the accreditation of its certificants, or other stakeholders, has been of value to hundreds of organizations for many hundreds of programs. The vast majority of programs that achieve accreditation will continue to maintain and renew their status, even in the face of the effort and expense of completing a full application for reaccreditation.

Because all organizations may not find great value to accreditation, there may be instances in which a self-evaluation will be sufficient. The first step of a self-evaluation is to consider the capabilities of organizational leaders to perform the evaluation, and the result of this consideration may be that external expertise is needed. For purposes of self-evaluation, it would be wise to start with a review of the most authoritative and comprehensive standards, those promulgated by AERA, APA, and the NCME. Hopefully, the result of the self-evaluation will be that the organization could be ready to apply for accreditation by one of the entities described here. If the credentialing organization does not have the expertise for a well-informed review of those standards, additional psychometric and other consultation could be the logical next step. Once well-informed about the AERA, APA, and NCME standards, the organization will be in a better position to review the accreditation standards, and then be able to reach a decision about which accreditation process is best for the organization.

**References**

American Board of Specialty Nursing Certification (2014). *Accreditation Standards.* Retrieved from: www.nursingcertification.org/accreditation.html

American Educational Research Association, American Psychological Association, & National Council on Measurement in Education (AERA, APA, & NCME) (2014). *Standards for educational and psychological testing.* Washington, DC: American Educational Research Association.

American National Standards Institute (ANSI) (2009). Guidance on psychometric requirements for ANSI accreditation (PCAC-GI-502, Revision 2). Retrieved from: www.ansica.org

Association of Real Estate License Law Officials (2011). *Basic item writing principles.* Retrieved from: www.arello.org/default/assets/File/BasicItemWritingPrinciples_4-4-11.pdf

Association of Real Estate License Law Officials (2012). *Guidelines for accreditation.* Retrieved from: www.arello.org/default/assets/File/EAP/3%20Accred%20Guidelines%20Rev%202012-10-26.pdf

Brauer, R. (2011). *Exceptional certification – Principles, concepts and ideas for achieving credentialing excellence.* Champaign, IL: Premier Print Group.

Equal Employment Opportunity Commission (EEOC) (1978) *Uniform Guidelines on Employee Selection Procedures.* Retrieved from: www.gpo.gov/fdsys/pkg/CFR-2011-title29-vol4/xml/CFR-2011-title29-vol4-part1607.xml

International Test Commission (2005). *International guidelines on computer-based and internet delivered testing.* Retrieved from: www.intestcom.org

Institute for Credentialing Excellence (ICE) (2009). *ICE 1100 Standard – ACAP standard for assessment-based certificate programs.* Retrieved from: www.credentialingexcellence.org

Institute for Credentialing Excellence (ICE) (2010). *Defining features of quality certification and assessment-based certificate programs.* Retrieved from: www.credentialingexcellence.org

Institute for Credentialing Excellence (ICE) (2014a). *National Commission for Certifying Agencies (NCCA) standards for the accreditation of certification programs.* Retrieved from: www.credentialingexcellence.org

Institute for Credentialing Excellence (ICE) (2014b). *2013–2014 Annual report: Growing the value of credentialing.* Retrieved from: www.credentialingexcellence.org/d/do/1118

International Standards Organization (2012). *International standard ISO/IEC 17024 Conformity assessment — General requirements for bodies operating certification of persons.* Retrieved from: www.ansi.org/

Knapp, L. G., & Kendzel, J. G. (2009). Future trends in certification. In J. Knapp, L. Anderson, & C. Wild. (Eds.), *Certification: The ICE handbook* (2nd ed., pp. 351–371). Retrieved from: www.credentialingexcellence.org/p/cm/ld/fid=11

Reid, J. B., Raymond, M., & Zara, A. R. (2009). Examination design and construction. In J. Knapp, L. Anderson & C. Wild (Eds.), *Certification: The ICE handbook* (2nd ed., pp. 149–182). Retrieved from: www.credentialingexcellence.org/p/cm/ld/fid=11

Society for Industrial and Organizational Psychology (SIOP) (2003). *Principles for the validation and use of personnel selection procedures* (4th ed.). Bowling Green, OH.

# 11 Legal Issues for Credentialing Examination Programs

*S. E. Phillips*

## Introduction[1]

The terms "licensure" and "certification" are often used interchangeably but actually refer to different kinds of tests. Licensure tests typically assess mandatory, minimum, entry-level skills and are scored pass/fail, while certification tests typically distinguish levels of achievement for awarding voluntary credentials and are scored on a continuous scale. Licensure tests are normally administered by state agencies; certification tests may be administered by public or private entities. In this chapter, the term "credentialing examination" refers to both licensure and certification tests.

Legal challenges to credentialing examination programs generally involve allegations of unfairness. This chapter is organized around the following four broad issues and corresponding questions related to major aspects credentialing examination programs that have been challenged in litigation.

1. **Protecting the Public**: Under what conditions is it fair to require *all* candidates to demonstrate prescribed knowledge and skills at or above a specified performance level on a credentialing test?
2. **Testing Accommodations Policies**: Who qualifies as disabled? What is a reasonable accommodation? How can a credentialing program ensure that test scores obtained with testing adaptations fully represent the intended construct and produce comparable scores?
3. **Test Security Policies**: What are defensible procedures for maintaining the confidentiality of test items, protecting the validity of test score interpretations from corruption by misconduct, and canceling scores for test security violations?
4. **Test Construction Procedures**: What options are available to a credentialing program pressured to adopt variations of discredited item selection criteria that minimize differential performance between majority and minority examinees?

Courts in the United States have generally addressed such issues by imposing limitations on the conditions under which a challenged action may be upheld or by accepting settlement agreements drafted by the parties. The remainder of this chapter explores these responses of the U.S. legal system after providing some background information about federal law.

### Constitutional and Federal Protections

A credentialing examination case may involve issues of federal and/or state law and may be filed in a federal or state court. A judicial decision applies only to cases that are factually similar and is binding only on lower courts and administrative agencies in the jurisdiction in which the case was decided, although judges in other jurisdictions have discretionary authority to cite and adopt its holdings. Cases accepted by the Supreme Court for argument where a written decision is issued are considered settled precedents that apply to all jurisdictions within the United States. Federal courts are generally reluctant to overrule earlier decisions and do so infrequently.

A common remedy sought by plaintiffs in credentialing examination cases is an injunction requiring the testing entity to take a specific action such as providing a requested testing adaptation or releasing a withheld test score. The purpose of an injunction is to prevent future injury; it does not provide monetary compensation for past injuries.[2]

Primary federal laws cited in credentialing examination challenges include the due process and equal protection clauses of the fourteenth amendment to the U.S. Constitution, Title VII of the Civil Rights Act (1964), Section 504 of the Rehabilitation Act (1973), the Americans with Disabilities Act (1990) and the Copyright Act (1976). Cases litigated under these federal laws may be broadly classified as racial discrimination, due process, disability discrimination or copyright infringement claims.

### *Professional Testing Standards*

Courts have routinely recognized the *Standards for Educational and Psychological Measurement* (*Standards,* American Educational Research Association [AERA], American Psychological Association [APA], & National Council on Measurement in Education [NCME], 1985, 1999)[3] as an appropriate source of authority for expert opinions in credentialing cases and competing interpretations have been offered and debated by expert witnesses. Although the *Standards* is aspirational rather than prescriptive, requires professional judgment to apply its general provisions in specific cases, and is not binding on any court, judges tend to be skeptical of expert opinions that seriously conflict with reasonable interpretations of the *Standards*.[4]

## Legal Issues Related to Protecting the Public

Legal challenges to the content, scoring or other technical aspects of credentialing examination programs have alleged discrimination and due process violations under federal law. These challenges and their requirements are discussed below.

### *Racial Discrimination Challenges*

The performance of examinees from some minority groups administered standardized tests for credentialing is often lower than that of majority group examinees. This differential test performance is labeled *disparate impact* when the difference in performance is large. Demonstration of disparate impact is a requirement in statutory civil rights and constitutional equal protection challenges alleging that the use of a specific test unfairly discriminates against the lower performing minority group.

#### *Title VII*

Title VII of the Civil Rights Act (1964) as amended prohibits employment discrimination on the basis of race, color, religion, sex or national origin. The original 1964 legislation held private employers liable only for intentional discrimination, known as *disparate treatment*, which occurs when a protected trait is the basis for an employer's unfavorable treatment of an employee with respect to compensation, terms of employment or workplace privileges. In a disparate treatment claim, the challenger must prove that the employer had a discriminatory intent or motive for the challenged employment action (Watson v. Ft. Worth Bank & Trust, 1988). A 1972 amendment extended Title VII to cover public employment.

Although the 1964 statute did not specifically prohibit facially neutral policies that were discriminatory in practice, in Griggs v. Duke Power Co. (1971) the Court interpreted the statute to cover situations, known as *disparate impact,* where members of a protected group are differentially subjected to unfavorable employment actions unrelated to job performance. In 1991, Congress amended the statute to incorporate the *Griggs* criteria for impermissible *disparate impact*. Federal courts have applied different standards of review to disparate impact challenges depending on the classification of the group alleging the violation. A stringent standard (strict scrutiny) is applied when racial/ethnic groups are affected while a more lenient standard (rational basis scrutiny) applies to socioeconomic classifications. Title VII also specifically makes it permissible for an employer to use a professionally developed test "provided that such test is not designed, intended or used to discriminate because of race, color, religion, sex or national origin" (42 U.S.C. § 2000e – 2(h)).

The testing requirements of Title VII were originally designed to apply to employers using tests to select applicants for specific jobs. The extent to which Title VII applies to credentialing tests and, if it does, the exact requirements for proving a violation remain unclear under prior federal decisions.[5]

*Shifting Burdens of Proof*

When Title VII does apply, a plaintiff can initially establish a presumptive violation by using statistics to show that a disparate impact exists (Hazelwood Sch. Dist. v. Kuhlmeir, 1977). The Supreme Court has held that the "proper comparison [is] between the racial composition of [the at-issue jobs] and the racial composition of the qualified ... population in the relevant labor market" (Wards Cove Packing Co. v. Atonio, 1989, p. 650). The plaintiff is not required to prove that the testing entity had discriminatory intent because Congress supplied the requisite intent by stating that the purpose of Title VII was to remedy past societal discrimination (Washington v. Davis, 1976).

Once the plaintiff has presented sufficient evidence of disparate impact, the burden of proof shifts to the employer to demonstrate a business necessity or justification for the challenged employment practice. In testing cases, this requirement translates into demonstrating the validity of the test score interpretations and the job-relatedness of the tested knowledge and skills. A federal court stated, "Title VII does not invalidate a test that has disparate impact if the test is reasonably calculated to measure a bona fide occupational qualification" (United States v. LULAC, 1986, p. 648-49).[6] Title VII requires more, however, than merely showing that the test was constructed by professionals.

If the employer provides convincing evidence of the validity of test score interpretations and measurement of job-related skills, the burden then shifts back to the plaintiff to argue that equally effective but less discriminatory alternatives are available. The Court has held that cost is one factor to be considered, concluding that "the judiciary should proceed with care before mandating that an employer must adopt a plaintiff's alternate selection or hiring practice in response to a Title VII suit" (Wards Cove Packing Co. v. Atonio, 1989, p. 661). In addition, equally effective alternatives are rare in credentialing examination cases because substitute tests are usually nonexistent, prohibitively expensive or measure different construct(s).[7]

## The Uniform Guidelines

As part of its Title VII enforcement responsibilities, the federal Equal Employment Opportunity Commission (EEOC) issued the *Uniform Guidelines on Employee Selection Procedures* (*Uniform Guidelines,* 1978). The *Uniform Guidelines* are interpretive regulations directly applicable to employment tests and applicable by analogy to some credentialing examinations. They detail the permissible boundaries of employment testing and specify requirements for demonstrating the criterion, content or construct validity of test score interpretations for a selection test. A job analysis is a required piece of evidence in all cases under the *Uniform Guidelines.*

Measures of practical and statistical significance are commonly used to assess disparate impact. The *Uniform Guidelines* create a presumption of practically significant *disparate impact*, commonly referred to as the *four-fifths* or *80% rule*, when the passing rate for the minority group is less than 80% of the passing rate for the majority group (§ 1607.4D). For example, if 90% of Whites and 70% of African-Americans pass a credentialing examination, there is a *presumption of disparate impact* because 70% is less than 80% of 90 = 72%. Statistical significance tests are appropriately applied to calculate the probability of true population differences when only a sample of the potential applicant pool has been tested.

For credentialing examinations, job-relatedness evidence is typically collected through job analysis surveys of stratified random samples of job incumbents who are asked to rate the importance and frequency of use of a list of relevant job tasks (compiled by reviewing training/practice materials and consulting experts) related to competent job performance (see Chapter 4). Job tasks rated highly are included on the test. The validity of the intended test score interpretations is supported by evidence that the scores are valid and reliable measures of the content identified in the job analysis (AERA et al., 2014).

## Reconciling Disparate Treatment and Disparate Impact

In Ricci v. DeStefano (2009), the Supreme Court in a 5 to 4 decision addressed a conflict in which the challengers alleged disparate treatment and the employer defended its actions as necessary to avoid disparate impact liability. The Court held that intentional discrimination against nonminority groups could not be justified by disparate impact liability when convincing evidence of job relatedness and the validity of test score interpretations established the business necessity of the test, and proposed alternatives were unavailable or involved impermissible adjustment of the test scores based on race.

The *Ricci* plaintiffs were 1 Hispanic and 17 White firefighters from New Haven, CT who had passed discarded promotion exams for lieutenant or captain rank. Each test consisted of a 100-item multiple-choice written exam (reading level below 10th grade) and an oral exam based on hypothetical job situations with responses rated by a panel of three higher ranking assessors (2 minority, 1 majority) from outside the state. Total scores were weighted 60% written exam and 40% oral exam. Passing rates were 58–64% White, 32–38% African-American, and 20–38% Hispanic.

The content of the examinations was based on initial interviews/ride-alongs and a follow-up job analysis survey for which minority job incumbents were oversampled.[8] A list of source materials covering the content identified in the job analysis and from which the test questions were drawn was compiled by the vendor, approved by the city, and shared with candidates three months prior to testing. By design, city staff members were not allowed to review the test items before administration due to allegations of prior test security violations.

Eight lieutenant and seven captain positions were vacant. Test results were rank ordered and the top three candidates were eligible for promotion to each position. Based on the test results, all 10 lieutenant candidates and 7 of 9 captain candidates eligible for promotion were White. The additional two captain candidates were Hispanic, leaving no African-Americans eligible for promotion.

Before deciding whether to certify the results, the city held several public meetings, requested additional information from the vendor, and consulted several experts regarding the substantial disparate impact in the test data. The city ultimately decided to discard the test results, believing that it would be subject to a Title VII lawsuit if these results were certified. In the ensuing legal challenge, the city argued that the potential for Title VII disparate impact liability justified the disparate treatment of the Whites and Hispanics whose passing scores were disregarded. The Supreme Court disagreed.

In establishing a standard for situations when Title VII disparate impact and disparate treatment prohibitions were in conflict, the Supreme Court adopted a *strong basis in evidence* standard allowing disparate treatment of nonminorities in the face of disparate impact on minorities only when evidence of job-relatedness is insufficient for the test in question. Applying this standard to the city's promotion exams, the Court found that the record included substantial, convincing evidence that the exams tested job-related knowledge and skills. The Court also credited the steps the vendor had taken to over-represent minorities in the job analysis survey and the scoring of the oral exams. The Court found the candidate ranking process to be fair, transparent, communicated sufficiently in advance, consistent with bargained union contracts, developed with broad minority participation and inclusive of reasonable criteria. The only outside expert firefighter who had reviewed the exams in detail stated they contained relevant questions. The Court also chided the city for electing not to produce the technical manual (including validity evidence) listed in the vendor's contract.

In addition, the Court was not persuaded by the alternatives offered by the city. The Court specifically rejected replacement of the exams with assessment centers recommended by a competitor of the vendor, banding the rule-of-three results to allow additional minority candidates to qualify for promotion and reweighting the written exam 30% and the oral exam 70% in computing the total score to allow three African-Americans to be considered. The latter two alternatives violated the Title VII prohibition on using race to adjust test scores. Thus, the strong evidence of job relatedness, evidence of the validity of test score interpretations, and the absence of equally effective, less discriminatory alternatives led the Court to find the city's promotion examination process defensible under Title VII despite evidence of disparate impact. The Court ruled that the city had violated the Title VII prohibition on disparate treatment when it refused to certify the examination results due to racial disparities. Having ruled in their favor on the Title VII claim, the Court did not address the challengers' additional equal protection claim.[9]

*Equal Protection*

The equal protection clause requires government agencies to treat similarly situated examinees equally. In addition to demonstrating disparate impact, equal protection challenges require evidence of discriminatory intent (Washington v. Davis, 1976). Discriminatory intent is generally harder to prove than disparate impact because there usually is no direct evidence that anyone intended to discriminate. Absent a law or official policy of discrimination, intent must be proven by all the surrounding facts and circumstances (Village of Arlington Heights v. Metro. Hous. Dev. Corp., 1977).

*Disparate Impact Challenges to Teacher Licensure Tests*

There have been many challenges to the fairness of teacher licensure tests for historically disadvantaged groups of examinees (Phillips & Camara, 2006). The following sections discuss three important cases from the 1990s in Alabama, 2000s in California and 2010s in New York.

**Richardson v. Lamar County Bd. of Educ.** (1991). Alice Richardson, an African-American teacher employed by the district for three years under temporary teaching certificates, alleged Title VII discrimination when the district failed to renew her teaching contract for a fourth year. She was not rehired due to layoffs related to the consolidation of two elementary schools and because she had been unable to pass the state teacher licensure test after multiple attempts. Richardson cited disparate impact statistics indicating that the African-American passing rate was only 45% to 53% of that of Whites, and she claimed that the Alabama teacher licensure test discriminated against African-Americans, was not properly validated, and employed an arbitrary passing standard unrelated to teaching competence. Richardson was issued a teaching license later when the court approved the Allen v. Alabama State Bd. of Educ. (1997) settlement of a class action challenging the disparate impact of the state teacher licensure tests (see *Test Construction* section below).

The district argued that Richardson's claim was preempted by the *Allen* Settlement, but the trial court disagreed because the district was not a party to that agreement. Although she had taken only three of the licensure tests, the trial court made extensive findings of fact related to the entire testing program. The trial court rejected the job analysis and content validity evidence offered by the state's contractor because it was based in part on judgments made by contractor staff rather than Alabama educators. Similarly, the court held the passing scores to be invalid and not consistent with acceptable professional standards because they were adjusted by contractor staff to produce acceptable failure rates.[10] The trial court's holdings were affirmed on appeal and the district was ordered to reemploy Richardson and provide her with backpay.

**Ass'n of Mex.-Amer. Educs. (AMAE) v. California** (2000). The AMAE challenged California's teacher licensure test claiming it discriminated against African-American, Hispanic and Asian minority candidates in violation of Title VII. The state argued that the test was valid and job-related.[11] At trial, the AMAE produced initial passing rate statistics (53% Asian, 38% African-American, 49% Hispanic and 73% White) that demonstrated a disparate impact under the 80% rule. The court held that the validity studies presented by the state were adequate to satisfy the job relatedness requirement in the *Standards* and the *Uniform Guidelines*. In reaching this conclusion, the court considered the state's job analysis, content validity evidence and procedures used for setting passing standards (review of Angoff method results and advice from an expert panel). The court rejected AMAE's argument that under the *Uniform Guidelines,* the state also was required to provide evidence of the criterion and construct validity of the test score interpretations. The court concluded that California's licensure test was an objective, cost-effective and valid method for assuring minimum basic skills for prospective California teachers.

The appellate court affirmed the trial court decision that Title VII applied to California's teacher licensure test and that it had been properly validated. The appellate court listed three steps it deemed essential for validating the job relatedness of a test: (1) identify what the test measures (test content specifications); (2) show that the measured knowledge and skills are important work behaviors (job analysis); and (3) demonstrate that the test satisfies professional standards for the validity of test score interpretations (content validity evidence).

**Gulino v. Bd. of Educ. of N.Y.C.** (2006). Another case from New York City highlights the continuing battle over whether state tests required for teacher licensure are employment tests subject to Title VII disparate impact challenges. The *Gulino* case began in the early 1990s when the state replaced the National Teacher Exam (NTE) with a state-developed test for teacher licensure. Until 1991, when a new licensing statute was adopted by the legislature, the city licensed its own teachers based on standards substantially equivalent to state standards. However, due to shortages, some teachers were allowed to continue teaching in the city on conditional or temporary licenses without having passed the required licensure exam. Subsequently, the state pressured the board to revoke the licenses of delinquent teachers. Due to continuing shortages, many continued to teach full time as substitutes in the same classrooms but with lower pay and fewer benefits. By 1996, all teachers were required to pass the new exam (aka the Liberal Arts and Sciences Test, or LAST) to obtain permanent licenses.

In 1996, a group of African-American and Hispanic candidates in the city filed suit against both the state and the district alleging that the new teacher licensure test discriminated against racial minority candidates. Statistics for the new test indicated that in the period from 1993 to 1999, White passing rates ranged from 91% to 94%, while the corresponding ranges for African-Americans and Hispanics were 51%–62% and 47%–55%, respectively. The passing rates for both minority groups were substantially below the four-fifths rule threshold of 73%–75% for presumed disparate impact under the Title VII *Uniform Guidelines*.

A trial was held in federal court in 2002–03 and the court ruled that Title VII applied to both the state and the district, found disparate impact, but held that the test was job-related and properly validated. On appeal, the challengers argued that it was improper for the city to require experienced teachers to take a test designed to license new teachers. The appellate court dismissed the state as a defendant, finding that only the district was liable under Title VII because it was both a licensor and employer. The appellate court also found that the trial court had not properly considered the validation issue and remanded the case for reconsideration.

The district then appealed the case to the Supreme Court, arguing that it was in the awkward position of being required to defend the psychometric quality of a test that it did not develop, administer or score. The Supreme Court was urged to consider the case because most federal courts that had considered such cases had concluded that Title VII disparate impact analysis did not apply to state licensure exams. Conversely, city teachers argued that the district was using the test as a de facto civil service exam and that such use constituted employment testing subject to Title VII Regulations. Without comment, the Supreme Court declined to hear the case.

On remand, the court granted in part the district's motion to decertify the class because a single injunction or judgment would not appropriately compensate individual class members requesting backpay and the award of licenses. The court chose to bifurcate the class action into a single determination of the board's liability to all class members under Title VII and a remedial proceeding to assess individual damages. Although no longer a party, the state filed a friend of the court brief arguing the new test had been properly validated.

The court held that evidence related to five factors must be presented to validate the job-relatedness of an employment test: a suitable job analysis, competent test development, test content related to job content, tested content representative of the job, and an appropriate performance standard for selecting competent applicants. After noting that professional expertise is required to assist a court in properly evaluating evidence related to the five factors, the court held that the new test was not properly validated because the vendor did not conduct a rigorous job analysis, did not competently develop the test, tested content unrelated to and unrepresentative of the job of teaching, and applied a passing standard unrelated to teaching competence.

The court found that the vendor's test framework developed by reviewing teacher education materials, consulting with education experts, and surveying teachers and college faculty asked to rate the importance of framework subtopics was flawed because the vendor did not start with a task analysis of teaching, had not documented the materials consulted or persons interviewed, pilot tested items on college students rather than working teachers, failed to link the tested content to minimum and representative content required for teaching competence, and set the passing standard based on a small subset of items with no definition of minimum competence or data relating test scores to student outcomes. Thus, the court concluded that the board violated Title VII when it required teachers to pass the new test to obtain permanent licenses. The decision was affirmed on appeal.

Subsequent to the court's finding of liability, the court conducted a hearing to determine appropriate remedial relief. The court also appointed a neutral expert to evaluate the job relatedness of a revised version of the discredited test to determine whether there were any remaining claims to be resolved.

### *Due Process Challenges*

Due process protections apply only to government entities. A property right or liberty interest is a threshold requirement. Due process claims may be procedural or substantive. Procedural due process requires adequate notice and an opportunity to be heard. Substantive due process requires fundamental fairness and government action that is not arbitrary or capricious. Procedural due process applies to the manner in which a testing program is administered while substantive due process relates to the test's technical qualities (e.g., validity and reliability of test score interpretations). Courts have given substantial weight to the *Standards* when deciding whether substantive due process requirements have been satisfied. Occasionally, criminal conduct is involved as when the court in Mahmood v. Nat'l Bd. of Medical Exam'rs (NBME, 2012) rejected a due process claim because NBME was not a state actor. The examinee had been given a three-year suspension from testing for starting a small fire in the restroom after experiencing difficulties with the computer monitor.

In 1988, the Supreme Court in Watson v. Ft. Worth Bank & Trust established that the professional standards for objective employment tests also apply to performance measures such as interviews, simulations and ratings. Performance assessments present unique psychometric challenges including adequate content representation, consistent and relevant scoring criteria, effective rater training, sufficient interrater reliability, and confidentiality of memorable tasks.

*Scoring Challenges*

Several due process challenges to credentialing examinations have focused on scoring. For example, in Grant v. NBME (2009), the court found it acceptable for examinee requested score rechecks to employ automated computer software and to be rejected if untimely. In Marquez v. Medical Bd. of Cal. (2010), an examinee challenging an NBME passing standard was allowed to retest because the state board had not formally adopted the standard as required by state statute. And in Turner v. Nat'l Council of State Bds. of Nursing (2014), the court found that the council's refusal to allow a score appeal caused actionable injury because the candidate was unable to obtain a nursing license. A computer scoring glitch had caused the shutdown of a computer adaptive test before the minimum number of items was administered. Incidentally, in that case the court also found no ADA violation because the injury was not connected to the examinee's dyslexia.

*Summary*

Under what conditions is it fair to require all candidates to demonstrate prescribed knowledge and skills at or above a specified performance level on a credentialing test?

Credentialing tests with disparate impact on racial minorities are most likely to be upheld when there is convincing evidence that the test measures job-related content judged important for safe and effective practice, the test items match the identified content, the test is developed and administered consistent with professional standards, there is no equally effective, less discriminatory, alternative assessment available, and a score appeal procedure is available.

## Legal Issues Related to Testing Accommodations Policies

Before considering accommodations cases of importance for credentialing examinations, the next sections briefly discuss relevant professional standards and trace the historical development of applicable federal law. This information highlights recent changes in professional standards and federal law that are beginning to impact litigation.

*Professional Standards*

When an individual with a disability is unable to access a test due to construct-irrelevant factors, as a matter of fairness, to support the validity of the intended inferences from the resulting test scores, and consistent with federal law, the *Standards* (AERA et al., 2014) requires testing accommodations to be provided (Standard 3.9). Judicial decisions have interpreted federal law consistent with the distinction in the 2014 *Standards* between *accommodations* that fully represent the intended construct and produce comparable scores, and *modifications* that alter the tested construct and result in scores that are not comparable to scores obtained from standard administrations of the original test.

The *Standards* (AERA et al., 2014) recommends that modified tests be treated as new test score interpretations for which the validity, reliability and other psychometric properties need to be independently verified (Standard 3.11). While modified tests may be useful in providing limited access to the tested construct for individuals with disabilities who would have no access otherwise, they may also create differential *opportunities for success* (Phillips, 2012) and be insufficient for the purpose of protecting the public from incompetent practitioners due to significant construct underrepresentation and the inability to establish comparable passing standards (AERA et al., 2014).

The *Standards* (AERA et al., 2014) places the responsibility on the testing entity for creating tests that provide full access to the construct with comparable scores when feasible (Standards 3.1, 3.2, 3.5). Nonetheless, eliminating construct irrelevant factors without creating construct underrepresentation may be less feasible for cognitive disabilities than physical disabilities when measuring achievement of academic knowledge and skills because cognitive disabilities often are coincident with the focal construct of the test. It may also be challenging in professions where automaticity and reasonable fluency with the construct, performance under time pressure, and work in distracting environments are expected in practice and are therefore important job-related competencies. According to the *Standards* (AERA et al., 2014), the key to defending a judgment of construct relevance and job-relatedness is a comprehensive job analysis that clearly defines the elements of the construct, and convincing content validity evidence linking tested content to it (Standards 11.2, 11.3, 11.13).

When a comparable alternative for measuring the full construct is not feasible for a requested testing adaptation, credentialing programs face a difficult choice between offering alternate/partial accommodations that may be rejected by the examinee and result in litigation, or granting the requested modifications and reporting annotated scores that may be challenged as invading the privacy of an examinee who does not want to be identified to third parties as disabled. In some cases, credentialing programs have been pressured to (1) offer modifications that, in the opinion of their licensed professionals, produced scores that meaningfully underrepresented the tested construct, and (2) forego score annotations describing these modifications (e.g., 50% extra time) to avoid potential stigmatization of candidates with disabilities who threaten lawsuits. Unfortunately, such actions may fail to adequately protect the public or ensure specialty area competence. The next sections describe how Congress and the federal courts have dealt with these issues.

## *Federal Disability Rights Legislation*

Beginning in 1973, federal disability law applied only to programs receiving federal funds. Subsequently, federal law was expanded in 1990 to include private and government entities. These federal laws and key interpretative legal decisions are summarized next.

### *Section 504 of the Rehabilitation Act (1973)*

Section 504 was the first federal statute to address discrimination on the basis of disability. Otherwise qualified individuals with impairments that substantially limited one or more major life activities were covered. Section 504 Regulations (1990) further provided that recipients of federal funds were required to make reasonable accommodations for otherwise qualified applicants or employees with physical or cognitive disabilities unless doing so imposed an undue hardship on the operation of its program (45 C.F.R. § 104.12). The Supreme Court further clarified Section 504 requirements.

In *Southeastern Community College v. Davis* (1979), the Supreme Court defined *otherwise qualified* as a person who, despite the disability, can meet all educational or employment requirements. The Court held that the college was not required to modify its nursing program to exempt from clinical training an applicant with an uncorrectable, severe hearing impairment because limiting her instruction to only academic courses would not even roughly approximate the training normally provided by a nursing program.

The Court was persuaded that the applicant was not otherwise qualified because she would not be able to safely care for patients or function effectively without close supervision. The *Davis* decision clearly stated that an educational institution was not required to lower or substantially modify its standards to accommodate a person with a disability, nor was it required to disregard the disability when evaluating a person's fitness for a particular educational program.

Subsequently, in Alexander v. Choate (1985), the Supreme Court clarified its interpretation of *otherwise qualified*. The Court held that programs must provide *meaningful access* and *reasonable accommodations* but were not required to substantially alter their requirements. Then in Sch. Bd. of Nassau County v. Arline (1987), the Court explained that a *reasonable accommodation* allows a person with a disability to receive the principal benefits of the program without imposing undue financial or administrative burdens, or requiring fundamental alterations in the nature of the program.

The *Arline* case involved an experienced elementary teacher who had been discharged after repeated hospitalizations for relapses of contagious tuberculosis. The Supreme Court held that Arline was disabled under Section 504 and entitled to an inquiry by the trial court to determine whether she was otherwise qualified for her job, and if so, whether the school district could reasonably accommodate her. The trial court was instructed to "defer to the reasonable medical judgments of public health officials" and to consider, among other factors, "the duration and severity of Arline's condition, ... the probability that she would transmit the disease, ... [and] whether Arline was contagious at the time she was discharged" (pp. 287–289).

### *Americans with Disabilities Act (ADA, 1990)*

The ADA, effective in 1992, extended the Section 504 provisions prohibiting discrimination against persons with disabilities in programs receiving federal funding to all public and private entities. The ADA made minor changes in the wording of Section 504, replacing the term *otherwise qualified individual* with the wording *qualified individual with a disability*. State credentialing programs are covered under the ADA Title II public services provisions and both government and private credentialing programs are covered under the ADA Title III public accommodations provisions enforced through Department of Justice (DOJ) Regulations. The ADA Title I employment provisions enforced through EEOC Regulations may also apply by analogy to work/employability issues.

The general provisions of the ADA define a *disability* as "a physical or mental impairment that substantially limits one or more major life activities ... ; [or] a record of such an impairment; or being regarded as having such an impairment" (§12102(2)). Section 12189 requires testing entities to offer credentialing examinations "in a place and manner accessible to persons with disabilities or offer alternative accessible arrangements." The corresponding ADA Regulation § 36.309 requires tests administered to persons with disabilities that impair sensory, manual or speaking skills to produce results that accurately reflected the aptitude, achievement or other factors the test is intended to measure rather than reflecting the individual's impairment *unless it is the factor that the test is intended to measure*. Testing entities are also required to provide appropriate auxiliary aids and services such as audio tapes or interpreters, Braille or qualified readers, and scribes for persons with impaired sensory, manual or speaking skills *unless* such aids would *fundamentally alter the tested skills* or create an *undue burden* (§ 36.303). The next sections review federal judicial decisions that addressed the definition of a qualifying disability under the ADA, mitigation with auxiliary aids or medication, amendment of the ADA, the identification of reasonable accommodations, score annotations for test adaptations, technological advances, documentation requirements and exemptions.

## Defining Disability

The ADA requires credentialing programs to make individualized determinations of the accommodations needed by examinees with disabilities. To establish an ADA violation, a claimant must provide evidence of an ADA qualifying disability for which a reasonable accommodation was denied by a covered entity (Cox v. Ala. State Bar, 2004). The ADA definition of disability consists of three parts: (1) an *impairment* (2) that *substantially limits* (3) a *major life activity*. DOJ and EEOC Regulations have provided further clarification with similar but not identical provisions. The 1999 DOJ Regulations listed "caring for oneself, performing manual tasks, walking, seeing, hearing, speaking, breathing, learning and working" as *major life activities* (28 C.F.R. § 35.104).[12] Some courts included test taking as part of working and reading/writing as part of learning (Bartlett v. N.Y. State Bd. of Law Exam'rs, 2000).

DOJ Regulations (1999) also described *substantially limits* as "when the individual's important life activities are restricted as to the conditions, manner, or duration under which they can be performed in comparison to most people" (28 C.F.R. § 35.104). With respect to working, the corresponding EEOC Regulations (1999) described *substantially limits* as "significantly restricted in the ability to perform either a class of jobs or a broad range of jobs … compared to the average person having comparable training, skills and abilities" (29 C.F.R. § 1630.2(j)(3)(i)). The question raised by the difference in wording between the two definitions is whether a person is to be judged substantially impaired with respect to most people or an average person with comparable skills. When selecting an appropriate comparison group for impairments related to learning, such as specific learning disabilities in reading and writing, courts have applied the DOJ *most people* standard (Kelly v. W.Va. Bd. of Law Exam'rs, 2010; Gonzales v. NBME, 2010) but when the impairment is related to the ability to work in one's chosen profession, courts have applied the EEOC *average person with comparable skills* standard with two caveats: (1) the impairment, not some other factor, must be limiting success; and (2) the individual must be foreclosed from all jobs within a professional category (Sutton v. United Airlines, 1999; Bartlett, 2000).

## Mitigation

There has also been disagreement about whether a physical or mental impairment should be judged with or without mitigation for conditions that can be corrected in whole or in part by auxiliary aids (e.g., corrective lenses, hearing aids) or medications (e.g., insulin, anti-hypertension drugs). Early ADA Regulations were silent on this issue but DOJ and EEOC Interpretive Guidance (1998) advised that disability should be assessed without considering mitigating measures such as reasonable accommodations, auxiliary aids and services, assistive or prosthetic devices, or medications (§35.104; §1630.2(j)). In 1999, the Supreme Court ruled that the EEOC and DOJ did not have the authority to modify the ADA definition of disability and held that "the determination of whether an individual is disabled should be made with reference to measures that mitigate the individual's impairment" (Sutton vs. United Airlines, 1999).

**Sutton v. United Airlines** (1999). In *Sutton*, twin sisters with severe nearsightedness who had been denied employment as global airline pilots challenged the requirement of uncorrected visual acuity of at least 20/100. Both had uncorrected vision of 20/200 to 20/400 but corrected vision of 20/20 or better with glasses or contact lenses. The sisters claimed disability discrimination in violation of the ADA but the trial court held they were not disabled because when their vision was fully corrected, they were not substantially limited in any major life activity and were not regarded as such. The trial court found that they were only regarded as having failed to meet the requirements of one specific job while remaining eligible to work as regional pilots or pilot instructors. The appellate court affirmed, creating a conflict with decisions in other circuits holding consideration of self-mitigation impermissible in disability determinations. The Supreme Court affirmed on appeal, holding:

> the approach adopted by the agency guidelines – that persons are to be evaluated in their hypothetical uncorrected state – is an impermissible interpretation of the ADA. Looking at the Act as a whole, it is apparent that if a person is taking measures to correct for, or mitigate, a physical or mental impairment, the effects of those measures – both positive and negative – must be taken into account when judging whether that person is "substantially limited" in a major life activity and thus "disabled" under the Act.
> 
> (p. 482)

The Court analogized corrected vision to medicated diabetics who are not substantially limited in major life activities unless they fail to take their insulin. The Court also explained that mitigation may create negative side effects (e.g., painful seizures from antipsychotic drugs) or incomplete correction that also must be individually evaluated. In addition, the Court observed that findings enacted by Congress when the ADA was passed estimated coverage for 43 million Americans with disabilities, a figure inconsistent with the 160 million or more that would have been covered if persons with corrected physical and health conditions had been included. The Court also found that a valid job requirement does not become invalid because it would cause a significant limitation in work opportunities if adopted by a substantial number of industry employers.

**Bartlett v. N.Y. State Bd. of Law Exam'rs** (2000). On remand after the *Sutton* decision, the appellate court reconsidered its earlier decision discounting self-mitigation in a disability determination. Bartlett, who claimed to have a reading disability, had earned a doctorate in education and a law degree. For the bar examination, she had repeatedly requested extended time, tape recording her essay answers and marking her multiple-choice answers in the test booklet, but her requests were denied based on an expert's opinion that her high reading comprehension scores and lower, but average word attack and word identification scores were inconsistent with a reading disability.

Bartlett failed the bar examination four times without accommodations. After filing suit claiming an ADA violation, she was offered limited accommodations and failed the exam again. At trial, Bartlett's expert provided results from a different reading test indicating an inability to read with the speed and automaticity of an average person and concluded that Bartlett's earlier work teaching phonics had allowed her to self-accommodate and achieve word skills scores higher than usual for a person with a reading disability.

The trial court determined that Bartlett was not disabled with respect to the major life activity of reading because compared to the general population, her self-accommodated reading skills were average on some measures. However, due to her slow reading rate and inability to compete on the bar examination, the trial court found her disabled with respect to the major life activity of work and ordered double time, use of a computer, circling answers in the test booklet and large print. This order was affirmed on appeal.

On remand, the appellate court changed its views holding that even with consideration of self-mitigation, the trial court had applied the wrong legal standard by relying exclusively on test scores and not considering clinical judgment to determine whether Bartlett's slow reading rate qualified as a reading disability. Data indicating a reading rate at the 4th percentile among college freshmen was of limited value, the court stated, because the proper reference group was the general population, not college students. Additionally, to support a substantial limitation for working, Bartlett was required to show that her inability to pass the bar exam was due to her reading impairment rather than other causal factors such as her education, experience or innate ability.

Two years later, the Supreme Court adopted a strict standard for deciding when an impairment substantially limited a major life activity. Toyota Motor Manufacturing v. Williams (2002) involved a plaintiff with carpal tunnel syndrome and tendinitis which a unanimous Court found interfered only in a minor way with performing manual tasks of central importance to the daily lives of most people. The Court further explained that a medical diagnosis by itself was insufficient; there must also be evidence of substantial limitations for that individual.

Later, in *Knapp v. City of Columbus* (2006), the appellate court upheld the denial of extra time and separate testing rooms for three firefighters with attention deficit hyperactivity disorder (ADHD) taking promotion exams. The firefighters each took prescription Ritalin but argued that the medication only partially alleviated their symptoms. Nonetheless, the court found they were able to perform ordinary daily tasks as well as most people. Even assuming they were disabled, an inquiry still would have been needed to determine whether their impairments in learning and concentration were job-related skills intended to be tested by the promotion exams and if not, how much extra time would reasonably compensate for the residual effects of their partially mitigated disabilities.

In 2008, Congress passed the ADA Amendments Act which adopted the original DOJ and EEOC guidance regarding mitigation. The Act requires disability determinations to be based on an individual's uncorrected state disregarding the ameliorative effects of mitigating measures such as medications, magnification, prosthetics, hearing devices, mobility devices, assistive technology, reasonable accommodations, auxiliary aids or services, and learned behavioral or adaptive modifications, *except* for ordinary glasses or contact lenses that fully correct visual acuity (§ 12102(4)(E)(i)(I)).

## The ADA Amendments Act (ADAAA, 2008)

The ADAAA was passed in response to a report by the National Council on Disability (2004), a federal agency charged with collecting and analyzing information about the effectiveness of the ADA. The report was critical of a series of Supreme Court decisions (including the *Sutton* and *Toyota* cases discussed above), arguing that the definition of disability and requirements for coverage had been inappropriately narrowed contrary to the intent of Congress and the objectives of the ADA. The purposes of the ADAAA as enacted by Congress were to reinstate a broad scope of available ADA protection by rejecting the Supreme Court's holdings in *Sutton* (evaluation with mitigation) and *Toyota* (demanding standard for qualifying as disabled) and reinstating the broad definition of disability applied by the Court in the Section 504 *Arline* case. Congress further indicated an intent for the determination of disability not to demand extensive analysis and for the focus of litigation to be on whether covered entities had complied with ADA requirements.

In addition to requiring disability determinations to be based on an individual's uncorrected state, substantive changes in the ADA codified by the ADAAA included:

1. Replacing references to discrimination "against a qualified individual with a disability" with discrimination "*on the basis of disability;*"
2. Expanding the definition of disability by

    a. Creating a nonlimited, statutory list of major life activities including those from the original ADA Regulations plus eating, sleeping, standing, lifting, bending, reading, concentrating, thinking, communicating, and the *operation of bodily functions* (immune system, normal cell growth, digestive, bowel, bladder, neurological, brain, respiratory, circulatory, endocrine and reproductive);
    b. Defining *regarded as having a disability* to include persons subjected to ADA prohibited actions because of an actual or perceived impairment irrespective of actual limitation, but not including transitory (duration ≤ 6 mo.) and minor impairments;
    c. Including impairments that are episodic or in remission if, when active, a major life activity is substantially limited;

3. Disallowing selection criteria based on uncorrected vision unless such criteria are job-related and consistent with business necessity;
4. Requiring *reasonable accommodations* for individuals with actual impairments or records of actual impairments but not for individuals qualifying for ADA coverage solely based on being *regarded as* having an impairment; and
5. Specifying that the DOJ and EEOC have the authority to issue regulations that implement the ADAAA definitions of disability and rules of construction.

The ADAAA also amended Section 504 to incorporate the ADAAA definition of disability and specified an effective date for the ADAAA of January 1, 2009.

## Post-ADAAA Litigation

The ADAAA has clearly expanded the breadth of impairments and the potential number of major life activities that may be substantially limited so that it is easier for an examinee to demonstrate a qualifying disability under the ADA. Virtually any recognized medical condition, evaluated without mitigation,[13] appears to qualify as long as it limits one of the many listed life activities and can be linked to test taking skills.[14] Congress expressed an intent for the courts to apply a lenient standard to this determination in order to shift the focus from qualification of the impairment to whether the appropriate accommodations have been provided. Nevertheless, because there is an incentive for struggling examinees to claim a cognitive disability to obtain more time or other assistance they believe will raise their scores, it continues to be important for credentialing programs to carefully examine an applicant's documentation to ensure that professional judgments and diagnoses are consistent with credible corroborating evidence. DOJ ADAAA Regulations (2010) state that documentation requirements must be reasonable and limited to the need for accommodations or auxiliary aids, and decisions should be timely and give considerable weight to past accommodations received in similar testing situations (§ 36.309(b)(iv–vi)).

Given the increased ease of demonstrating a disability, credentialing programs may find it useful to shift their focus to the connection between the examinee's impairment and the requested testing adaptation(s). The ADAAA did not change the requirements for an individual determination of appropriate accommodations, a causal connection between the impairment and the specific testing activity that is substantially limited, the duty of the examinee with a disability to explain how the requested adaptation(s) will address the specific limitations the impairment causes, the expectation that a testing adaptation will be provided only when it does not fundamentally alter the tested construct, or the defense of undue burden when a requested testing adaptation would create a financial or administrative hardship for the testing entity.

However, to invoke the *fundamentally alter* or *undue hardship* defenses, the testing entity must be able to document convincing evidence to support its position. For construct definitions, courts will look for clear ties to documented job skills, descriptions of test purposes and specifications, and expert opinions identifying and explaining the importance of tested skills judged construct-relevant. When undue financial or administrative burden is claimed, courts will consider the testing entity's resources and revenues, detailed documentation of actual or estimated costs, and credible evidence of future impacts or unintended consequences. Nonetheless, to be successful such claims must involve hardships that are substantial and cause unintended consequences that cannot be readily eliminated or managed by the testing entity.[15] The cases involving screen access software reviewed in the section on *Technological Advances* illustrate the skepticism of courts about financial hardships when the testing entity has substantial resources.

As of this writing, only one federal case has applied the ADAAA to a credentialing examination. In addition, several recent federal cases have reinterpreted the DOJ *best ensure* standard with respect to technological advances. These cases provide some preliminary insights into the possible effects of the ADAAA on credentialing litigation.

**Jenkins v. NBME** (2009). Kirk Jenkins was a third-year medical student with a reading impairment who was denied extra time on the Step 1 medical licensure exam. He had received formal and informal accommodations on tests throughout his education, including 50% extra time for the ACT Assessment and the Medical College Admissions Test (MCAT). In 2002, the trial court applied the strict *Toyota* standard and found that although Jenkins was a slow reader who had difficulty reading under time pressure, he did not have an ADA qualifying disability because he was unable to identify any major life activities, such as reading newspapers, for which he was substantially limited by his impairment from performing as well as most people.

The ADAAA was enacted while the case was pending on appeal and the court held it applied to Jenkins's case because he was seeking prospective relief requiring the NBME to grant extra time for tests to be administered in the future. The appellate court stated that resolution of the case depended on the ADA definition of *substantial limitation* as amended, noting that Congress had overturned the strict *Toyota* standard when it enacted the ADAAA and directed the courts to apply a more inclusive standard. The court remanded the case to the trial court for reconsideration, stating:

> If the [trial court] finds that Jenkins is disabled under the more inclusive terms of the amended ADA, [it] must still determine specifically what NBME must do to comply with the requirement that a professional licensing board offer [accessible examinations].
> (p. 7)

Presumably, the construct-relevance of reading, the degree of discrepancy between Jenkins's ability and reading achievement, the accommodations he received in medical school, and any strategies he has developed to aid his reading will be relevant in determining what testing adaptations are reasonable and appropriate, and will *best ensure* that construct-irrelevant skills are not being tested.

In an earlier case in which the trial court affirmed the denial of double testing time, recording multiple-choice answers in the test booklet and a separate room to minimize distractions for a bar applicant with a questioned reading impairment related to visual processing, the court stated:

> The Court ... finds some merit to the argument that a disparity between [ability and achievement] may, in some circumstances, permit the inference that an individual has a learning disability, even though that individual's performance has met the standard of the ordinary person. The Court is not persuaded, however, that such a disparity compels that conclusion as a matter of law, especially since [it] could reasonably be the result of many other factors, such as stress, nervousness, cautiousness and lack of motivation. Indeed, to hold otherwise would compel the conclusion that any underachiever would by definition be learning disabled as a matter of law.
> (Pazer v. N.Y. State Bd. of Law Exam'rs, 1994, p. 287, citations omitted)

Crediting the board's expert, the court also found that Pazer's percentile ranks of 62 on the timed Woodcock–Johnson Spatial Relations test and 64 on the timed Reading Comprehension test were in the average to superior range for adults and inconsistent with a reading disability requiring extra time. The court also cited similar college GPAs of 2.9 in the first two years of college without accommodations and 3.1 in the last two years with accommodations as further support for its position. Moreover, the court held that Pazer had provided no evidence for his claim of dysgraphia, including failure to provide results from any figure drawing tests best suited to confirming his alleged eye-motor coordination problem.[16] In a footnote, the court addressed construct relevance stating "It is ... at least arguable that reading is a skill necessary to be a lawyer and that it is reasonable to expect that a bar applicant, whether learning disabled or not, have the reading capacity of the ordinary person" (p. 288).

This opinion suggests that some federal courts may not be persuaded by experts who fail to support their diagnoses of learning disabilities with convincing assessment data and may be open to evidence that reading skill is job related (construct relevant) and falls within the exception to the requirement for reasonable accommodations "where those skills are the factors that the examination purports to measure" (28 C.F.R. § 36.309(b)(1)(i) (2010)).[17] In essence, the court appeared to be suggesting that timed tests administered in a large group setting may simulate the real-world, job-related skills of reading and applying important content knowledge and skills under time pressures in distracting environments that are normally expected of practicing doctors, lawyers and school teachers in their daily work.[18]

### *Identifying Reasonable Accommodations*

Required accommodations under the ADA were initially interpreted by the courts using a *reasonable accommodations* standard similar to that for Section 504. Past accommodations in an educational program or on similar types of tests were relevant but not dispositive (Cox v. Ala. State Bar, 2004). Mitigation, although not relevant to establishing a qualifying disability under the ADAAA, should still be relevant for identifying reasonable accommodations. For example, reasonable accommodations for a bar examinee with

*Legal Issues for Credentialing Examinations* 245

visual acuity of 20/40 with corrective lenses and attention deficit hyperactivity disorder (ADHD) fully corrected with medication and behavioral therapy might include large print test materials but not extra time, a reader or a separate room. Similarly, reasonable accommodations for an examinee with a hearing impairment fully corrected with a hearing aid and a specific learning disability in writing (dysgraphia) might include a computer word processor for an essay test not measuring writing but no accommodations for a computer-administered multiple-choice test. Deciding when the tested construct has been fundamentally altered requires a clear definition of the tested construct and statement of the test's intended test use (AERA et al., 2014, Standard 1.1).

*Construct Fragmentation*

When a testing adaptation would *fundamentally alter* the skills intended to be tested, an examinee with a disability is not entitled to an accommodation under the ADA. Determining whether a specific testing adaptation fundamentally alters the tested construct requires the testing entity to clearly define which skills are elements of the construct and which are not. For credentialing programs, the issue may be whether the tested skills should focus broadly on simulating application of the tested skills in a realistic, job-related environment or whether such tests should be limited to measuring narrowly defined academic content such as knowledge or application of specific information. With a narrow focus on academic content in isolation, testing adaptations such as a separate room without distractions, double the standard response time, readers, word-processing software, multiple extra breaks or individual assistants may be reasonable accommodations, but with a broader focus on real-world applications under simulated job-relevant conditions, they may not be.

From the viewpoint of an examinee with a disability, the purpose of an *accommodation* is to provide greater access by removing or compensating for any effects of the impairment. But the term *access* is ambiguous because psychometricians typically view it as meaning access to the tested content while advocates for the disabled may have in mind access to professional occupations for which the credentialing examination is a gatekeeper (Phillips, 2012). However, if *construct-relevant assistance* is provided to examinees with disabilities to increase their test scores so they will have greater access to professional opportunities, the test scores will have diminished validity as indicators of the acquisition of important job-related competencies, may fail to ensure safe and effective practice and may mislead the examinee about the likelihood of obtaining gainful employment.

In addition, allowing multiple testing adaptations in various combinations produces test administrations that measure different aspects of the construct depending on which elements are removed or receive assistance. For example, a timed statistics test will measure different mathematical competencies with a calculator and a formula sheet than it will with a reader and extra time. The former does not measure memorization or calculation, but does require reading skill and efficiency while the latter does just the opposite. Although one might argue that each element by itself is not essential to the essence of the construct, the *construct fragmentation* created by the accumulation of adaptations in different combinations may create differentially underrepresented constructs that do not measure the original construct equally and do not produce comparable test scores (Phillips, 2011, 2010). The *Standards* (AERA et al., 2014) state:

> [I]f the construct is changed, criterion-based score interpretations from the modified assessment (for example, making classification decisions such as "pass/fail" ... using

cut scores determined on the original assessment) will not be valid.... When a condition limits an individual's ability to perform a critical function of a job, an accommodation or modification of the licensing or certification exam may not be appropriate (i.e., some changes may fundamentally alter factors that the examination is designed to measure for protection of the public's health, safety, and welfare).

(p. 61, 177)

Deciding when the examinee has performed the essential functions of the task and when the tested skills have been fundamentally altered are difficult judgments for which there is considerable disagreement. Even judges do not always agree. For example, in Martin v. PGA Tour (2000), the Supreme Court held that the essence of a golf tournament was shot-making so allowing a waiver of the walking rule for a player with a mobility impairment was not considered a fundamental alteration. The Court also found that other golf tournaments (e.g., the Senior PGA Tour) allowed carts. However, two judges dissented, arguing that there was no rational basis for deciding which competition rules were non-essential.

Similarly, in Palmer College of Chiropractic v. Davenport Civil Rights Commission (2014), the court held that the college was required to provide a blind student with a sighted assistant for reading and interpreting X-rays. But the dissent argued:

The majority elevates political correctness over common sense. Obscured in its lengthy decision is the fact [we] are requiring [the College] to permit a student, blind since birth, to interpret X-rays based on what an untrained reader tells him the X-ray films depict and treat patients through vigorous spinal adjustments relying on that interpretation.... A misinterpreted X-ray could lead to improper treatment and life-long paralysis. X-ray interpretation requires training and skilled judgment to reach correct conclusions based on shades and shadows of complex bony structures.... The majority's intrusion into academic judgment on professional health care standards is unprecedented.... The majority fails to confront the well-reasoned decision of the Ohio Supreme Court applying [Section 504] to uphold a medical school's decision to deny admission to a blind student who, like [the Plaintiff here], requested a personal assistant to read X-rays and help with clinical examinations.

(p. 16)[19]

Litigation before and after the ADA Amendments has required courts to evaluate the reasonableness of requested testing adaptations for inventive and novel impairments. The examples that follow illustrate the mixed results produced by these types of cases.

In Unlimited Time/Interactive Test Administration: Pandazides v. Va. Bd. of Educ. (1994), after graduation from college with a degree in special education, Sophia Pandazides had been granted a one-year probationary license to teach emotionally disturbed students on the condition that she pass the National Teacher Examination (NTE) during that year. Pandazides was unable to pass the communication skills subtest and was diagnosed with a learning disability affecting auditory processing and test anxiety in a group, timed setting. Pandazides requested a reader and unlimited time, and the Educational Testing Service (ETS) granted her 50% extra time, a written script of the audio tape for the listening section, a recorder that played the tape at a slower speed and a separate testing room. She retested twice, first under standard testing conditions and then with the testing adaptations offered by ETS and failed both administrations with similar scores. Pandazides then consulted a psychologist who recommended unlimited time and an interactive administration by a test examiner so she could paraphrase her thoughts. ETS denied the request, characterizing it as "extraordinary." She was not rehired, filed suit alleging a Section 504 violation, lost and appealed.

The appellate court held that Section 504 was intended to protect individuals with disabilities from being denied employment based on stereotypes or prejudice, and required the court to look behind the stated qualifications to the actual job requirements. The trial court was directed to conduct an individualized inquiry into her ability to perform the essential functions of the job of a school teacher, determine whether the required licensing test measured those essential job functions and determine whether the requested testing adaptations were reasonable for the job of teaching, and if so, whether disallowing them for testing had arbitrarily denied her meaningful access to a teaching job.

On remand, the trial court made findings of fact about the communication requirements of the job of a teacher and the connections between those requirements and the skills tested by the NTE. The court also evaluated Pandazides's disability and concluded that it did not qualify as limiting a major life activity as required under Section 504 because (1) it was not listed in the professional diagnostic manual used by psychologists, and (2) her claimed auditory processing deficit was contradicted by communication test scores that were higher for listening than reading or writing both with and without testing adaptations. The court also held that even if Pandazides were disabled under Section 504, the testing adaptations provided by ETS were reasonable and appropriate. The court stated:

> Unlimited time would not be a reasonable accommodation because similar modifications could not be expected in the job of teaching .... Similarly, interaction with the examiner would have been a fundamental change to the test design which would compromise the integrity of the test as a measure of minimum skills.
>
> (pp. 803–804)[20]

In Double Time versus Time and a Half: Kelly v. W. Va. Bd. of Law Exam'rs (2010), Kelly was diagnosed with a reading disability after acceptance to law school and received 50% extra time for exams. He then transferred to another law school where he was reevaluated and given double time for exams. Kelly had not received any accommodations in college or for his college and law school entrance exams. He also passed the required legal ethics portion of the bar exam without any extra time.

For the remainder of the West Virginia bar examination, Kelly requested double time but was only granted 50% extra time. A member of the board testified that working under time constraints was a job-related skill intended to be tested and that the vast majority of examinees used all the allotted testing time, including some who did not finish. He also testified that board members received accommodations training and based their decision on the nature and extent of the disability and the prior history of accommodations. Kelly failed the exam twice with time and a half and then successfully appealed to the Kentucky Board to grant him double time for its bar exam while pursuing a lawsuit against West Virginia for disability discrimination under the ADA.

In deciding the case, the court had to evaluate the relative credibility of the expert opinions provided by the two parties. Kelly's expert diagnosed a severe learning disability based on a Wechsler full-scale ability score of 105 and achievement test scores between 90 and 100, and recommended that Kelly receive unlimited time. The board's expert diagnosed a right brain learning disorder impacting non-language based cognitive tasks but found his functioning to be in the low average range compared to the general population. He opined that time and a half was a reasonable accommodation but stated that Kelly's primary deficit of inattentiveness would not be helped by extra time, recommending that the only effective accommodation would be a separate room.

Weighing the testimony of the experts, the court found that the conclusions of Kelly's expert were undermined by his test scores and that the opinions of the board's expert were more credible. The court held that granting Kelly "more time than is required to accommodate his disability would give him an unfair advantage over other applicants" and was not required by the ADA (p. 9). The court also found relevant the fact that Kelly had received no accommodations in college or for standardized tests until law school. The court concluded that Kelly's request for double time was unreasonable and that the board was not required to have an appeals procedure or hold a hearing to allow him to contest his failing exam score. Nonetheless, allowing an applicant to petition the board for reconsideration may be helpful to a credentialing examination program in avoiding litigation.

In a similar case of conflicting expert opinions, an applicant with dyslexia and ADHD was denied double time for the Alabama bar exam (Cox v. Ala. State Bar, 2004) despite having received it for the LSAT, law school exams and the South Carolina Bar Examination which he passed. With Alabama's allowance of 50% extra time, Cox failed twice. The court refused to order double time and held that its reasonableness must be decided at trial.

*Extra Break Time for Breastfeeding*

In Currier v. NBME (2012), on the Step 2 medical licensure examination, a medical student and nursing mother sought extra testing time for dyslexia and ADHD, and extra break time so she could pump breast milk for her five-month-old daughter. For her learning disabilities, the NBME offered to replace the eight, one-hour segments of multiple-choice questions usually computer-administered in a single day with eight, two-hour segments administered over two days (double time) in a separate room. In response to her request for 60 extra minutes of break time each day to pump breast milk, the NBME offered the standard 45 minutes of single-day break time for each of the two test days, a separate room with a power outlet to pump milk and permission to bring food into the testing room.[21]

Currier accepted the two-day test administration for her learning disabilities but rejected the options for pumping breast milk as insufficient to avoid painful breast engorgement and possible infection from blocked milk ducts. She had taken and failed the examination by a few points the previous spring and stated that she would be unable to begin her residency program in clinical pathology until she achieved a passing score.

**Annotating Test Scores**

Currier filed suit in state court seeking a preliminary injunction requiring the NBME to provide an additional 60 minutes of break time each day for expressing her milk. She provided affidavits from experts stating that she needed to pump milk twice during each test administration day and that each pumping session would require 25 to 30 minutes. The NBME argued that maintaining uniform break-time limits was necessary to protect the integrity of the testing program and because a computer-administered test form allowing both double time and extra break time was unavailable.

Legal Issues for Credentialing Examinations   249

The trial court refused to grant the requested preliminary injunction and Currier appealed. The appellate court vacated the trial court's ruling and granted the requested injunction, stating:

> As break time is only permitted after the completion of [an exam segment], the two thirty-minute sessions for breast milk expression will not give [Currier] any additional advantage on the exam segments. In contrast, the denial of [Currier's] reasonable request for break time solely for the expression of breast milk places her at a significant disadvantage in comparison to her peers [men and nonlactating women].
> (pp. 20–21)

Subsequently, Currier unsuccessfully tested with the ADA accommodations offered by the NBME and the extra break time ordered by the court. A year later, she tested again without the extra break time and passed. Although after she passed the test the case was technically moot, the trial judge exercised his discretion to provide a final ruling because the issue was important and likely to recur. The judge decided in favor of the NBME and Currier appealed. The appellate court held that lactating women were covered under the state equal rights act and found the issue of whether intentional discrimination had occurred might be inferred from exceptions made by the NBME for other temporary medical conditions and should be decided at trial. Although no ADA violation was found, the court did hold that the NBME had violated the state public accommodations law by "discriminating against her on the basis of her 'sex' in a place of public accommodation" (p. 841) because Currier was required to be present at the test center for a lengthy period of time and the NBME had provided no evidence that reasonably accommodating her would create an undue hardship.

### *Poor Performance on Timed Tests*

In another state case decided in federal court, Baer v. NBME (2005) involved a medical student with high IQ scores was denied 50% extra time to take Step 1 of her medical licensure exams because the NBME's experts believed she had not provided adequate evidence to substantiate her claimed reading disability and ADHD. In denying her request for an injunction requiring the extra testing time, the court held:

> While Baer has shown that she likely suffers from some ... impairment that adversely affects her ability to read, comprehend and process written material quickly, she has not shown that she is likely to succeed in demonstrating that her impairment has such a severe impact on her that it can properly be regarded as "substantially limiting" her in a "major life activity" .... Poor performance on exams might also be attributable to numerous other factors, such as anxiety, stress, nervousness, cautiousness, poor organization, poor time management, lack of motivation, lack of appropriate preparation, or weakness in a particular subject matter .... Some of these factors are present in Baer's case .... Her claim is that she is disadvantaged when required to take standardized tests under regulated time pressure .... Even if taking timed tests could be considered a "major life activity," the record is ambiguous .... Baer's scores on the timed SAT, which she took three times without any accommodations, were more or less in line with the national mean score for female test takers. She did, however, perform relatively poorly on the MCAT [without accommodations], the [Step 1], and in

math and science [college classes] which she says involved timed tests. This evidence may suggest that any impairment she has substantially limits only her performance on timed math and science tests, not timed tests generally.

(pp. 45–49)

*Application of State Disability Law*

Four examinees with dyslexia, ADHD, and other learning disabilities who were denied extra time for the MCAT sued the association that administers it (Sorrel, 2009). They claimed the denial violated California disability law which provides more expansive protections than the ADA. A state appellate court sided with the association holding that requests for extra time from examinees with learning disabilities should be decided under uniform, nationwide ADA standards rather than state law. In 2009, the state's highest court declined to review the case. Two of the challengers were granted extra time after providing additional documentation and the other two tested without accommodations and achieved percentile rank scores of 90–92 and 69–74. The association annotates scores received with extra time or in a separate room to facilitate accurate interpretation by medical schools.

Annotations on test score reports signal users that the test was administered with modifications that changed the underlying construct and produced noncomparable scores. The *Standards* (AERA et al., 2014) state:

> When there is clear evidence that scores from regular and altered tests or test administrations are not comparable, consideration should be given to informing score users, potentially by [annotating] the test results to indicate their special nature, to the extent permitted by law.

(p. 61)

Often a score annotation does not identify the specific testing adaptations provided to avoid revealing the examinee's impairment. However, because testing adaptations are provided only to examinees with disabilities, score annotations alert the recipient that the examinee has a disability.

Courts have wrestled with the appropriate balance between a user's need to know to properly interpret test scores and the examinee's right to privacy. Two related cases involving extended time reached different conclusions and created fallout that continues to affect the testing industry. At the time these cases were litigated, the *Standards* (AERA et al., 1999) recommended that when evidence of score comparability was lacking, test score annotations should identify the altered testing conditions (but not the disability) to facilitate appropriate score interpretation by test users (Standards 10.11, 10.4).[22]

*Annotations for Extra Time for Physical Disabilities*

In Doe v. NBME (1999–2006), John Doe requested extra time for his medical licensure tests to compensate for problems with fine motor coordination, muscle spasticity and bathroom urgency caused by multiple sclerosis diagnosed during his junior year in college. The request was granted but his reported scores were annotated by the NBME to indicate that a nonstandard test administration had been provided. Doe objected to the annotations as invading his privacy by identifying him as disabled against his will and alleged in federal court that the annotations violated the ADA. The NBME believed that the extra time provided Doe with a performance benefit relative to candidates tested with standard time limits. Although Doe conceded that it was theoretically possible for him to think about the test questions while taking mini-breaks, he also stated he was unable to read the test materials or mark his answers while massaging his cramping muscles.

A trial court order requiring the NBME to remove the annotations from scores reported in the future was reversed on appeal because Doe had failed to provide sufficient evidence of score comparability for his scores. On retrial, Doe's expert provided evidence supporting the essential comparability of Doe's scores while the NBME's expert argued that credible empirical evidence of score comparability for a group of similarly situated examinees was lacking.

While his case was still pending, Doe was licensed in multiple states and was accepted to his chosen residency program with the annotated scores. The court then held that any potential future harm from possible use of the annotated scores for additional fellowship programs or licensure in other states was too speculative to justify ordering the NBME to remove the annotations. The decision to dismiss the case for lack of a judicially cognizable injury to Doe was affirmed on appeal without consideration of the comparability of his scores.

*Annotations for Extra Time for Cognitive Disabilities*

In Breimhorst v. ETS (2000–2002), Breimhorst requested extra time and a trackball for the computer-administered Graduate Management Admissions Test (GMAT) to compensate for having no hands. ETS annotated his reported scores and was sued under the ADA after refusing to remove the annotation. The suit alleged that the annotation was improper because ETS had no evidence that the scores were not comparable. The earlier *Doe* case had held that the ADA did not prohibit score annotations but the *Breimhorst* court ruled that the ADA was focused more broadly on equal opportunity and required tests to equally measure the abilities of examinees with and without disabilities regardless of the burden to the testing entity. The court reserved for trial the question of whether a score annotation for a modified test could still be permissible if a testing entity's best efforts did not produce equal results.

Unexpectedly, ETS settled the case by agreeing to discontinue score annotations for extended time on several of its admissions and licensure tests. The College Board also agreed to convene an expert panel to consider the same action for examinees with learning disabilities who were allowed extra time on the SAT. The expert panel consisted of two psychometricians, three disability researchers, one college administrator and a nonvoting chair. Splitting 4–2, the expert panel recommended that SAT scores not be annotated when examinees with learning disabilities were allowed extra time (Gregg, Mather, Shaywitz, & Sireci, 2002).

The majority opinion appeared to argue that the lack of reading fluency exhibited by examinees with learning disabilities was construct-irrelevant and should be compensated for with extra time to provide more valid measurement of potential college success. However, the same logic was not applied to slow readers who lacked reading fluency for unknown reasons and were not allowed extra time.

Judging reading fluency to be construct relevant for nondisabled slow readers but construct irrelevant for examinees with learning disabilities represented a *construct shift* from a property of the test to a property of the group to which the examinee was a member (Phillips, 2010, 2011). This position was inconsistent with the 1999 *Standards* that defined construct-relevance as a test-centered, not a group-centered, characteristic (Standard 1.2; 2014 *Standards*, Standard 1.1).

Moreover, the majority did not argue that examinees with learning disabilities would be denied access to the test without the extra time but rather that their scores would be improved by removing the effects of their lack of reading fluency. The majority ignored the possibility (and limited empirical evidence) that scores obtained with extra time might over-predict college success because reading fluency and processing speed are relevant to the ability to handle the reading load and work speed expected at the college level. Nonetheless, the majority opinion concluded that "there are situations when it is necessary to treat people differently in order to treat them equally and [this situation] is one of them" (p. 10).

The two psychometricians were in agreement that the ETS score annotation policy was consistent with the 1999 *Standards*, SAT administrations with and without extra time had similar factor structures and reliabilities, and score interpretations from standard administrations demonstrated higher predictive validity (Psychometric Committee, 2001). Having reached similar conclusions that evidence of comparability was lacking and applying Standard 10.11, one might have expected the two psychometricians to have agreed that scores obtained with extra time should be annotated. Instead, apparently giving differential weight to the lack of comparability evidence and other nonpsychometric factors, they split their votes, one voting in favor of retaining the score annotations and the other voting to remove them (Brennan, 2002; Sireci, 2001).

Subsequently, the College Board announced that it would no longer annotate any SAT scores obtained with testing adaptations (College Board, 2002), and ACT followed suit announcing it would no longer annotate extended time administrations of the ACT Assessment (American College Testing program, 2002).

At the time the College Board made its decision, other alternatives existed that would have preserved score comparability and the privacy of examinees who did not want their disabilities revealed. These alternatives included (1) administering the test with extra time for all examinees and (2) allowing all examinees to choose between a timed administration or extra time with annotated scores.[23] In addition, ETS and the College Board could have chosen to defend their annotation policy in court. Although it may have been appropriate to settle with Breimhorst because his need for the extra time due to a physical disability gave him a colorable claim of score comparability, this author believes that a court decision requiring all score annotations to be removed was a remote possibility, particularly at the Supreme Court level.[24] However, a court decision permitting score annotations for examinees with learning disabilities allowed extra time would not have resolved the troubling question of whether to continue to annotate the scores of the much smaller number of physically disabled examinees (e.g., *Doe* and *Breimhorst*) who needed the extra time to deal with the non-cognitive, physical manifestations of their disabilities (Phillips, 2010).

*DOJ Regulations*

In 1992, the DOJ released ADA Regulation § 36.309(b) requiring examinations to be:

> selected and administered so as to *best ensure* that ... the examination results accurately reflect the individual's aptitude or achievement level ... rather than reflecting the individual's impaired sensory, manual, or speaking skills (*except where those skills are the factors that the examination purports to measure*) .... [emphasis added]

The *best ensure* standard survived in the ADAAA Regulations in addition to references to *reasonable accommodations*. Courts are likely to defer to this regulation because the

ADAAA expands coverage for persons with impairments and explicitly gives the DOJ authority to formulate regulations implementing the ADAAA definition of disability. The *Breimhorst* (2000) case and the *Technological Advances* cases decided post-2008 (discussed below) did so, holding that the *best ensure* standard requires more than reasonable accommodations for accessing the test. These decisions interpreted the DOJ language to place an affirmative duty on testing entities to provide test administrations for examinees with disabilities that minimize the effects of the impairment while enabling the fullest possible demonstration of the tested construct.

*Recent Score Annotation Ruling*

In Dept. of Fair Employ. & Hous. (DFEH) v. LSAC (2012), the DFEH alleged in a class action that the Law School Admissions Council (LSAC) was annotating test scores obtained with extra time in violation of the ADA and California's more expansive civil rights act. The court referenced the *Doe* and *Breimhorst* cases and noted their differing conclusions and assigned burdens of proof.

The *Doe* Court found that the ADA and its Regulations did not prohibit score annotation nor were scores obtained under nonstandard test administration conditions required to be declared psychometrically comparable to those obtained under standard conditions. To remove the annotation, the *Doe* Court placed the burden of demonstrating score comparability on the examinee. Conversely, despite the clear indication in the 1999 *Standards* that affirmative evidence of comparability was necessary to avoid annotating test scores, the *Breimhorst* Court held that the *best ensure* standard in the ADA Regulations required affirmative action by the testing entity to produce a test that appropriately measured the tested skills for persons with disabilities, avoiding the need for score annotations. Retention of score annotations would be permitted, the court indicated, only if the testing entity demonstrated that it had made a good faith effort to meet the *best ensure* standard and produced evidence that the resulting scores still were not comparable. Which party (examinee or testing entity) is assigned the responsibility for producing comparability evidence and what evidence (comparability or noncomparability) is required make a difference both legally and practically. The party with the burden of evidence production will have the greater expense of information collection and analysis and will not prevail if unable to produce the required evidence.

The *DFEH* Court adopted the position of the *Breimhorst* Court, holding that LSAC had not met its burden of demonstrating that its test *best ensured* that the abilities and achievements of examinees with and without disabilities were measured equally. The court stated:

> Under *Breimhorst*, the test provider has the burden of proving it best ensured that the test equally measured abilities of disabled and non-disabled test takers.... [T]he DOJ's regulation ... likewise requires *test providers* to "best ensure" that the examination accurately reflects aptitude or achievement levels, not impaired skills.... While the precise contours of the "best ensure" standard are not clear, it is more exacting than a "reasonableness" standard.
>
> (p. 869, emphasis in original)

Additionally, the court agreed with the plaintiffs that score annotations discouraged examinees from requesting testing adaptations and punished those whose requests were granted. The court refused to dismiss the case and the DOJ intervened. Reminiscent of

ETS in the *Breimhorst* case, LSAC chose to settle the *DFEH* case out of court to avoid a trial.

In the settlement announced in May 2014, LSAC agreed to pay $7.73 million in civil penalties and damages to compensate approximately 6,000 examinees denied testing adaptations nationwide over the previous five years. LSAC also agreed to permanently end all score annotations for extra time, to automatically grant most accommodations received previously by an applicant on a post-secondary admissions test,[25] and to implement the recommendations of an expert panel convened to identify best practices for evaluating testing accommodation requests. Future research may clarify the extent to which LSAT scores obtained with and without extra time are actually comparable.

*Technological Advances*

The *best ensure* standard has been interpreted in recent cases to require testing entities to change their testing accommodations policies when technological advances create improved methods of compensating for the effects of specific disabilities.[26] As indicated in the *Breimhorst* and *DFEH* cases, courts have held that the *best ensure* standard goes beyond the *reasonableness* standard previously applied by analogy from ADA employment discrimination and Section 504 cases while retaining reasonableness as a separate and important factor (U.S. Airways v. Barnette, 2002). In *Barnette*, the court applied a reasonableness standard for accommodations separate from consideration of undue hardship, holding that "an accommodation could be unreasonable in its impact even though it might be effective in facilitating performance" (p. 1522). The court rejected Barnette's argument that *reasonable* means *effective*, finding that the term *accommodation* denotes effectiveness and *reasonable* modifies it.[27]

Testing entities have historically provided Braille, large print, audio CDs and human readers as accommodations for examinees with visual impairments. But in recent years, many individuals with visual disabilities have begun using screen access software such as JAWS (Job Access with Speech), Kurzweil and ZoomText that they say allows them to focus on the content rather than the reading process, and to simulate the automaticity and fluency of sighted readers of complex text. JAWS and Kurzweil are screen-reader programs that vocalize text, allow users to control the speed, volume and timber of the voice as they independently navigate through text using a modified keyboard, and provide audio cues indicating the layout and organization of the text. ZoomText is a screen magnification program that employs a high-visibility cursor and permits the user to control the font, size and color of the text. These screen access software programs are often the primary reading method used by professionals with visual impairments, especially if they became legally blind after learning to read and are not skilled at reading Braille.

In 2011, several cases involving the National Conference of Bar Examiners (NCBE) on both the east and west coasts considered a testing entity's obligation to provide screen access software for multistate components of state bar examinations. The *best ensure* standard was applied and other factors, including the examinee's prior success with standard accommodations, minimizing test security risks and undue burden, were weighed.

*West Coast Cases*

**Enyart v. NCBE** (January, 2011). The *Enyart* case set the stage for subsequent assistive technology challenges. This case involved a California law school graduate who had been legally blind since age 15 and used a combination of JAWS and ZoomText as her primary reading method. To accommodate her visual impairment for the bar examination, Enyart requested testing adaptations consisting of extra time, a private room, hourly breaks, use of personal items including a lamp, digital clock, yoga mat and migraine medication, and the JAWS and ZoomText assistive technology software. California approved all of Enyart's requested adaptations for the state-specific portion of the exam, but notified Enyart that use of the screen access software would not be allowed on the Multistate Professional Responsibility Examination (MPRE) or the Multistate Bar Examination (MBE) because the NCBE was reluctant to provide electronic versions of these exams.

The NCBE argued that its offer of a human reader or audio CD, and closed circuit TV magnification or large print text provided the reasonable accommodations required by the ADA, and that Enyart had successfully used readers and audio tapes for past exams. Enyart countered that her progressive condition rendered the exams inaccessible to her with the proffered alternatives which she characterized as "vastly inferior" and ineffective because the audio and visual inputs could not be synchronized and their use would cause her "severe discomfort and disadvantage" in the form of eye fatigue, disorientation and nausea within minutes. The NCBE responded that granting use of the requested software would create an undue burden because to minimize security risks, the test and software would have to be loaded by NCBE staff on a laptop computer owned by the NCBE at an estimated cost of $5,000 per test administration.

Contingent on the posting of a $5,000 bond for each administration, the trial court ordered the NCBE to administer the MPRE and MBE to Enyart on a computer equipped with JAWS and ZoomText for two test administrations. The NCBE appealed and the order was affirmed. Meanwhile, Enyart passed the MPRE on her second attempt but failed the MBE twice with the ordered adaptations. In response, the trial court granted her a permanent injunction requiring the NCBE to provide her with the ordered adaptations for all future administrations of the MBE.

The court credited expert testimony from an assistive technology consultant, a professor of cognitive psychology, a research professor specializing in rehabilitation, and an ophthalmologist to certify Enyart's visual impairment and support the need for assistive technology to best ensure that her examination results accurately reflected her achievement rather than her visual disability. The court was unconvinced by arguments about past uses of other accommodations, her past exam failures with the assistive technology or the NCBE's assertion of undue burden, noting that the NCBE could outsource the work to an assistive technology vendor and pass on the cost to individual state bars or to all examinees in the form of increased fees.

**Elder v. NCBE** (February, 2011). The *Elder* case involved another candidate for the California bar who was legally blind but formerly sighted, and who had been denied the use of the JAWS screen access software for the MBE. Elder had previously passed the MBE portion of the Maryland Bar Examination using a human reader, but stated that the duration of the exam had been prolonged by the reader's frequent mistakes and increasing frequency of breaks.[28] Assistive technology was Elder's primary reading method in law school and in his employment as a disability rights fellow in a Maryland law firm. An accessibility specialist who had observed Elder described him as an advanced to expert user of the JAWS software.

Opposing Elder's request to use screen access technology, the NCBE presented similar arguments to those given in the *Enyart* case. The trial court cited the *Enyart* case as controlling precedent and again rejected the lower *reasonable accommodation* standard urged by the NCBE for licensure examinations. The court ruled that Elder was entitled to his requested adaptation because the screen access software was necessary to *best ensure* his chances of success on the bar examination. In its ruling, the court noted that compared to Maryland, the California bar examination presented a greater challenge for Elder due to its 50% longer length and lower passing rate. The court also found that NCBE could adequately minimize the security risks of providing the test in an electronic format by supplying a laptop without wireless access to the Internet and by establishing protocols requiring the state bar to handle the laptop with security precautions similar to those mandated for paper test booklets containing secure items.

*East Coast Cases*

**Bonnette v. D.C. Court of Appeals** (July, 2011). Bonnette gradually lost her vision and became totally blind after learning to read visually. JAWS became her primary reading method for complex text at school and work. In a two-year period, Bonnette took the California Bar Examination four times with a human reader and failed. She attributed her lack of success in part to difficulties working with the reader. Her MBE scaled scores ranged from 132 to 142, high enough to be successful on the D.C. bar examination which required a combined score of 266 on the MBE and essay portions.

As in prior cases, Bonnette's request to use JAWS for the MBE portion of the D.C. Bar Examination was denied with NCBE offering the same alternatives and making similar arguments to those it made in the earlier cases. A computer science professor having extensive experience with electronic voting machines opined that NCBE's security concerns could

> be easily remedied through precautions such as password encryption and observation by proctors.... . [W]ith these precautions, it would be virtually impossible for the security of the MBE to be compromised without the collusion of the examiners – a risk that is equally present for paper-based examinations.
>
> (p. 172)

Other experts proffered by Bonnette opined that the complexity of the MBE required many more shifts back and forth between questions and previously read text than for ordinary text and could only be accomplished effectively with screen access software. An offer by the District to reimburse the NCBE for the costs of providing the screen access software was declined.

Based on the ADA Regulations, the court held that a testing entity is not required to provide examinees with disabilities their preferred adaptations but must provide accommodations that are at least equally as effective, a criterion not met by the alternatives offered by the NCBE in this case. The court stated "Bonnette is entitled to an auxiliary aid that allows her to perform at her achievement level, not just one that might be good enough for her to pass" (p. 184).[29]

**Jones v. NCBE** (September, 2011). Jones was an older law student who had been legally blind since childhood and also had a reading disability. Her primary reading method used the ZoomText and Kurzweil screen access software. She took the LSAT with double time and a reader but found the experience exhausting and only scored at the 37th percentile. For the MPRE, she requested a computer equipped with screen access software, triple time and other accommodations. The NCBE granted all Jones's requests except the use of the screen access software and instead offered her a choice among the usual options provided to visually impaired examinees. Jones declined these options as unsuitable and not meeting her needs. The NCBE continued to be concerned about test security plus the cost of configuring a secure laptop computer and loading the requested software.

The court was not persuaded by NCBE's arguments and held that testing with the screen access software would best ensure measurement of Jones's knowledge of the tested content rather than her skills in coping with her impairments. Citing NCBE's 2009 revenues in excess of $13 million and net assets in excess of $50 million, the court was not convinced that NCBE's estimated costs of $5,000 for a single administration or $300,000 annually for an anticipated 60 requests constituted an undue burden. The court held that the options offered by the NCBE did not provide Jones with an equally effective opportunity to access the test as her nondisabled peers and ordered the NCBE "to keep pace with the rapidly changing technology of the times" by providing Jones with her requested screen access software. The court also denied the NCBE's motion to informally advise Jones of her score but withhold the written score report until after the trial and a final ruling by the court.

### Significance

The appellate court in the *Enyart* case observed that "assistive technology is not frozen in time; as technology advances, testing accommodations should advance as well" (p. 23). With technology advancing at a rapid pace and new assistive software being released and revised in increasingly short development cycles, continued litigation in this area is likely. In such cases, the court will be asked to balance the test security risks and financial burdens of providing specific technologies to multiple examinees in idiosyncratic configurations with the *best ensure* language of the ADA Regulations requiring a needs analysis of what is required to make a specific examination accessible to a specific examinee.

### Documentation

Credentialing programs typically require examinees requesting accommodations to complete an application form and submit verification of the disability from a professional with appropriate expertise. This documentation generally includes the expert's professional qualifications, a diagnosis based on current test results standardized on adults, a description of the applicant's current functioning, the relationship of the disability to test taking skills, and recommendations for specific adaptations with an explanation of why they are needed and how they will address the effects of the disability for the test in question. The ADA Regulations state that "any private entity offering an examination covered by this section must assure that any request for documentation ... is reasonable and limited to the need for the [testing adaptations] requested" (§36.309(b)(1)(iv)). Cases from California and New York present contrasting views of the *reasonable and limited* documentation standard.

### Sufficiency versus Burden

In the *Bartlett* (2000) case, an appellate court held that a testing entity is not liable for offering accommodations if the applicant fails to provide sufficient evidence to substantiate the disability. Subsequently, in another New York case, Shaywitz v. American Bd. of Psychiatry & Neurology (2012), the trial court found that the board was not required to offer accommodations on the live-patient clinical portion of a certification test to an examinee with dyslexia who failed to check the box on the application requesting accommodations and to submit the required documentation. Although the examinee had received accommodations on an earlier written portion of the exam, the court held that the board's policy of requiring a separate application for the clinical exam was reasonable because the applicant might not need the same accommodations for an oral exam as for a written exam.

Conversely, the *DFEH* (2012) case held that requiring applicants with cognitive impairments to undergo a full psychoeducational and neuropsychological evaluation and explain any failure to take their prescribed medications during the evaluation constituted unreasonably burdensome documentation and improper mitigation pressure under the ADA. However, as the *Gonzales* and *Ware* cases reviewed below demonstrate, even when documentation is adequate, disagreements among experts about the severity of the disability may create disputes about which adaptations must be provided.

*Matching Accommodations to the Severity of the Disability*

In Gonzales v. NBME (2000), Gonzales was diagnosed with a learning disability in college and received double time on tests, assistance with note taking and permission to tape classroom lectures during his first two years of medical school. He had scored well on the SAT and MCAT timed tests without accommodations. The NBME denied his request for extra time on Step 1 of the medical licensure exam because his impairment did not substantially limit a major life activity. Gonzales tested without accommodations, failed, and was reevaluated. His diagnostic test scores included a full-scale IQ of 109 and reading test scores in the average to above average range compared to most people, but he was again diagnosed as having a learning disability in both reading and writing. The NBME's expert reviewed the reevaluation report and again determined that Gonzales did not have a qualifying disability because there was no evidence of a significant discrepancy between ability and achievement.

Gonzales retested without accommodations, failed again, and filed suit in which the court credited NBME's experts and denied relief. He retested and failed a third time without accommodations. Gonzales appealed claiming that the court erred in finding no reading, work or writing disabilities. The appellate court affirmed, holding that the findings of the trial court were reasonable given the credible testimony of the NBME's experts and the diagnostic test score evidence provided by Gonzales's own experts, indicating he was not *substantially limited* because he could read as well as the average person. Citing *Pazer* (1994), the court also indicated that even if the score discrepancy had been larger, performance similar to most people normally would be dispositive; otherwise, any underachiever would be found disabled even if the poor performance was the result of other factors such as motivation, effort, emotional issues or social problems.

In Ware v. Wyoming Bd. of Law Exam'rs (1997), the trial court held that the board had complied with the ADA when it offered an applicant with multiple sclerosis, whose fine motor hand coordination and vision were impaired but who had no cognitive impairment, the adaptations recommended by her treating physician, even though they did not exactly match those she had requested. At issue was the amount of extra time required for responding and for bathroom breaks. The board had offered large print, a separate room and 30 minutes of extra bathroom break time per test session (with carryover of unused time) *plus* dictation to a court reporter with simultaneous large print screen projection for the essay portion and marking answers in the test booklet for the multiple-choice Multistate portion. Based on the treating physician's recommendation of 10 extra seconds per page for turning pages, additional testing time of 6 minutes for the essay portion and 20 minutes for the Multistate portion was also granted.

Ware had received 50% extra time, large print test booklets, a scribe and a separate testing room for the Utah Bar Examination which she failed. In law school, she had received 50% extra time for essay exams and marked her answers in the test booklet for objective tests. Ware's physician had indicated an additional time extension would be needed if she had to write her own answers and blacken ovals on an answer sheet, but the board believed those needs had been fully addressed with the court reporter and test booklet marking accommodations. Ware argued that the ADA required the board to grant her request for 50% extra time based solely on her documentation of a disability.

In response to Ware's concern about accuracy of transcription, the board offered audiotaping of her essay dictation and witnessing of the transfer of test booklet responses to the answer sheet with retention of the test booklet for rescoring if requested. The board also offered her an opportunity to practice with the court reporter in advance using a prior essay test item. Ware objected to the former and refused the latter.

In finding for the board on Ware's claim of ADA discrimination (affirmed on appeal), the trial court also dismissed additional challenges to the licensing statute and claims of racial discrimination, due process violations and intentional infliction of emotional distress. But the trial court did observe:

> It is hoped that future timely communication between [Ware] and her health care providers will inform them of the exact accommodations she believes she needs, the reason [each is needed], and the necessity of submitting those recommendations to the Board in specific and detailed form.
>
> (p. 1358)

## Exemptions

A federal case pending on appeal, Binno v. American Bar Ass'n (ABA, 2012), has presented the court with a novel argument for exempting visually impaired examinees from portions of the LSAT. Binno sued the ABA because its accrediting standards for law schools require all applicants to be administered a valid and reliable admissions test and provide that law schools who grant waivers are subject to sanctions. Virtually all law schools require the LSAT to avoid the responsibility of demonstrating the validity and reliability of score interpretations from an alternative admissions test. Binno, who is legally blind, claims that these ABA policies violate the ADA because correctly answering the 25% of LSAT items testing analytical reasoning requires perception of spatial relationships and diagramming of visual concepts, skills for which blind examinees are significantly disadvantaged relative to their sighted peers.[30] Binno scored poorly on the LSAT, was denied admission to three Michigan law schools and was unable to obtain a waiver of the testing requirement. He was employed by Homeland Security with a high-level clearance and fluency in three languages.

The trial court dismissed the case, finding that Binno's claim should have been directed at the law schools that denied him admission or the LSAT providers. No mention was made of whether any adaptations exist that would make the analytical reasoning items accessible to a blind examinee. Nor did the court consider psychometric alternatives such as linking LSAT scores without the analytical reasoning items to the full LSAT scale or substituting other types of reasoning items for the analytical reasoning items and linking the revised test to the full LSAT scale.

## Summary

Who qualifies as disabled? What is a reasonable accommodation? How can a credentialing program ensure that test scores obtained with testing adaptations fully represent the intended construct and produce comparable scores?

Guidance for legal defensibility can be synthesized from the varied testing accommodation cases and the ADA Amendments Act. The ADAAA has expanded the number of individuals with qualifying disabilities and the application of the *best ensure* standard by federal courts in recent cases suggests that the number and variety of requests for testing adaptations will continue to increase. Credentialing examination programs may best serve their constituencies and minimize litigation by considering the following recommendations.

- Accept documented impairments listed in the ADAAA or associated enforcement regulations as qualified disabilities and focus attention on identifying accommodations that are reasonable, appropriate, improve accessibility and satisfy the *best ensure* standard. An examinee's preferences, primary methods of compensation and prior history of testing adaptations on similar tests are relevant but not dispositive.
- Request sufficient, verifiable and detailed test data and clinical observations from qualified professionals to evaluate the extent and severity of the disability. Use this information to tailor specific accommodations to what the applicant with a disability actually needs to best ensure measurement of the intended knowledge and skills in a manner that fully represents the tested construct, produces valid scores and minimizes the construct-irrelevant effects of the disability. But note:
    - Although ADAAA qualifying disabilities must be determined in the applicant's uncorrected state, information about the applicant's current functioning with any mitigating corrective aids, medications or adaptations is relevant to identifying reasonable accommodations that compensate for the effects of the disability without providing an unfair advantage.
    - Testing entities are not required to provide testing accommodations for impairments that do not affect test taking or access to the test site, are in remission, or are fully corrected with auxiliary aids or medications in use by the applicant. But under some circumstances, additional breaks or a separate room may still be necessary for the examinee with a disability to use the aids or administer the medication.
    - Normally prohibited personal items may also be needed by an examinee with a disability and should be vetted using pre-established, systematic preapproval and test site security clearance procedures.
- Match accommodations to the effects of the impairment directly related to the demands of testing or the accessibility of the test site. Reasonableness is still relevant and includes documentation of a causal connection between the impairment, its effects on test taking, and the ability of the requested testing adaptation(s) to minimize those effects while fully representing the construct intended to be tested, producing comparable scores and avoiding an undue burden.
- Be proactive in keeping current on new research and technological advances that support the most effective strategies and aids for enabling examinees with disabilities to function as similarly as possible to their nondisabled peers in the testing environment. Large testing entities with substantial resources may find it difficult to argue *undue hardship* and should set aside resources to:
    - Acquire and maintain computers with technical software and necessary peripherals to administer tests in new formats being used regularly by persons with specific disabilities.

*Legal Issues for Credentialing Examinations* 261

- ○ Train and deploy additional test proctors as necessary to ensure test security and provide individualized administration of new testing adaptations where appropriate.
- ○ Arrange for larger test sites with adequate space to provide separate testing rooms when needed for specialized equipment or a distraction-free environment.
- Refrain from burdening applicants with complicated request forms, excessive documentation requirements or extra costs. But courts have indicated that it may be acceptable to pass on the additional costs of expensive accommodations to all examinees in the form of nominal increases in per person test administration fees.
- Conduct and document thorough and detailed job and public safety analyses to identify and provide supporting evidence for tested skills judged necessary to fully represent the focal construct. Use universal design principles to provide all examinees with access to testing features likely to improve performance but not create underrepresentation of the tested construct.
- Consider establishing an internal appeal procedure (short of a formal hearing) to check that policies have been applied consistently and to provide a final opportunity to resolve conflicts without litigation.

## Legal Issues Related to Test Security Policies

Fair enforcement of reasonable test security policies is an essential activity for ensuring the validity and integrity of the intended test score interpretations for all examinees (AERA et al., 2014, Standard 6.6). In general, courts have upheld the right of testing organizations to cancel scores for which the validity of the intended test score interpretations is questionable provided they have fairly considered all available evidence, including that supplied by the examinee whose scores have been questioned, and have followed procedures accepted by the examinee during the registration process.

Examinees and test administrators each have important rights and responsibilities. Examinees have the right to a fair test and fair treatment, but they also have a responsibility to follow directions, not disclose test items, be courteous to other examinees and avoid any conduct that produces scores that misrepresent their actual levels of knowledge and skills. Test administrators have a right to expect fair dealing, respect and integrity from examinees and a responsibility to act in good faith, strictly adhere to established test administration procedures, and ensure that no examinee obtains an unfair advantage by proactively seeking and investigating evidence of misconduct (AERA et al., 2014, Chapters 8 and 9). Courts have upheld score cancellations when a proctor reported a failure to follow directions (ETS v. Hildebrant, 2007) and dismissed minor disruptions unless a proctor needlessly interrupted an examinee (Mindel v. ETS, 1990).

Test security violations involving credentialing tests have typically involved examinee or test preparation program misconduct. In cases with published decisions, the particular facts and circumstances were critical to the outcome, and testing entities were successful most often when written policies were followed and the evidence was substantial and consistent.

### *Examinee Misconduct*

The methods used by testing entities to identify cases of examinee misconduct usually involve vigilant proctoring, videotaping, identification of large retest gains, similarity analyses of the responses of adjacent examinees, documenting violations of test center rules, monitoring the Internet and social media for test content, handwriting analysis and detailed identification procedures to detect impersonation. While individually such methods may not prove that cheating occurred, they provide important circumstantial evidence to guide further investigation of suspected misconduct and may be convincing when multiple methods produce convergent evidence.[31] When convincing evidence casts doubt on the validity of test score interpretations, credentialing programs usually offer an examinee a variety of options, including score cancellation, a free retest to confirm the scores, submission of additional information and arbitration. In rare cases, civil or criminal charges may result.

There are few published decisions involving examinee misconduct because most cases investigated by credentialing examination programs involve threatened score cancellation and are settled confidentially out of court or through mandatory arbitration. Thus, the cases reviewed below represent only the small fraction of examinee misconduct cases in which a court issued a published opinion. The review begins with a sample of the more frequently reported teacher licensure cases.

*Teacher Licensure Examinee Misconduct Cases*

In Shirer v. Anderson (1950), during the February 1949 administration of the NTE, proctors at multiple locations across South Carolina confiscated crib sheets from seven examinees. ETS compared examinees' answer sheets with a composite crib sheet, noting similarities in correct, incorrect and omitted answers, and compared the performance of examinees on sets of items included and not included on the crib sheet.[32]

From these analyses, ETS determined that the answer sheets of 801 (about one-third) of the African-American examinees in the state "followed the [composite crib sheet] so closely that the correspondence could not reasonably be explained on any honest basis" (pp. 860–861). The suspects were interviewed by the board and 131 admitted cheating. Most of the remaining suspects were found guilty of the charges in hearings before the board and their teaching certificates were revoked.

Pearl Shirer filed a class action lawsuit on behalf of all African-American teachers whose licenses had been revoked despite their protestations of innocence, claiming that the board violated their fourteenth amendment due process rights. Shirer's similarity analysis demonstrated that on one subtest for which the crib sheet provided answers to the first 10 of 45 items, Shirer's answers were identical to the crib sheet for the first ten items (90% correct), and of the 33 remaining items she attempted, she answered only seven (21%) correctly.

The trial court held that the board had acted legally, stating:

> Inquiries … made of suspected teachers resulted in confessions which disclosed the existence of a widespread conspiracy to cheat. Those who were suspected but who did not admit guilt were given a full opportunity to be heard and to produce evidence in answer to the charges and to be represented at the hearing by counsel of their choice. A few were successful in persuading the Board that they were not guilty. As to the others, it is absurd to say that the Board's action was not supported by the evidence or was arbitrary or unreasonable.
>
> (pp. 861–862)

The court also found that "the possibility of the similarity between [Shirer's] examination paper and [the composite crib sheet] being accidental or coincidental is so extremely remote as to be almost infinitesimal" (p. 863). The court denied relief and dismissed the complaint.

In Tolleson v. ETS (1992), Mike Tolleson was an applicant for teacher licensure in social studies in South Carolina. He took the NTE five times within two years and received scores of 450, 440, 320, 420 and 650. ETS investigated the 230-point score gain from the previous administration and found that out of 150 items, Tolleson had 98 identical correct answers and 31 out of 38 identical incorrect responses to a test taker seated near him, an event with a probability of less than 0.00000001.

Tolleson rejected all the usual options and filed suit against ETS claiming violation of his due process rights and seeking release of his scores to the state licensing authority. The trial court ruled in favor of ETS, holding that ETS was not a state actor because the state did not exercise control over ETS's security and testing procedures, ETS had no authority to make licensure decisions, and there was an insufficient nexus between the state and ETS. The court concluded that Tolleson did not have a cognizable due process claim.

In *ETS v. Hildebrant* (2007), an examinee administered that the PRAXIS principal licensure test had signed the standard certification agreeing to the testing conditions set forth in the registration bulletin. However, during the test, she twice refused to stop writing when the proctor called time. The first time, the proctor gave her a warning, but the second time, which lasted more than 30 seconds, the proctor filed an irregularity report.

Based on the proctor's irregularity report, ETS sent a letter providing the examinee with an opportunity to respond. The examinee stated that the proctor was mistaken and that the alleged violations had not occurred. ETS was not convinced and elected to cancel her scores. She sued, and the court held that her unsworn general denial was insufficient evidence to create doubt that ETS had acted in good faith or to establish a motive for the proctor to lie. The court held that ETS had acted within the terms of its contract in relying on the statements of its agent that the examinee had engaged in misconduct sufficient to justify score cancellation.

*Group Invalidation*

In Doe v. Nat'l Bd. of Podiatric Medical Exam'rs (2005), this case is an example of group invalidation of test scores due to misconduct for which it was impossible to determine which examinees had benefited. The case involved a podiatry licensure exam administered by ETS via computer at a New York college test center during a four-day testing window. The registration bulletin prohibited reproduction of test questions and provided for score invalidation in the event of such a security breach. Nevertheless, some students who tested early in the testing window posted their recollections of test content in emails sent to a website accessible to all members of the college podiatry class. ETS was sent the emails anonymously and determined that the content of secure test items had been compromised. The scores of all of the examinees who had tested at the college were invalidated and examinees were denied individual hearings because the board believed the decision would be the same no matter what transpired at any hearing.

Students at the college were retested six months later. Although they all had passed the computer version of the test, five students failed the paper-and-pencil retest and several filed suit against the board and ETS alleging breach of contract. The plaintiffs sought to force the board and ETS to validate and release the original scores and to provide each plaintiff an individual hearing.

Plaintiffs argued that the students who tested on the first day could not have benefited from the emails sent afterward. They also contended that a hearing was necessary to individually consider whether a student had access to and had read secure test information prior to testing, how many of the compromised items were on that student's test, whether the student passed with a high enough score to indicate that knowledge of the compromised items was irrelevant, and whether that student had been guilty of improperly communicating secure test content to others. The board and ETS argued that the appeal procedure was not applicable because it applied only to individual examinee misconduct, not group invalidation due to secure test items being compromised.

The trial court disagreed, stating that the right to a hearing applied to the invalidation of scores and that the purpose of such a hearing was to determine if an examinee's results had been tainted by misconduct. Nonetheless, the court acknowledged that under these circumstances, the board and ETS could legitimately invalidate the scores of examinees whose innocence could not be verified. The court also found that the potential harm to examinees from the invalidation of their scores had been mitigated by the free retest. Thus, the trial court declined to order release of examinees' initial scores but held that those who renewed their requests for an appeal hearing must be given one. When one examinee who had requested a hearing challenged an adverse ruling, the court cited the *Standards* in support of its conclusion that the board and ETS had acted consistent with industry standards and that neither could "vouch for the reliability and validity of [his] test results" because "the entire testing process was tainted by the misconduct which occurred" (pp. 8–9).

*Osteopathic Licensure Test Challenge Backfires*

In an interesting twist, an examinee's scoring challenge resulted in the discovery of misconduct and cancellation of his scores (Apoian v. S.D., 1975). The examinee had taken the basic sciences portion of the South Dakota osteopathic licensure test with a friend from school. He passed several parts but challenged his failing score on the anatomy section. He requested that it be rescored believing that the wrong form code may have been used. In the process of responding to this request, the testing agency discovered evidence leading it to believe that he had copied answers from his friend on the test sections he had passed.

The licensure board cancelled his scores for all sections of the test and he appealed. The court held that the licensure board had acted within its authority and had provided an adequate due process hearing for which he had notice but chose not to attend. Had he not questioned his score on the failed section, his misconduct might not have been discovered, and he would only have been required to retake the one test section he failed.

**Test Preparation Program Misconduct**

Preparing candidates for licensure tests in some fields is big business. Over the years, there have been organized attempts by some test preparation programs to surreptitiously acquire current secure items to provide an advantage to their course clients and increase future business. Testing entities have fought back with federal copyright infringement suits.[33] The following sections chronologically review noteworthy credentialing cases.

In ETS v. Simon (1999), the PRAXIS Multiple Subjects Assessment for Teachers (MSAT) was being used to license elementary teachers in California. Best-Prep, a teacher licensure test preparation business, compiled a workbook of practice items substantially similar to MSAT items that they obtained by debriefing former students who had taken the MSAT. ETS filed suit and the court held that Best-Prep had copied the "creative 'heart' of each infringed question," including 19 of 22 essay questions from one MSAT form, and had given their course participants an unfair advantage. The court issued a detailed order prohibiting Best-Prep from copying and selling ETS test items in any form without permission and from debriefing examinees about test content.

In NCBE v. Multistate Legal Studies (2006) preliminary Multistate Bar Review (PMBR) offered three-day MBE preparation courses in multiple locations. Student testimonials in promotional materials attested to the similarity of the PMBR practice items to actual MBE items. After a proctor caught a PMBR examinee leaving the testing room with scratch paper, the NCBE investigated and concluded that more than 100 MBE items had been copied. The NCBE sued for copyright infringement and the trial court upheld the claim.

The court questioned the credibility of PMBR's claims that its employees were providing superior instruction and writing their own practice items because these same employees had failed the MBE multiple times. The court also found substantial similarity between the infringing items and the actual MBE items, with many items reproduced nearly verbatim and others with only trivial changes. For example, one PMBR question referred to *X-10 gidgets*; the corresponding MBE item used *X10 widgets*. The court awarded NCBE a portion of PMBR's profits as damages for the infringement and enjoined PMBR from any further copying or distributing of MBE items. The court also prohibited its employees from taking the test for other than bar admissions purposes. The court stated "By exposing its students to questions likely to appear on the MBE, PMBR undermined the integrity of the bar examination, possibly causing the admission of unqualified applicants" (p. 262).

*Recent Technology-related Cases*

Examinee misconduct using technology to misappropriate item content has been the focus of two recent test preparation program misconduct cases. In NBME v. Optima University (2011), unusual response patterns and low scores on the computer-administered Step 1 medical licensure exam (e.g., 82% of items answered "A") led to examination of videotaped test administrations showing suspected examinees in Romania and Hungary holding an electronic device up to the screen to photograph the items. The suspects had registered using the same New Jersey address that the owner of the test preparation company used to test repeatedly. The NBME sent an undercover agent to attend the test preparation program and found at least 50 items from the Step 1 pool in the program's course materials accessible only on a secure computer.

The program attempted to evade prosecution by relocating to Tennessee, remotely shutting down the server and refusing to comply with court orders. Eventually, verbatim copies and screen shots of secure items were discovered among program materials and NBME filed a copyright infringement suit. The program failed to respond, its owner reportedly having fled to Egypt. The court ruled in favor of NBME, awarded statutory damages of $2.4 million for willful infringement, permanently enjoined program staff from any further copying of items or test taking for other than licensure purposes, and ordered all electronic and paper copies of the stolen items to be returned to NBME counsel for destruction.

In American Registry of Radiologic Technologists v. Bennett (2013), a test preparation program owner requested that participants email questions post-exam to be shared with future course participants. However, because the emails did not name the test and the recalled questions were similar but not identical to actual test questions, the court held that a trial was necessary to weigh the evidence. However, the court ruled that a valid copyright of an item bank includes all the questions individually.

### Negligent Test Security Procedures

Testing entities have on occasion been the victims of organized attempts to capitalize on negligent test security procedures. The misappropriation of test items from the American Board for the Certification of Teacher Excellence (ABCTE) during a 2003 field test is an example (Mathews, 2003). ABCTE was formed and federally funded to develop a portable teaching credential intended primarily for career changers from other fields. Unfortunately, a mistake by the vendor during Web-based field testing of new items inadvertently provided an opportunity for critics to obtain unauthorized copies of field test items. One critic distributed copies of the items at a professional meeting. Believing the compromised items to be worthless, ABCTE refused to pay the vendor for the items, changed vendors, replaced the disclosed items with new items and conducted a new field test. The organization estimated that the security breach cost them approximately six weeks of work and $1.2 million in item replacement expenses. Some board members believed that the real purpose of the disclosure had been to delay the new ABCTE tests from reaching the market (Mathews, 2003).

### Summary

What are defensible procedures for maintaining the confidentiality of test items, protecting the validity of test score interpretations from corruption by misconduct, and canceling scores for test security violations?

For secure tests to remain useful for the purposes for which they are intended, testing entities must continue to take seriously and respond to all threats to the validity of test score interpretations. As technology evolves, test security will require added vigilance and sophistication to deter, detect and sanction violators. Score cancellations are most likely to be upheld when applicants have agreed to written procedures, evidence of misconduct is convincing and the testing entity has acted in good faith and followed its written procedures. Copyright infringement cases are most likely to succeed when the testing vendor holds a registration certificate for the pirated items, there is clear evidence the suspect was exposed to those items and the suspect is in possession of copies of the actual or substantially similar items.

## Legal Issues Related to Test Construction Procedures

In addition to alleging racial discrimination directly based on disparate impact statistics, challengers have also used settlement agreements to force test developers to adopt procedures that minimized majority/minority item performance differences with the expectation that such procedures would translate into higher test scores for minorities. Although such procedures have been discredited by psychometricians and the *Standards* (AERA et al., 2014, Standard 3.6C), variations still surface occasionally, so testing entities need to be informed and vigilant.

### The Golden Rule Case and its Progeny

The *Golden Rule* procedure was part of an out-of-court settlement in a lawsuit challenging an Illinois insurance licensure test (Golden Rule Life Ins. Co. v. Mathias, 1980). A test revision by a new vendor sparked the controversy.

## Background of the Golden Rule Case

Under a contract with the Illinois Insurance Department, ETS began administering a new licensure test for insurance agents in the state. Initially, the passing rate dropped from approximately 60–70% to 31% but returned to the 70–75% range after the exam was revised. On behalf of five applicants who had failed the test, the Golden Rule Insurance Company filed suit against ETS and the department. The suit alleged constitutional violations of the fourteenth amendment due process and equal protection clauses and statutory violations of the Civil Rights Act but did not directly allege a Title VII violation, perhaps because there was some doubt as to whether Title VII applied.

The challengers sought a permanent injunction barring any further administration of the insurance licensure tests. The insurance company claimed that the individual challengers (three of whom were African-American) were fully qualified in all other respects but had been denied employment as insurance agents solely because they failed the required state licensure test.

Statistics for the two versions of the test indicated a disparate impact in White/African-American passing rates of 55%/40% (difference = 15%) for the original test and 77%/52% (difference = 25%) for the revised test. But note that at the time these data were compiled examinees were not required to provide racial classification data. The data reported here were compiled by sorting applicants into categories based on pictures required to be submitted with their test application forms.

Because the court found that ETS was a partner with the department in a testing program that was *the* criterion for employment, the court held that ETS was a state actor subject to the fourteenth amendment. The court indicated that because the statute mandating the test was facially neutral, the required proof of discriminatory intent would involve consideration of all the facts and circumstances. The challengers argued that the department and ETS knew or should have known that there were substantial White/African-American differences in performance on the new licensure exams and that despite this foreseeability, no corrective action was taken (Rooney, 1987). However, in a constitutional challenge to a test required for admission to teacher education programs in Texas, a federal Court had held that "an action does not violate the equal protection clause simply because the decision maker knows that it will have a disparate impact on racial or ethnic groups" (U.S. v. LULAC, 1986, p. 646). Thus, even if proven, foreseeability alone would not have established the required discriminatory intent.

The *Golden Rule* case was settled out of court as the result of a settlement agreement in which the testing entities made no admissions regarding any of the challengers' allegations (*Golden Rule* Settlement, 1984). An ETS spokesperson emphasized that the settlement was limited to only two of four required tests and estimated the additional procedures agreed to would cost ETS $150,000 over its seven-year duration. The settlement required items with White/African-American percent correct (p-value) differences of less than 15% and p-values in both groups of at least 40% in a content category to be used first. No adjustments were made to compare groups of equal ability.

Supporters of the challengers believed that the settlement achieved its twin goals of opening the test development process to greater public scrutiny and decreasing performance differences between majority and minority groups (Shapiro, Slutsky & Watt, 1989). The insurance company announced a victory and predicted that the settlement would affect many other testing programs nationwide (*New York Times*, 1984). FairTest, an organization financed in part by the insurance company, began a campaign to convince other states to utilize the *Golden Rule* procedure (Friendly, 1986).

Three years later, ETS President Gregory Anrig declared that the *Golden Rule* settlement was a mistake (Anrig, 1987). Anrig cited three unintended consequences in support of his belief: 1) some testing critics had interpreted the settlement as an admission of guilt on the part of ETS; 2) procedures narrowly tailored to only a portion of one testing program were being cited as precedent for action and legislation in other states; and 3) the *Golden Rule* procedure, though not compromising the validity of test score interpretations for the specific tests to which it was applied, was cumbersome to implement, had not substantially reduced the performance differential between African-Americans and Whites, and precluded the use of state-of-the-art statistical procedures for detecting differential item performance.

ETS was not alone in criticizing the precedential value of the *Golden Rule* settlement; the psychometric profession was virtually unanimous in its condemnation of the *Golden Rule* procedure as a bad precedent (Bond, 1987). Moreover, settlement agreements are binding only against the parties, and no court has ever mandated the *Golden Rule* procedure. Nonetheless, the *Golden Rule* procedure was extended to teacher licensure testing in an out-of-court settlement of an Alabama case specifying item selection criteria that were more stringent than those in the *Golden Rule* case.

In Allen v. Alabama (1986), this was a class action suit by minority teachers who had failed the Alabama teacher licensure test and alleged that their failures were due to discrimination. Prior to trial, attorneys for the parties reached a tentative settlement agreement and communicated it to the court. However, under adverse political and public pressure, Alabama officials subsequently repudiated the settlement, the challengers filed a motion to enforce it and an appellate court held that it was enforceable.[34]

In the Alabama Settlement, the procedure agreed to by ETS in the *Golden Rule* Settlement was modified to be much more stringent by preferring items with only a 5% difference in performance between majority and minority examinees, and prohibiting the use of any items with subgroup differences exceeding 15%. Because there was no trial, the challengers were never required to produce evidence that items with smaller subgroup differences were more job relevant and more accurate measures of the skills of minority candidates.

Had the case gone to trial, Alabama may have been able to rebut the challengers' disparate impact statistics by showing that its teacher licensure tests were job related and properly validated. If so, the court would have been asked to determine whether the *Golden Rule*-type item selection criteria proposed by the challengers created a less discriminatory but equally effective alternative. It is likely that Alabama could have demonstrated that this alternative would produce test scores that were less valid and less able to accurately identify candidates who did and did not possess the required minimum skills identified as important for competent teaching (Shepard, 1987).

On appeal, the court held that the Alabama settlement was enforceable. However, it was never fully implemented because the parties continued to litigate its requirements. Alabama again sought to have the settlement vacated or modified based on changed circumstances, but the court refused this request because it felt that the state had not made a good faith attempt to develop tests that satisfied both the settlement terms and psychometric standards. Alternatively, the challengers sought an injunction to bar the state from adopting legislatively mandated, nationally normed tests, but the court also refused this request on the grounds that the settlement did not proscribe such an action. In 2000, the court reluctantly approved an amended settlement allowing Alabama to administer basic skills tests and subject-matter tests (in five years) with 50% weighting of GPAs for nonpassing candidates and no individual item selection criteria.[35]

## Legislative Action

Despite abandonment by testing professionals and the *Allen* parties, the original settlement's item selection criteria were used to pressure other testing entities to adopt *Golden Rule*-type item selection procedures. Various versions of the *Golden Rule* procedure were introduced into proposed testing legislation, but ultimately were defeated in several states, including California, Massachusetts, New York, Texas and Wisconsin (Faggen, 1987).

The proposed *Golden Rule* legislation in New York was supported by test critics but criticized by measurement experts. Dr. Richard Jaeger, then President of the National Council on Measurement in Education (NCME) and writing on its behalf, criticized this approach in a letter to legislators (also shared with California legislators considering similar legislation; Jaeger, 1987). Jaeger questioned the assumption inherent in the legislation that items having statistics outside specified arbitrary ranges were necessarily biased against the lower scoring group and argued that research evidence did not support such a procedure for detecting potential bias against minority groups. He further argued that such procedures would decrease the reliability and validity of individual test score interpretations for all examinees and were contrary to the intent of the *Standards*. Jaeger also stressed that differential performance for a test item only indicates potential bias if such a difference is found for majority/minority examinees of *equal achievement*.[36]

The final legislation in New York provided that item functioning for individual test items "take into account differences in overall test performance" (N.Y. Educ. Law, 1987). Because the *Golden Rule* procedure did not consider differences in overall test performance, it did not fall within the requirements of the legislation. Since then, no other state has mandated the *Golden Rule* procedure through legislative or legal action, although some expert witnesses have unsuccessfully attempted to persuade the court to mandate variations of this procedure (GI Forum v. Tex. Educ. Agency, 2000).

## Summary

What options are available to a credentialing program pressured to adopt variations of discredited item selection criteria that minimize differential performance between majority and minority examinees?

Periodically, advocates have proposed variations on the *Golden Rule* procedure to remedy alleged discrimination manifested by disparate impact statistics. Credentialing tests with strong job-related and content validity evidence, items reviewed for language or content that might disadvantage minority examinees, appropriate differential item performance screening based on groups of equal ability, and minority participation at all stages of the item development and review process will be most likely to defend against the imposition of such discredited and ineffective alternatives.

# Conclusion

As the brief overview of litigation presented in this chapter indicates, the legal issues facing credentialing examination programs are many and varied. Technology continues to change rapidly impacting test administration, accommodations, test security and score reporting. Settlement agreements in one venue may be used to pressure other testing entities to follow suit. Credentialing examination programs have learned much from prior litigation and have improved their legal defensibility substantially over the years. As attorneys learn more about psychometrics and psychometricians increase their knowledge of legal requirements, more constructive substantive negotiations about testing issues may be facilitated between parties, resulting in more frequent resolution of disputes outside the courtroom. Awareness of future judicial decisions will also be important in evaluating the legal defensibility of a credentialing examination program.

**Notes**

1. Portions of this chapter have been adapted from Phillips (2010). This chapter is not intended to provide specific legal advice. Its purpose is to provide a broad outline of the legal, psychometric and policy issues involved in the topics discussed. In applying these principles, testing entities are advised to seek individual legal counsel.
2. The legal criteria for obtaining a preliminary injunction include: 1) a likelihood of success on the merits at trial; 2) likely irreparable injury absent an injunction; 3) greater harm to the challenger without the injunction than to the testing entity with the injunction (balance of the equities); and 4) the injunction is in the public interest (Enyart v. NCBE, 2011). A preliminary injunction may become permanent if the plaintiff succeeds at trial.
3. The appropriate edition of the *Standards* for evaluating a specific test is the one in effect at the time the test was constructed and administered. For most cases discussed in this chapter, that was the 1985 or 1999 editions. The 2014 edition of the *Standards* (AERA et al. 2014) is applicable to tests developed and administered after its release. Standards from the 2014 edition of particular relevance to past or future legal decisions are discussed in applicable sections of this chapter.
4. Expert witnesses, who are qualified by training and experience to offer opinions, are distinguishable from fact witnesses such as agency and vendor staff, who are qualified by job description to testify about factual matters related to a credentialing examination program. When evaluating the credibility of expert opinions, judges typically consider the expert's qualifications, demeanor on the witness stand, quality and quantity of supporting evidence, and ability to withstand cross-examination.
5. Compare Woodard v. Virginia Bd. of Bar Exam'rs, 598 F.2d 1345 (4th Cir. 1979) (holding that governmental licensing boards are not employers, and therefore, not covered by Title VII) and Ass'n of Mex.-Amer. Educs. (AMAE) v. California (2000) (holding that Title VII applies to a California teacher licensure test).
6. Citing Griggs v. Duke Power Co. (1971), p. 431.
7. A construct is the knowledge, skills or competencies the test is intended to measure (AERA, et al., 2014, p. 11). The *Standards* (2014) define an *equally effective* test as one for which the degree of construct representation and the validity of test score interpretations, including freedom from construct-irrelevant variance, is equal to that of the original test (Standard 3.20). In such cases, subgroup differences may be considered when choosing a test.
8. Nonetheless, 67% of the job analysis survey respondents were White, while the applicant pool was approximately 58% White, 22% African-American and 20% Hispanic.
9. A concurrence in the case argued that on the evidence, a reasonable juror could find that concern about Title VII disparate impact liability was a pretext for intentional discrimination to placate a "politically important racial constituency" (Ricci, 2009, p. 2688). Apparently, the mayor had the final decision-making authority and had vowed privately to overrule the city if it certified the exam results.
10. In the credentialing cluster of standards in the *Test Standards* (2014), Standard 11.16 states that the "level of performance required for passing a credentialing test should depend on the knowledge and skills necessary for credential-worthy performance in the occupation or profession and *should not be adjusted to control the number or proportion of persons passing the test*" (p. 182, emphasis added). See also Phillips (2012). However, impact data may be considered among other contextual information in a content-based standard setting process (Standard 5.22C).
11. *Note:* In 1995, the mathematics subtest was revised to remove higher order skills such as geometry to make the test easier. The most difficult multiple-choice item on a resulting form was "How many students at a school can be served a ½ pint of milk from 5 gallons of milk?" In contrast, the apparent easiest item on an 1895 eighth-grade constructed-response final examination in Salina, Kansas, was "Find the cost of 6,720 lbs. of coal at $6.00 per ton." One might infer from this information that

more mathematics skill was required to graduate from eighth grade in the 1890s than was required for college graduates to obtain an initial teaching license in California in the 1990s (AMAE, 1996, p. 1400, 1403; Phillips, 2010, pp. 99, 101).

12. This list was considered "illustrative and not exclusive" (Reeves v. Johnson Controls, 140 F.3d 144 (2nd Cir. 1998)).

13. Potential unintended consequences of ignoring mitigating measures when evaluating impairments include discouraging mitigation where feasible and encouraging greater reliance on disability labeling and use of accommodations.

14. The EEOC ADAAA Title I Regulations (2010) and corresponding Interpretive Guidance applicable to employment discrimination cases include a non-exhaustive list of conditions that are predictable or virtually always disabilities, including a few involuntary bodily functions (29 C.F.R. § 1630.2(j)(3)). Declaring certain impairments virtually always disabilities would seem to run counter to the ADAAA requirement for individualized disability determinations. However, individualized decisions will still be needed to evaluate what accommodations are reasonable for each person with a predictable disability.

15. *Note:* The DOJ ADAAA Regulations (2010) state that "[a]lternative accessible arrangements may include, for example, provision of an examination at an individual's home with a proctor if accessible facilities or equipment are unavailable" (28 C.F.R. § 36.309(b)(4)).

16. Accord, Price v. NBME, 966 F. Supp. 419 (S.D. W.Va. 1997), denying extra time and a separate room for the Step 1 medical licensure exam to medical students with alleged ADHD and reading disabilities because "plaintiffs are able to learn as well or better than the average person in the general population" (p. 422). The court held that plaintiffs, who were gifted/honor students, earned good grades without accommodations and had recent disability diagnoses, had "not exhibited a pattern of substantial academic difficulties" or received a differential diagnosis ruling out alternative explanations for their symptoms (p. 423–424).

17. *Note:* In rare cases a court may find an accommodation *unreasonable*. Such was the case for a male volunteer at a nursing home who had Asperger's syndrome and had sexually harassed female staff members. The court ruled that his requested accommodations—"talking to his therapist about helping him to change his conduct and counseling his associates to better tolerate his behavior—were unreasonable as a matter of law" (McElwee v. County of Orange, No. 10 Civ. 00138(KTD) at 6 (S.D. N.Y. 2011)).

18. One might wonder if a surgical patient would receive good care from a doctor with a learning disability who needs extra time, frequent rest breaks and a distraction-free environment to recall and apply the correct procedures for an operation or emergency resuscitation. The potential risk to public safety in this case may be relevant for licensure.

19. Ohio Civil Rights Comm'n v. Case Western Reserve Univ., 666 N.E.2d 1376 (Ohio, 1996). *Note:* The California Unruh Civil Rights Act, Cal. Civil Code § 51 et seq. (1959), a more expansive state statute, mandates such assistance.

20. *Epilogue:* The sole issue on appeal was whether Pandazides had a right to a jury trial and the court held that she did. Prior to commencement of that jury trial, she again retested with the testing adaptations provided previously and passed. Having obtained her teaching license, Pandazides apparently chose not to pursue the case further.

21. The Step 2 exam referenced here was one of the exams involved in the Doe v. NBME (2006) case discussed below.

22. *Note:* The *Standards* (AERA et al., 2014) state that "there is little agreement in the field on how to proceed when credible evidence on comparability does not exist. To the extent possible, [testing entities] should collect [empirical, qualitative, and/or judgmental] evidence to examine the comparability of regular and altered tests or administration procedures for the test's intended purposes" (p. 60–62).

23. *Note:* The College Board was reluctant to grant extra time to all examinees by increasing allotted testing times due to the added proctoring costs associated with administering longer tests and concerns about potential increases in security violations and testing room disruptions by examinees who finished early (Camara, 2008, personal communication).

24. A Boston, MA, attorney specializing in education law made an even stronger statement, asserting that "[t]he College Board's unfortunate and puzzling action – an action that no court was likely to order if the case had gone to trial – deserves far more scrutiny than it has received so far. While private and without legal standing, this settlement involves giants in the testing industry and may have a chilling effect on validity and technical standards in the nation's … testing programs … . [A] court would most likely defer to educational experts, uphold standards supported by evidence of the SAT's validity, reliability, and technical underpinnings, and find [score annotations] not to be unlawful discrimination" (Freedman, 2003, pp. 2–3). Freedman also reported that "79% of college admissions officers opposed the College Board's decision" (id.).
25. The automatic accommodations included, among others, Braille, large print, screen access software, reader, scribe, computer/printer/spell check for writing samples, private room, stop-the-clock breaks, ability to pace around the room and up to 100% extra time (with no score annotation) previously granted on ACT, SAT, GED, GRE, GMAT and MCAT.
26. DOJ ADAAA Title III Regulations for Public Accommodations, 28 C.F.R. § 36.309(b)(1)(i) (2010). Section 36.303 requiring the provision of auxiliary aids and services lists screen reader and magnification software as examples.
27. See also Vande Zande v. State of Wis. Dept. of Admin., 44 F.3d 538 (7th Cir. 1995) (holding that an accommodation that is not an undue burden could still be unreasonable).
28. Elder asserted that use of a human reader placed him at a competitive disadvantage compared to sighted examinees but his score of 161 on the Maryland MBE obtained with a reader placed him at the 86th percentile nationally.
29. *Note:* The *Bonnette* (2011) case interpretation of the ADA requirements for licensure exams scored pass/fail contrasts with the decision in Bd. of Educ. v. Rowley, 458 U.S. 176 (1982) holding that educational accommodations under the Individuals with Disabilities Education Act (IDEA) require educational benefit, not maximum performance. Rowley was a "B" student with a hearing impairment who wanted the school to provide her with a sign language interpreter.
30. The following is a sample LSAT analytical reasoning question from the LSAC website (www.lsac.org). Seven piano students—T, U, V, W, X, Y, and Z—are to give a recital, and their instructor is deciding the order in which they will perform. Each student will play exactly one piece, a piano solo. In deciding the order of performance, the instructor must observe the following restrictions:

    - X cannot play first or second.
    - W cannot play until X has played.
    - Neither T nor Y can play seventh.
    - Either Y or Z must play immediately after W plays.
    - V must play either immediately after or immediately before U plays.

    If U plays third, what is the latest position in which Y can play?

    A. first;
    B. second;
    C. fifth;
    D. sixth;
    E. seventh.

    The correct answer is D. One recommended method for solving problems of this type is to construct a two-dimensional grid with playing positions listed horizontally and players listed vertically. Using the given information, cells representing impossible combinations can be marked and permissible orders deduced by a process of elimination. Binno argued that this is an extremely difficult task for a blind examinee who cannot see such visual representations. However, blind examinees often excel at spatial ability tests and one sighted workshop participant correctly solved this item without any written notes.
31. See Buss, W. G. & Novick, M. R. (1980). The detection of cheating on standardized tests: Statistical and legal analysis. *Journal of Law & Education*, 9(1): 1–64, for a discussion of the limitations of statistical methods used to detect cheating on college admissions and professional licensure tests.

32. See also Pettiford v. S.C. State Bd. of Educ., 62 S.E.2d 780 (S.C. 1950) (related case in which a state court upheld the board's decision and found the similarity between the crib answers and Pettiford's answers so extensive and so striking that it provided ample evidence of cheating even though she had not been caught in possession of a crib sheet).
33. To prevail on a copyright infringement claim, a testing entity must establish: 1) ownership of the pirated items and 2) direct or indirect evidence of copying by the defendant. When the evidence of copying is indirect, the testing entity must establish a substantial similarity between the infringing and original items (NBME v. Optima Univ., 2011).
34. See Phillips (2010) for a more complete discussion of the facts of the Allen case, its settlement terms, subsequent developments and a chronology of events.
35. *Note:* No attempt was made to justify the use of subjective GPAs with objective test scores by claiming that they measured the same skills or that GPAs would be equally effective at protecting the public from incompetent teachers. Rather, although GPAs may reflect relevant competencies useful in teaching, their primary function was as a convenient measure for qualifying more minority candidates for licensure. *Epilogue:* In 2004, the *Allen* settlement agreement was modified to permit subject matter testing of teachers with the ETS Praxis II tests to satisfy the No Child Left Behind (NCLB) Act, 20 U.S.C. § 6301 et seq. (2002) "highly qualified" mandate. There was also agreement to begin granting teaching licenses based on the test results. At that point, three new African-American candidates petitioned the court to intervene in the case, and the state's testing plans were again put on hold. On December 14, 2004, the trial court approved an agreement between the plaintiffs and the state education department permitting the use of the Praxis II subject specific tests for initial teacher licensure. The new requirements were implemented in April 2005.
36. Test items are typically evaluated for possible racial bias using a two-step process. First, a racially diverse panel of content experts is asked to review each item and identify any offensive language or cultural context that might disadvantage examinees from particular minority groups. After completing recommended revisions, the items are field-tested and a statistical comparison of the performance of majority and minority group examinees of *equal ability* is used to identify items with differential performance in the two groups. Items with large differential performance not likely due to chance are usually revised or discarded. But note that differential performance by itself does not necessarily indicate racial bias because other factors, such as different instruction or course selection, in the two groups may have caused the differential performance. In cases where an item has been judged to clearly and appropriately measure an important skill and minority reviewers concur that it is acceptable and appropriate for minority examinees, the item may be retained for use on a test form when it is needed to satisfy the test specifications and no better item is available (Phillips & Camara, 2006).

## References

Alexander v. Choate, 469 U.S. 287 (1985).
Allen v. Ala. State Bd. of Educ., 976 F. Supp. 1410 (M.D. Ala. 1997), aff'd, 164 F.3d 1347 (11th Cir. 1999), inj. den'd, 983 F. Supp. 1084 (M.D Ala. 1997), amen'd settle., 190 F.R.D. 602 (M.D. Ala. 2000).
American College Testing Program (2002, July 26). *ACT will end practice of annotating test scores under extended time.* Iowa City, IA: Author.
American Educational Research Association, American Psychological Association, & National Council on Measurement in Education AERA, APA, & NCME (2014, 1999, 1985). *Standards for educational and psychological testing.* Washington, DC: AERA.
American Registry of Radiologic Technologists v. Bennett, 939 F. Supp.2d 695 (W.D. Tex. 2013).
Americans with Disabilities Act (ADA), 42 U.S.C. § 12101 et seq. (1990).
ADA Amendments Act (ADAAA), 42 U.S.C.A. § 12101 et seq. (2008).
ADA Interpretive Guidance, 28 C.F.R. App. A, § 35.104 (EEOC 1998); 29 C.F.R. App. § 1630.2(j) (DOJ 1998).
ADA Regulations, 28 C.F.R. § 36.101 et seq. (EEOC Title I 1991); 29 C.F.R. § 35.101 *et seq.*, § 36.101 et seq. (DOJ Title II, Title III 1992).

ADAAA Regulations, 28 C.F.R. § 36.101 et seq. (EEOC Title I 2009); 29 C.F.R. § 35.101 et seq., § 36.101 et seq. (DOJ Title II, Title III 2010).

Anrig, G.R. (1987). ETS on "Golden Rule." *Educational Measurement: Issues & Practice*, 6(3), 24–27.

Apoian v. South Dakota, 235 N.W.2d 641 (S.D. 1975).

Ass'n of Mex.-Amer. Educs. v. California, 937 F. Supp. 1397 (N.D. Cal. 1996), *aff'd*, 231 F.3d 572 (9th Cir. 2000).

Baer v. NBME, 392 F. Supp.2d 42 (D.C. Mass. 2005).

Bartlett v. N.Y. State Bd. of Law Exam'rs, 226 F.3d 69 (2nd Cir. 2000).

Binno v. American Bar Ass'n, Case No. 11-12247 (E.D. Mich. 2012), appeal pending.

Bond, L. (1987). The Golden Rule settlement: A minority perspective. *Educational Measurement: Issues & Practice*, 6(3), 18–20.

Bonnette v. D.C. Court of Appeals, 796 F. Supp.2d 164 (D.D.C. 2011).

Breimhorst v. Educational Testing Service, No. C-99-3387 WHO (N.D. Cal. 2000).

Brennan, R. L. (2002). *On the comparability of extended-time vs. standard-time scores for College Board standardized tests: Psychometric report submitted to the blue ribbon panel on flagging*. New York: College Board.

College Board (2002, July 17). *The College Board and Disabilities Rights Advocates announce agreement to drop annotating from standardized tests.* New York: Author.

Copyright Act, 17 U.S.C. § 101 et seq. (1976).

Cox v. Ala. State Bar, 330 F. Supp.2d 1265 (M.D. Ala. 2004).

Currier v. NBME, Case No. 07-J-434 (Mass. Ct. App. 2007), *vac. & rem.*, 965 N.E.2d 829 (2012).

Dept. of Fair Employ. & Hous. v. Law Sch. Admissions Council, 941 F.Supp.2d 1159 (N.D. Cal. 2013), Consent Decree (Settlement), Case No. CV 12-1830-EMC (N.D. Cal. 2014).

Doe v. Nat'l Bd. of Medical Exam'rs, No. 99-4532 (E.F. Pa. 1999), *rev'd*, 199 F.3d 146 (3rd Cir. 2000), *on rem.*, No. 99-4532 (E.D. Pa. 2005), *aff'd*, 210 Fed. Appx. 157 (3rd Cir. 2006).

Doe v. Nat'l. Bd. of Podiatric Medical Exam'rs (Doe III), No. 03 Civ. 4034 (RWS) (S.D. N.Y. 2005). See also Doe I (2003) and Doe II (2004).

ETS v. Hildebrant, 923 A.2d 34 (Md. 2007).

ETS v. Simon, 95 F. Supp.2d 1081 (C.D. Cal. 1999).

Elder v. NCBE, Case No. C 11-00199 SI (N.D. Cal. 2011).

Enyart v. NCBE, No. 3:09-cv-05191-CRB (N.D. Cal. 2010), *aff'd*, 630 F.3d 1153 (9th Cir. 2011), *cert. denied mem.*, ___ U.S. ___ (2011), *perm. inj. granted*, 823 F. Supp.2d 995 (N.D. Cal. 2011).

Equal Educational Opportunity Commission, *Uniform guidelines on employee selection procedures* (Title VII Regulations), 29 C.F.R. § 1607.2B (1985).

Faggen, J. (1987). Golden Rule revisited: Introduction. *Educational Measurement: Issues & Practice*, 6(2), 5–8.

Friendly, J. (March 11, 1986). Standardized-test makers shift course in response to critics. *New York Times*. A14.

GI Forum v. Texas Education Agency, 87 F. Supp.2d 667 (W. D. Tex. 2000).

Golden Rule Life Ins. Co. v. Mathias, 408 N.E.2d 310 (Ill. App. 1980); Settlement Agreement.

Golden Rule Life Ins. Co. v. Washburn, No. 419–76 (Ill. Cir. Ct., November 20, 1984).

Gonzales v. NBME, 225 F.3d 620 (6th Cir. 2010).

Grant v. NBME, Case No. 7:07-cv-996 (N.D. N.Y. 2009).

Gregg, N., Mather, N., Shaywitz, S. & Sireci, S. (2002). *The annotating test scores of individuals with disabilities who are granted the accommodation of extended time: A report of the majority opinion of the blue ribbon panel on annotating*. New York: College Board.

Griggs v. Duke Power Co., 401 U.S. 424 (1971).

Gulino v. Bd. of Educ. of N.Y.C., 236 F. Supp.2d 314 (S.D. N.Y. 2002), *aff'd in part, rev'd in part*, 460 F.3d 361 (2nd Cir. 2006), *on rem.*, Opinion & Order, Case 1:96-cv-08414-KMW (S.D. N.Y. 2012), *aff'd*, Summary Order, No. 1301001-cv (2nd Cir. 2014).

Hazelwood Sch. Dist. v. Kuhlmeir, 433 U.S. 299 (1977).

In Re Police Sergeant, 819 A.2d 1173 (N.J. 2003).

Jaeger, R. M. (1987). NCME opposition to proposed Golden Rule legislation. *Educational Measurement: Issues & Practice*, 6(2): 21–22.

Jenkins v. NBME, No. 08-5371 (6th Cir. 2009).
Jones v. NCBE, 801 F. Supp.2d 270 (D. Vt. 2011).
Kelly v. W.Va. Bd. of Law Exam'rs, Case No. 2:08-00933 (S.D. W.Va. 2010).
Knapp v. City of Columbus, 192 F. App'z. 323 (6th Cir. 2006).
Mahmood v. NBME, Case No. 12-1544 (E.D. Pa. 2012).
Marquez v. Medical Bd. of Cal., 182 Cal.App.4th 548 (2010).
Martin v. PGA Tour, 204 F.3d 994 (9th Cir. 2000).
Mathews, J. (2003, June 10). Education effort meets resistance – Leaders say teacher certification test was sabotaged. *Washington Post.* A8.
Mindel v. ETS, 559 N.Y.S.2d 95 (N.Y. Sup. Ct. 1990).
Nat'l Bd. of Medical Exam'rs (NBME) v. Optima University, No. 1:09-cv-01043-JDB-cgc (W.D. Tenn. 2011).
Nat'l Council of Bar Exam'rs (NCBE) v. Multistate Legal Studies, 458 F. Supp.2d 252 (E.D. Pa. 2006).
National Council on Disability. (2004). *Righting the ADA.* Washington, DC: author.
N.Y. Educ. Law, §§ 341-a – 346-a (1987).
*New York Times* (November 29, 1984). Test service accepts safeguards against bias. *New York Times,* B17.
Palmer College of Chiropractic v. Davenport Civil Rights Commission, ___ N.W.2d ___ (Ia. 2014).
Pandazides v. Va. Bd. of Educ., 752 F. Supp. 696 (E.D. Va. 1990), *rev'd,* 946 F.2d 345 (4th Cir. 1991), *on rem.,* 804 F. Supp. 794 (E.D. Va. 1992), *rev'd on other grounds,* 13 F.3d 823 (4th Cir. 1994).
Pazer v. N.Y. State Bd. of Law Exam'rs, 849 F. Supp 284 (S.D. N.Y. 1994).
Phillips, S. E. (2010). *Assessment law in education.* Phoenix, AZ: Prisma Graphic, available at www.SEPhillips.dokshop.com.
Phillips, S. E. (2011). U.S. legal issues in educational testing of special populations. In S. N. Elliott, R. J. Kettler, P.A. Beddow, & A. Kurz, (Eds.), *Handbook of accessible achievement tests for all students* (pp. 33–68). New York: Springer.
Phillips, S. E. (2012). Legal issues for standard setting in K–12 educational contexts. In G.J. Cizek (Ed.), *Setting performance standards: Foundations, methods, and innovations* (2nd ed., pp. 535–569). New York: Routledge.
Phillips, S. E. & Camara, W. J. (2006). Legal and ethical issues. In R.L. Brennan (Ed.), *Educational measurement* (4th ed., pp. 733–755). Westport, CT: Praeger.
Psychometric Committee (2001). *Blue ribbon panel on flagging: Report of the psychometric committee.* New York: College Board.
Ricci v. DeStefano, 557 U.S. 557 (2009).
Richardson v. Lamar County Bd. of Educ., 729 F. Supp. 806 (M.D. Ala. 1989), *aff'd,* 935 F.2d 1240 (11th Cir. 1991).
Rooney, J. P. (1987). Golden Rule on "Golden Rule." *Educational Measurement: Issues & Practice,* 6(2), 9–12.
Sch. Bd. of Nassau County v. Arline, 480 U.S. 273 (1987).
Section 504 of the Rehabilitation Act [Section 504], 29 U.S.C. § 701 et seq. (1973).
Section 504 Regulations, 45 C.F.R. § 84 (1990).
Shapiro, M. M., Slutsky, M. H., & Watt, R. F. (1989). Minimizing unnecessary racial differences in occupational testing. *Valparaiso U. L. Rev., 23,* 213–252.
Shaywitz v. American Bd. of Psychiatry & Neurology, 848 F. Supp.2d 460 (S.D. N.Y. 2012).
Shepard, L. A. (1987). *A case study of the Texas teacher test: Technical report.* Los Angeles, CA: UCLA Center for the Study of Evaluation.
Shirer v. Anderson, 88 F. Supp. 858, 860 (E.D. S.C. 1950).
Sireci, S. G. (2001). *Equating non-standard and standard SAT test administrations: Opinion paper submitted to the Blue Ribbon Panel on flagging.* New York: College Board.
Sorrel, A. L. (2009, Mar. 2). Calif. court denies extra MCAT time for students with learning disabilities. *American Medical News.* Retrieved from: www.amednews.com/article/20090302/profession/303029971/6/
Southeastern Community College v. Davis, 442 U.S. 397 (1979).
Sutton v. United Air Lines, 527 U.S. 471 (1999).
Title VII of the Civil Rights Act, 42 U.S.C. § 2000e et seq. (1964).

Tolleson v. ETS, 832 F. Supp. 158 (D. S.C. 1992).
Toyota Motor Manufacturing v. Williams, 534 U.S. 184 (2002).
Turner v. Nat'l Council of State Bds. of Nursing, Case No. 13-3088 (10th Cir. 2014).
United States v. LULAC, 793 F.2d 636 (5th Cir. 1986).
U.S. Airways v. Barnette, 122 S. Ct. 1516 (2002).
Village of Arlington Heights v. Metro. Hous. Dev. Corp., 429 U.S. 252 (1977).
Wards Cove Packing Co. v. Atonio, 490 U.S. 642 (1989).
Ware v. Wyoming Bd. of Law Exam'rs, 973 F.Supp. 1339 (D.Wyo. 1997), *aff'd*, 161 F.3d 19 (10th Cir. 1998).
Washington v. Davis, 426 U.S. 229 (1976).
Watson v. Ft. Worth Bank & Trust, 487 U.S. 977 (1988).

# Index

Added to a page number 'n' denotes a note.

ability: and CATs 56; estimating from a pool of calibrated items and tasks 109, *see also* knowledge, skills and abilities (KSAs)
access/accessibility 94, 155, 238, 245
accountability 4, 17
accountants 7, 71
accreditation 17–18, 212, 213, 216; benefits of 218; graduation 5; standards 17; test design 45
Accreditation Board for Specialty Nursing Certification (ABSNC) 214, 216; standards 214, 220, 222, 225
accuracy 36, 181
actionable injury 236
Acute Care Physical Therapy 71
adaptability: of tests 43
adaptations 94
adaptive testing 186–7
administration: of items 51, *see also* test administration
administrative fees 6
administrative hardship 243
adverse impacts: testing programs 21
affective CIV 99
agencies (credentialing) 2, 28
Agile philosophy 101
agreements: relating to paper-based tests 184–5, *see also* Candidate Agreements; non-disclosure agreements
*Alexander v. Choate* (1985) 238
algorithms 31, 127, 187, 189–90
*Allen* Settlement 233
*Allen v. Alabama* (1986) 268
Almond, R.G. 79
alpha coefficient 30, 54, 144
American Board for the Certification of Teacher Excellence (ABCTE) 266
American Board of Dental Examiners (ADEX) 2

American Board of Nursing Specialties (ABNS) 214
American Board of Psychiatry and Neurology 91
American Educational Research Association (AERA) 210, *see also Standards for Educational and Psychological Testing*
American Institute of Certified Public Accountants (AICPA) 92
American National Standards 214, 225
American National Standards Institute (ANSI) 213, 217, 221
American Nurses Credentialing Center 218
American Physical Therapy Association (APTA) 3
American Psychological Association (APA) 210, *see also Standards for Educational and Psychological Testing*
*American Registry of Radiologic Technologists v. Bennett* (2013) 265–6
Americans with Disabilities Act 1990 (ADA) 229, 238–9; disability definition 238, 239; violations 236, 239
Americans with Disabilities Amendments Act 2008 (ADAA) 241–2, 260
analysis: psychometric 35, *see also* data analysis; practice analysis; statistical analysis
Angoff methods 113
angry applicants 170–1
annotating test scores 248–57
Anrig, G. 268
answer copying 186, 197
answer keys *see* keys
answer similarity analysis 197
*Apoian v. S.D.* (1975) 264
appeals: test result reports 170
applicants: communicating with 154–8
appropriate action 201
Architect Registration Examination 59

## Index

arcsine transformations 149
argument-based validation 23–6
artificial intelligence 127
Ash, R.A. 79
Assessment Engineering (AE) 79
assessment literacy 16–17
assessment-based certificates 9–10, 214, 216
assistive technology challenges 254–7
*Ass'n of Mex.-Amer. Educs. (AMAE) v. California* (2000) 233–4
Association of Real Estate License Law Officials (ARELLO) 214–15, 216, *see also Guidelines for Accreditation*
Association of Test Publishers (ATP) 187
assumptions 25, 30, 31
asynchronous remote item review 172
attention deficit hyperactivity disorder (ADHD): testing accommodation 241, 245, 249–50
attorneys 5, 7
audits: credentialing programs 217; of proctors 196
authority 174, 229
automated scoring 93, 107–8
automatic accommodations 272n25
auxiliary aids and services 238, 239, 242, 256, 260

back-reading 107
background checks 6, 193
backing (warrants) 24
badging 2, 10–11
*Baer v. NBME* (23005) 249–50
bar graphs 164–5
Baron, P.A. 79
*Bartlett v. N.Y. State Bd. of Law Exam'rs* (2000) 240–1, 257–8
*Basic Item Writing Principles* (ARELLO) 221
Becker, K.A. 101
Belov, D.I. 198–9
Bennett, N. 79
'best ensure' standard 252–3, 254, 255–6, 260
best practices: in candidate check-in 193–4; communicating with volunteers 173; content development 95, 101; crisis communication 173; guidance relating to 18; item writing 50, 95; physical security 185; test development 190
beta testing 99
bias: freedom from 22; in practice analysis 78, *see also* cognitive bias; social bias
binary scoring evaluators 131
*Binno v. American Bar Ass'n* (2012) 259

biometric information 193–4
biserial correlations 131, 132, 135
blind candidates 94
Bloom's cognitive taxonomy 86
Body of Work method 114
*Bonnette v. D.C. Court of Appeals* (2011) 256, 272n29
Bontempo, B. 159, 163
Bookmark method 114
borderline minimally competent candidates 165
boundaries: domain specifications 46
Brain, D. 66
braindumps 191–2
Brauer, R. 217–18
break areas 196
breaks: extra time for breastfeeding 248–9; maintaining security during 196
breastfeeding: extra break time for 248
*Breimhorst v. ETS* (2000-2002) 251, 253, 254
Brennan, R.L. 116
Breyer, F.J. 107
Brunner, B. 101
bubble charts 168
Buckendahl, C.W. 11, 12, 17, 43, 192
budgets (test security) 182
build-list-and-reorder items 126
Bunch, M.B. 111
burden of proof: racial discrimination challenges 230–1
Buros Center for Testing 216
Buros Institute for Assessment, Consultation and Outreach (BIACO) 216
business: of credentialing 18–19
Buss, W.G. 199–200

calibrated item pools 109, 117–18
calibrated scoring models 107
California Department of Healthcare Services 218
call centres 155
Camara, W.J. 18
CAN-SPAM laws (US) 175–6
candidate(s): check-in 193–5; credential worthy 110, 111, 112, 113, 114; evaluation 22, 114; handbooks 155–6; maps 167; minimally competent 3, 15, 59, 111, 114, 165; perspective 36, 38; predictable cycle 170; purpose of seeking credentials 2; variance, and score reliability 54, *see also* failing candidates
Candidate Agreements 182
*Candidate Guide* 183–4

Index 279

candidate volume: estimating expected 44; item bank needs 51; test delivery 56
CanMEDS framework 75
carpal tunnel syndrome: testing accommodation 241
Carpenters International Training Fund 9
Case, S.M. 95, 202
case-based items 92
categorization: topic performance 168
Center for Association Leadership 173
certification 7–8; development 4; distinguished from assessment-based certificate program 214; five benefits of 217–18; in higher education 4; public protection 1, see also specialty certification
certification examinations 7; multiple-choice items 89; proposed use of test score 85; publicity material 155; and security see test security
Certified Financial Institute (CFI) 92
challenges: test result reports 170
cheating 36; culture 181; definition 179; detection 197–201; increasing frequency of 181; organized and professional 178; responding to 201–2; testing industry responses to 178; types of 197
Cheating in the News 181
check-ins 193–5, 196
check-outs 196
Cialdini, R. 174
circle-arc equating 117
Cisco Networking Academies 93
Cizek, G.J. 111, 179, 180
claims (inference) 23, 25
Classical Test Theory 114, 117, 143–5
classification errors: in standard setting 112–13
classification (item) 88–9, 108
clearance procedures 260
clinical tests 13, 92–3
clinical videos 91
cluster analysis: similarity data 197
cognitive bias 68
cognitive CIV 98
cognitive complexity 51, 85–6
cognitive demand 49, 53, 71–2, 85–6
cognitive disabilities: testing accommodation 237, 251–2, see also learning disability
cognitive measurement 13–15, 27
cognitive processing tests 55
cognitive task analysis (CTA) 74–5
cognitive tasks 92
cognitive taxonomy (Bloom's) 86

collaborative meetings: in test design 42
collegial review: items written in training 96
collusion/detection 195, 197–8
combinatorial optimization 198–9
combining scores 108, 109–10
comfort aids 171
Committee on conformity assessment (CASCO) 213
committee-based practice analysis 69, 78
Common Item method (data collection) 117
communication 153–76; with applicants 155–8; documentation 173–4; during crises 173; with examinees 158–71; with potential applicants 154–5; privacy and confidentiality 175–6; sources of influence 174; with subject-matter experts 171–3; terminology 154; validation framework as a source of 13
comparability: across modes of administration 118; of assessment 221, 223; of scores 253
comparative information 164–6
compensatory scoring models 10, 58–9
competency 6; demonstrations 2, 5, 7, 8, 9, 10
competency modelling 75–7; listing of behavioural themes 76; orientation towards future goals 76; prescriptive aspect 76; strive to inspire maximum performance 76; top-down aspect 76
competency statements 76
competitive landscape 7, 18–19
completion of tests: time constraints 55
complex assessments 114
compromised items 200
computer software: test development 86
computer-administered examinations 99
computer-based testing (CBT): beta testing 99; items across response constraint continuum 89–93; monitoring for over-exposure of items 190; proctoring requirement 186; security advantage 190; selected response measurement opportunities 126; test delivery 185; test design 124; testing windows 57, see also test security
computer-delivered simulations 31
computerized adaptive testing (CAT) 55, 117; algorithms 187, 189; distinguishing principle 56; fixed length 109, 187; goal of 189; item analysis 139–40; standards for 112; test design 124; test security 186–7
computerized simulations 93
conditional means 130, 137
conditions of rebuttal (warrant) 24
confidence intervals 33, 166
confidentiality 169, 175, 223

conflicts of interest 193
*Conformity Assessment - General requirements for bodies operating certification of persons see* ISO/IEC 17024
conjunctive scoring models 10, 58–9
consensus 174
consistency 174
consistent metrics 112
constitutional protections 228–9
construct fragmentation 245–8
construct irrelevance 237
construct irrelevant variance (CIV) 93–4, 98–9, 184
construct relevance 237, 243–4, 251
construct relevant assistance 245
construct underrepresentation 31, 89, 237
construct validation 23
construct validity 107, 231, 233
constructed response items 98, 117, 131
constructed response measurement opportunities 126
consultation 217
content alignment 51
content development 85–101; considerations in item selection 93–5; design strategies, novel item types 100–1; item types 88–93; process 95–100; standards and guidelines 221; typical cycle 86–8; and validity 85–6
content piloting 52–3
content review 97–8; ARELLO program 215
content sampling 30, 89
content specifications: and practice analysis *see* practice analysis; presentation 65–6; purposes 64–5; translation schemes 77–8, 79
content validity 21, 73, 107, 231, 233, 234, 237
content-area subscores 115
content-by-process matrices 65–6
contents: of test results 159
continuing education: and maintenance of credentials 7
continuous innovation 101
continuous testing 57, 170, 188–9
control: credentialing as 4
copyright 91
Copyright Act (1976) 229
copyright infringement 202, 273n33
copyright protection 182
correlations 131–2
Cosmetology/Barber, Esthetics, Electrology and Nail Technology Licensing Board 5
cost(s): budgets for covering 182; item specification 49; validation questions 25
Council on Certified Nurse Anesthetists 73

Council for Licensure, Regulation and Enforcement (CLEAR) 173
create-a-tree items 126
credential worthy candidates 110, 111, 112, 113, 114
credentialing/programs: basic function of 21; business of 18–19; communication *see* communication; decisions 21; emergence of 19; examinations/tests *see* tests; expansion of 1; focus of 4–11; grey area 3, 18; integrating policy and practice 16–19; legal considerations 18, 228–73; overlap with education and employment testing 3–4; perspectives on 35–8; purposes 2, 64; semantic confusion 4, 7, 9; sponsors 2–3; stakeholders 13; standards *see* standards; validation *see* validation; websites 155, *see also* accreditation; certification; licensure; registration
credentials: credibility of 1; emerging yet poorly defined class of 2; gatekeeping role 181; test security and integrity of 181, *see also* micro-credentials
credibility 1, 3, 69, 216
criminal conduct 235
crisis communication 173
criterion-referenced comparison 164, 165
criterion-referenced standard-setting 222
criterion-related inference 35
critical incident techniques (CIT) 69–70, 79
critical review: of IUAs 25
Cronbach, L.J. 23, 25
Cronbach's alpha 54, 144
CTT-ATT solver 140–1
currency: of credentials 6–7; item types 119
*Currier v. NBME* (2012) 248–9
curvilinear transformations 110
cut scores 109, 111, 142, 143, 164; establishing 113; and Goldilocks Criterion 21; as reflection of minimal competence 114; scale properties 110, *see also* standard setting

DACUM 72–3
data: scope and types of 127–8
data analysis 123–50; data extraction views for 128–9; data preparation 123–9; high quality data 124; item analysis 129–41; reporting scores 147–50; scale analysis 141–7; statistical 34
data extraction views 128–9
data integrity 124, 125
data preparation 123–9
data quality control 123–5

data queries 123
data structures 124
data visualization 163
data-collection designs 117
database structures 128
datum (inference) 23
de-regulation 5
decision accuracy 54, 144–5
decision consistency 54, 144
decision inferences 24, 25, 29–30, 31–2, 34–5
decision procedures 37
decision rules 10, 30, 34–5, 38
decision-making: drag-and-drop items 92; multiple response items 90; objectivity in 37; scale properties 110
declarative knowledge 86
decoy items 190, 191
defensibility: score interpretations 110; of test programs 18, 61
democratic societies: credentialing in 22
demonstrations of competence 2, 5, 7, 8, 9, 10
dental licensure program (example) 12–16; anticipated, unintended interpretations and use 15; illustrative validation activities *14, 16*; intended interpretation and use 13–15; purposes 13; rational for each intended use 15
Department of Health, Education and Welfare (US) 6
Department of Justice (DOJ) regulations 238, 239, 242, 252–3
*Dept. of Fair Employ. & Hous. (DFEH) v. LSAC* (2012) 253, 258
design strategies: content development 100–2
detection: of unusual similarity 187
detection strategies: funds for covering 182
diagnostic feedback 160
diagnostic information 115, 116
dichotomous scoring 58, 90, 93, 113, 131
differential opportunities for success 236
digital badges 10
dimensionality 10
Direct Consensus Method 113–14
directness 49
Director of Test Security 182
disability: definitions 238, 239, 242; determinations 239, 240, 241, 242, 260; discrimination 237, 238, 240, 247; exemption from extrapolation inference 34
disability rights: federal protections 237–9
disabled test takers 24; and accessibility 94, *see also* testing accommodation
discrete hot spot items 91–2
discrete option multiple choice (DOMC) 191

discriminatory intent 233
disparate impact 229, 230, 267; assessing 231; challenges in teacher licensure tests 233–5; liability 231, 232; reconciling disparate treatment and 231–2; *Uniform Guidelines* and presumption of 231
disparate treatment 229–30, 249; reconciling disparate impact and 231–2
distractor patterns 136
'do not contact' requests 175–6
documentation: ABSNC accreditation 214; communication 173–4; content outline 155; intent behind standards 224; scoring guidelines 107, 110; in test design 41, 43, 44, 49–50; test specifications 220–1; testing accommodation 257; of unusual events during testing 195
*Doe v. Nat'l Bd. of Podiatric Medical Exam'rs* (2005) 263–4
*Doe v. NBME* (1999-2006) 250–1, 253
domain analysis 119
domain critical errors (DCEs) 59, 70–1
domain specification 46–8
Donahue, B.E. 202
*Double Time v. Time and a Half: Kelly v. W. Va. Bd. of Law Exam'rs* (2010) 247–8
Downing, S. 41, 90, 94
draft test design 42
drag-and-drop items 91–2, 126
dual accreditation 224
due diligence 59
due process 229
due process challenges 235–6, 262, 263, 264, 267
Dunnette, M.D. 67
DuVernet, A.M. 77

East Coast cases: involving technological advances and the NCBE 256–7
editorial review 97, 98
educational programs: assessment policies 4; communication 154; item writing guidelines 95; overlap of credentialing with 3–4; passing scores 22; scenario-based item sets 92; similarity of assessment-based certificates to 9; test design 54
educational requirements 6, 8, 156
Educational Testing Service (ETS) 246; *Golden Rule* case 267, 268
effectiveness 22, 35
efficiency 35
80% rule 231
*Elder v. NCBE* (2011) 255–6, 272n28
electronic file security 185

electronic test result reports 159, 162
eligibility requirements 2, 3, 6, 8, 43–4, 192–3
email communication 170
empirical evidence 25
employment: assessment-based certificates 9; credentials and 2, 6, 8; discrimination 229–30
employment provisions (ADA) 238
employment testing: guidelines 215; overlap of credentialing with 3–4, 8; permissible boundaries 231; top-down selection procedures 22, see also job-relatedness
enabling competencies 75
end of course (EOC) assessments 17
entities 127
*Enyart v. NCBE* (2011) 254–6, 257
equal ability 273n36
Equal Employment Opportunity Commission (EEOC) 215, 231, 239, 242
equal protection 229, 232–3, 267
equally effective test 270n7
equated score scales 142–3, 161
equating 116–17, 222–3; data collection designs 117; error 33, 116; statistical methods 117–18
equipercentile equating 117
equivalence of results 223
error(s): equating 33, 116; false negative 54, 145; false positive 54, 58, 113, 145, 194; psychometric perspective 36; in standard setting 112–13, see also domain critical errors; measurement error(s); random errors; standard errors
error risk 54
error variance equalizing transformations 149
essay prompts 191, 192
essays 27
estimated latent score 29
*ETS v. Hildebrant* (2007) 263
*ETS v. Simon* (1999) 264–5
evaluation: test specifications 80
evidence: on lack of comparable 271n22; of learning, credentialing as 2; regarding cheating 200–1; sources of 6, 8; for validation 13, 25–6
Evidence Centered Design (ECD) 79
evidence-based on response process 180
Examination Accreditation Program (ARELLO) 214–15, 216
examinations *see* test-takers; test(s)
expectations: accreditation standards 17
expected percent score (IRT-based) 149
'experience' requirement 6, 8, 156

experimental innovation 101
expert witness 270n4
external input: in test design 44–5
extra break time for breastfeeding 248–9
extra time for cognitive disabilities: accommodation cases 258–9; annotations for 251–2
extra time for physical disabilities: annotations for 250–1
extrapolation inferences 24, 25, 29, 31; from scaled score to USE of KSJs in practice 33–4; plausibility 36
extreme scores 59, 149, 161

Fabrey, L.J. 17
face-to-face item writing workshops 96–7
failing candidates: interpretive information 164–9; investigating prevalence of 55; provision of feedback 44; use of test result reports 160, *see also* pass/fail decisions
failing rate 165
fairness 35, 36, 37, 38, 44, 98, 221; challenges to 233–4
FairTest 267
false negative error 54, 145
false positive error 54, 58, 113, 145, 194
familiarity: with formats 31
'far from passing' 164
federal protections 228–9; disability rights 237–9
Federation of State Boards of Physical Therapy (FSBPT) 2, 166
federations (sponsor) 2–3
fee schedules 225
feedback: diagnostic 160; item writing training 96; normative 162, 165; score reports 41; and test design 41, 44
Feinberg, R.A. 116
fidelity: in credentialing 48–9, 50, 92
field testing 99–100
file formats 50
financial analysts 7
financial hardship 243
Fine, S. 72
fingerprint scanners 194
fingerprinting 193–4
firewalls (electronic) 185
Fitzgerald, C.T. 182
fixed date testing 188
fixed-length CAT approaches 109, 187
flagging criteria 132, 134–5
Flanagan, J.C. 69
flawed multiple choice items 90
Fleishman Job Analysis Survey 66

food safety management program 9
format: test delivery 55–7; test result reports 162–3
forward-thinking competencies 77
Foster, D. 190
Foster, D.F. 191
Foundations (*Standards*) 211
four-fifths rule 231
Fowles, M.E. 192
freedom from bias 22
functional job analysis (FJA) 72–3
'fundamentally alter' 238, 243, 245, 246
future validation: consideration of 12

gap analyses: item replenishment 96
gatekeeper role: of credentials 181
generalization/scaling inferences 24, 25, 29, 30–1; from task scores to a scaled score 32–3; plausibility 36
generalized partial credit (GPC) 109
*Generally Accepted Principles of Examination Development* (ARELLO) 214
Gerrow, J. 192
Gifford, B. 108
globally-administered tests 116
*Golden Rule* case 266–8, 269
Goldilocks Criterion 21, 35
*Gonzales v. NBME* (2000) 258
government issued identification (ID): at check-in 193
governmental organizations: participation in ISO and IEC activities 213
GPAs 273n35
Graduate Management Admissions Council 191
graduation: accredited training 5
*Grant v. NBME* (2009) 236
graphical assets: items with 90–1, 92
graphs: data communication 163, 164–5
GRE essay prompts 192
*Griggs v. Duke Power Co.* (1971) 230
group invalidation 263–4
group item writing training 96
group performance reports 169–70
group work (remote) 172–3
*Guidance on Psychometric Requirements for ANSI Accreditation* 213
guidelines: item specification 49–51; item writing 94–5
*Guidelines for Accreditation* (ARELLO) 214, 220, 221, 222, 225
*Guidelines for Computer-Based Testing* 217
Guild system 4–5

Guille, R.A. 101
*Gulino v. Bd. of Educ. of N.Y.C.* (2006) 234–5

Haberman, R. 161
Haberman, S. 116
Haladyna, T. 48, 86, 94, 95
Hambleton, R.K. 113
Hamdy, H. 91
hard copies: testing materials 184
health advocates: of CanMEDS framework 75
healthcare 4, 216, 218
hearing impairment: cases involving 237–8, 245
help desks 157
Henderson-Montero, D. 12
hierarchical relationships (data) 127
hierarchy of cognitive demand 86
high quality data analysis 124
high response constraint items 89
high-fidelity simulations 28
high-quality test content 102
high-scoring candidates 115
high-stakes examination programs 86, 118
higher order thinking skills 86
highest obtainable scale scores (HOSS) 149
histograms 165
Hoffart, N. 74
holistic judgements: of candidate performance 114
homogeneous candidate populations 54, 138, 189, 220
hot-spot items 91, 126
House, E.R. 23
$H^T$ person-fit measures 198
human judges 31, 107
humane policies 171
Hunt, R. 202

ICE 1100:2010(E) 214, 224–5
identification (ID) 193
Illinois Insurance Department 267
image collections 50
images 94
impairment 239, *see also* disability
Impara, J.C. 190
impartiality 37
incompetent practice 201
incompetent practitioners 2
independent trialing 100
inductive approach: in practice analysis 74
industry regulators: in test design 42
inferences (scoring) *see* scoring inferences
influence: in communication 174
information: privacy and confidentiality 175–6

information theory: in cheating detection 198–9
information yield: in validation 25
injunctions 229
innovation aspects: validation framework 12, *14*, 16
innovations: in automated scoring 107–8
innovative items 88, 93–4; design strategies for content development 100–2; scoring 108; security threats 53
Institute for Credentialing Excellence (ICE) 17, 173, 211, 224, *see also Standard for Assessment-Based Certificate Programs*
institutional perspective 35–6, 37–8
instructions: about multiple response items 90; item writing 96
intact test forms 119
integrated approaches: practice analysis 78–9
integrated item sets 92, 93, 96
intellectual property protection 185
intended interpretation and use: dental licensure program (example) 13–15; micro-credentials and badges 10
intended use: and test design 43–4
intent: behind standards 219–24
intentional discrimination *see* disparate treatment
inter-item correlations 131
interactive tasks 92
intermediate constraint items 89
internal appeal procedures 261
internal consistency reliability 54
international certification 7
international credential programs 112
International Electrotechnical Commission (IEC) 213
International Organization for Standardization (ISO) 17, 212–13, *see also* ISO/IEC 9.3.1; ISO/IEC 17024
Internet: discovery of copyright infringement on 202
Internet-based testing: test delivery 185–6
interpretation: test result reports 163–9
interpretation/use arguments (IUAs) 23–4; acceptance of 26; for credentialing tests 29–32; critical review 25; evaluation of 32–5; KSJ test task performance 27; necessary and sufficient conditions for validity 25–6; test development 28–9; validity arguments 25
*Interpretive Guidance* (EEOC, 1998) 239
interrater reliability 30, 32, 235
intrusion detection software 185
investigations: prior to sanctioning 200, 202

irregularity reports 195, 201, 263
irrelevant variance 34
ISO/IEC 9.3.1 221
ISO/IEC 17024 17, 212–13, 219, 221, 222, 223, 224
item(s): calibration 124; currency 119; development *see* content development; exposure, LOFT and reduction in 56–7; misappropriation 265–6; racial bias evaluation 273n36; specifications, in test design 48–51; statistics, in test construction 140–1; types 88–93; usage, and security 189–90; use of performance statistics in training 96
item analysis 124, 129–41; answer key and rubric validation 125, 134–6; common issues in 137–9; IRT theory 136–7; purposes 129–30; special issues in 139–40; statistical indices 130–4
item authoring 96–7; tools 86–7
item banks 86; asynchronous remote item review 172; candidate volume 51; computerized adaptive tests 56, 187; development 189; funds for replacing compromised 182; gap analyses to determine replenishment 96; maintenance 118–19; security 189–90; testing windows and control of exposure to 57
item databases: search capability 119
item delivery: design security 190–2; security in 185–90
item difficulty indices 130, 131
item discrimination indices 130, 132–3
item functioning 269
item harvesting 186, 187, 190, 197, 199
item mean 130, 131, 132, 133–4, 137, 140, 141
item pool flooding 191–2
item response theory (IRT) 124, 164; -based expected percent-correct score 149; estimated latent score 29; item analysis 136–7, 139–40; scale quality analysis 145–7; score scales 143; scoring 109, 110, 113, 114, 115; test unidimensionality requirement 30
item review 97–9
item reviewers 95
item selection 93–5
item selection algorithms 189–90
item writers 49–50, 86, 92; selection 95; training 95–6
item writing: assignments 96–7; guidelines 50, 94–5; re-examination of conventional 190; standards 221; workshops 96–7
item-level scoring 106–7

item-total correlation 131–2, 133
iterative item design 101

Jaeger, R. 269
JAWS (Job Access with Speech) 94, 254–5, 256
*Jenkins v. NBME* (2009) 243–4
job analysis 119, 219–21, 231, 237, 261, *see also* practice analysis
job descriptors 67–8
Job Element Inventory 66
job performance 99, 115, 230, 231
job-relatedness 13, 18, 64, 231, 234, 235, 236, 237, 244
Joint Commission on National Dental Examinations (JCNDE) 92
*Jones v. NCBE* (2011) 256–7
Jozefowicz, R.F. 95
judgemental equating 142
judgements: regarding test items 111–12; scoring involving 24, 35, 113, 114, *see also* human judges; knowledge, skills and judgements (KSJs)
judicial decisions 228–9
'junkies' 159
jurisdictions 6, 7, 8

Kane, M.T. 13
Kaplan, S.H. 187
Karabatsos, G. 198
Kendzel, J.G. 218
key validation 124, 130
key validation analysis (KVA) 134–6
key verification 98, 125
keys: supporting information 97
Knapp, L.G. 218
*Knapp v. City of Columbus* (2006) 241
knowledge: length of test and assessment of breadth of 54–5; objective 37
knowledge, skills and abilities (KSAs) 39; practice analysis 66, 73–4; test design 47, 48, 51
knowledge, skills and judgements (KSJs): assessment 26–8; domain critical errors 59; extrapolation from scaled score to use of 33–4; licensure examinations 22, 27; test tasks 39; validation concerns 21
Kolen, M.J. 110, 116
Kurzweil 254, 256

large volume testing programs 117
latent scores 29, 30, 161
Law School Admissions Council (LSAC) 253, 254
learning: credentialing as evidence of 2

learning disability: reasonable accommodations 245; testing accommodation cases 246–8, 250, 251–2, 258
legal counsel 171
legal disclaimers 219
legal fees 182
legal issues 18, 228–73; professional testing standards 229; public protection 229–36; test construction procedures 266–9; test security policies 261–6; testing accommodation policies 236–61
length of tests 53–5
Leucht, R. 161
level playing field 36
leverage: validation questions 25
Levine, E.L. 76, 79
license holders: currency 6–7
licenses: number of occupations requiring 1
licensure 5–7; development of 4; in higher education 4; predictive evidence 26; public protection 1, *see also* dental licensure program
licensure examinations: automated scoring 108; disparate impact challenges 233–5; KSJ domain 27, 28; medical 22, 30; misconduct cases 262–3; multiple-choice items 89; proposed use of test score 85; and security *see* test security
liking 174
Linden, W.J. van der 198
linear equating procedures 117
linear transformations 110, 142, 148–9
linear-on-the-fly testing (LOFT) 55, 56–7, 109, 112, 117, 124
linguistic analysis 127
linkage exercise 73
linking 116–17
linking calibration 143
location: credential recognition 43
logistics: test design 45–6
longer test lengths 54
lost and confused applicants 157
low scores: inferences 180
low-fidelity simulations 28
lowest obtainable scale scores (LOSS) 149
LSAT test 272n30

Magnet Recognition Program 218
*Mahmood v. Nat'l Bd. of Medical Exam'rs* (NBME, 2012) 235
maintenance requirements (credential) 6–7, 8, 9
major life activity 239, 240, 241, 242

mandatory accreditation 18
market-based incentives: for credentials 2
*Marquez v. Medical Bd. of Cal.* (2010) 236
*Martin v. PGA Tour* (2000) 246
mastery tests 161
mastery-based focus 106
matching algorithms 127
Maynes, D. 197, 198
Meade, R.D. 185
mean equating 117
meaningful access 238
measurement: focus, of licensure 6; goals, item specification 49; need for breadth of understanding of 1–2
measurement error(s) 10, 38, 144, 161, 166–7
measurement opportunities (MOs) 126–7, 139
media assets: items with 90–1
medical licensure tests 22, 30
medical speciality certification 7, 8
Meehl, P.E. 23
membership association sponsors 3, 5
memory effects 53
*Mental Measurements Yearbook* 216
meritocratic societies: credentialing in 22
metadata: items 97
micro-credentials 2, 10–11
Miller, H.L. 191
minimally competent candidates 3, 15, 59, 111, 114, 165
minimum competency 5, 6, 8
'minute per item' rule 55
misappropriation (item) 265–6
misconduct: budgets 182; identifying 261–2; legal cases 262–6, *see also* cheating
miskeyed items 130, 133
Mislevy, R.J. 79
mitigation 239–41, 242, 244, 258
mixed format assessments 114, 117
mixture item response models 198
mock candidates 55
modified tests 236
monitoring: of proctors 195–6; statistics 107; test times 55
'most people' standard 239
motivations: for accreditation 17–18
Mulkey, J.R. 182
multimedia 50–1
multiple categories: candidate performance 114
multiple choice items/tests 27, 28, 31, 37, 55, 66, 88, 89–90, 90–1, 93, 100, 106
multiple constructs: single competencies as an amalgamation of 76
multiple response items 90, 93

Multiple Subjects Assessment for Teachers (MSAT) 264
multiple test forms 116
multiple variables: tabular communication of 163
multiple-choice rules 94
multistage testing (MST) 55, 57, 109, 124, 139–40, 187–8

NAEP Science Assessment 92
*National Assessment of Educational Progress* 11
National Board of Medical Examiners (NBME) 92
national certification 7
National Commission on Certification of Physician Assistants (NCCPA) 2
National Commission for Certifying Agencies (NCCA) 17, 163, 211–12, 217, *see also* Standards for the Accreditation of Certification Programs (NCCA)
National Commission for Health Certifying Agencies (NCHCA) 211
National Conference of Bar Examiners (NCBE): technological advances and cases involving 254–7
National Council of Architectural Registration Boards (NCARB) 2, 92
National Council on Disability 241
National Council on Measurement in Education (NCME) 210, 269, *see also* Standards for Educational and Psychological Testing
National Council on Measurement Used in Education (NCMUE) 210
National Dental Examining Board (NDEB) of Canada 191–2
National Education Association 210
National Organization for Competency Assurance (NOCA) 211
National Physical Therapy Examination 166
National Restaurant Association 9
National Strength and Conditioning Association (NSCA) 3
*NBME v. Optima University* (2011) 265
*NCBE v. Multistate Legal Studies* (2006) 265
'near the cut score' 164
negative decisions 38
negative scoring 90
negligent test security procedures 266
'newbies' 159
'next generation' assessments 202
nominal weighting 109–10
non-adaptive testing 186

non-compensatory scoring models 110
non-disclosure agreements 184; sample 204–5
non-disclosure policies 53
non-discrete hot spot items 91–2
non-equated raw score scales 142
non-governmental organizations: participation in ISO and IEC activities 213
non-linear transformations 149
norm-referenced comparison 164
norm-referenced tests (NRTs) 85
normal score equivalents 142
normalized percentiles 148
normative comparisons 165–6
novel item types *see* innovative items
novelty effects 53
Novick, M.R. 199–200
numerical computation tests: time requirement 55
numerical values: scores reporting 164
nursing certification 214

O*NET online method 66
objectivity 22, 37
observation notes (proctor) 195
observations: cognitive task analysis 75
occupations: number requiring licenses 1
official test results 162
'on the basis of a disability' 242
'on-demand' testing 188–9
one-to-one relationships (data) 127
1:N matching 194
online communication 171
online item development 184
open-ended response items 89, 96
'operation of bodily functions' 242
operational aspects: validation frameworks 11–12, *14*, 16
operationally innovative items 108
Operations (*Standards*) 211
opportunities for success 236
optimization software 141
optimum test length 53–4
order effects 52
ordinal groups: score reports 60
organizational leaders: test design 42
organizational self-evaluation 216
organizational sponsors 2, 3
organized cheating 178
osteopathic licensure test: misconduct case 264
otherwise qualified 237, 238
outcomes: reporting 160
overall plan: test design 41
overall scores 60, 160–1, 165

*p*-value statistics 114, 131, 132, 137, 139
*Palmer College of Chiropractic v. Davenport Civil Rights Commission* (2014) 246
paper-and-pencil tests 86, 124, 184–5
Parshall, C.G. 101, 108
partial credit scoring 90, 93, 135–6
participation: in accreditation programs 17–18
pass/fail decisions 22, 108, 110, 114, 142, 148, 160, 190, 222
passes: KSJ tests 27–8
passing candidates: use of test result reports 160
passing rate 165, 231
passing scores 22, 35, 38, 105–6, 222
passing standards 54, 105, 106, 120n2, 161, 166, 222, 223, *see also* cut scores
passwords 185
pattern scoring 109
*Pazer* (1994) 244, 258
Pazer's percentile ranks 244
Pearson product-moment correlation 132
peers: normative information and definition of 165
percent-correct scores 142, 149, 161
percentile rank 165, 244
percentile rank transformations 148
performance assessments 26, 28, 92–3, 107, 235
performance information 60
performance level: for passing tests 270n10
performance level change: cheating detection 197–8
performance standards 73
performance tasks 27, 29, 32, 96, 107, 117, 128, 139
performance-based tests 7, 13, 37, 98, 114, 117, 126
permissible boundaries: employment testing 231
person-fit: cheating detection 198; IRT scale analysis 146–7
person-oriented descriptors 67, 68
personal belongings: secure storage for 194
personally identifiable information (PII) 175
personnel (security) 182
Phillips, S.E. 8, 18
physical CIV 98–9
physical disabilities: annotations for extra time for 250–1
physical security 185
physical walk-throughs: testing centers 195
physicians 5, 7, 30
piloting strategy 52–3

PISA assessment of Scientific Literacy 92
Pitoniak, M.J. 113
Plake, B.S. 17, 61
planning: for test security 180–1
plausibility: of scoring inferences 36
point-biserial correlations 131, 132, 135
policies and procedures: accommodations 171; communications 174; educational sector 4; test administration 193; test security 181, 201, 261–6
policy aspects: validation frameworks 12, *14*, 16
policy-makers 35
policy/practice integration 16–19
polytomous scoring 58, 90, 131
pool-based tests 113; ability estimation 109; standards for 112, *see also* computerized adaptive testing (CAT); linear-on-the-fly testing (LOFT)
poor performance: on timed tests 249–50
Porter, T. 37
Position Analysis Questionnaire 66
post-ADAAA litigation 242–4
potential applicants: communication with 154–5
Powers, D.E. 192
practical knowledge 66
practice analysis 220; approaches to 69–77; bottom-up aspect 76; choosing among approaches 77–80; defining domains prior to 46; descriptive aspect 76; evaluating study results 80; expert panels 78; expert review 79–80; focus on the present 76; foundations of 66–9; impact of study design decisions 77; language 72; repeated standard setting 112; results 76, 77; specificity 68; study design decisions 67; and test development activities 64
practice domain: definition of, in test development 28
practice(s): performance assessments in 26, 28
PRAXIS principle licensure test 263
pre-assembled fixed test (PFT) forms 124
pre-equating 109
pre-testing 52–3, 99–100
precision 36, 37, 54, 105, 161, 166, 189
predictive evidence 26
predictive inferences 35
preknowledge 187, 197; detection 197–9; protection against 190–2
preliminary injunctions 270n2
Preliminary Multistate Bar Review (PMBR) 265
preliminary test results 162
presumption of disparate impact 231
presumptive inference 23–4

presumptive violations 230
prevalence of failure 55
prevention strategies 182, 199
principled test design (PTD) 79–80
*Principles for the Validation and Use of Personnel Selection Procedures* (SIOP) 215
printed test booklets: unique identifiers 185
prior uncertainty: in validation 25
prioritized questions: in validation 25
privacy 169, 175
probabilistic information: on cheating 200, 201
problems: test tasks framed in terms of 28–9
procedural due process 235
procedural fairness 36, 37
process assessment 92
process-oriented practice analysis 78–9
proctoring 186, 194, 195–6
*Proctoring Best Practices* 196
product assessment 92
product-moment correlation 132
profession-specific activities: and maintenance of credentials 7
professional cheating 178
professional performance model (PPM) 74
proficiency estimates: precision 189
proficiency scores: IRT-based 136–7, 139, 143
profile plots 134
program structure 41
prohibited items 194, 260
properties (entity) 127
protection: test security and 181
psychometric analysis 124
Psychometric Consulting 216–17
psychometric perspective 35, 36–7
psychometric practice 10
psychometric quality 10, 21, 130, 234
psychometrics: challenges, performance assessments 235; expertise in test design 42; information about multiple response items 90; standards for 213–15
psychomotor measurement 27; dental licensure 13–15
public accommodations (ADA) 238
Public Law 106-50 (Montgomery GI Bill) 218
public protection 2, 5, 201; certification 7; legal issues related to 229–36; licensure 1, 6; registration 8; test security 181
public safety analyses 261
publicity material 154–5
purpose: in test design 43–4

'qualified individual with a disability' 238; judicial decisions relating to 239–61

qualifiers (warrant) 24
qualifying disabilities 260
qualitative feedback: item writing training 96
qualitative qualifiers 24
quality assurance 107, 125
quality control: before providing test result reports 162; human scoring 107, 116–17; score reporting 149–50, *see also* data quality control
quantitative qualifiers (warrant) 24, 33
quartiles 166
questionable inferences and assumptions 25
questionnaires: in practice analysis 66, 68, 70, 71–2, 73–4, 78
questions: prioritizing, in validation 25
quintiles 133–4

racial bias evaluation 273n36
racial discrimination challenges 259; due process 235–6; equal protection 232–3; reconciling disparate treatment and disparate impact 231–2; shifting burdens of proof 230–1; Title VII 229–30; *Uniform Guidelines* 231
random errors 33, 36, 38
'random group' assumption 142
Random Groups method (data collection) 117
random seeding 52
randomization-based selection methods 190
rank/ranking 3, 22, 160, 165
Rasch and Rasch Partial Credit (PRC) 109
Rasch-based IRT methods 117, 136
rater calibration 107
rating dimensions: appropriate for FJA 72
rational basis scrutiny 230
raw scores 108, 110, 115, 161
raw-score-to-scaled score conversion table 117
Raymond, M. 68, 220
Reading Comprehension test 244
reading impairment: testing accommodation cases 240–1, 243–4, 249–50
reading speeds 171
real-time normative feedback 162
real-time test assembly 124
reasonable accommodations 237, 238, 242, 244, 260; identifying 244–8
reasonableness standard 254, 260
recall 86
recentering: standardizing transformations 148
reciprocity 174
recognition credentials 10
recommended actions 167–8
recruitment: volunteer SMEs 172

reference groups 138–9, 148
reference/requirement restrictions 51
'regarded as having a disability' 242
registration 7, 8–9, 124
registration process: information in candidate handbooks 156
Reid, J.B. 220
relationship variables: graphical communication of 163
relevance 26, 36, 37, 38, 97
reliability 36, 37, 54, 143, 144, 269
reliability index 140
remote SME volunteers: working with 172–3
replacement of items 190
representative samples: survey populations 71
representativeness: content sampling 89
request forms (testing accommodation) 261
rescaling: standardizing transformations 148
rescores 170
research: test design decisions 42
research bases: decision rules 34
resources: developing and maintaining test programs 45; setting aside for testing accommodations 260–1
response constraint items 88–93
response constraint taxonomy 108
response time(s) 55, 91, 167, 198, 199, 200, 245
restriction of range: in item analysis 138
retake policies 57–8
retake range 166
retakers 158
retests 262
review(s): accreditation 214, 215, 225; item 97–9; practice analysis 79–80; structured/organized 216; tasks 34; topics 168
reviewers 95, 225
*Ricci v. DeStefano* (2009) 231–2
*Richardson v. Lamar County Bd. of Educ.* (1991) 233
Rigging and Signalers Certificate 9
*Rights and Responsibilities of Test Takers* 183
risk(s): purpose of credentialing 2; test design 45–6
Robustelli, S.L. 79
Rodriguez, M. 48, 86, 94
role-based permissions 86
Royal College of Physicians and Surgeons of Canada (RCSPC) 75
rules: scoring *see* scoring rubrics; for test days 158
rules of thumb: scale points 110; updating job analyses 119

sample competency 75
sampling across items (tasks) 31
Sanchez, J.I. 76
sanctioning 200, 201
SAT scale 161
scale points 110
scale properties 110
scale quality analysis: classical test theory 143–5; item response theory 145–7; other quality control steps in 147
scaled scores 29–30, 109–10, 161
Scalise, K. 108
scarcity 174
scenario-based items 92, 100
*Sch. Bd. of Nassau Country v. Arline* (1987) 238, 241
scheduling testing 188–9
Schmitt, K. 1, 4
Schraagen, J.C. 75
Scicchitano, A.R. 185
score(s) 105–20; annotations, testing accommodation 248–57; cancellations 201, 202, 261, 262, 264, 266; in certification and licensure examinations 85; educational programs 22; estimating 106–10; holding of suspicious 201, 202; information about how and when to get 158; institutional perspective 36; intended interpretation and use, dental licensure 13, 15; interpretation and use of 26–32; interpreting 110–16; maintaining the meaning of 116–19; monitoring appropriateness of test content 119; psychometric models 35, 36; rechecks 236; security and the accuracy and meaningfulness of 181; Standards' definition 160; test design and intended/unintended use of 44; in test result reports 160–1, *see also* cut scores; latent scores; overall scores; passing scores; rescores; scaled scores; subscore(s); true scores; universe scores
score reporting: periods 169–70; quality control 149–50; scale transformations 148–9; standards relating to 223–4; subscores 115–16; test design 44, 59–60, *see also* test result reports
score scales 22; building and maintaining 141–7; transformations 110, 142, 148–9
score-differencing approach 198
scorer training 107
scoring: algorithms 31, 127; in beta testing 99; design 107; due process challenges 236; item-type selection and use 93; security in 197–202; test design 58–60

scoring evaluators 125–7, 131, 139
scoring inferences 10, 116; evaluation 32–5; and validity 23–4, 179–80, *see also* decision inferences; extrapolation inferences; generalization/scaling inferences
scoring rubrics 24, 25, 29, 30, 96, 107, 109, 110; validation 134–6
screen access software 94, 254; cases involving 254–7
search capability: item databases 119
search engine optimization 171
seating: in test rooms 194–5
secondary identification checks 194
secret shopping 196
Section 504 of the Rehabilitation Act (1973) 229, 237–8, 247
security: concerns, in test design 45–6; of information 59–60, 175, *see also* test security
security hotlines 199
selected response items 91–2, 106, 113
selected response (SR) measurement opportunities 126
selection algorithms 189–90
self-evaluation (organizational) 216
self-mitigation 240, 241
self-regulation 5
semantic confusion 4, 7, 9
Semko, J.A. 202
sensitive information 59–60
sensitivity review 97, 98–9
ServSafe® 9
severity of disability: testing accommodations 258–9
sex discrimination 249
*Shaywitz v. American Bd. of Psychiatry & Neurology* (2012) 257–8
Shimberg, B. 1, 5–6, 15
*Shirer v. Anderson* (1950) 262–3
similarity: detection of unusual 187
similarity data: cluster analysis 197
simulations 27, 28, 29, 31, 92, 93
Single Group design (data collection) 117
single test forms 116
single testing windows: reporting periods 169–70
single-source databases 128
Sinharay, S. 116, 161
Sireci, S.G. 113
situation-specific behaviours: and CIT approach 69
Six Universal Principles of Influence 174
skills *see* knowledge, skills and ability (KSAs)
small samples: in item analysis 138

small-scale testing programs 90, 117, 123
social bias 68
social media 171
Society for Industrial and Organizational Psychology (SIOP) 215
sociological trends: and frequency of cheating 181
sources of evidence 6, 8
*Southeastern Community College v. Davis* (1979) 237–8
Spearman-Brown formula 54, 144
special needs applicants 157
speciality certification 2, 7, 8
specialized expertise: test security planning 181
sponsors 2–3, 181
stakeholders 13, 42, 44–5
*Standard for Assessment-Based Certificate Programs* (ICE 1100:2010(E)) 214, 224–5
standard errors 33, 36, 110
standard setting 111; additional considerations 112; Angoff and related methods 113–14; Body of Work method 114; Bookmark method 114; general process of 111–12; important caveat 112–13; logic of 111; remote 172; standards relating to 222–3
standardization: criticism of 48; focus on test administration 223; institutional perspective 37, 38; organizational promulgation 213; psychometric perspective 36
standardized work samples 107
standardizing transformations 148
standards 210–26; brief history of selected 210–15; cautions regarding use of 219; comparison of 224–7; use of 215–24
*Standards for the Accreditation of Certification Programs* (NCCA) 211–12, 213, 220, 221, 222, 223, 224, 225
*Standards for Educational and Psychological Testing* 210; 2014 edition 211; accreditation 17; annotating test scores 250, 252; Buros standards based on 217; candidate guides/test books 183; challenges and appeals 170; communication 153, 173–4; consistency of other standards with 212, 214, 215; construct fragmentation 245–6; construct relevance 251; cut scores 113; documentation in test design 41; due process challenges 235; employment testing 3, 6; equally effective test 270n7; first three editions 210–11; group performance reports 169; instructions about measurement error 167; intent behind 219; investigating prior to sanctioning 200; job analysis 220; lack of comparable evidence 271n22; legal considerations 18; legal disclaimers 219; passing scores 222; psychometrics 213; purpose of credentialing 64; score definition 160; score equating 222–3; score interpretation 164; score precision on test result reports 166; score validity 105, 107, 143; simulations 93; as a source of authority 229; specific test evaluation 270n3; standardization of test administration 223; test development 98; test result report contents 159; test specifications 81, 119; testing accommodation 236–7; universal design 94; valid test score interpretations 180; validation 11; validity definition 85
*Standards for Educational and Psychological Tests and Manuals* 210
state disability law 250–7
statistical indices: item analysis 130–4
statistical methods: detection of cheating 197–201; equating 117–18; field testing 99; key verification 125; in practice analysis 77; psychometric perspective employment of 36–7; score scales 144, 145; scoring inferences 25, 30; testing data 34
statistical significance measures 231
statistical tests (timed) 245
Steinberg, L.S. 79
stimuli: integrated item sets 92
stopping rules 190
storage security 184, 194
strategic management: content development 101
stratification-based selection methods 190
strict scrutiny 230
'strong basis in evidence' standard 232
structured interviews: cognitive task analysis 75
structured/organized reviews 216
style guide: item development 50
subject matter experts (SMEs): ARELLO guidelines 221; communicating with 171–3; content review of ARELLO program 215; currency of item content 119; field testing 100; item reference requirement/restrictions 51; item writers and reviewers 49, 95; practice analysis 66, 68, 69, 72, 73, 78, 80; security obligations 184; standard setting 111–12, 113; test design 42
subscore(s) 160; error 166; evaluations based on 4; normative information 165–6; reporting/communicating 60, 115–16, 161–2
'substantially limits' 239, 240, 241, 243, 250

substantive due process 235
sufficiency versus burden: in testing accommodation cases 257–9
Sulaiman, N.D. 91
summary data: test difficulty 157–8
summed scores 108, 109
Supreme Court 229, 230, 231, 232, 235, 237, 238, 240, 241, 246, 252
survey-based practice analysis 71–2, 78
suspected breaches: budget for covering costs of 182
*Sutton v. United Airlines* (1999) 239–40, 241
Swanson, D.B. 95
systematic errors 36

tables: data communication 163
Tannenbaum, R.J. 79
target pilot test population 52
task format 27, 31
task inventory 71–2
task lists 72, 74–5
task-based simulations 92
task-level scoring 106–7
task-oriented descriptors 67–8
task-oriented practice analysis 78
tasks: in KSJ domain 27, 33; review and editing of 34; successful performance 39; in test development 28–9, *see also* cognitive tasks; performance tasks
taxonomy: Bloom's cognitive 86; innovative items 108; of item writing rules 94–5
teaching licensure examinations: disparate impact challenges 233–5; misconduct cases 262–3
technical criteria 35, 36
technical explanation: on test result reports 168–9
*Technical Recommendations for Achievement Tests* 210
*Technical Recommendations for Psychological Tests and Diagnostic Techniques* 210
technological advances 254; cases involving the National Conference of Bar Examiners 254–7; keeping current with new research 260
technology-enhanced items 88, 108, 126, 128, 135, 139
technology-related misconduct 265–6
terminology 154
test(s): budget for monitoring and analysis 182; delivery models 186–8; difficulty, summary data on 157–8; items *see* item(s); length/time 53–5; maintenance decisions 60–1; modality and security 185–6; performance level for passing 270n10; performance-based *see* performance-based tests; proctoring during 195–6; scores *see* score(s); tasks *see* tasks, *see also* certification examinations; licensure examinations
test administration 57, 142–3; comparability 118; implications for data processing 124; security during 192–6; standards related to 223
test administrators 193, 261
test blueprints 85, 86, 97, 111, 112, 168
test construction: item statistics in 140–1; legal issues related to 266–9
test days 158
test delivery: format 55–7; item specification 48; quality control 124; security in 185–90
test design 41–61; decisions 28, 41, 46–61; goal 28; implications for data processing 124; importance of 41; influences on 43–6; maintaining 60–1; phases 41, *42*; process 41–3; test security 34, *see also* principled test design
test development 9–10; best practices 190; computer software 86; construct irrelevant variance 98; interpretation/use arguments 28–9; in KSJ domain 27; practice analysis 64; resource availability 45; security during 183–5; standards related to 221, *see also* content development
*Test Handbook* 183
test information function (TIF) 145–6
test preparation program misconduct 264–6
test result reports: angry applicants 170–1; challenges and appeals 170; contents 159; delivery method 162; development and evaluation 158; feedback on 41, 44; format 162–3; group performance 169–70; helping with interpretation 163–9; timing of provision 162; types of results to include 160–2
test results: communicating 158–9
test security 178–205; budgets 182; comprehensive plans 183–202; credentialing context 179; identification of breaches in 162; legal issues related to 261–9; planning 180–1; sample agreement 203–4; standards related to 223; test design 34; validity concern 179–80
test specifications: definition of 81; job analysis 220; updating 119, *see also* content specifications

virus detection software 185
visual impairment: and accessibility 94; reasonable accommodations 245; testing accommodation cases 239–40, 254–7, 258
visual inspection: of candidates before entering test rooms 194
visual representations: of errors, in test result reports 166
voluntary certification 8, 9
volunteer SMEs 171–2

Wainer, H. 116
*Ware v. Wyoming Bd. of Law Exam'rs* (1997) 258–9
warrants (inference) 23–4, 29–30, 33
*Watson v. Ft. Worth Bank & Trust* (1988) 235
web monitoring 199, 202
web-based images 50
web-based meetings: item writing 97
websites: braindumps 191–2; and communication 155, 162

weighting schemes 108, 109–10
West Coast cases: involving technological advances and the NCBE 254–6
Wiley, W.W. 72
Williamson, W.M. 107
Wilson, D. 159
window-dressing 50
Wise, L. 61
Wollack, J.A. 197
Woodcock-Johnson Spatial Relations test 244
Woodcock's Test Construction Nomograph 54
Woods, C.Q. 74
Woolsey, L.K. 69
word clouds 168
Wright Map 168
written examinations (clinical) 13

Xi, X. 107

Zara, A.R. 220
ZoomText 254–5, 256

test tampering 197
test-takers: communicating with 158–71; eligibility 124; misconduct *see* misconduct; rights and responsibilities 261; test design 43–4; 'testwise' 90
test-taking behaviour 167
testing accommodation: automatic 272n25; humane policies 171; interpretation/use arguments 24; legal issues related to 236–61; recommendations 260–1; requests 57, 157
Testing Applications (*Standards*) 211
testing centers 193, 194, 195
testing data *see* data
testing policies 193
testing windows 57, 116, 142, 188
testlets 57, 92
'testwise' test takers 90
thermometers: for comparative data 164–5
think-aloud protocol 180
third-party accreditation 18
threats: to test security 45–6, 181, 184, 190–1
three-parameter logistic (3PL) 109
threshold competency 10
time constraints: test completion 55
time frame: piloting stage 52
timed tests 244, 245, 249–50
timelines (test design) 45
timing: provision of test results 162
Title VII of the Civil Rights Act (1964) 229–30, 232, 234
tolerances 127
*Tolleson v. ETS* (1962) 263
top-down selection tests 22
topic performance: categorization 168
topic reviews: information on 168
topics: in candidate handbooks 156
total score(s) 131, 142
Toulmin, S. 23
*Toyota Motor Manufacturing v. Williams* (2002) 241
trace lines 134
trade group sponsors 3
training: item writers 95–6; in proctoring 195; scorers 107; in standard setting 111
training specifications 73
transformations (score scale) 110, 142, 148–9
translation: of tests 43
translation schemes: content specification 77–8, 79
transparency 22, 36, 37, 38, 184
Trojan Horse method 198
true scores 30, 36, 54, 110, 144
Tukey's box plot 166

*Turner v. Nat'l Council of State Bds. of Nursing* (2014) 236
two-parameter logistic (2PL) 109
Type I and II errors 54
'typical performance' focus: of practice analysis 76

unauthorized remote access: electronic files 185
unconstrained integrated item sets 93
uncorrected state: disability determinations 240, 241, 242, 260
undue burden 238, 243, 254, 255, 257, 260
undue hardship 237, 243, 249, 254, 260
unidimensional tests 30
*Uniform Guidelines on Employee Selection Procedures* (EEOC) 215, 231, 233
unintended interpretations and use: dental licensure program (example) 15
unique identifiers: printed test booklets 185
United States Medical Licensing Examination (USMLE) 31, 65–6
universal design 94, 156, 261
universe scores 30
*Unlimited Time/Interactive Test Administration: Pandazides v. Va. Bd. of Educ.* (1994) 246–7
*U.S. Airways v. Barnette* (2002) 254
usability studies 94

validation 9–10, 21–39; argument-based 23–6; conceptual analysis in 26; concerns in 21; evaluation of interpretation/use arguments 32–5; interpretation and use of test scores 26–32
validation framework 11; application (clinical example) 12–16; innovation aspects 12, *14*, 16; operational aspects 11–12, *14*, 16; policy aspects 12, *14*, 16
validity 269; for certification 8; content development 85–6; fail/pass decisions 222; item writer expertise 95; licensure 6; necessary and sufficient conditions for 25–6; score interpretation 105; score scales 143, 144; scoring 107; sensitivity review 98; test design decisions 41; test security 179–80
variance (candidate) 54
variance restriction 132
verification (key) 98, 125
video items 91
video samples 50
vignettes 92
violations of security 184
virtual patients 93